THE BIGGEST TWITCH

'Birding is hunting without killing, preying without
punishing, and collecting without clogging your home.'
Mark Obmascik

Alan Davies

Ruth Miller

21/2/13

This book is dedicated to Cecile Miller, without whose enormous generosity *The Biggest Twitch* would never have been concluded. Not only did she ensure the success of *The Biggest Twitch*, but she also had a major part in supplying half the personnel! We are forever grateful.

We also wish to thank Iain Campbell, once described as a manic genius, who is perhaps the person most responsible for our year of non-stop birding; a better friend would be impossible to find.

The list of birds seen on *The Biggest Twitch* in 2008 was based on the 2007 edition of *The Clements Checklist of the Birds of the World*. However, for ease of reading, the species' names in the book are those commonly used in the relevant field guides. A full list of species seen is available on our website, *www.thebiggesttwitch.com*.

THE BIGGEST TWITCH

ALAN DAVIES AND RUTH MILLER

CHRISTOPHER HELM
LONDON

Published 2010 by Christopher Helm, an imprint of A&C Black
Publishers Ltd.,36 Soho Square, London W1D 3QY

Reprinted 2010, 2011

www.acblack.com

ISBN (print) 978-1-4081-2387-4
ISBN (e-pub) 978-1-40801-3404-7
ISBN (e-pdf) 978-1-4081-3432-0

A CIP catalogue record for this book is available from the British Library

This book is produced using paper that is made from wood grown in
managed sustainable forests. It is natural, renewable and recyclable. The
logging and manufacturing processes conform to the environmental regulations of the country of origin.

Commissioning Editor: Nigel Redman
Project Editor: Jim Martin
Copy Editor: Mike Unwin

Design by Mark Heslington Ltd, Scarborough, North Yorkshire
Cover artwork by Robert Gillmor

Printed and bound in Great Britain by MPG Books Group

10 9 8 7 6 5 4 3

Contents

Part Six: Latin reprise

Part Seven: Back to Africa

Part Eight: End game

Foreword

Seen from the outside, a birder's preoccupation with lists would be easy to misinterpret. I have heard it said that we reduce birds to mere numbers, checking them off so we'll never have to look at them again. But most of us love seeing birds over and over. Otherwise it would be hard to explain the popularity of year lists.

I have been birding almost my whole life, and almost every year on the first of January I feel the urge to start a list for the new year. It's a way of appreciating the birds all over again: yesterday that bird was just another robin or sparrow, but today it's a new one for the annual tally. As the year goes on, the list furnishes an excuse for getting out. Maybe I've seen scores of Long-eared Owls in the past, but I haven't seen one *this* year, reason enough to go seek out this trim, spooky owl and admire it afresh.

Practised on a local level, as in our home county, the year list keeps us on top of local bird happenings. The game becomes more intense when we shift from just *keeping* a year list to actually *working on* one, and the game become crazier as we play it in larger and larger areas. I learned this the hard way as a teenager, when I set out to break the year-list record for all of North America. The year that I turned nineteen, I spent more time travelling than birding, in an exhausting, madcap dash around the continent. Was it, as some suggested, an insane and useless stunt? Sure. But I would not have traded that adventure for anything.

For bird lists, the ultimate arena is the world: no fussing with arbitrary boundaries, just go for the whole planet. When I was a kid, few of us thought seriously about trying to bird the world. The number of bird species globally was considered to be about 8,600, but in the 1970s it was almost impossible to find illustrations or precise localities for most of them. If anyone had asked, we would have said that the style of birding practised in the U.K., northern Europe, Canada, and the United States simply couldn't be applied elsewhere.

By that point, however, a few people already were actively birding the world. One of the most influential was the late G. Stuart Keith. Stuart was an intrepid British ornithologist and birder who had moved to the United States and had become the first president of the American Birding Association. I was lucky enough to go birding with Stuart when I was still a teenager. I was tremendously impressed by him, and even more impressed a few months later when he published a landmark article entitled 'Birding Planet Earth: A World Overview.' For many young birders, that article changed everything. Stuart wrote about adventures around the globe, and made it clear that birding the planet was not only feasible but irresistible. He made it clear that anyone could travel and find life birds by the thousands. Indeed, Stuart himself had just become the first to hit 'half', listing 4,300 of the then known 8,600 bird species in the world.

Looking back, it's stunning to see how birding has changed. With better understanding of classification, bird species worldwide are now considered to number about 10,000. Almost all are now illustrated in field guides. Travelling birders, scouring the globe and sharing tips, have turned up reliable sites for most; rather than 'somewhere in the Andes' or 'somewhere in the Outback,' they are known from specific stakeouts where you can find them if you work hard enough. In the 1970s, Stuart Keith asked whether it was even possible for a life list to reach 7,000; today dozens of birders have surpassed that mark, and a few have reached 8,000.

But what would happen if the new reality of world birding were combined with pursuit of a year list? For the answer to that, again we turn to intrepid British birders. Alan Davies and Ruth Miller had already decided to quit their jobs and spend 2008 birding around the globe, but their focus changed after a fateful conversation with Iain Campbell, one of the mad geniuses behind the tour company Tropical Birding. Iain is infamous for big ideas, and his response to Alan and Ruth's travel plan was typical: while you're at it, why don't you try to break the world record?

Sensible people would have rejected the idea. Alan and Ruth embraced the suggestion and ran with it. The previous record of 3,662 had stood for 19 years, but Alan and Ruth blew it away and kept going. From dawn on 1 January through to the end of December, they grabbed 2008 and squeezed it out for every possible drop of fun and excitement, zigzagging around the globe to see a dizzying and glorious galaxy of birds.

They also encountered a terrifying galaxy of obstacles, from unexpected weather and vanishing reservations to comically bad rental cars and absurd levels of logistical disaster. Ordinary people would have given up and gone home. This extraordinary duo laughed at the challenges and kept going, buoyed up by all the fabulous birds they were seeing. They ended with a one-year tally strikingly close to the 4,300 that Stuart Keith had considered a worthy lifetime achievement back in 1974.

This account of their quest is a page-turner, jam-packed with excitement. If you've ever been intrigued by a bird or by the idea of travel, you'll be swept up by this book, with its exotic landscapes, astounding birds and amazing people. The most memorable characters in the story are Alan and Ruth themselves, plucky and resourceful, and filled with good humour in the toughest of circumstances. The fact that they were able to survive this intense level of togetherness for a full year proves that they are both wonderful people, and both crazy, in a delightfully compatible way. In *The Biggest Twitch* they have graciously invited us along with them on the ultimate birding adventure.

Kenn Kaufmann

Kenn Kaufman is quite simply a birding legend. His epic book, Kingbird Highway, *which describes Kenn's North American year-list odyssey as a penniless teenage hitchhiker, has both inspired and motivated us to head out on our own great birding adventure.*

Introduction (Ruth)

If we'd been given a pound every time we were asked why we were doing it, what countries we were visiting and how we were funding it, we'd be rich by now. We would pay off our debts and set out on *The Biggest Twitch Two*. Everyone seemed to find it a staggering idea to give up everything and spend a whole year birding around the world. To us, though, it quickly became second nature.

In fact, we hadn't originally thought of trying to break a world record. In 2006, after visiting the international stands at the British Birdwatching Fair, we had simply wanted to do more travelling and spend more time birding. Just working on the Tropical Birding stand with our friends Iain Campbell, Christian Boix and Keith Barnes had seen us surrounded by images of mouth-wateringly exotic birds, and the Herring Gulls and Jackdaws back at home just didn't cut the mustard.

Once we'd thought of taking a whole year out of work to travel the world, however, we found that we couldn't come up with a really good reason for *not* doing it. Soon we had compiled a wish list of countries and had started drooling over the field guides.

Then came a pivotal conversation with Iain Campbell and we made what was either the best decision or biggest mistake of our lives. We mentioned to Iain our idea of leisurely birding our way around the world for a year and all the birds we might see on the way. "If you're going to do that," he replied, "you might as well try a bit harder and break the world record."

For a heartbeat there was silence. Alan and I looked at each other. We'd never thought of that. Research revealed that the world record for the highest number of bird species recorded in a single calendar year was 3,662, set in 1989 by the American birder, Jim Clements, author of the celebrated *Clements Checklist of Birds of the World*. It was a daunting figure, but when we looked again at our list of countries and estimated realistically how many species we might see it already came to around 3,000. Perhaps Iain was onto something.

Once we'd mentioned it there was no going back. Everything clicked into place. Suddenly our 'gap year for oldies' had a purpose: it wasn't just a self-indulgent drift around the world any more, it was an attempt to break a world record, something much more serious.

First, we set some ground rules. If we were going to break Jim Clements' record then we should follow his rules too. This meant that we could count only birds that were alive, wild and free flying; road-kills and caged birds were out. Jim had included birds that he had only heard, even if he hadn't seen them, so we would too. Ultimately, though, for a species to make our list we would have to be happy that its identification was verified either by our field guides or recordings, not just by the word of a guide. And it seemed only fair to use Clements' own taxonomic list, as he had been instrumental in creating a scientific list of the birds of the world – even though this made life tougher, as it recognised fewer species than some other popular world bird lists.

As the two of us were in this together, we added an extra rule just for fun: we *both* had to see or hear the bird for it to count. This meant that we would have to spend the entire year living in each other's pockets. For 366 days, because 2008 was a leap year, we would be able to stray no more than a few feet from each other's sides. Wherever one of us went the other would have to go too, because if only one of us saw a new bird it couldn't go on the list until the other had also seen it. We both had to get up and go to bed at exactly the same time; even going to the bathroom alone might be risky.

Next, we needed a name for our adventure. That was easy. Iain Campbell and Nick Athanas had already done *The Little Twitch* in May 2001, a one-month birding frenzy in nine countries setting a record that still stands. Sean Dooley, an Australian birder, had carried out *The Big Twitch*, spending 2002 birding his way across Australia to set a new year-list record, a grand total of 703. So there was only one possible name for our adventure: *The Biggest Twitch*. It had a certain ring to it.

Finally, we needed an itinerary. Our quest dictated our choice of destinations. If we wanted to break the record we needed to visit the birdiest countries and the best birding hotspots around the world at just the right times of year. Catching up with spring migration was going to be crucial to our success, and we had a lot of springs in 2008.

We planned out the year on the living room floor – and it's lucky we have a long living room. First we put down one very long strip of paper and marked it with a square to represent every week of the year. Then we cut up separate squares for each week, and wrote on them the names of the countries we would visit. If we needed four weeks in a country, we used four squares of paper. By the time we'd laid all of these end to end we'd mapped out over eighteen months' worth of travel. Nice, but impossible, so we had to change things. Out went countries with not enough new birds and in came more bird-rich countries to give us more birds in quick time. At our second attempt, we plotted the key destinations against the critical times of year: Texas in April, Finland in May/June, eastern Australia in October, India in November/December and so on. Then the less time-critical countries were slotted into the gaps to give us our schedule of twenty-seven birding countries in twelve months.

This had a huge impact on our budget. Instead of a simple round-the-world tour, we would be zigzagging our way backwards and forwards between continents to be in the right place at the right time. It meant many more flights on different airlines, trebling the cost and the complexity. While I booked up many of the European flights myself, I wasn't up to scheduling our madcap dash around South America, for example, so we asked the help of the professionals. I don't think Trailfinders had ever been asked to book such a complicated schedule of international flights either, but our Man in Manchester, Steve Alban, was brilliant in breaking down our year's travel into manageable chunks and booking us the best deals available.

Meanwhile, I spent many hours on the internet, fixing up accommodation and hire cars around the world. At about this time *The Long Way Down* was shown on TV, featuring Ewan McGregor and Charlie Boorman travelling by motorcycle from John O'Groats in Scotland down to Cape Town over the course of three months. Watching this became a bit disheartening. OK, so Ewan and Charlie are film stars and had a film crew covering their eighteen-country adventure. But they also had a warehouse for all their kit, and a complete team of organisers and fixers to arrange everything from flights and visas to clothing and luggage. We had just the two of us in our spare time, with a laptop, a telephone and our dining table. There was no comparison. Did we really think we could manage it?

Going for the world-record gave us a good story, however, and made it easier to ask for support. I had done some freelance marketing work for the Conwy-based web and design agency blahdblah design, so when it came to building a website for *The Biggest Twitch* there was, of course, only one place to go. Not being particularly web-savvy, we explained what we were looking for with no idea of its cost or complexity. Neil Rylance, the MD, appreciated the potential of our idea and just how much it meant to us, and was able to reduce the cost to something we could afford. The result was a brilliant website that showcased *The Biggest Twitch* and kept us in touch with our growing group of global followers.

Critical to the success of our trip would be our optics. We needed binoculars and telescopes that were light enough to carry easily, but robust and reliable enough to last a year on the road. They also had to be excellent quality: we'd stated up-front that we'd only include birds on our list where we were both happy with the ID, so we really needed to be able to see the birds as clearly as possible in all conditions. We approached Swarovski with a proposal, and they immediately bought into the idea and let us have two pairs of 8x32 EL binoculars and two 65mm ATS HD telescopes.

Clothing was pretty important too. We couldn't take much luggage, as the field guides took up most of our space, so what clothing we did take had to be versatile, long-lasting and quick to wash, dry and wear again. We'd known Maria Chilvers, who owns Country Innovation, for many years and she provided us with some fleeces to model in her catalogue and take around the world with us. In an interview for BBC Radio Wales, presenter Jamie Owen teased me about whether I could fit a year's supply of handbags and high heels into our luggage. If only! We didn't miss much from home as we travelled, but I must admit, after a year of living in khaki and walking boots, I couldn't wait to change into something frivolous and girlie – preferably bright pink!

But optics, clothing and a website wouldn't do us any good if we weren't in the right place for the birds, so we played our trump card. Over many years of birding around the world, we had built up a huge network of friends and birders in all sorts of useful places. Now we needed to call in favours from as many friends as possible. Not least of these was Tropical Birding. Alan had been friends with Iain Campbell, one of the founders of TB, for years. Maybe we would be living out Iain's own dream of spending a whole year birding while the responsibilities of being a father kept him closer to home. Whatever the reason, Iain and all the guys at Tropical Birding would be fundamental to the success of *The Biggest Twitch*, providing both advice on our itinerary and practical support on the ground in some of the toughest countries. Our final schedule turned out to be a mix of birding with friends, joining tours and relying on our own experience in countries we knew well.

But while we were very grateful for all the practical support we received, *The Biggest Twitch* was still a self-funded expedition. We had not only given up our jobs to follow our dream but also sold the house to help fund it, putting every penny we had into this adventure. We didn't know what we would be coming back to, but that was a problem for 2009. We were sure that something would turn up.

Luckily, we are better at birds than we are at budgets. Had we known before we left just how much the rising cost of fuel and the global economic meltdown would increase the total cost of *The Biggest Twitch*, we might never have left home. Thankfully we remained blissfully ignorant of the looming recession and so, with light hearts and heavy bags, we pulled the front door shut behind us and headed off on our adventure of a lifetime.

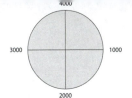

Prologue: 1 January, 4am, Arizona

It is cold and dark. We are waiting. Nobody speaks as all three of us stare at one spot. Slowly the first grey fingers of dawn creep across the Tucson sky. Tension mounts. Will it show?

As the light comes, all we can make out is the prickly outline of a cactus. But this is not just any old cactus. We are staring at it for a very good reason.

There! Under the bush. It's a Cactus Wren. The very first bird of *The Biggest Twitch*. Our scouting has paid off: we knew that a pair were nesting here at the Sweetwater sewage works and wanted Arizona's state bird to be our very first species.

High fives all round, then we're off. We have a world record to set and need to get off to a flying start on day one. The race is on: can we top 3,662 species before the year is out?

PART ONE

New year, new world

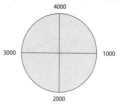

1–3 January, Arizona, USA (Alan)

No time to hang about. We had a world record to set and had to hit the ground running. With Cactus Wren on the list we were free to bird like crazy. Turning around, Sora Rail was bird number two, feeding in a ditch just yards away. Dashing around the pools at Sweetwater we soon had 40 species, including Blue-winged, Green-winged and Cinnamon Teal among the wildfowl, and a family of Harris's Hawks sat out in open view, just where we wanted them.

Madera Canyon was next and we birded it from bottom to top. Unfortunately it was slower birding than on our recce trip a few days earlier, but we still scored some great birds, including Arizona Woodpecker, Magnificent Hummingbird and both Olive and Black-throated Grey Warblers. A Golden Eagle soared overhead and Wild Turkeys scuttled about under the trees, the latter reminding us of our farmyard birds back home.

Then we blasted down to Kino Springs, where although our staked-out pair of Hooded Mergansers let us down (how *could* they?), we did have a fine male Phainopepla feeding in mistletoe. This large silky-flycatcher is a quite a looker, with his jet-black plumage, crimson eye and funky crest.

Patagonia Lake was next up and hopes were high for a big boost to our growing list. A scan of the lake itself gave us Greater Scaup, Common Merganser, Eared Grebe and Neotropical Cormorant, while a short walk along the trail brought us a real treat in the form of a pair of dapper little Black-capped Gnatcatchers. The species only has a toehold in the US and this was *the* place to see it.

As always on big days, the time soon started slipping away. Despite missing several birds at Patagonia Lake we realised that we had to cut and run; there were more sites to visit with, we hoped, nailed-on birds. So, with the sun already heading for the western horizon, we rushed over to Paton's Birder's Haven where, sure enough, birds were lined up on the feeders waiting to be ticked: soon Lazuli Bunting, Blue Grosbeak, White-throated Sparrow and Anna's Hummingbird were all on the list. Phew!

But we were not quite finished; the man who runs Paton's – Robin, appropriately enough – had news of a Gray Hawk that had been seen nearby. This is another very rare bird in the US, so we were off. (Thanks, Robin!) With the daylight almost gone we scanned the scattered woodland – and suddenly Ruth had it, flying directly towards us. Wow! We had a real close-up of this beautiful raptor as it passed low overhead, no doubt heading for its roost.

It was a great finale to day one, and we finished with 119 species. Keep this up and 3,663 should be easy.

The next day dawned grey and chilly with a howling wind. This was not the plan. Ruth had developed a bad cold overnight and the thought of a day in these conditions did not fill her with joy. A day in bed would have been the sensible thing. We decided to head into town in search of some powerful remedy to help get Ruth through the day. While there, we went looking for internet access in order to update the blog and share news of day one. As was often to be the case over the coming year, this took far longer than planned. We ended up having to use wi-fi in McDonald's, of all places. But we thought it essential to keep the website updated. After all, not to have reported back on day one would have been a very poor start.

Our guide in Tucson was Moez Ali. Originally from Kenya, he was now heavily involved in the local birding scene and knew all the best sites. Moez was itching to get going – and at last we headed out to look for birds.

Back at Carr Canyon the wind was still ferocious and birds were keeping their heads well and truly down. A Brown Creeper did eventually show but we needed numbers fast. At nearby Ash Canyon it was the same story: almost birdless. We tried some feeders near the bottom of the canyon, where it was a little more sheltered, and after a short wait we added Canyon Towhee and Cassin's Finch to our list.

It was time to cut our losses and abandon the canyons, despite having missed numerous species. We dropped down to the grasslands in the hope of better weather. As we drove the wind died and we felt sure we could get back on track. Whitewater Draw in the Sulphur Spring Valley was our next destination. This nature reserve is famous as a roost site for Sandhill Cranes and even before we reached the car park we could see large numbers flying in. These majestic birds stand some five feet tall and are powder grey with a splash of red on the forehead. In flight, the long slender neck is held outstretched and the legs trail behind as the huge wings beat out a slow rhythm.

Stepping from the car we were greeted by the magical bugling calls of the cranes as flock after flock cascaded from the grey winter sky and bounced to land alongside the lake. They gathered along the shoreline, many leaping into the air with open wings. Meanwhile our scopes revealed that the small flock of geese on the open water in front were mostly Snow Geese, with two Ross's Geese and a single White-fronted Goose among them – all new for the list. Scanning the far side of the reserve we picked up a magnificent adult Bald Eagle slowly circling a rough field, a causeway brought us close views of Least and Spotted Sandpipers, and in a willow copse we were able to scope a communal roost of at least eight Barn Owls – unusual for this species. Back at the car park we added our second owl of the day, a huge Great Horned Owl, roosting in an open sided barn. And all the while more and more Sandhill Cranes were dropping in, calling excitedly. It was quite a place.

Moez next suggested we drive the quiet farm roads in the hope of finding sparrows and raptors. We were also hoping for a Greater Roadrunner, which he had assured us would be easy around Tuscon ('They're all over the place,' were his words). First up were Sage Sparrows and a Ferruginous Hawk. And then we had a stroke of luck: a lump on a pylon up ahead turned out to be a Prairie Falcon. This was one bird we really had hoped to see: rather similar to a Peregrine, it is both a charismatic bird and a formidable hunter. We watched transfixed as the falcon eased into the air and, with a few deep wing beats, was gone.

Bendire's Thrasher was next on the list, finally popping up in full view after we had spent a few frustrating minutes of watching movements in the scrub. This species is restricted to the Southwest in the US, and is one of the shortest-billed thrashers with a lovely pale yellow iris. But the sun was sinking fast so we couldn't hang around. We made a dash to Willcox, only to find the wind had caught up with us again. The pools that should have been full of birds were white with waves and almost empty, making Ring-billed Gull our only addition. By way of compensation, Moez's sharp eyes picked out Scaled Quail on the road-side, and we enjoyed great views of this cute, diminutive game bird.

Our final site was Benson's Sewage Ponds, where we found just one new species: a male Vermillion Flycatcher, glowing red in the fading light. It was a cracking bird with which to end any day, but heading back to Tucson in the dark it was clear that Moez was pretty fed-up. The slow start, with the wasted – in his opinion – time in the morning then the poor finish in high winds had taken its toll. Ruth and I had had a great day, of course, but bird guides are a strange breed.

Day three, and we picked up Moez on what was thankfully a calm morning. It was still pitch black and the canopy of stars in the clear desert air was dazzling. Whether it was the stars or the improved weather, Moez was back on form and once again his usual happy smiling self. Meanwhile the power of American medicine had worked wonders and Ruth was also back on her game.

We headed again for the Santa Catalina Mountains, where Moez had back-up. Liz Payne and her mother Jean have a fantastic home on the edge of the desert – well *in* the desert really, as they count Mountain Lion among their neighbours. The bungalow was surrounded by native vegetation and well-stocked feeders festooned the lovely garden.

Liz and Jean greeted us like old friends. Tea, cake and fruit all appeared as we scanned the feeders for new birds. This was birding in style. A Curve-billed Thrasher hopped, rather awkwardly, onto one of the bird tables as a Cactus Wren climbed the garden fence. Gambel's Quails, with their ridiculous question-mark crests, squabbled over another hanging bird table. A Costa's Hummingbird suddenly appeared on one of the sugar-water feeders literally a couple of feet from our faces. We feasted our eyes on this little gem as at least two others buzzed around the garden. Anna's Hummingbirds also vied for our atten-tion, but we were on the lookout for something else. We waited and waited, then – in a flash of blue and green – it arrived: a Broad-billed Hummingbird. This is another really tough bird to see in the States and here it was in a garden right in front of us.

With our target bird under our belts we ventured out of the garden. The desert here is stunning, with Teddy-bear Cholla, Prickly Pear and Saguaro Cactus. Saguaro are the real cowboy-movie cacti, with huge arms reaching skywards. Some must be hundreds of years old. A dry streambed behind the house looked promising and sure enough we were soon watching a pair of Black-tailed Gnatcatchers calling excitedly from some mesquite scrub. But still no road-runner. Liz and Jean told us how they often see them crossing the driveway. Surely we could not miss Arizona's most charismatic bird? We bid our farewells and thanked Liz and Jean for their wonderful hospitality and – more impor-tantly – their new birds.

Back in Tucson Moez had a very nice bird lined up for us at the zoo. Nothing captive, of course, but a nearby park had some very tall trees that attract wood-peckers. We had just stepped out of the jeep when in flew a Lewis's Woodpecker. What a great-looking bird! Nearly eleven inches long, with a twenty-one inch wingspan, this is a good-sized woodpecker, and with its iridescent black plumage, red head and pale collar it has to be one of the finest. Unusually for its kind, Lewis's often catches flying insects on the wing – and it was strange to watch a woodpecker twisting and turning through the air in pursuit of some juicy fly. We were hooked, watching it climb palm trees, sit on a pylon and chase a Gila Woodpecker around the park. Moez had to drag us away.

Next we searched the nearby desert for Gilded Flicker, another handsome woodpecker, and once again for roadrunner, but neither was playing. Moez was now becoming worried about the roadrunner – so much so that we were starting to feel guilty. Did he see this dip as a slight on his birding ability? Or was it perhaps possibly a visa violation to miss such an easy bird? But hey, birds have wings (and legs) so these things happen.

North of Tucson we reached a rather eerie stretch of very flat farmland. We were sure we had seen this place used in some gruesome thriller, perhaps with a terrified heroine, tumbleweed and the sound of a distant banjo. The sun was gone and a low grey sky did nothing to enhance the mood. Moez assured us the place had birds, so on we went. We came to an area of stock pens where cattle were being raised intensively: a grim sight as they squeezed into small pens deep in their own dung and were fed something that was certainly not grass. It was a very sorry picture. Nonetheless these cattle concentration camps did attract birds. Thousands of starlings and doves fed around the pens. In one small tree a flock of Inca Doves were joined by a single Ruddy Ground-dove, just as we had been hoping.

Leaving this ugly place behind us we returned to cruising the farm tracks. Raptors were plentiful and we had more great views of Prairie Falcons and Red-tailed Hawks. Three Crested Caracaras strutted around a ploughed field and were great additions to our list, as was a distant White-tailed Kite hovering over rough grassland. But still no roadrunner and now time was fast running out. We screeched to a halt alongside a Burrowing Owl standing on the roadside, who returned our stare with piercing yellow eyes.

Moez had one more target bird to try for out here in this agricultural desert, where there was nobody in sight and the fields stretched to the sky. An area of turf fields was our next stop. This seemed strange: the close-cropped grass was criss-crossed with irrigation pipes and there was not a bird to be seen. With the light going fast we did not want to end the day on a dip, so drove slowly up and down, scanning hard. And there they were: a flock of 23 large, beige-coloured plovers scattered over one of the turf areas. Our first ever Upland Plovers. Brilliant – and not only a great bird for *The Biggest Twitch* but a lifer too! Now let's get out of here, we thought, before the bogeyman comes.

We rolled back into Tucson well after dark, tired but very happy with our birding. We had recorded 161 species in just three days, proving what a great place Arizona is and, of course, what a great guide Moez is. We celebrated back at Moez's house with his wife Beth and their irrepressible labradoodle, Luna. The food tasted good and we felt that *The Biggest Twitch* had got off to a flyer.

So, three days in and how did we feel things were going? Well, no problems with the birds. OK, missing Greater Roadrunner was painful, and that lovely pair of Hooded Mergansers seen on 30 December should really still have been there on New Year's Day. But we have been birding long enough to know you never see everything on the agenda and 161 species in three days was a very satisfying start.

We were already realising, however, that keeping up the website diary was going to be tougher than we had thought. It was a great way to keep the birding world in touch with our progress but it ate up time. Typing up a diary at the end of a long day in the field and then finding internet access to upload it to the website was clearly going to be quite a job. But we both agreed that it was essential for the success of the project. We wanted to create a buzz about *The Biggest Twitch* and we couldn't do that unless we shared our adventure with the world. It seemed to be working, with around 800 hundred hits per day on the site the first few days. Emails were coming in thick and fast from around the world with lots of encouragement and questions. We were determined to reply to them all. But we needed to find a way of doing this without becoming slaves to the computer.

Another problem had also emerged: too much luggage. We needed to find a way of reducing our three large bags. One large bag each and our hand luggage would be much easier to move around – and to find stuff in. But one thing we could not leave behind though was our mascot, Toco the Toucan. This realistic-looking soft toy proved very popular with people we met and made for some great photo opportunities – none better than when we perched him on a cactus!

161 species

4–11 January, Mexico (Ruth)

I looked at my watch one more time. Where was he? The airline staff watched us with frustration. Why didn't we just board the plane? At last we shrugged and gave up the wait. It looked as though Michael wasn't going to make it.

As we stepped onto the aircraft, there he was: Michael Retter, large as life, sitting in the front row of first class and grinning broadly. 'I was worried you guys had missed the flight,' he said, as he sank back into his seat. We were ushered back to our places in cattle class, the last two passengers to board. Forty rows of eyes glared at us for having held them up.

Michael Retter works as a bird guide for Tropical Birding and knows Mexico – and especially the Yucatan Peninsula – like the back of his hand. We knew we were in for a bird-filled time over the next few days. It was a relief to see him; birding on our own for the first time in this area would have been tough.

Alan's and my bags appeared first on the carousel and we loaded them onto a trolley. Then Michael's luggage started to arrive: not one, not two, but three huge black bags were piled high onto a separate trolley. And we thought *we* were travelling with too much kit! What did he have in there – a dead body?

In fact it was nothing so dramatic. Michael was running two tours back-to-back in Mexico so he needed plenty of gear. He showed us how he'd loaded his field guides into a cool box inside a black holdall, Russian doll-style. But over the next few days, boy, did we curse the six pieces of check-in baggage, three day-sacks and two telescopes we hauled around!

First stop was the car hire desk, and here began the first of many painful relationships with car hire companies worldwide. At first, the computer said no. But after much muttering and glaring at the screen a vehicle was eventually produced. To call it a car, however, would be over-stating things. Our luggage and the three of us already filled the office to bursting point, so there was no way that we could compress ourselves into the toy vehicle they were offering and we refused to budge. Even more muttering and stabbing at the keyboard followed until, finally, a slightly larger vehicle was offered: a Dodge Attitude. Great name, we thought, and took it. Next we had to try packing it, and as none of us was a Tetris expert, it took three attempts before we managed to fit in all the bags, three people and close all the doors. Eventually we managed it and Michael headed out into the Cancun traffic. At that point we thought our car hire problems were over.

Our first destination was the ferry terminal at Playa del Carmen, a few hours' drive away. This was the jumping-off point for the island of Cozumel, our final destination for the day. Having reached the town in the early evening, our first priority was to park the car somewhere that we could leave it securely for a day. Finding a walled courtyard serving as a car park, we paid the security guard and staggered with our luggage along the busy streets towards the local ferry port. We joined the end of a long queue for the catamaran to San Miguel on Cozumel Island and settled down to wait.

Up until now, the weather hadn't really brought itself to our attention, but standing waiting in line we had plenty of time to study it. The sun was sinking below the horizon, making the heavy purple clouds seem particularly sinister. The wind was blowing sharply, whipping the waves up into rows of white crests. These hurled themselves against the wooden jetty and periodically, one would completely douse the pier in cold salty spray. Kitted out for birding, we wore fleeces and outdoor trousers so didn't find it cold, though the sun-kissed holidaymakers around us in shorts and strappy sandals began to shiver. Alan, a bad sailor who can feel queasy just watching ocean footage on the television, began to fidget nervously in anticipation of a rough crossing ahead. Complete darkness fell and, beyond the glare of the harbour buildings, we could only see the lurching lights of ships moored out to sea. At least we couldn't see the waves any more but we could still hear the rising pitch of the wind. One set of lights detached itself and the outline of a large catamaran hoved into view. Deckhands rushed out to catch the mooring ropes. The doors opened and the passengers burst out onto dry land, gulping in the fresh air. They looked seriously rough: haggard and green with seasickness, as if they'd just endured the funfair ride from hell.

Then it was our turn and Alan's stomach sank as we braced ourselves to leap across the gap onto the heaving catamaran. Below decks, the air was hot and stuffy and the acrid whiff of vomit made it clear just how much the previous passengers had suffered. Alan held my hand hard, curled up against me, his head on my shoulder, and closed his eyes to shut out the world. This was to become a familiar routine whenever we went to sea.

Anyone who has been birding with Alan will know that he and boats do not get on. But recently, after years of suffering crippling seasickness on even the shortest boat rides, he had discovered the miracle of ear patches. Peeled open and stuck on the skin behind the ear, these patches release chemicals into the bloodstream that counteract the imbalance caused by the sea's motion. The result for Alan: no seasickness at all.

This time, unfortunately, Alan had not expected a boat trip so had not brought his patches. Instead he had to hunker down and endure it as, for an hour, the catamaran fought its way through the waves. But even the longest hour does pass, and eventually Alan's torture was over – he'd survived the crossing without being sick, a major achievement – and we were let loose on Cozumel Island.

Cozumel did not seem like our natural habitat. All around us trendy bars like Monsieur Frog's were offering cocktail happy hours and holidaymakers were wearing new suntans and ethnic jewellery. We clomped past them in our walking boots, outdoor clothing and fleeces. Where on earth had Michael brought us?

Once again picking up our hire car proved hard work. We'd booked it weeks earlier and had arrived well within business hours, but the hire car office was closed and in total darkness. Clearly there was nothing doing here. While we pondered plan B, a short Mexican, complete with drooping moustache, sidled up to us. 'You want car?' he murmured from the side of his mouth, furtively scanning the street from side to side. 'I find you car!' We hung around on the street corner – after all, what was there to lose? Then, just as we were about to give up on him, he reappeared. 'You like VW?' A VW would do just fine, so we followed him as he led us on a crazy route across town until finally he brought us out onto a narrow but busy street, lined with parked cars all the way.

'There!' he said proudly, opening his arms wide to display our transport for the next two days. It was a VW all right, but not as we knew it. A Beetle: well past retirement age, a torn black soft top, no locks on the doors, no windows on either side and – as we were to find out – no brakes. And it was pink. Bright, Barbie pink! Not exactly the ideal bird-mobile. But beggars can't be choosers, so we filled in the paperwork, piled our gear into the 'Pink Peril' and chugged out very cautiously into the San Miguel traffic, Alan at the wheel.

Stopping the car once we'd located our backstreet hotel was quite a challenge. In fact, the only way to come to a complete halt was to run the wheels into the kerb, so we did just that. The day had been quite long enough and we were ready to collapse into our very comfortable beds at the welcoming Hacienda San Miguel.

The next day began abruptly with loud hammering on the door to our room. 'Wake up!' shouted Michael from the other side. Had we overslept? We checked our watches: 5.30am. But no, according to Michael – and the rest of San Miguel – it was 6.30am. Why hadn't anybody told us about the different time zones across Mexico?

Now, I've got a bit of a confession to make. I'm not very good at getting up in the morning. In fact, let's be honest here, that's an understatement. I am appalling at getting up in the morning. My idea of morning starts about 7am-ish, preferably with a steaming cup of tea brought to me in bed, and ideally with a half-hour or so to come round slowly, maybe reading a book or something. Anything before 7am isn't morning but part of the night before, so I was already seeing parts of the day I hadn't realised existed. For the rest of the year that was to follow, the alarm would go off at 5am, 4am, 3am, even once at 2.30am, and I would stumble about like a zombie trying to get ready. I soon learned to lay out everything the night before to minimise the need for pre-dawn thinking, but still I'd find myself with T-shirts on back-to-front and my feet in Alan's socks. And as for trying to put in my contact lenses, you could open the vaults at the Bank of England easier than I could prise open my eyelids at those ungodly hours.

Alan, on the other hand, enjoys getting up early in the morning. The second the alarm goes off, he's wide awake and irritatingly chirpy, and he stays that way all day. Or at least he does if there are birds to go for. He sees a 4am alarm call to go birding as no problem at all, but a 4am alarm call to catch a plane is a different matter. As far as I'm concerned, 4am is still oh-my-god o'clock whatever you're supposed to be doing.

But, as it happened, the loss of time that morning didn't matter, as there was some great birding right in the courtyard itself. Surrounded on three sides by terracotta-coloured rooms, the pretty courtyard had raised flowerbeds, ornamental pools and full-size palm trees that the local warblers were taking full advantage of. While we tucked into hot coffee, tea and croissants, we enjoyed close-up views of Yellow-throated and Yellow-rumped Warblers, while a fidgety gang of Blue-grey Gnatcatchers flicked their way through the branches. Then the star bird, a male Black-throated Blue Warbler, showed off for us, with his black face and throat, rich blue head and mantle and a shockingly bright white wing patch. If this was the standard of Mexican birding, we were in for a real treat.

The reason for our excursion to Cozumel was to add the island's endemics to our list, and Michael knew just the place to look for them. We had only half a day to tick them though, so breakfast and courtyard birding over, we jumped into the Pink Peril and headed out of town. Luckily, given our lack of brakes, Cozumel turned out to be mostly flat, and by trundling along in a low gear we managed to avoid most of the tourists who stepped out in front of us. Driving along the seafront we dodged pedestrians and added our first Ruddy Turnstone to the list.

Soon we were through the built-up area and out onto the open road. Alan risked changing up into second gear and the wind through the open windows ruffled our hair. After a short drive we came to a turning. 'Left here!' instructed Michael from the back seat. Just as Alan indicated and started to turn the wheel, a honking blast burst from behind and a huge lorry thundered past just inches from his wing mirror.

'Oops, sorry!' said Michael. 'I forgot to warn you about that. If you want to turn left in Mexico, you pull off to the right first and then cross over when the road is empty,' he explained. 'Indicating left here means please overtake me.' Another piece of information that would have been useful in advance. Still, no harm done, and we crossed over safely and drove down the side road.

No sooner were we out of the car than we heard the singing of Cozumel Vireo, our first endemic. But even with much patience and some tape playback the bird remained obstinately hidden from view, so we continued on our way. Some other interesting clucks and squeaks in the bushes turned into a Black Catbird, and a Cozumel Bananaquit showed off in a spindly tree – a nice bird but as a sub-species, we couldn't count it towards *The Biggest Twitch*, unless it is split in the future. The next call rang out and again Michael played his tape. Obligingly the bird flew in and the next endemic, Cozumel Wren, added itself to the list. As it is the only wren on the island there is no mistaking this one.

More birds kept coming. White-crowned Pigeons and Yucatan Woodpecker shared a dead snag, a pair of Caribbean Doves shot low across the road in front of us and a trail into the bushes brought us a Caribbean Elaenia. Ten minutes' patient wait by a massed bank of flowering bushes was rewarded with a smart male Cozumel Emerald, which flew in and buzzed the red blossoms. With a green body, red bill and deeply forked tail, this hummingbird was handsome indeed.

We puttered back to the town and bounced the Pink Peril into the kerb outside the hire shop. We're not saying it looked abandoned, but as we passed it again only five minutes later with our luggage, people had already started throwing their litter into it.

Next day, back on the Yucatan Peninsula, we jumped back into the Attitude and headed to the Mayan ruins at Cobá. Now, the thing I liked best about the Yucatan Peninsula is the way birding comes with culture. To Alan, culture is something you grow on a petri dish in science class at school; it has nothing to do with birding. But in Mexico you can combine the two. In fact, you have to. The natural habitat across much of the country is too dense to penetrate on foot. But if you visit a Mayan temple site you can follow well-maintained trails right into the heart of the jungle and enjoy birds all around you. And magnificent temples too, of course.

Mixed flocks were passing through the trees over our heads but so far up that we couldn't see them in enough detail to identify. Then someone had a brain-wave. Why not climb the pyramid ruins until we were eyelevel with the canopy? Clearly the Mayans were keen birdwatchers. Why else would they have built the most perfect canopy towers: large blocks of chiselled grey stones layered in steps to form pyramids, making it easy to climb up to exactly the right height for birding the canopy flocks? Now we could look at the birds face-to-beak, and we enjoyed great views of a myriad warblers: Black-throated Green Warblers, Black-and-white Warblers, American Redstarts and Northern Parulas, plus Masked Tityras and Yellow-throated Euphonias.

Tearing ourselves away from warblers, we headed off down some less-trodden paths and were rewarded with two excellent new birds. First up, Rose-throated Tanagers called in the branches overhead. This is a species that has becoming increasingly hard to see as its habitat has been disturbed by a succession of hurricanes, so we were delighted to enjoy a good view of its distinctive plumage, with sharply demarcated rose-coloured patches on its crown, throat, wings and tail. Then, in the midst of another mixed feeding flock, we encountered a Grey-collared Becard, another very tricky bird. Michael was certainly pulling out all the stops today.

There are just too many birds in Mexico. The next morning, we had planned to head straight for Rio Lagartos and another boat trip, but birds kept distracting us en route. A flock of hundreds of passerines was flushed out of the roadside, so naturally we had to take a closer look. It was as if we'd stepped into a paintbox. At first it was variations on a theme of blue, with Indigo Bunting and Blue Grosbeak, whose names give a good idea of their appearance. But then the blue cloud parted and we saw an incredible rainbow spectacle in the middle. Give a six-year-old some felt tips and a colouring book, and they will instinctively create a Painted Bunting: a cobalt blue head with a red eye-ring; a scarlet throat, belly and matching rump; yellowy-olive over the mantle shading to darker green on the wing; and a grey tail, just to make sure all the colours are used. That's the male, of course; as usual the female is much less colourful. (I'm so glad to be a member of a species where the female has the more attractive plumage!) As we feasted our eyes on this paint-by-numbers bird, Michael – ever the hard-core bird guide – insisted we stop drooling over this 'trash bird' and concentrate on a Yucatan Flycatcher in the tree overhead. OK, it was a Peninsula endemic, but boy was it drab in comparison.

We finally made it to Rio Lagartos, where Michael had arranged for us to go out on another boat. No chance of seasickness this time though, as we would be exploring the marshy inlet that stretches for miles either side of the town. We piled into the open-top dinghy and our captain fired up the outboard. A chunky chap, he obviously enjoyed life and had an infectious chuckle, his belly wobbling in time with his laugh. He was used to taking tourists out on the water, most of whom wanted close-up views of the thousands of American Flamingos that congregate here, but he knew we were after more specialist stuff and he knew just where to find it. His binoculars were slung around his neck, though he didn't need to lift them once, birding almost by ESP.

First we reached a shorebird-covered mudflat, where we worked our way contentedly through flocks of Marbled Godwits, Short-billed Dowitchers, Royal Terns and Black Skimmers. Cutting the motor, we paddled silently in amongst the mangroves. Away from the cooling breeze out on the open water, the heat became oppressive and the trees seemed to lean over to smother us. I pulled my hat down firmly to cover the back of my neck and tried to ignore the headache that was developing. Even so, I was glad when we regained the open water and at least the illusion of a breeze. Here we found an area of exposed mudflat so packed with Wilson's Plovers and other waders that all we could see was a carpet of grey-brown backs and heads, spiked with chunky black bills and the occasional brown chestband. Then the colour changed, taking on the deep pinky-orange of American Flamingos. The lurid carpet rippled as the birds paced slowly forward, heads down in the classic croquet mallet posture of *Through the Looking Glass*, swaying their necks from side to side as they sifted tiny shrimps from the shallow brine. Wooden posts stuck out of the water at intervals, each topped by a Royal Tern busy preening.

The captain turned the boat around and we headed back towards the town. By the time we climbed ashore I was beginning to feel pretty rough. My head was thumping now, my eyes were sore and my stomach was making those ominous gurgling noises that had me nervously checking out the distance to the nearest bathroom. While Alan and Michael gulped down toasted sandwiches at the restaurant where we'd landed, also conveniently owned by our birding captain, I stuck to soft drinks, hoping I was just suffering from dehydration. I made it as far as the car park before the first rush to a toilet. It was clean and even had toilet paper – a real bonus, though by now I was packing a loo roll in each trouser pocket, just in case.

Soon, though, Michael had to start the long drive to our next destination, while I hunkered down in the back seat amongst the luggage and hoped to sleep things off. Some chance! Luckily for me, we were driving along a main road with plenty of petrol stations. Petrol stations meant toilets, and we needed to stop at every one. The distances between loo stops became progressively shorter and the time spent in the cubicle longer. I must be empty by now, I kept thinking, as my body turned itself inside out to rid itself of whatever had caused the upset.

I must have dozed off at some point, as it was dark when I woke up. Something was clearly very wrong and it was about to become to be explosive. 'Stop the car now!' I shouted, and before we'd even come to a halt I hurled myself out of the vehicle while the last remains of my insides hurled themselves out of my body at both ends. This must be the lowest moment of my life, I thought to myself, gasping for breath and wiping my face clean. Surely it can't get any worse, can it? Only two weeks into our big year and here I am, feeling like I just want to shrivel up and die. How totally humiliating!

At least it was dark, so my very public misery was only lit up for seconds at a time as headlights flashed past. This was no simple case of sunstroke; Montezuma was getting his full revenge. Who did I feel most sorry for: myself in such a mess or Alan who had to clean me up? No contest, I was feeling very, very sorry for myself as I changed into clean clothes and climbed shakily back into the car. I don't remember much of the journey after that, though I do remember shuffling into the hotel like an old crone, curled up with cramps, and collapsing almost comatose into bed while Alan and Michael went off in search of supper.

Even the hardest of hardcore bird guides has a soft heart, and Michael was no exception, so I was allowed a bit of a lie-in the next morning to recover. Nothing too excessive – after all, we had a race to run – but it was at 11am rather than dawn that we arrived at our next birding destination. And what a destination: Calakmul, the largest ruined Mayan city on the Yucatan Peninsula. Given that we'd missed the best birding time and arrived at the hottest part of the day we didn't have high hopes of our birding here, but how wrong we were. The drive down the entrance road alone took over an hour and had us leaping out the car several times to catch up with new birds.

Our progress once we'd finally reached the ruins wasn't much quicker. No sooner were we out of the car park than we started hitting flocks of birds: Grey-throated Chat, Northern Bentbill, Magnolia Warbler, Hooded Warbler, Scrub Euphonia, Ivory-billed Woodcreeper, Bright-rumped Attila, Violaceous Trogon: gorgeous birds and great names, coming in so thick and fast that Alan could barely keep up recording them on the dictaphone for that evening's bird list. 'What looks like a small wren with a very long bill? he asked Michael. Long-billed Gnatwren, of course, doing just what it says on the tin. Another one on the list.

Suddenly four large birds stepped onto the path ahead of us. We froze, hardly daring to breathe: a male and three female Great Curassows strutted out. What incredible luck! The male was such a striking bird. Apart from his white belly, he was black all over, topped off with a funky black crest that curled forward as if he'd combed it in place with Brylcreem. The finishing touch was a stonking great banana-yellow bill with a knob on top. His ladies were more discreetly coloured in shades of brown, with a subtler black crest and yellow bill. We felt privileged to have seen them, and were so excited that we even managed to get their name wrong in the blog that night. It's an easy typo to make, swapping Cassowary for Curassow, and it wasn't until we had some frantic phone calls from Nick at the Tropical Birding office in Ecuador that we realised we'd managed to ship four extremely large birds all the way from Australia to Mexico by mistake.

The highlight for your average visitor to Calakmul is the Gran Pirámide, the largest Mayan building anywhere. Gasping for breath, and a little light-headed from the exertion on an empty stomach, we finally reached the top and turned to admire the view. It was awe-inspiring. Nothing at ground level had prepared us for this and we were reduced to total silence as we contemplated the immense vista. In all directions we could see rainforest stretching into the distance, a seamless green carpet of domed canopy tops, punctuated only by a handful of grey pyramids poking up through the vegetation, marking the sites of other Mayan ruins – one even as far away as Guatemala. It was thrilling to see so much undisturbed habitat. No wonder the birding here was so good.

Once again, the Mayan canopy tower didn't disappoint as we enjoyed eye-level views of the wildlife. I caught sight of an unmistakeable rainbow of colour flashing through the vegetation: orange, green, yellow and black – it was a Keel-billed Toucan, a new bird for Alan and me. I had no doubts about the ID. After all, this was the bird on the front cover of our Mexican field guide, something I'd pored over for hours on the plane. Alan was scanning the treetops through his scope and drew me over to take a look. Across the Grand Plaza from us, a Bat Falcon was perched up, enjoying the peace on top of a less-visited pyramid. Maybe he too appreciated the eye-level views of other wildlife. Then Michael started laughing. Following his pointing finger, we saw a gang of young Black-handed Spider Monkeys fooling about on the top of yet another pyramid. They were playing tag, taking it in turns to pull each others' tails and then run away before getting caught, ambushing each from behind pillars and dropping down from overhead branches. Mayan ruins obviously made perfect playgrounds as well as birding sites. We could have watched their antics for hours, with toucans in the canopy and Black Hawk-Eagles soaring overhead, but we had miles to cover and were behind schedule.

Michael's driving, I should mention, was not for those of a nervous disposition. Maybe it had to do with the long distances and tight schedule or maybe he's just a speed junkie. And perhaps it was drivers like Michael that the speed cops had in mind when they introduced 'topes', Mexico's answer to 'sleeping policemen'. No matter how small the village, be it only a couple of tin shacks and a donkey, there are 'topes' on the road in and 'topes' on the road out, to make sure you cut your speed. Sometimes they are painted with yellow warning stripes, sometimes there are road signs to alert you, and sometimes they are unmarked, simply lying in wait to trap the unwary motorist. When the crawling lorry in front of us started to slow down even more on a perfectly straight stretch of road, Michael didn't hesitate. He dropped a gear, gunned the accelerator and we shot out past the lorry. And that's when we hit it at full speed: Mexico's largest 'tope', unmarked, unsigned and massive. The world went silent as all four wheels left the ground and spun uselessly beneath us. For a moment we were breaking all records for a flying car – until BANG! All four wheels hit the ground with a huge thump. The car seemed to hesitate, shake itself like a dog while we waited for something to fall off, and then carried on down the road as smoothly as if nothing had happened. What a car! Move over, Dukes of Hazzard, here comes Michael with Attitude!

It became my job to keep the driver awake on our long drives. Michael always underestimated the time it would take to drive to our next stop for the night, and we always made the mistake of believing him when he said we'd arrive in time for an early supper. We soon got used to arriving at 10pm, with just time to grab a bite, update the bird list and write a quick blog before collapsing in bed for a very short night's sleep – then starting all over again the next day. However, the upside of the long drives was that this gave us plenty of time to catch up with Michael's news. He was very excited as his partner, Matt, a geneticist from London, had recently moved over to the States and they'd set up home in Indiana. Two nations divided by a common language: there had apparently been a few crossed wires at first, something to do with pants and just where to wear them, and the perils of walking on the pavement rather than the sidewalk, but Michael was gradually ironing out Matt's Britishness.

Michael and I got on famously, and I was to realise as our Big Year progressed how refreshing it was to chat about something other than birding at the end of a long day in the field. Now don't get me wrong: I'm as keen to talk up the day's birds as the next man, but I did find that if you put Alan and a bird guide (usually a bloke) together, the conversation would invariably range from birds to birds and more birds, with the odd digression into football for light relief. With Michael, however, we talked about everything from music (you can learn a lot about someone from what's on their iPod) to fashion, and why there is no such thing as stylish birding clothes. Even Trinny and Susannah would struggle.

Another day, another temple, but this time it was an adventure just getting there. First we travelled down the Rio Usumacinta in a *lancha*, a narrow wooden boat with a very pointed prow, a tin roof and a bench down either side, which swept along the river at high speed powered by a noisy outboard motor. The riverbank on our left was Mexico, the one on our right was Guatemala, so we added a few birds such as Mangrove and Ridgway's Rough-winged Swallows to our Guatemalan list as we sliced our way upstream.

When we reached the site, we scrambled up a set of slippery steps cut into the high riverbank and set off along a trail through the rainforest. The undergrowth was dense and the trees closed in over us. The atmosphere was cool and green, and we experienced a great sense of isolation, as if no-one ever came here. Suddenly our path was blocked by a high moss-covered stone wall with a narrow arch at its base. A dark and dank tunnel led us on, a pinpoint of light showing at the far end. We stumbled our way through, running our hands along the damp stone walls to guide us and prevent ourselves falling on the roughly hewn floor. There was a movement of air as something brushed our heads: bats! Ahead of us we could hear blood-curdling roars. What dread place was Michael bringing us to?

Then we burst out of the tunnel into the Great Plaza of Yaxchilán and found ourselves surrounded by incredible ruins, half smothered in greenery, with immense fig trees overshadowing the gently crumbling stonework. We were the only visitors, and it felt as though we were the first to discover this wonderful place, with its overwhelming sense of peace, calm and incredible green-ness. The peace didn't last long, however. Howler monkeys, those blood-curdling callers we'd heard from the depths of the tunnel, announced very loudly their displeasure at our arrival, and a flock of noisy, pheasant-like Plain Chachalacas crashed about in the canopy overhead before flying off in disgust.

One particular fruiting fig tree held our attention. In fact, for the next three hours we were unable to move any further as bird after bird came into the tree to feast on its bounty. First up, more colourful Keel-billed Toucans showed off. I hesitated to drag Michael away to look at a dull grey bird, but it was an imma-ture Lovely Cotinga, and as an adult male flew in to join it I could see how it deserved its name – and top place on Michael's most-wanted Mexican list. A cobalt blue body and a plum throat and belly, it was lovely indeed. Two Collared Araçaris arrived, smaller members of the toucan family with a serrated bill and a banded belly making them look like they were wearing one of their mum's knitted jumpers. Noisy Montezuma's Oropendola showed next: a large, crow-sized brown bird with a wickedly pointed red-tipped bill and the distinctive yellow outer tail feathers of its family. Red-legged Honeycreeper shot through, its name pointedly overlooking its obvious bright blue body and green cap. All of these birds and more came in to enjoy the fig tree before we had reluctantly to tear ourselves away as the afternoon drew to a close. The sunset boat trip back brought a spectacular flypast by squadrons of Red-lored, Mealy and White-crowned Parrots. And as the sun dropped below the horizon, Lesser Nighthawks came out to feast on the insects swarming over the water, swooping low over the boat and racing us as we scythed our way downstream.

The next day we had another long drive, and a few birding stops en route, so it was well after dark when we reached San Cristóbal for the night. By the light of the streetlamps it looked to be a very attractive town, with a beautiful church set in an impressive square and narrow cobbled streets lined with elegant buildings. Not that we had time to play the tourist. After finally finding a parking space, we checked into our hotel and went through the bird list as we waited for dinner, a well-earned margarita definitely helping the process!

By now, even I was ready for a change from temples, and San Cristóbal provided just that. Here we were birding high-elevation pine woodlands just outside town. We drove the car a short way up the track into the woods and continued on foot. All around us the forest was silent. At this early hour and at this higher altitude the air was surprisingly cold, which was quite a shock after the lowland warmth. It wasn't until the sun began to filter through the trees that the birds began to appear. They were worth the wait. A handsome male Garnet-throated Hummingbird displayed amongst the bromeliads, its irides-cent ruby-coloured throat flashing in the sunlight. Michael played a quick burst of tape to encourage a calling Rufous-collared Robin to show itself and we were rewarded with a close view. We hadn't really noticed the trogon call in the background of the robin tape, but a male Mountain Trogon certainly had and he flew in directly overhead, showing off his fine ruby belly. Was it the surroundings that encouraged red-coloured birds to thrive particularly here? We didn't know, but our last bird here was definitely the best: the astonishing Red-faced Warbler. His bright-red face above a white body and grey back shone out like a traffic light through the pine branches and really made Alan's day. This was a bird he had drooled over for many hours as a young boy in North Wales, thumbing the pages of American field guides and dreaming of brighter warblers than Chiffchaffs.

By mid-morning we were on the road again and heading for the spectacular canyon of El Sumidero. As we climbed up this steep ascent we experienced a real change of habitat. We started in the foothills in an area of dry thorn forest. Here, exposed among the short scrub, we really felt the heat of the sun, which was such a contrast to our nippy start to the day. Not ideal conditions for birding but that wasn't going to stop Michael. He started to hoot.

Much of our year would turn out to be spent in the company of people and tapes imitating small owls. Pygmy owls of various types accompanied us as we birded in nearly every continent of the world and became a regular soundtrack to our birding. At the sound of the call – usually a metronome hoot or beep – small passerines flock in to mob the owl and move it on, and a human imitation can work nearly as well as the real thing. Michael was no exception and his rendition of Ferruginous Pygmy-Owl brought in a succession of hummingbirds, flycatchers, wrens and tanagers, and even a real pygmy-owl keen to see off the artificial intruder.

As we gained altitude, the habitat became lusher, wetter and, thankfully, cooler. Bamboo replaced the scrub, and it was here we were lucky enough to find two of the area's endemic species: Belted Flycatcher and Blue-and-white Mockingbird. We also followed the raucous calls to track down a family party of handsome Green Jays. Parking in a layby, we took a path through the bushes to a viewpoint. A vast canyon suddenly opened up before us, making us catch our breath. A sturdy stone wall prevented us from straying too far but we had to lean over the wall on our bellies to see right down into the depths of the canyon where a blue strip of river snaked through the gorge. Nonchalant locals lounged on the wall, dangling their legs over the wrong side of the wall; they clearly hadn't heard of vertigo. We tried to take the appropriate tourist photos but we just couldn't capture the scale of this immense landscape. Way below us Black Vultures soared on the thermals. It seemed bizarre to be looking down on these large birds as they circled far above the valley floor, appearing sparrow-sized, but they added real perspective to the sense of just how high we had climbed.

No time to linger, we had to jump back in the car and head for our final overnight stop, in Villahermosa. We'd heard of the appalling flooding in the region while still in the UK in December, but as always with world news it hadn't stayed long on our TV screens so we didn't know what to expect six weeks later. As it was, much of the flooding had receded, leaving a legacy of potholes in the roads and the debris of fallen trees and broken fences and buildings. The shortest route took us straight across a huge low-level area of open grassland. Initially the floodwaters were a good distance from the road, but as we descended they crept closer and closer to the edge of the road itself.

Coming round a sharp bend we were greeted with a large lake. Our road disappeared straight into it and we could see how it continued on the other side, but blocking the way was a smooth sheet of water some 50m wide. How deep was it? Just as Michael was considering rolling up his trouser legs and wading in to test the depth, a local bus came rolling round the corner. With only a slight touch of the brakes it ploughed straight in. We waited for it to stutter to a halt in the middle but it was driving so fast that the waters parted like the Red Sea and the bus continued out the other side without a problem. Clearly that was the technique and Michael needed no encouragement. He backed up and floored it, and we ploughed through the water and out the other side.

We arrived in Villahermosa after dark, and checked into our hotel. The whole place throbbed to the beat of the nightclub downstairs but we were so tired that not even an earthquake would have kept us awake once our head hit the pillows.

The next morning we arrived at the airport in plenty of time. In fact we were so early that the check-in desks weren't even open so we dozed on the benches until they opened up for the day. Here we had to part ways with Michael, Alan and I heading back to Houston in Texas while he flew on to another part of Mexico. We'd had an amazing whirlwind tour with him and had encountered a stunning array of birds, adding 270 to our year list in just ten days' birding. We'd enjoyed warm Mexican hospitality and superb Mexican cuisine everywhere we went; we'd come face to face with the Mexican chilli and survived, and had even experienced Mexico's famous stomach upsets and recovered. We were also learning just how hard it could be to find internet access on the road to update our blog – and were realising just what a task we'd made for ourselves by keeping a daily diary and a complete bird list for the day. This could be a real slog at the end of a long day in the field, but over the year it would prove its worth in making sure we kept the most accurate record possible of our grand tally.

We waved goodbye to Michael and his three enormous bags, then headed off to Houston. Already we were on 413 species and it was only 11 January.

413 species

11–12 January, Houston, USA (Ruth)

Houston, Texas, is the hometown of Rainbow Moon Under Sun. Ms Moon Under Sun, presumably known as plain Rainbow to her friends, is renowned internationally as a five-star psychic. Had we known this on our 24-hour stopover in Houston, we could have asked her exactly where we should go to see Red-cockaded Woodpecker. As it was, we had to rely on the excellent ABA/ Lane guide *A Birder's Guide to the Texas Coast* and a large helping of luck.

Much of our time in Houston, however, was spent in George Bush Intercontinental Airport. In fact, it being a major airline hub, much of our year was spent in the place. Perhaps the name of the airport is significant. Just as GB Senior and Junior both managed to upset many countries around the world with their foreign policies, so does Homeland Security manage to seriously piss off many foreign visitors. We can't be the only ones who've looked at airline schedules to try and avoid going through the US en route to another country. If you want somewhere to spend at least two-and-a-half of your three hours between flight connections, Homeland Security is just the place to do it. You meet the nicest people in the queue, and by the time you finally make it through, you have made new friends around the world and boosted your address book considerably. Americans returning home are processed separately and are probably blissfully unaware of what we 'aliens' have to go through, even if we're only in transit. In fact, just for writing this I will probably be banned from entering the USA ever again; making a joke about Homeland Security will generally see you taken away by burly officers for interrogation in a dark room.

First, there's the paperwork, which starts with the tricky question 'Are you a terrorist?' Hm, that's a toughie. Wonder how many terrorists are caught out by that one? Next you are asked if you are smuggling snails into the country. French gourmets beware! Then there's the fingerprinting – fingers and thumbs of both hands – followed by the retina scan. Several loud and authoritative stamps on forms and passports later and you are finally allowed on your way. We did this so often that we were soon on first-name terms with one particular Homeland Security official, Carlos (not his real name, lest he be carted away by those burly officers), who always made a point of asking how our birding was progressing and regaling us with tales of his fishing trips to Costa Rica.

Next, you have to reclaim your baggage from the carousel and queue up at Customs with your declaration form. 'Has anyone interfered with your baggage ma'am?' asks the official. Well, anything's possible in the last two hours while I've been queuing with your officials upstairs, I think to myself, but know better than to say it out loud. Finally you walk through a door and hand the luggage straight back to yet another official who re-checks it for your next flight. All that's left to do is run as fast as you can to the departure gate, which will of course be the one furthest away.

This time we were overnighting in Houston and, given our limited time for birding, wanted to stay near the airport. We headed straight for W.G. Jones State

Forest to the north of the city. The Lane guide advises asking staff at the Texas Forest Services Headquarters for information on where to look for our target birds, Red-cockaded Woodpecker and Brown-headed Nuthatch. Sure enough, Ray Uballe knowledgeably advised us exactly what direction to take. It was late afternoon by now, not ideal, but with nothing to lose we set off on foot through the woods.

We followed a trail through the tall pine trees, which towered ramrod-straight over us, sunlight slanting between the trunks and casting long angular shadows across the ground. It was still warm, perfect T-shirt weather, and it was great to stretch our travel-cramped legs and stride along the bouncy needle-carpeted footpath. Just one thing was missing: birds. The forest was totally silent, not a whistle, trill, *tseep* or *tzitt*, never mind the drum of bill against wood. We walked and walked, finally coming to a number of trees wearing orange cummerbunds that marked nesting sites, where we spent a long time peering up into the branches. But still nothing. We continued until we reached the far edge of the forest. From beyond the boundary fence came the steady sound of knocking on wood. No, this was not the elusive woodpecker but a man working hard on his DIY. We turned around to retrace our steps. This was the cue for a woodpecker to swoop in over our heads and up into the top of a tree. Could this be our target bird? Had he been attracted by the DIY hammering? We frantically focused our bins and immediately realised we had Red-headed Woodpecker in our sights, his head immediately giving the game away. He was a very handsome chap indeed and obligingly stayed put long enough for us to photograph him. His plumage was divided into distinct blocks of colour: red on the head, white on the belly, black on the back and tail, and a striking white patch on his wings.

This signalled a change in our luck and the specialist birds started appearing in quick succession. The very next bird to show was a male Red-cockaded Woodpecker. This rare bird flew overhead towards another belt of trees. We ran and caught up with it as it jerked its way up the trunk. It was black-and-white all over: black-with-white-bars on the back and white-with-black-bars on the flanks, a white belly, white cheeks and a black cap. It also had a distinctive black V running from its bill to its shoulder, but where was its red cockade? Well, somewhere on the back of its head was a tiny red patch, but as this is usually invisible we weren't going to worry ourselves too much about this; it was a rare bird and it was now on our list.

Next up was Brown-headed Nuthatch, which – surprise, surprise – was a nuthatch with a brown head. Then along came a Carolina Chickadee, looking to our European eyes very much like a Marsh Tit. The prize for cutest bird of the day went to Tufted Titmouse, a spirited little bird with a pointy crest and bright button eyes. With Pine Warbler making it onto the list just as we got back to the car park, we felt very pleased with ourselves: we'd scored some pretty hard-to-see birds and we'd done it completely on our own.

The reward for our success was a slap-up meal at Joe's Crab Shack, where we didn't fully appreciate the implications of their 'Dish to Share' menu and hungrily ordered enough of their delicious food to feed the whole restaurant. We waddled back to our motel and filled most of the king-size bed. The next morning we just had time to catch up on laundry and admin before heading off to the airport. Only eleven days into our trip and we were already on 422 species. If we kept up this average rate of 38 new species a day we'd be breaking the record in just over three months. What would we do for the rest of the year? We packed up and headed back to George Bush. Ecuador, and some exciting, fast-paced birding awaited us.

422 species

12–27 January, Ecuador (Alan)

It was dark when the plane banked steeply and began its rapid descent into Quito Airport. The airport lies right in the heart of the city and it is always a little disconcerting to be passing buildings on either side as the plane enters the crowded urban sprawl of the capital. At nearly 3,000m the air is pretty thin, and the engines howled in protest as full reverse thrust brought the plane to a halt before overshooting the runway. Thankfully the formalities of arriving in Ecuador are quickly dispensed with and by 11pm we were making our way towards the exit. Iain Campbell, our great friend from Tropical Birding, was there to meet us.

It is always good to see a smiling face when you arrive in a new country. Iain was straight on our case, wanting to know exactly how many species we had seen so far and whether we had missed anything in Mexico. 'We'll have to go like crazy,' he added, before we'd even had time to draw breath. 'We really need to build your total before you leave here.'

We had guessed as much. There was no way Iain and the other Tropical Birding guides were going to take it easy on their home turf. They were determined to show us and the birding world just how great Ecuador is. And the mission was under way immediately. Despite the late hour and the prospect of a 5am start, Iain insisted we try for Band-winged Nightjar before hitting the sack. Crazy, but what can you say? The man was trying to boost our list and we needed the nightjar. So, off we went into the dark suburbs of Quito armed with a flashlight and a tape of the bird's call. Luckily we didn't encounter any police or we may have had some explaining to do: driving around playing the torch beam on every tree while blasting out weird noises at full volume may not have been their idea of birdwatching. No nightjars could be found, however, and luckily Iain saw sense and we headed back to his place for some much-needed sleep.

Way before dawn we stumbled into the 4WD and were once again in the dark streets of Quito. A few blocks away we picked up Nick Athanas, also from Tropical Birding. Nick was wide awake, having very sensibly turned in early the night before, and he grilled us just as Iain had done. Numbers, misses and best birds were duly trotted out. Iain guided the 4WD uphill out of the city, and we climbed steeply, leaving the chaos of the capital behind. The first signs of dawn crept across the sky from the east, and we had a spectacular view across Quito to the high Andes beyond. We were heading for Yanacocha, a nature reserve high on the slopes of Pichincha Volcano, towering above the city at 4,784 metres. The reserve had been established to protect pristine temperate forest, and holds some very special birds. First light revealed our first bird of the day: Rufous-collared Sparrow. One of the commonest birds in Ecuador, perhaps, but right now a new bird for *The Biggest Twitch*.

The forest was cloaked in low cloud, a common condition here, and it was eerily quiet as we set off on the wide, level trail. We didn't have to wait long for our next new bird, as a gang of Rufous Wrens burrowed through the dense vegetation just below the path then exploded out across the trail right next to us. Next, a flash of colour announced a Scarlet-bellied Mountain-Tanager, flaunting splashes of blue on rump and wing, as well as the eponymous scarlet belly. A small flock of these beauties moved quickly through the treetops above us, leaving us hungry for more.

With mist still shrouding the trail, we moved farther along, scanning ahead for any telltale movement. A hummingbird popped into view, but just as quickly dropped below the edge of the path. We waited, and sure enough it returned and hovered by a tiny yellow flower, allowing us a few seconds to enjoy this colourful sight. It was a Rainbow-bearded Thornbill, a real gem of a hummer that does indeed have the colours of the rainbow on his throat.

Suddenly, our attention was caught by a shout from Nick: 'Sword-bill!' Another hummingbird swept past and we just had time to make out an enormous bill, like a medieval knight's lance. We hurried along the track and soon found this bizarre bird sitting on a bare branch. Through our scopes, we could marvel at this miracle of evolution. How does a bird with such an enormous bill live out its daily life? How does it preen and feed its young? Someone should make a documentary on this species, we mused. But our reflections ended with a curt 'Move!' from Iain.

Soon the cloud began to lift and we glimpsed the stunning views that Yanacocha has to offer. From our height of nearly 3,500m we could see range after range of hills sweeping away to the distant horizon. Sadly, however, many of these have been deforested to make way for cattle pasture – which just served to underline the importance of this great forest reserve.

At the end of the level trail, we had a choice of retracing our steps or plunging down the Spectacled Bear Trail, which winds back through the dense forest to the car park. For our guides the choice was easy, so down we went, slithering in the wet mud. The main trail provides great birding with easy viewing, but to see some of the skulking species you have to get in amongst the trees, and this return route certainly did that. It was hard going, and we slipped and stumbled as we tried to look ahead for movement. Something dark shot across the path. Nick was pretty sure what it was, and signalled for silence. We waited as he spun the wheel on his iPod to select the required track, and stared at the bank of dense vegetation where the bird had dived for cover. A burst of song from Nick's speaker. Nothing. We waited. Still nothing. Another burst of song. Bingo! There it was: a small black bundle of rather wren-like proportions. It was a Blackish Tapaculo and a new bird for the list. After taking a good hard look at us and the offending loudspeaker, the tapaculo ducked back out of sight.

Iain and Nick know this trail well and further along they told us to sit on the edge of the path and watch a stand of bamboo. Out came the iPod again, and a call was played softly. The reply came almost instantly and we could soon see movement at the base of the stems. The bird was clearly very close – and suddenly it popped out into view: a cracking Rufous Antpitta. We had only seconds to soak it up before it hopped back into the bamboo and vanished. By now rain was falling steadily and, after adding a lovely Stripe-headed Brush-Finch, we decided it was time to get off the mountain.

That night we collapsed into bed and were asleep instantly. Only two weeks into *The Biggest Twitch* and already we were exhausted. The prospect of another fifty weeks like this was worrying. But we were seeing amazing numbers of birds: 487 so far. That's more than a lifetime's birding back home in the UK, and we had done it in just two weeks. In fact, in just thirteen days.

Our small jet roared out of Quito the next day – later than scheduled – and turned sharply, giving us stomach-churning views of the city and mountains on all sides. It is only a short flight to Coca, and we soon began our descent. We could see immediately why our flight had been delayed: the area was flooded with standing water. Obviously there had been torrential rain earlier and we were glad the airline had not tried to land in those conditions. As it was, the plane skidded when it hit the wet tarmac and we were relieved when it came to a safe stop. We piled out into the steamy, humid air of lowland Ecuador – very different from the thin dry air of Quito.

Soon we were on a motorised canoe, roaring away from the busy quayside at Coca and heading down the Napo River for Sacha Lodge with high expectations. Out on the river proper, we settled back to take in river life, with lots of other local boats ferrying people, beer, vegetables and timber to and from who knows where. Two hours later we jumped ashore and set off into the jungle, leaving our heavy bags for the porters. A boardwalk led us through wonderful, pristine rainforest alive with weird calls and strange-looking plants and insects. Our leader was on a mission and there wasn't much time to stop for birds, though we did pause to enjoy a handsome Double-toothed Kite and to laugh at the antics of a gang of squirrel monkeys scampering through the trees.

Soon we found a cluster of dugout six-seater canoes moored beside a small channel and gingerly stepped into one of them. Our boatman expertly manoeuvred our craft along the channel and soon we broke out onto a blackwater lake. As we paddled serenely across, a large bird flapped about in the low trees at the water's edge. It was a Hoatzin. This amazing creature resembles a cross between a turkey, a pheasant and a reptile, and fossil remains suggest it has evolved very little since prehistoric times. The young even have a claw on their tiny wings when they hatch, which they use to clamber among branches around their nest. This was a great bird to welcome us to Sacha – and soon we saw for the first time the thatched buildings of the lodge. Marcelo, our local guide, met us for a welcome drink. We had met Marcelo at the previous year's ABA conference, where he was also guiding for Tropical Birding. As a native of the Amazon, Marcelo knows the birds here better than anyone and has the eyes of a hawk.

The alarm woke us at 4.30am on 15 January and we were quickly down for our first excellent breakfast at Sacha. We met up with Tim and Janet, our birding companions for the next few days. They were of good Lancashire stock, so we knew would get along just fine. They seemed really pleased to be a part of *The Biggest Twitch* and were keen to hear about our adventure so far. It was at that moment, however, that we discovered how rainforest got its name. Thunder roared overhead, lightning flashed, and the heavens opened. Not just rain but torrential rain. Marcelo decided we should wait a while and we gratefully agreed.

After half an hour the rain eased and we ventured out. Donning ponchos and wellington boots we slipped and squelched our way along the trail to the canopy walkway deep in the forest, soon discovering that the rain passed straight through our ponchos. After half an hour of slogging through the mud we were soaked and the rain was torrential again. Worse, we hadn't seen a single bird, let alone any year ticks. Finally, we reached the base of one of the walkway towers. Thankfully, a shelter here gave us respite from the downpour, and we huddled inside and glumly watched the rain. At last it eased to a light drizzle and Marcelo gave the word to start climbing. What a climb: 180 steep steps up a slippery, swaying metal tower, clutching scope and tripod. It was pretty scary. Of course Marcelo was used to this and it was several minutes before we caught him up at the small metal platform above the canopy. Even in these grim conditions, though, the view was breathtaking. A green carpet of leaves stretched away as far as we could see. Now we could look down on birds that from the ground would have been neck-breaking to see.

The platform was a little cramped for five, so Ruth and I decided to head across the walkway to the next tower, which was considerably bigger. I found it very scary stepping off the platform onto the swaying suspended walkway. Ruth, however, had no such problems and was happily leaning over the ropes snapping pictures. I found the best strategy was to look straight ahead and keep moving. It was about 100m to the next platform, though it felt a lot longer as I inched my way across the swaying path, thinking daft thoughts. When was the last safety check on all these ropes? Did it normally bounce so much? Why was the hand rope so low?

Of course we made it across safe and sound to the next platform and were very glad to find that it was much larger and we could set up the scopes. But just as my knees had stopped wobbling and we were ready to get stuck in to some birding at last, the heavens opened again. This wasn't funny. We needed birds. We stood and waited again for the tap to be turned off, amusing ourselves by trying to dry out our optics under the shelter of the roofed plat-form. Despite the downpour, a pair of White-throated Toucans climbed up into a dead tree and see-sawed their calls out across the forest, while a Russet-backed Oropendola swooped past the tower and vanished below the carpet of the canopy.

At last the rain eased. As if on cue, a colourful bird landed in the top of a nearby giant tree. And what a bird it was: Paradise Tanager, and aptly named, with its bright green head, glowing turquoise underparts, blue and black wings, and startling crimson rump. This was the kind of beauty we had come for. And scarcely had we recovered from the shock than Marcelo called 'Spangled Cotinga!' Another stunner was sitting out on a dead snag and we filled the scope with more turquoise blue, this time set off by a plum throat. Amazing birds came thick and fast: Bare-necked Fruitcrows, Gilded Barbets and Yellow-tufted Woodpeckers all vied for bird of the morning.

Time had flown by and soon we realised it was no longer morning but after-noon. Reluctantly we made our way down and headed back to the lodge for a very late lunch. Marcelo was not finished yet though, and he took us off the path into the forest and pointed. Incredibly, two Crested Owls were sitting looking back at us not twenty yards away. These are surely among the funkiest owls in the world, with their huge Groucho Marx eyebrows. How a day can change, from the depression of the morning rain to our total elation at seeing these mega birds. We floated back to the lodge buzzing with excitement.

Next morning the four of us again waited for the torrential rain to ease before setting off along the Napo River in search of parrots. These amazing birds were coming to earth banks to supplement their fruit diets with mineral-rich beakfuls of clay. The first clay lick we saw was from the boat on a steep, exposed bank of the main river and views were a little distant. Mealy Parrots were flying above the cliff and occasionally dropping down onto the exposed earth to grab a chunk of clay. The next lick, however, was a very different setup. We landed and jumped ashore, then took a short trail to a hide below another exposed mud cliff. Here we had jaw-dropping views of the action. At first the parrots were reluctant to come down, and sat in nearby treetops squabbling, with a barrage of raucous calls. Then one lovely Blue-headed Parrot took the plunge and dropped down to grab some clay. That was the signal for the masses to descend, and an army of green bodies tumbled out of the trees and onto the clay. What a sight! Parrots fought and pushed one another for the best position, becoming a heaving mass of bills, wings, tails and feet – like a single creature moving on the exposed mud.

By looking carefully both at the cliff and up into the trees, we were able to pick out several species. There were not only Mealy Amazons and Blue-headed Parrots, but also Yellow-crowned Parrots and smaller Dusky-headed Parakeets. Watching individual birds, it soon became apparent that each had a different method of getting the clay it needed. First, there were the bully-boys who barged straight to the point, knocking less dominant birds flying. Then came more timid birds, which fed around the edge of the flock and avoided the battle in the centre. There were even acrobats who swung upside-down from a low branch above the cliff and grabbed billfuls of clay like circus performers on a trapeze. Hundreds of birds were involved and the noise was deafening. This frenzy was surely one of nature's great spectacles.

We then explored a forest trail that proved to be amazing for manakins. First up was fine male Striped Manakin high in the canopy, with striped breast and a neat red crown. Next was a stunning Golden-headed Manakin, the male jet black with a head of lovely bright yellow that extended onto the neck. Last, but by no means least, was Blue-crowned Manakin. Again, the male was black but this time finished off with a lovely royal blue crown.

With Marcelo going to guide another group the next day, young Ivan stepped up to chief guide status. Ivan has amazing eyes and can spot the tiniest movement in the gloom of the forest under-storey. We set off into the forest and Ivan led us to a new canopy tower. This one was wooden and wrapped around a giant kapok tree like a belt. It was a solid structure and, after our high-rise walkway experience, a piece of cake. We reached a sizeable platform, which encircled the tree, giving a wonderful vista over the endless forest canopy. Wow! There was a flash of blue in the leaves right at eye level and we were watching a gorgeous male Blue Dacnis, a warbler-sized bird glowing blue with black wings, mantle and chin, and a crimson eye.

The next attraction was not avian at all but a mammal. A three-toed sloth was clinging to a tree trunk half-hidden in the foliage. Through the scope, we could see those toes curled around the branches: a good subject for some digi-scoping. We got out the camera and focused the scope, but just at that moment the sloth had an attack of camera shyness and was off down the trunk, moving like an Olympic athlete among sloths. It was impossible to get a clear shot as the woolly beast made quick progress down the tree. How embarrassing: we could not even get a photo of one of the slowest animals on earth. Better not give up the day job. (Hang on, we already have!)

Putting our failure behind us, it was back to birds. A stunning Cream-coloured Woodpecker soon swept in and landed on a bare sunlit branch for us to drool over – a butter-yellow bird with chestnut wings and a black tail finished off with a funky crest. To see a bird like this was just staggering. When I started birding some forty years ago I never imagined that I would be standing on a canopy tower in the Amazon Rainforest, Ecuador, watching such a creature.

As the heat and insect numbers rose, so the bird activity slowed, and we climbed down and took a short walk through the forest. We scored with a cracking view of a Spix's Guan balanced on a bough above us. Imagine a huge female pheasant, dark brown, with a speckled throat and scarlet throat wattle. Sacha just kept throwing up mind-blowing avian wonders.

Next we took the canoe across a mirror-like lake, its waters reflecting the surrounding jungle and the high, thin clouds that stretched like a spider's web across the blue sky. As the boat glided towards the landing stage, a movement caught our eyes and Ivan applied a few rapid backward strokes, stopping the canoe in its tracks. We sat motionless, watching and waiting, as a thrush-sized bird clambered up through the vegetation to reveal itself as a Black-capped Donacobius. The bird hopped about in full view, showing off its handsome combination of black cap, warm buff-yellow breast, sparkling yellow iris and full black tail, then dropped back down out of sight.

We disembarked at the end of the channel and birded along the trail to the Napo River. Birds came thick and fast, the highlight being a brace of Marbled Wood-Quail that proved tough to see. A recurring problem of writing about birds is how best to describe calls. The Marbled Wood-Quail has a great one, and if you have a CD of Ecuadorian bird calls on your bookshelf then I recommend you pause a moment and play it now. Pretty good, eh? For those of you that don't have that CD to hand, the best description I can manage is the bubbling up of a tumbling stream, but with more bass, followed by an *Ooh-loo-woo-loo-hoo-loo*, repeated fast and with the gobbling quality of a turkey. Got it? Probably not. But perhaps you get the idea. Either way, standing in the forest and hearing that from just a few metres away was incredible.

So we had Marbled Wood-Quail on call, but we wanted to see the owner of that voice. The calls stopped as we peered deeper into the dense vegetation, but suddenly Ivan was beckoning us excitedly and we quickly joined him. Unexpectedly he pointed up. We had been scouring the forest floor, but there on a branch about two metres off the ground were two Marbled Wood-Quail snuggled up together, looking like cute bantam hens. They had gone to roost, and it was only then that we realised how quickly time had passed.

Dusk was falling fast but we still had time for one more exciting sighting: not a bird but a Tayra. This large member of the weasel family popped up on a dead tree just two metres away. Almost as big as an otter, it was black with a creamy patch on its throat, and a new mammal for us.

Sadly, the next morning –19 January – we had to drag ourselves away from Sacha Lodge. Ivan took us down to the River Napo to catch the motorised canoe back to Coca. As we walked through the forest one last time, we collected two more species: a Citron-bellied Attila and a Solitary Black Cacique. We left with our year list having risen to 712 species after just nineteen whirlwind days.

Back at Quito, Nick was waiting at the airport with the engine running and we were off. We climbed steeply towards the high mountain of Papallacta. At 4,000m it was bitterly cold and windy, a startling change from the steamy humidity of the Amazon. With the wind and rain increasing we changed plans and headed down the other side of the pass to more benign climes. At Guango Lodge we sat and watched the busy hummingbird feeders over a welcome cup of tea. Already Sacha seemed a long time ago. A Mountain Avocetbill was the star of the show. This small green hummer has a unique upturned end to its fine bill, and was both new for 2008 and a lifer for us both.

The road back out was spectacular, passing through steep winding gorges with waterfalls spilling furiously down the rock faces. Nick told us to watch the river below for Torrent Ducks and seconds later we had some. Screeching to a halt, we bailed out and frantically set up scopes to focus on these amazing birds. Luckily the ducks were happily sitting on their boulder mid-stream, and we soaked up views of the handsome male, with his striped head and bright red bill, and the lovely dark orange underparts of the female.

We found a small, grotty, run-down hotel in a small, grotty, run-down town, but we were tired and anything would do. It didn't do meals so we set out that evening in search of food and soon found a small restaurant. There were no other customers – never a good sign – and the staff did not look thrilled to see three hungry people. Menus were studied and Nick gave us the rundown on what culinary delights awaited us. When we came to place the order we were greeted with a series of negatives: no beef, no lamb and no chicken – even though the latter is a staple in Ecuador. Finally we asked what they had. 'Trout!' proclaimed the waiter proudly. We looked at each other and decided trout would be just fine.

The next day began at the Virgin Viewpoint, though there was no view to be seen at dawn. Perhaps Virgins need more sleep than birders? We crept silently along a narrow forest trail so Nick could use his superhuman hearing to identify and locate birds. We have never, by the way, known anyone with a knowledge of bird calls like Nick. One call that we did recognise, however, was the harsh rasp of an Ocellated Tapaculo. Now this is a bird and a half, and was very high on Ruth's wish list for *The Biggest Twitch*. For years, Ruth had looked at a picture in our living room of an Ocellated Tapaculo by Ian Lewington. This painting has also featured on the front cover of a Tropical Birding catalogue. We moved along the trail to a point where a clearing might allow us a glimpse and Nick played his tape. The tapaculo responded immediately. The calls came closer and closer and then suddenly there it was: an Ocellated Tapaculo in its full, binocular-filling glory. Ruth could not believe her eyes. We had told her to expect just a brief glimpse, if we were lucky. This amazing bird is like a cross between a small bantam and a wren, with startling white dots all over its dark-brown, almost

42

black body, and a bold orange head and rump. This bird was showing off. 'Just like the picture on the wall,' as Ruth said.

The next day we took longer than usual to dress. Today we were birding at high altitude and wanted to be as well prepared as possible. With our limited number of outfit options layers were the key. Just about everything went on, including overtrousers, hats and gloves. We set off climbing steeply up the road and were soon enveloped in a heavy drizzle and cold wind. Ugh! Birds were not showing and as we stumbled about at over 4,000m gasping for breath, we wondered what on earth we were doing here? A Puna Hawk, a buzzard-sized raptor, flapped heavily past, no doubt heading for shelter. We moved back down a little and stood by the roadside, staring at some stunted trees through the mist and drizzle. It was so cold and each time a truck passed we got sprayed in icy water.

Then suddenly Nick had our target bird: a Giant Conebill. We were immediately on to it. This species, with its blue-grey upperparts and chestnut underparts, looks rather like a nuthatch as it climbs about in *Polylepis* woodland at high altitude. Today, mind you, it was little more than a grey shape in the rain. By now we had been out for some three hours and even Nick had to admit some breakfast might be a good idea. As if to underline this point, the rain came on even harder as we legged it back to the car. We returned down the twisting road, keeping a sharp lookout for anything resembling a café.

Soon we found a building that met this description and stopped. Inside, however, it was grim and barely warmer than outside. We sat around a plastic picnic table on plastic chairs and surveyed our surroundings: concrete floor and walls, a small cracked window. We could see no Michelin stars displayed, nor any other customers to recommend the house special.

Still, looking out at the rain and wind, it was better in here than out there. At least the staff looked pleased to see us, and soon set about preparing some very welcome hot drinks. Nick did not seem to think there was a menu, so we just took pot luck. Surprisingly quickly, bowls of hot chicken soup appeared. We could tell this is what it was from the roughly hacked chunk of bird that squatted in each bowl of hot soupy water. But we were hungry and cold, so what the hell. Once we'd removed any edible meat we could find on the chicken – not easy – our bowls were whisked away and replaced by cheese rolls. Next came scrambled eggs, which must have come from different chickens as they tasted fine. All this washed down with tea and coffee, and then came the bill: US$14 in total. Now it tasted even better. Nick thought they had probably bumped up the price for non-Ecuadorians. No worries: by UK standards, this was incredibly good value and if they made a little extra out of us, fine. Judging by the smiles and waves when we drove off, it looked like Nick was right. They probably shut for the rest of the day and partied hard on their spoils. Good luck to them!

Back up the pass the weather had not improved, but at least we were warmer on the inside. We hiked across the paramo and reached a lake. Well, it should have been a lake. Given the low cloud, we could only see a few metres of water and no birds. Occasionally a strong gust of wind parted the grey curtains and we had a tantalising glimpse, but just as quickly it was gone. By scanning fast in these openings of the clouds, we did manage to see Andean Coot and Andean

Ruddy Duck, but no sign of the hoped-for Silvery Grebe. The rain came again, so we headed back to the car.

Nick decided it was time to head for the radar station even higher up. With no sign of improvement, he was worried conditions could get worse. Worse than this? Luckily, a dirt track runs up to the collection of grey squat buildings crouched against the biting wind and rain. Unluckily, we had to get out of the vehicle if we were to see any birds. Nick was out and off, but we were more hesitant. Sure, we wanted new birds, but this was grim. As we tried to catch up with Nick striding away on his impossibly long legs, we gasped for breath in the high altitude and could barely shuffle let alone hurry. Soon both our guide and the car had vanished in the swirling mist, and there were certainly no birds.

Suddenly Nick's ghostly outline emerged through the fog and, like some wizard parting the clouds, he shouted to follow him quickly. Quickly? Doing our best, we caught up to where Nick was pointing down a slope. At first we could see nothing, but then movement caught our eyes. Creeping across the rock face were two Rufous-bellied Seedsnipe. This is what we had suffered for. It is truly amazing how the sight of a good bird changes your outlook on a day. In an instant, the cold, wet and altitude were all forgotten and we were high on adrenaline. We knew we were very lucky to see these elusive birds. Back in September 2007 the ABA conference had failed to find them and no further sightings were known to Nick. Many people suspected the birds had left this site, and some speculated that they had been shot or trapped, so it was wonderful to find them again.

Now on a high, we headed back down to Quito and the allure of warm sunshine and blue skies. The car had barely stopped for Nick to jump out when our new guide Scott jumped in. Scott is from Connecticut, USA, but left the States to learn the birds of South America. Tropical Birding was rotating its guides like some European football manager to ensure fresh legs for fast-paced birding. The only problem was that the two of *us* could not bring on any substitutes.

Soon we were speeding out of Quito towards Tandayapa Bird Lodge, one of our favourite places. Once into the Tandayapa Valley, however, we made a brief diversion up a side valley in search of a very special bird. And a scan of the forested hillside soon produced just what we were looking for: a telltale flash of bright orange, which materialised through the scope into an amazing male Andean Cock-of-the-Rock. This is one of those birds that makes you rub your eyes with disbelief. Predominantly a shocking bright orange, with striking black flight feathers and silver tertials, it also has a bulbous crest that extends around its bill in a fan of orange, looking like some bizarre helmet that has slipped forward. And it makes wonderful noises, too: raucous cat-like calls that attract attention to the lek, where males prance and posture in the hope of attracting the dowdy females. This show takes place twice a day: at dawn, then again in the afternoon. Away from the lek, however, these gaudy birds are surprisingly hard to see – which is yet another thing that makes them so intriguing.

With time against us, as ever, we made our way back up the valley and climbed the steep slope to the lodge. We were exhausted but happy, with some amazing birds under our belts. Could it really be only this morning that we had been watching Giant Conebill and Rufous-bellied Seedsnipe? It seemed days ago.

The next day, we birded the Tandayapa Valley hard and fast, seeing an impressive number and variety of species. Highlights included Plate-billed Mountain Toucan and the very elusive Tanager Finch, both up in the cloud forest above the lodge. Lower down, we were privileged to see a Scaled Antpitta on its nest. In the afternoon we sat and watched hummers at the feeders, oblivious to the heavy rain. Exquisite Booted Racket-tails buzzed around just inches from our face, revealing fluffy white boots covering their tiny feet and rackets on their forked tails. Other great hummers included Fawn-breasted Brilliant, Buff-tailed Coronet, Purple-throated Woodstar and Violet-tailed Sylph, all at point-blank range. We watched this living kaleidoscope from beneath the roof of the deck as we drank wonderful coffee: the perfect way to spend a rainy afternoon.

Early on 23 January we left Tandayapa and headed lower to the wonderful reserve at Milpe. This is owned and managed by the Mindo Cloudforest Foundation, the charity for which we were raising funds during *The Biggest Twitch*. The foundation was established in December 2001 to conserve and promote the Chocò area of northwestern Ecuador, one of the world's most diverse and threatened Endemic Bird Areas. Their projects to-date include the Nono-Tandayapa-San Tadeo Ecoroute (El Paseo del Quinde), an eco-scenic route for nature tourism, plus Bird Sanctuaries at Milpe and Rio Silanche.

It was great to see where our funds would be spent, and we were keen to explore and find out how the reserve was developing. It was a good sign to find well-maintained buildings and enthusiastic staff who greeted us warmly. Better still there were wonderful birds! A lek for Club-winged Manakins was just 100m away from the entrance so we headed there first. It didn't take long to track down the telltale buzzing; not a call, but a mechanical noise these birds make by flicking their wing feathers forward above their back. Seeing one, however, proved trickier. We crept into the forest and crouched down to await the next buzz. At last we could make out one of these weird little, robin-sized birds, with its dark red-brown body, black-and-white wings and bright red crown. Even better: it did its party trick right in front of us, leaning forward, lifting its wings and buzzing. Wow! We had never seen anything like it.

And there was more. We were walking down a forest trail, already reeling from tanagers, hummingbirds and woodpeckers, when a small traffic cone dropped onto the path in front of us. At least it was the colour of a traffic cone: shocking bright orange and white. We stared open-mouthed at this latest amazing bird. How could it be this colour? We knew it was a tanager, but which one? With Scott some distance ahead we grabbed the field guide – and there it was: Scarlet-and-white Tanager, number 19 on plate 86 of *The Birds of Ecuador* by Ridgely and Greenfield. Personally we would have named it 'Orange-and-white Tanager' but it was a stunning bird by any name, its luminous orange plumage contrasting shockingly with its white belly and bright red eye. Luckily the bird stayed in view long enough for Scott to enjoy it as well. He was thrilled, as this species is rarely seen in Ecuador. Thank you, Mindo Cloudforest Foundation! Now we were now even more enthusiastic about our fundraising.

24 January, and Scott had already told us that today would be different. Birding, yes, but not as we knew it. We arrived at our destination, Paz de las Aves Refuge, just after dawn. But we were not the first birders here; a small coach was already in

the car park. Scott explained the others had probably come early to see the Andean Cock-of-the-rock lek, something we had already seen, so we were not missing anything. It was hard to keep our footing on the steep, slippery path, and we grabbed tree branches to prevent ourselves from falling headfirst down the trail. The other birders must have done this in the pre-dawn dark and we expected to find a pile of crumpled bodies at the bottom. Eventually we slid to a stop by a small shelter, where a group of American and Canadian birders were sheltering from the rain, some wrapped in bright yellow ponchos with hoods pulled down over their faces, looking like some alien species that landed in the forest.

We were told that the star bird had not yet shown, and that the local guide had gone to search for it. So Scott, never a man to stand idle, switched straight to plan B. We set off along a side trail to find two Rufous-bellied Nighthawks fast asleep on a horizontal branch at eye-level. And while enjoying great views of these hard-to-see nocturnal birds one of the local guides came along the path, trailing behind him came a gang of six Dark-backed Wood-Quail. Unbelievable! This shy species generally hides away deep in the undergrowth – but clearly this group had not read the field guide. They pottered along the trail just metres away. We were stunned. The guide was feeding them worms and leading them back along the trail so the group could enjoy them.

We returned to the shelter and good news. The other guide had found the star bird and was hoping it would show soon. We took our places on the bench and waited in tense silence. Then we heard a call; not a bird call, but a man shouting 'Maria' over and over again. What on earth was going on? Round the corner of the muddy wet forest trail came the guide, still calling 'Maria, Maria, Maria!' This guy was also throwing worms behind him, and seconds later the object of his calling bounced round the corner and into full view: a Giant Antpitta. We stared in disbelief. This bird is nearly impossible to see under normal circumstances, yet there it was just a few metres away.

The Giant Antpitta is one bird that really earns its name, being huge compared to most other members of its family. It stands very upright on long grey legs, has reddish-brown underparts, chocolate-brown upperparts and a massive black bill more reminiscent of a Night Heron than an antpitta. Maria, as this individual was obviously called, stood boldly in front of us and picked up the chopped worms from the path, beating them against a tree root to ensure they were dead. This fascinating bird – a species we had never dreamed of seeing – held us spellbound. Sadly, the heavy rain and poor light made good photos impossible, but we will never forget Maria.

As our group climbed slowly back up the narrow muddy trail, a Scaled Fruiteater was spotted above. Panic ensued as everyone tried to get into position for a glimpse. One guy swung round, knocking Ruth with his rucksack and sending her flying into me. I reeled backwards into another birder, Charlie Hess, who thankfully thumped into a tree, breaking all our falls. Others were not so lucky, however, and as one person tumbled over into the next, Charlie's group began to go down domino-style. It was chaos, with people grabbing at anything to stop themselves sliding all the way back to the bottom. Amazingly the bird sat there throughout, probably far too entertained to think about flying off.

After all the excitement and climbing back up that hill we were starving.

Luckily breakfast was included in the birding circus and we were served hot chocolate, deep-fried maize-and-chicken balls, delicious cheese empanadas and fruit salad. Just the job. Then a Yellow-faced Grassquit decided to hop out and show itself just as Ruth had nipped to the loo. Scott dashed over and called her to hurry up, but the door was jammed. Disaster! As Ruth struggled, the Grassquit hopped into the deep grass and vanished. By the time she broke free – with a final superhuman effort – and dashed over to join us, we were simply staring at grass. Luckily, after a tense few moments, out it popped again. And a very nice little bird it was, too, with its bright green body and yellow face.

Heavy rain made the rest of the day's birding hard work and new species were slow to come, a pair of Esmeralda's Antbirds being the highlight. But when we got back to our hotel there was just enough light for a final unexpected burst, with Pied Water-Tyrant, Pacific Hornero and Pacific Parrotlet all appearing in the hotel garden. Our total now stood at 971 species after just twenty-four days. We were sure to break the one thousand mark before the end of January. It was hard to take in. We had seen so many birds so quickly.

The next morning we met up with Jose Illanes, another Tropical Birding Guide. We have known Jose a long time and it was good to catch up with him. Jose was guiding a group, and several of his clients had been following our adventure via the website and were keen for firsthand news. Next we headed for Rio Salanche, another area of pristine forest and another changeover point for our guides. Nick was taking over from Scott, once again, and was now being joined by another of our great friends, Sam Woods.

Sam, who is English, works from Quito as a full-time guide for TB and travels the world in pursuit of a life list of five thousand species. He is great company and always ready for a laugh. But Sam is also a born worrier – about anything and everything, but mostly about birds. It does not matter how rare or wonderful the latest sighting is, you know that he will immediately start worrying about what he might miss next. In turn we worry a little about Sam, as he says his life will be over when he sees five thousand species and he is getting very close. Fair enough to throw in the towel after seeing all the world's birds, of course. Job done. But after only half? That's just not right!

Personally, I would never want to see all the world's birds. I love the thought that there are still thousands of amazing new species out there. They are adventures waiting to happen, reasons to get up in the morning and reasons to go to work to earn cash to fund those adventures. I would be very sad if that all came to an end.

Once the three guides got together, they immediately went into a tight huddle to discuss tactics. Our input was obviously not required; this might be our big year but right now the guys were calling all the shots. Scott was due to return to Quito, but there was no way he was leaving without that prized number 1,000 on our list. He did not have to wait long. With five of us now birding like crazy, new birds came every few minutes and we struggled to keep count. Then suddenly we had 999 species. Cue a drum roll: what would the next bird be?

Number 1,000 turned out to be a Slate-throated Gnatcatcher. Perhaps not the most beautiful or charismatic species, but at that moment it was just brilliant. This warbler-sized bird feeds high in the canopy of humid forests in northwest

Ecuador where it is a scarce resident. It is also a real neck-breaker to see! There were high fives all round, and then Scott said farewell and headed for home. But there was to be no resting on our laurels. Despite the intensifying downpour, Nick and Sam got straight back into the birding and kept playing tapes of more birds we needed (just in case any species equipped with snorkels and flippers could be tempted out, perhaps). We again met Jose. By now his whole group knew who we were and all gathered round for a photo with *The Biggest Twitch*. It seemed very odd to be treated like this. But it began to sink in that we were doing something very special.

The next morning, 26 January, we drove northwest with Nick, Sam and Nesta, our driver. We were heading for the Pacific coast of Ecuador, not far from the Columbian border – a new area for us. Mid-morning brought our first views of the inviting blue sea and white curling breakers as we sped north along a coastal road. We stopped for lunch in a rough-looking town on the coast. It had the feel of Africa rather than South America, with a large black population, presumably descendants of slaves. We ordered seafood, figuring that – just a few hundred metres from the ocean – it would be safe, and sat back to enjoy our wait in the hot early afternoon sunshine. After so much rain recently, it felt really good to feel the sun on our pale skin. The food was excellent, too: prawns and rice, with various other bits of fish thrown in for good measure. Nick got into an argument over the bill, though, his fluent Spanish proving useful as he rumbled the waitress who had tried to overcharge us.

Our route now took us inland. And, guess what, there were black clouds gathering ahead. Down came the rain again. We reached an area of protected forest and left Nesta to guard the truck while we set off along the dirt road in search of birds. A huge lorry hauling logs roared into view and we hurried out of the way. Nick explained that there was still plenty of illegal logging up here near the Columbian border, despite this being a so-called protected area. The loggers are very powerful and don't let conservation get in the way of big business. We just stepped meekly aside as another illegal load was shipped off to market leaving another piece of habitat destroyed. It was a reminder of the importance of Mindo Cloudforest Foundation and why we were raising money for them.

Despite the loggers, we found some great birds deeper into the forest. Five-coloured Barbet was the first. Restricted to this area in Ecuador, it had been high on our wanted list. Views were difficult in the dense vegetation, with its constant movement frustrating our attempts to direct one another. It was a bit like doing a jigsaw: one second you saw a wing, then a belly, next a head and finally a tail. The trick was to fit all these fragments into a mental picture of the whole thing. A decent view finally revealed that our bird was the size of a large finch, with yellow underparts, a pale throat, blackish upperparts and a neat red skull-cap to top everything off.

Next up was a male Blue Cotinga. Like many of its family, this species likes to perch where it can see and be seen, so there he was on top of a dead branch, resplendent in bright blue, with his plum-coloured belly patch and throat. This was another species found only in the northwest of Ecuador. We were doing well.

Then a flash of white through the canopy brought an immediate 'Where the hell did it go?' response from Nick. We knew this must be something good and quickly moved along the trail to try and relocate it. 'There it is,' called Sam. Sitting high in another tree was a pure white bird, its black primary tips just visible through the scope. Black-tipped Cotinga. We could also see the soft orange-yellow eye and neat black bill through the scope. Then a deep slow call had us on alert for a Slaty-tailed Trogon, another local speciality that we were after. Trogons are strange birds: they sit still for ages, just turning their head slowly to scan for fruit or a juicy insect and uttering their weird call that sounds more distant than it is. As usual, it was Ruth who spotted it; she has a mysterious knack with trogons. This species was as wonderful as any of its family, with its green chest and head enclosed in a smart black mask, plus a red eye-ring, yellow bill, red belly, charcoal tail and dark grey-green wings.

As we left the forest we passed another huge lorry being loaded by crane with more fresh-cut timber. These guys were blatant in their destruction of the forest. A machine-gun would have put a swift end to it. Sadly we had none – though I'm not sure the same could be said for them.

The next morning we were on the road by 5am. Nothing new there. Picking up the aptly named Stub-tailed Antbird at dawn, we then went exploring. Nick and Sam had heard about a new trail in an area of forest that neither of them had birded before and they were keen to see what the area held. Following a tip-off about the muddy trail we stopped in a village and purchased Wellington boots – being ripped off to the tune of US$28, a fortune in Ecuador. Of course by the time we got there, it was raining and we had some trouble finding the start of the trail. This should have sounded warning bells – and it did to us – but Nick and Sam were keen to push on. We first crossed an area of very wet grassland, where each step involved a major effort not to fall over in the glutinous mixture of mud and cow dung. Our money was now looking very well spent.

At last we reached the forest edge, but our hopes evaporated as we saw the so-called trail. 'River of mud' would have been a better description. Surely we were not going down that? But Nick and Sam ploughed on, leaving us to struggle in their wake. Our ill-fitting Wellingtons were nearly pulled off each time we tried to extract them – as though the evil mud wanted to drag us down into its depths. Meanwhile the rain got heavier and birding became nearly impossible. And this was for fun? Unbelievably, the mud got worse. We were now reduced to stepping on logs as the mud was higher than our boots and we didn't dare look upwards for birds. After the umpteenth time one of Ruth's boots had come off, leaving her hopping on one leg, we decided enough was enough. So back we went to the car, with Nick and Sam storming ahead of us, not happy at our wimping out. It was nice to see Nesta coming down the trail to make sure we were OK. We set off back towards Quito, having abandoned our stinking wellies by the roadside. But spirits rose when our long drive was very pleasantly interrupted by the sight of a juvenile Andean Condor soaring among Black Vultures well away from its normal range.

We rolled back into the capital well after dark and said our goodbyes and thanks to the Tropical Birding team who had pushed us so hard. They are a tough bunch but boy, they deliver the goods. Just what we had wanted. We were now on 1,050 species for 2008, with only twenty-seven days gone.

1,050 species

PART TWO

African adventure

28 January–1 February, North Wales (Alan)

Throughout the year, our airline route between birding destinations frequently brought us back to the UK for a brief 24-hour stopover between flights before we headed off to our next target country. Just long enough to do our laundry and repack our bags and, if we were lucky, squeeze in some birding. This leg was no exception.

Britain was damp and grey, but we soon brightened up when we saw John Roberts waiting for us at Manchester Airport arrivals. John is an old friend, and always upbeat and jolly. He lifted our spirits so much that, despite being very tired, we decided to go birding instead of straight to bed.

Not far off our route home from the airport is the Dee Estuary, which forms the northern border between England and Wales. This huge tidal area is thronged with birdlife and is always a great birding venue. Today though, we were after just one species: Bewick's Swan. Given our proposed route for the rest of the year, today was likely to be our one and only shot at this winter visitor from Siberia. Thankfully John had done his homework and knew just where to look.

Soon we were standing on the edge of a vast grazing marsh scanning for white blobs. The good thing about swans is that they are large and white, so we quickly spotted a flock. But it is not as simple as that. Three species occur here and they often form mixed feeding flocks, so we now had to sort through them. The Mute Swans are easy, with their bright orange bills. The Whoopers and Bewick's are a little trickier, though, as both have black and yellow bills and the flock was distant. Using the scope on 60-times magnification did the trick: we could clearly see the Whoopers' diagnostic yellow triangle that extends in a point towards the tip of the black bill, while the Bewick's revealed their more rectangular patch of yellow that ends well away from bill tip. Happy with all three species on our list – and especially with the Bewick's – we headed for home.

We were tired and jet-lagged after a month of hard travel but there were new birds that needed to be seen. So we got up early the next day and headed down to the nearby RSPB Reserve at Conwy for some local home patch birding. Our friends, Ken Croft and Steve Culley, were already in the car park and fired up to boost the list. We left the reserve with a cheery 'back later' and headed onto the busy A55 dual carriageway that runs along the North Wales coast. With Steve driving like a man possessed we were soon at our first site. It was not the prettiest of spots – an industrial estate with small factories under construction and patches of rough grassland strewn with litter – but the next bird we saw more than made up for it: a Short-eared Owl came drifting over the grassland, looking gorgeous in the winter sun. Despite our hurry, this was one bird that should always be savoured. We watched as the owl quartered the ground, occasionally twisting back on its long wings to recheck some unseen noise in the grass, before it finally dropped into a patch of long grass and was gone. Then, seconds later, so were we.

We dashed back to RSPB Conwy to find the place packed out with the monthly farmers' market. Steve managed to find a parking place and we elbowed our way through the shoppers and out towards the hides. As always, Conwy held plenty of birds and we boosted our list nicely. Progress was slow, however, as many people stopped to ask us how *The Biggest Twitch* was going and all offered warm encouragement. It was great to see so many old friends, but we really needed to push on. Back at the car we found Steve and Ken already tucking into pork pies and sandwiches. Late breakfast or lunch? Both.

Soon we were at Aber Ogwen North Wales Wildlife Trust reserve just east of Bangor, where the River Ogwen flows into the sea. A small pool behind the beach usually holds a good selection of birds and today it gave us a silvery winter-plumaged Spotted Redshank amongst a gang of Greenshanks, plus a graceful Little Egret stepping delicately through the shallows. Flocks of Knot and Dunlin wheeled over the estuary, flashing white then grey as they banked through the air like a single creature. How on earth do they not collide?

We dashed across onto the Isle of Anglesey, hoping there was no speed camera on the bridge. Steve used all his knowledge of the island to get us to Red Wharf Bay double-quick, and we were glad when the car came to an abrupt stop as we were beginning to feel a bit carsick. The saltmarsh here is good for Jack Snipe and we quickly scored three of these diminutive waders amongst some forty Common Snipe that flew out from the wet grass. All too soon we were back in the car as Steve sped north for more birds, pausing only when Ken spotted a Red-legged Partridge in a small field. On again, and we raced over to northwest Anglesey and Holyhead. This is Ken's home turf and he knew just where to find the birds we wanted. At Beddmanarch Bay we soon had Slavonian Grebes in our scopes, followed by Pale-bellied Brent Geese and Bar-tailed Godwits, while Holyhead Harbour quickly delivered Black Guillemots at the fish quay. Unfortunately all the fast driving had taken its toll and as we pulled into the main harbour car park, I was out of the car even quicker than usual. I just made it to the low seawall before the contents of my stomach ejected spectacularly over the stone-work and splattered onto the rocks below. We hadn't eaten much, so where had all that come from? Feeling slightly better, I got down to scanning the harbour. We were in luck and quickly picked out a Great Northern Diver and a Red-throated Diver. Excellent. Let's go!

South Stack RSPB Reserve next and, not fancying a car-full of vomit, Steve was now driving a little slower. The wind was very strong and the sun had gone. Could we find any birds? Yes, we could. A gang of Red-billed Choughs was tumbling in the wind above the cliff edge, a gale posing no problem for these charismatic corvids. Nearby, the resident Hooded Crow – the only one in Wales, as far as we know – was striding across a grass field. Job done. We moved on fast.

As I was feeling grim, we agreed I should take the wheel for the return drive to Conwy. Ruth joined me in the front as she was now feeling queasy too. Back at the reserve, we thanked Ken for helping boost our year list and Steve for making me throw up for the first – but surely not last – time in 2008. It had been a great day and we had really enjoyed the guys' company, as always. Of the day's 98 species, 58 were new for *The Biggest Twitch*. This meant that with one day of January left we had already moved onto 1,122 species for the year.

1,122 species

2–26 February, Ethiopia (Ruth)

We all know what Ethiopia looks like. We've seen it on the television so many times: tented refugee camps, dust and flies, starving children everywhere and UN Aid handouts as the country suffers another drought and famine. These images were playing through our heads as we touched down; Ethiopia seemed an unlikely birding destination. As we were to discover, though, there is so much more to the country than aid appeals.

There were certainly plenty of children. Wherever we stopped, within seconds we found ourselves mobbed by a gang of youngsters all crying out 'You!' You! You!' right in our faces. Where did they come from? Were they like the swallows of ancient myth, hiding in the mud at the bottom of ponds to emerge as we appeared? We were mobbed everywhere we went, a crowd of dishevelled children holding out their hands and tugging at our clothes. This was the legacy of aid: a white 4WD jeep meant hand-outs, so to them a convoy of five such jeeps must have meant untold goodies and they all intended to get their share. The only things we had in ready supply were empty plastic water bottles and these were highly prized; the kids would run alongside the vehicle, clinging to the door handles to keep up, if they thought they had a chance of getting one. We learned later that just under half Ethiopia's population is under fourteen years old, and as we drove around the country it seemed as though most of them latched onto us.

But I'm getting ahead of myself. We landed safely at Addis Ababa after a long and uncomfortable overnight flight from London. Well, at least Alan and I did, but there was no sign of our luggage. Quite a few people were still hanging around long after the last bags had been claimed from the carousel and together we all shuffled over to the Lost Luggage counter. They checked our tags against the computer.

'Sorry madam, but your luggage is still in London,' said the official. 'The plane was overloaded so we took your luggage off. It will arrive tomorrow afternoon. Come back then to collect it. Next please!'

Now I'm not saying this is a regular occurrence, but the fact that they had a special Offloaded Luggage Claim Form suggested it was hardly the first time. We were later told that the flight from London to Addis is often overloaded, so bags are selected at random to be left behind at Heathrow and sent on the next day. This time, unfortunately, ours had been the randomly selected bags. We thus arrived with only the clothes we stood in, already rather crumpled and smelly, plus our optics in our hand luggage.

At least our lack of luggage meant we waltzed straight through customs and were promptly met by a representative of Ethop Travel, who took us to the Ghion hotel, our base for the next couple of nights. For this leg, we were joining a fixed departure tour run by Tropical Birding and the Ghion was our starting point.

We checked into our room and jumped straight in the shower. Luckily the hotel shop sold toothbrushes and toothpaste so we were able to freshen up. To keep the smell to a minimum, we washed our clothes and spread them out on the sunny windowsill to dry. Thank heavens for quick-dry outdoor clothing. But what could we do to pass the time while it dried? The TV worked, but our Amharic wasn't quite up to the Ethiopian equivalent of *EastEnders*. And sadly our field guide was in our luggage in London so we couldn't mug up on Ethiopian birds. So we did what any red-blooded naked couple would do in the circumstances – that is until the door burst open with a sudden bang and the chambermaid breezed in with fresh towels.

'Oh!' she exclaimed.

It's the same in Amharic as it is in English, the universal noise of surprise made by someone walking in on a couple *in flagrante*. Luckily she only had a fine view of Alan's buttocks before she dropped the towels in embarrassment (he prefers to think it was in awe) and backed out of the room. Later on, we studied all the female staff closely to see if any of them giggled when they saw us, but there wasn't a flicker. Perhaps she didn't recognise Alan with his clothes on.

Luckily, hot sun dries clothes quickly so we were soon able to wander the hotel grounds to try to find our first Ethiopian birds. They didn't take much finding. A gang of Wattled Ibises were feeding on a sunny patch of grass just outside the front door. What a start! This was our first endemic for Ethiopia, a bird that we could only hope to see – and therefore add to our list – in this country. If we missed these specialities here we would never have a second crack at them. Wattled Ibis was also the first endemic we could tick off in our copy of the *Guide to Endemic Birds of Ethiopia and Eritrea* by Jose Luis Vivero Pol. This book had been a present from my decidedly non-birding friend Debbie, who'd challenged us to see all the endemics before returning home. This is a pretty tough challenge given that the photo on page 35 shows only a wing. How were we supposed to recognise the rest of the Nechisar Nightjar, even if a whole bird actually exists?

Although a self-confessed non-birder, Debbie played an important role in *The Biggest Twitch*, supplying a touch of sanity and humour while we were on the road. I couldn't wait to read her next email with its updates on life in England – the weather, the traffic, the politics – and her non-birding take on our adventures. She kept a list of her favourite bird names, choosing them purely by the sound or the implication of the name that we birders just take for granted. 'Imagine the complex *you'd* have if you went through life called a thick-knee,' she'd write. Or 'I'm feeling a bit of a Drab Hemispingus myself,' if she was having a particularly tough week at work. In fact, so good were her emails that she nearly found herself writing this book for us.

Anyway, it wasn't just Wattled Ibis that we found in the hotel grounds. We also caught up with Christian Boix. We greeted Christian like the old friends that we are and he introduced us to his parents – which revealed immediately where he gets his seemingly limitless enthusiasm and bounce from, plus his ability to keep going long after the rest of us mere mortals have run out of steam. Born in Spain but now living in Cape Town, Christian speaks English with that slight foreign accent that makes it sound so sexy. He is a gifted storyteller and will have you in stitches as he tells the tale of some death-defying escapade or another. But do not be fooled by his relaxed appearance. Inside is a birder so hardcore that he makes concrete look soft. He will dig you out of your bed in the wee small hours and make you run around after birds all day in the heat of the sun. Food and drink is for wimps. This man is driven, but he gets the birds, and birds were just what we needed on this trip.

We also met three more of our group. Steven and Ann were the most charming of English couples you could ever hope to meet. Steven was a doctor, which we found very reassuring, given the remote areas we were due to visit, and they were both old Tropical Birding hands, having previously enjoyed a TB trip to Australia. We also met Ian, a keen birder and photographer from Scotland.

Breakfast was at 5.30am the next day, a time that we were all too familiar with. By now the rest of the group had arrived, and we all piled into a minibus to take us to our first destination, a reservoir on the outskirts of Addis. This was some bus. All the windows had tasselled curtains, and at the front, keeping watch over us, were images of Jesus Christ and the Madonna. A little divine protection never goes amiss but perhaps God was too busy elsewhere that day to pay attention to this one little bus. It just refused to start, no matter how many times the key was turned and the pedal pumped. Never mind. The hotel was at the top of a hill and there were plenty of staff around to give it a push. With a hiccup, a burp and a fart, the engine kicked into life and we spluttered our way out into Addis.

Early it might have been, but the city was already buzzing. The main activities seemed to be jogging, stretching, playing football and generally keeping fit, preferably all in the middle of the road. At least the middle was generally tarmac, albeit with deep potholes. The edges, by contrast, crumbled into a broad blanket of thick dust. Butchers' shops were already doing a good trade, with fly-blown carcasses swinging in the open air. Beside them were coffin shops open to the street, where piles of ornate, garish coffins were stacked to the ceiling. It seemed an odd juxtaposition of businesses, but obviously trade was booming.

We reached the reservoir and showed the guard on the gate our official entry permit. He was having none of it and refused to open the gate. Nobody had told him to expect us and no official entry permit was going to persuade him we should be allowed in. Heaven knows what we might get up to inside. So we had to turn around and bird from the road. Of course our tripod was in our luggage so Alan tried to balance the scope on my head, but despite my best efforts his views were extremely shaky. Not one to let a mere fence get in the way of his birding, however, Christian soon found a way to approach the other side of the reservoir and our Ethiopia list quickly shot up. We added Sacred, Hadada and Glossy to our ibis collection. We ticked off Blue-winged Goose, another endemic, which looks just as you'd expect from the name, and a few waders who'd feel at home – if a little cooler – in Welsh waters, including Little Ringed Plover, Black-tailed Godwit and Ruff.

Back to the hotel for lunch, and then the group went off in separate directions. Alan and I had to return to the airport for our luggage while the others went back out in the bus to try a nearby forest area. We were miffed at missing some birding, as we were moving out of town the next day, but retrieving our luggage took priority just this once.

Our taxi ride to the airport was hilarious. We hopped in the back of an enormous ageing Mercedes driven by a very distinguished-looking elderly gentleman, with grizzled hair and beard. He juggled the wheel constantly between his hands, spinning it left and right, left and right, left and right. In fact, he was moving it so violently from side to side that the car should have been swerving all over the road, but instead it continued in a perfect straight line down the centre. Were any of the wheels connected? This was classic cartoon stuff: Parker chauffeuring Lady Penelope, just without the peaked cap.

We hadn't entertained high hopes of seeing our luggage again so we were very surprised to find it lined up waiting for us at the airport. After being waved through customs, Parker drove us back to the hotel, and we settled down with a beer to wait for the others. We waited and we waited. An hour passed, then another. The beers slipped down and we amused ourselves watching a collection of large 4x4 jeeps arriving, all loaded up with extra fuel tanks on the roofrack and chunky spare tyres on the back. It looked like somebody was going to be heading off for a very tough expedition in the wilds.

A taxi arrived and two familiar figures hopped out: Keith Barnes and Ken Behrens. Keith and Ken were two more Tropical Birding guides from South Africa who were going to be joining us on the tour. Keith is another old friend; Alan had birded with him before in South Africa, while I'd also met Keith a few times at the UK Birdfair and in Ecuador. He's very tall, with legs that go on forever and can cover the ground extremely quickly, and he has piercing blue eyes that miss no bird. He is also a storyteller; in fact if there's anyone who can beat Christian at telling great tales, it's Keith. This trip was going to be a riot.

We'd also met Ken before – in Ecuador, a couple of years previously, when we were all guiding at the ABA conference. He's an American who now lives in Cape Town, but what I remembered most about him from our first acquaintance was that he was another tall guy. Now, at five foot seven I'm not short, but beside some of our male guides during *The Biggest Twitch* I often felt vertically challenged. Ken also had a very dry sense of humour. As the Ethiopia tour progressed, we got to know him pretty well, and we definitely enjoyed his wry take on life and came to appreciate just how quick he was to pick up and photograph birds.

A few beers later and we all had a ravenous appetite, so although the birding party still hadn't arrived, we headed inside for supper. It was bedtime before the rest of the group materialised, and they were more than a little disgruntled. Apparently JC and the Madonna hadn't given them much protection after all, as the bus had broken down several times and had then burst a tyre. Unable to get the engine going and replace the tyre, they'd been forced to abandon the bus and wave down a series of taxis to take them back into town. They'd seen some good birds but the bus breakdowns had totally spoiled their fun. Perhaps our trip to the airport hadn't been such a bad thing after all.

Bright and early the next morning we were all assembled outside the hotel with our luggage. In addition to the two of us, there were nine other clients, plus the three Tropical Birding guides and what looked like an army of local drivers, minders and fixers. By now there were also five 4WD jeeps lined up in a row, all looking suitably rugged, with their spare tyres, jerry cans, ropes and tarpaulins. It was obvious that we were to be the ones taking that tough expedition into the wilds.

Then the morning ritual of loading up the trucks and sorting out the passengers began for the first of many times. With five vehicles and only three guides, it was now obvious there couldn't be a guide in every truck, so to ensure everyone had a turn in each vehicle, Christian had worked out a fiendishly complicated rotation system. Pole position was with him in the front truck, the only vehicle in which dust from the others didn't obscure the view. This rotation system meant that Christian sometimes had to split couples across vehicles and, while all vehicles looked the same from the outside, some were definitely comfier inside than others. And, of course, the further back you were in the queue, the more dust you suffered. There was definitely a pecking order to the trucks, and woe betide the driver or passenger who tried to jump the queue.

Alan and I were in the fifth and last vehicle with Ken. This had distinct advantages. For a start, we had our own guide. Despite being only in his twenties, Ken seemed to have been birding for at least forty years, so good were his birding skills, and although Ethiopia was new territory for him, he'd made a recce trip with Keith only weeks before so was already familiar with the key birds. We also had the same truck each time, so we always knew where to sit or put our luggage. Of course, as we both had to see or hear a bird for it to count, we were both kept together in the same vehicle at all times. This meant we had to stay so close to each other that you couldn't pass a cigarette paper between us. We had started the year as partners, closest friends and lovers, but how long would this last in such close confinement?

With only two of us in the back seat, we also had more room to spread out – though sometimes, when the road was really rocky, a third person to wedge us in place might have been welcome. We had our own fixer, too. Masula could always rustle up the essentials, such as safe bottled water or bananas to keep us going. With our independent vehicle, we also had the flexibility to peel off from the main group and chase additional birds for our grand total, and this greater independence proved invaluable a few times.

Why were we so privileged? This was thanks to the guys at Tropical Birding, who were so keen for us not only to break but totally *smash* the world record that they went all-out to help us.

There were also distinct disadvantages to this arrangement, however. Being last in the line meant we were smothered in dust from the other vehicles pretty much all day, every day. And if our driver hung back so he could see where he was going, we'd risk missing a bird because we had fallen too far behind the others. In fact, on several occasions, we'd pull up behind a row of empty vehicles and have to run at full speed through the bush to catch up with the others and find out what we were supposed to be looking for.

Anyway, back to the hotel. By now our chief fixer, Solomon, had at last sorted us into some sort of order. Finally, with all the passengers inside and all the luggage on top, we were on our way.

Our first destination was Debre Libanos, several dusty hours' drive away. When we arrived, we squeezed our vehicles into a patch of shade under a tree and jumped out. All around us was a mass of humanity; hundreds of people dressed in white rags, who squatted or slept on the ground, or stood in lines leaning on wooden staffs. The centre of their attention was a historic monastery, founded in the thirteenth century. Inside was the tomb of Saint Tekle Haymanot. According to legend, he had spent so long praying while standing on one foot (anywhere between seven and twenty-nine years, depending on who's telling the tale) that his other foot had fallen off – though no one seems sure whether it was his left or right.

The centre of our attention wasn't the monastery itself, however, but the juniper woodlands on the steep hills beside it. Making sure to use both our feet equally, we scrambled up and started looking for birds. Looking up was hazardous, though. With so many people packed into a small space, many of the pilgrims also climbed up the hillside amongst the bushes to find a quiet bathroom spot and you needed to watch where you put your feet. Both of them. The birding made it all worthwhile, however, as we added White-cheeked Turaco and Abyssinian Oriole, as well as Abyssinian Woodpecker and Banded Barbet – two more Ethiopian endemics – to our list.

With no time to stop and enjoy the culture, we were soon on to our next birding site, called the Portuguese Bridge. This is a narrow humpback bridge made of rough stones, just about wide enough for a well-laden donkey, which spans a narrow gorge carved by a small stream before it tumbles over a sheer cliff into the Jemma River Valley far below. No one seems sure of the origins of this bridge. Some say it was built in the sixteenth century by the Portuguese; others by the Ethiopians under their emperor, Menelik, in the nineteenth century. Whatever its history, it is certainly an incredibly dramatic birding location.

Christian had collected some bones from one of those open-air butchers back in Addis Ababa. (Had it been later in the trip he might have been tempted to pick up a coffin, too.) While we ate our packed lunch on the edge of the cliff, he threw them far out into the air as bird bait, and we had breathtaking views of raptors as they swooped in low to catch them. Rüppell's Griffons, White-headed Vultures, Black Kites and ravens wheeled over our heads and swooped down right past our faces. Most impressively, a Lammergeier turned up for the show, and shot past so close that we could see its bristly 'beard'.

The next morning saw us down in the Jemma River Valley, lined up in a row looking back up at the escarpment. A francolin-type bird had been seen briefly scurrying between bushes on the steep cliff but had disappeared from view before anyone had really got onto it. There was only one thing for it: the boys had to go mountaineering. Christian had shimmied up the cliff like a rat up a drainpipe and was already close to the top. Keith, with his rather longer legs, was taking things more carefully, and he seemed to be stuck about halfway up. Just at that moment, Christian shouted and there was more scurrying movement on the cliff. Following his frantic arm waving, we focused on the indistinct shape. Through the scope it took on an identity: an Erckel's Spurfowl. A great bird, and well worth the climb by the boys, we all thought, as we happily trotted back to the vehicles, abandoning Keith and Christian stranded halfway up the precipice.

As we drove across the countryside, it was fascinating to study the changing landscape. Every area that wasn't vertical was under cultivation. At the lower altitudes it was mostly cereals, with stone-walled terracing used to squeeze every last inch of arable soil out of the landscape. Each village comprised a small collection of huts surrounded by a hedge, or *boma*, made of poplar or eucalyptus – or even tall, slim euphorbias in particularly dry areas. Inside, the huts varied slightly according to the regional design but were usually round, with mud or stone walls topped off by a thatched roof. Close to the villages, rows of gum trees stood like soldiers on parade. These alien trees are popular because they grow quickly and their straight trunks can be used in building, scaffolding, fencing and just about everything. And then there were goats and cattle everywhere: mixed herds of scraggy-looking animals wandered along the roads and over the fields, loosely guarded by diminutive, equally scraggy-looking children brandishing sticks, their older brothers and sisters already having been pressed into farming or water-gathering duties.

Rural life looked hard, particularly so for the women, whose day was mostly taken up with collecting water from the nearest well or pump, which might be several miles away. Somehow they managed to balance on their heads substantial jerry-cans of water which I would struggle even to lift, and walk barefoot along well-worn dirt paths with all the elegance and poise of a cheetah. In contrast, the men seemed to work equally hard at leaning against trees to make sure they didn't fall over (the trees, that is). Glad there aren't too many trees back home in Llandudno or it might catch on.

Back to the birding, however, and our next target bird was the Ankober Serin. After another cruelly early start, we dropped off our luggage at our next hotel while it was still dark without really seeing where we were to stay, and then drove on to the Ankober escarpment. Ethiopia excels in dramatic scenery. The ground just fell away beneath our feet as the plains ended in a sheer drop that marked the edge of the Great Rift Valley. Miles below, a patchwork of fields stretched away into the distance. This was where the rare and range-restricted endemic Ankober Serin called home. Somewhere out on those sheer rock faces was a handful of small streaky-brown birds and our job was to spot them without slipping over the cliff.

I must admit I was distracted by watching the significantly easier-to-see Gelada Baboons, which were scrambling all over the vertiginous ravine as though taking a walk in the park. Technically not true baboons, these shaggy Old World monkeys spend the nights on the relative safety of the cliff face – you assume they don't fall off in their sleep – and climb up onto the plain to graze like antelope on the grass shoots in daylight, when they can keep an eye open for predators. Today they are as endangered as their serin neighbours: not only is their habitat very restricted but their pelts also make excellent hats – at least according to the locals, who tried to persuade us to buy some. I'm sure they would keep you very warm at this bitterly cold altitude, but I'm equally sure they keep the monkeys warm too, and they fitted them so much better than us that we easily resisted the temptation to go shopping.

Back to the task in hand and someone – undoubtedly Keith or Christian – had picked out the tiny brown speck that was an Ankober Serin inching its way along the far cliff face, obstinately hiding behind tussocks to make itself even harder to spot. Pretty drab it may be, but pretty rare too, so it had a special place on our list. By now the inevitable bunch of children had found us, and they were gawping at our every move. Our hotel had supplied us with packed lunches, but it felt hard to eat our filled rolls under the close scrutiny of a handful of grubby and probably undernourished children. So we did the generous thing and unanimously donated our lunch to them. They timidly crept forward, snatched the food and retreated a safe distance to eat it. But after just one mouthful they spat it out and threw it back at us. So much for aid handouts.

Ethiopia amazed us by how near we could get to the birds. There is no hunting in this country – it's against religious beliefs – so a deep respect for birds is part of the culture. Even birds as large as an Abyssinian Ground Hornbill, an impressive metre-long black beast, will strut along the ground close to human habitation with little fear – though one could probably feed a whole family. In fact, these birds seemed totally fearless, and we laughed to see a pair stalk regally right through a petrol station forecourt. Wonder if hornbills run on diesel or unleaded?

It was dark when we returned to the hotel. We'd not yet seen it in daylight, so it felt like Blind Man's Buff as we stumbled along in darkness, holding hands in crocodile file up a narrow footpath that spiralled around a hill to the top. If only we'd had a torch. We reached a wooden door in a stone wall that encircled the hill and paused to catch our breath, chests heaving. Had we arrived? No, this wasn't it. Next we climbed some steep steps, thankful that we weren't carrying our luggage. At last we reached a terrace and there was Christian, up ahead, holding a paraffin lamp. This was the first of three levels of chalets, and the main hall and restaurant were still somewhere out of sight above us at the summit. Where on earth had Christian brought us?

Rooms were allocated on the basis of fitness. Those clients Christian thought could survive several trips up and down the mountain between meals and rooms without expiring were given the lowest. Those who could only make the ascent once were coaxed straight up to the rooms at the top on the same level as the restaurant. Clearly having given an illusion of fitness, we settled into our cosy little rooms on the lowest level and freshened up. It took us only seconds to get soaped up in the shower before the power went off and then we had a mad scramble to find candles, matches, torches and towels. Once dried and dressed, we took the torch from our room and fumbled our way in the dark up yet more steps to the restaurant, where candlelight shed a romantic glow over the scene. Supper was a breathless affair in the hall at the summit, surely an impressive building if only we could see it. It was also a slow affair. Presumably they had only candles to heat the food, but when it arrived it was tasty and extremely welcome. There was safety in numbers, we thought, as we made our way cautiously back down the hill in the darkness. But even with the combined power of several torches, the light was so dim that we all completely missed our chalets and walked right past them to find ourselves back down at the bottom of the mountain. Never mind: at least this unexpected cardiovascular workout made for a good night's sleep.

It was still dark when we set off back up the hill for breakfast the next morning but again the candle-powered kitchen took so long to rustle up scrambled eggs for 16 hungry people that it was daylight by the time we'd all eaten. And what a magnificent sight the daylight revealed! This was the site of the former Ankober Palace, and the hotel had been lovingly recreated by local craftsmen in the style of the original palace of Menelik II, Emperor of Ethiopia until his death in 1913. Menelik II is something of a hero in Ethiopia, as he had managed to defeat the occupying Italian forces in 1896, the first time an African power was able to overthrow a colonial invader.

The commanding views over the surrounding countryside were equally impressive, as we could see for miles over the Great Rift Valley, with a patchwork of pocket-sized fields below us and in the distance, the legendary Afar Plains. Sadly we didn't have time to take up the lodge's kind offer of experiencing local culture through grinding our own corn and making our own *injera*, as we had to cross those plains before nightfall.

It's time for a short word about *injera*, the staple diet of Ethiopians and something we encountered at every mealtime. *Injera* is made from *teff*, a tiny cereal grain that is grown all over the country, and is served as a flat, grey, spongy pancake with all the flavour and texture of carpet underlay. For foreigners, it is served as a large circle on a plate, dotted with dabs of sauce called *wat* in varying shades of brown or green, all highly spiced. For the locals however, it doubles as both plate and tablecloth, with a communal disk flopped over a bare wooden table and the sauces slopped in the middle. The approved approach is, using your right hand only, to tear off a piece, dip it into a sauce and then eat it with gusto. Having tried *injera* during previous business trips to Ethiopia, I was already familiar with its cleansing effect on my digestive system and had no desire to eat it again. Alan, being a conservative eater, wasn't even going to risk tasting it so, capitalising on the Italian legacy, we ate well-cooked spaghetti every day – the one thing that Ethiopia's brief colonisers seem to have taught effectively. Sometimes spaghetti came with tomato sauce, sometimes with meat sauce, sometimes just with more spaghetti, but every day without fail, wherever we sat down for dinner, we could be sure of a decent dish of pasta. Ken, on the other hand, isn't the sort to play it safe, and he worked his way through miles of carpet underlay each evening.

Now it was time to brave the Afar Plains. We'd heard much about this barren area and the fierce tribespeople who lived here, and Christian's briefing before we set off did little to reassure us. The Afar have chosen to make the dusty, inhospitable plains their home, far from other communities, and they jealously guard their privacy. Unluckily for them, they are a particularly photogenic people: tall and good-looking, with a stunning traditional dress of white robes thrown dramatically over one shoulder for the men, and colourful drapes in red and blue for the women. Their looks make them the perfect subject for photography, but they dislike this so much that they have been known to shoot tourists who've tried to take a snap. Oh yes, the most popular modern accessory for the menfolk is an AK47 over one shoulder and a bandolier of bullets over the other. So Christian told us all very sternly that as long as we were crossing the Afar plains, we weren't going to stop, we weren't allowed to use our cameras and we certainly weren't to point our bins or scopes anywhere near any people. All of which was going to make it hard to look for birds.

Suitably warned, we set off across the plains. Within seconds, we disappeared into a cloud of dust – and that's pretty much how things stayed for the rest of the day. A fine red dust crept in under the door, through the cracks in the window, up through the floorboards and began to coat everything. It got in your mouth and made your teeth crunch; it got up your nose and made you sneeze; it got in your eyelashes and made your eyes water. Bramo, our driver, turned the wipers on full speed to try to clear a patch on the windscreen but he was driving through a red fog. We just prayed that the vehicle in front didn't make an emergency stop.

Of course we had to make a pit stop at some stage, and we pulled up close to a suitable area of thorny scrub. A distant settlement of Afar people was still in sight but hopefully we were far enough away not to pose a threat. All the ladies in our group dived into the bushes while the men stayed by the vehicles, looking for birds without bins and scopes. We emerged from the undergrowth to find the men enjoying close views of Northern Carmine Bee-eaters sallying after insects from their perches atop the scrubby bushes. These beautiful bird looked slightly out of place against the harsh background: a riot of colour, with a salmon-pink belly, brick-red back and turquoise face, all set off by a bandit mask across the eye and a wickedly sharp bill.

But it wasn't long before we found that we had company. A line of five white jeeps was obviously an intriguing sight to the locals, who had wandered over for a closer look. Covering our binoculars with our hands we watched nervously as Christian walked forward to meet the gun-toting Afar tribesmen. Far from being fierce and unfriendly, however, they were curious to know what we were looking for and soon gathered around us, nattering away. Curiosity overcame their reserve as we set up a telescope for them to peer through. Clearly they'd never experienced anything quite like this before, and it was highly amusing to see them take a sudden step backwards in alarm as they found themselves suddenly face-to-face with something they thought was a long way away.

We said goodbye to our newfound friends and headed back into the dust. Our route across the featureless flatlands was far from obvious, and how our lead driver knew his way we'll never know, but as the sun was beginning to dip we joined something resembling a track. Soon this developed into something closer to a road and by nightfall we had reached the town of Metahara, our home for the next few nights.

The hotel looked quite comfortable as we checked into our rooms before heading straight out for supper. The only restaurant that could offer Western food for a hungry birding group was a short walk away, across a railway line that lurked cunningly in the darkness. No matter, we thought, there can't be much train traffic out here. With supper over, we blundered through the darkness back to the hotel and, setting the alarm for another early start, crashed into our beds.

Two a.m. The sound of gunfire tore the night apart and we rocketed out of bed. Opening the door a little we peeked out to see what was going on. Crack! Zap! Crack! Crack! Shots ripped through the darkness in quick succession from both left and right. It sounded as though we were in the midst of a Wild West movie and the bad guy had just ridden into town. Then, just as suddenly as it had started, it stopped. Silence fell as heavy as a blanket. We eased the door shut and huddled together under the bedclothes, shaken by what had just happened and hoping our guides weren't out owling.

We were all up early for breakfast the next morning, eager to compare notes and find out what had been going on. Keith and Christian's curiosity had already led them to the market to get the latest gen on the night's adventure. It transpired that a heavily laden freight train had lumbered into town during the night, heading for Addis Ababa. As it had stopped just outside our hotel, local bandits had tried to raid one of the wagons. But unbeknown to them, the police had received a tip-off and were lying in ambush. The raging gun-battle had broken out as the police drove off the thieves into the night, and the train was eventually able to continue on its way with its cargo intact. We checked the ground thoroughly for telltale pools of blood and dead bodies, but were disappointed not to find any. And the precious cargo that had given rise to such a shoot-out? Apparently, it had been a consignment of DVDs heading for the high life in Addis.

That morning Christian took us to the moon. At least that's what it looked like. A vast sea of lava from the nearby volcano of Fantale had left a bizarre landscape of misshapen black volcanic boulders that spread as far as we could see. Not a single bush, shrub or tree broke up the jungle of angular rocks. Surely there couldn't be any birds in this hostile habitat? But there were, and they were special birds too. Sombre Chat was restricted to just this spot, though the confusingly similar-looking Blackstart was also found here. This was a real test of our attention to detail as the two birds were both small, grey and inconspicuous, nearly identical in both looks and behaviour. A Blackstart was the first to appear and we all took a good look at it. Then Christian and some of the group picked their way out onto the lava field to look for the rarer chat. The footing was treacherous, the razor-sharp rocks ripping their hands as they scrambled awkwardly forward. Alan and I stayed on the raised causeway of the railway track and from this elevated viewpoint we watched the others' progress through our binoculars. This proved a good move, as we soon found ourselves watching a small speck of a bird leading them a merry dance round in a big circle right back to where we were standing. The Sombre Chat perched upright on a boulder just feet away from us, and found himself on *The Biggest Twitch* list.

The scenery on the other side of the causeway was much friendlier and we birded the Beseke Crater Lake. The water's edge provided us with a flurry of new waders, including Little and Temminck's Stints and Kittlitz's Plover. Alan was in his element, being a huge wader fan, but then a rather unpleasant smell sneaked into our nostrils and wouldn't let go. We didn't have to walk far before we saw the source of the stench. The corpse of a hyena was lying out in the open, swollen with gases and, bizarrely, with a rope around its neck. Who had done this and why had they chosen to leave the body here? These weren't questions to bother the Hooded Vultures who stood on top of the corpse. Unable to break through the tough hide, they were waiting for the corpse to explode, in the meantime contenting themselves with picking out the eyes. Yum! The smell and sight was appalling but, somehow, strangely compelling. We took photo after photo of the gruesome scene, and had great difficulty in tearing ourselves away.

Back at the hotel in Metahara, we found ourselves facing a double whammy. No electricity – which meant no water either, as it couldn't be pumped into the town. So it was a dirty and rather smelly group who made their way over the tracks to dinner, and we packed our bags by candlelight ready to move on the next day.

By now our group of fellow birders were emerging as distinct separate characters and we were gradually remembering their names – though with so many new bird names to contend with, people's names were proving very difficult. Firstly there were Gordon and Maxine from Canada. Gordon didn't seem to bear a grudge about our calling him Howard for most of the trip, and he and Maxine were keen travellers, dedicating several months of the year to birding in other parts of the world to avoid their bitterly cold Canadian winters.

Chuck and Nancy from Colorado, USA made a significant impact. We'd met Chuck the previous year at the ABA conference in Quito and he had endeared himself to us as a very amiable gentleman with a jolly, Santa-like laugh and plenty of tales about his time in the Foreign Office. In fact, he had worked in so many key countries around the world in the diplomatic service that we decided he just had to be an undercover CIA agent. But aren't secret agents meant to be, well, secretive? And since Chuck was so much larger than life, there was no way he could possibly hide in a crowd. Perhaps that was his best disguise, as an 'over-cover agent', who was just too obvious ever to arouse suspicion. (Oops, do I hear the approaching feet of those burly Homeland Security Officers again?)

We'd not met Chuck's wife Nancy before, though, and we soon learned that her place was always at the front of the queue right behind Christian, where, armed with an enormous camera, she hoped to get the best shots of the birds we saw.

Now, if Alan and I are avid tea drinkers, then Chuck and Nancy are coffee addicts, and no day could start before they'd had their caffeine fix. Thanks to Chuck, we can now all speak some Amharic, as shouting out '*Buza buna!*' ("more coffee!") became the regular breakfast routine. Having louder voices than most, Chuck and Nancy didn't always endear themselves to the rest of the group – especially before their breakfast coffee. But you certainly couldn't over-look them, and I can personally vouch for Nancy's kindness when she gave me the last of her cough medicine after I'd developed a hacking cough and completely lost my voice.

In complete contrast were Oz and Gail, a quiet and unassuming but actually rather remarkable couple from Denver, USA. They were that rare phenomenon: husband and wife who not only birded together but worked together too. They seemed to live life as the perfect complement to one another. Once I asked them their secret. 'Always say please and thank you,' Gail whispered to me after some thought. 'And always be sure to appreciate the other person.' Wise words indeed and something I tried (and usually failed) to remember as Alan and I coped with life on *The Biggest Twitch* joined together like Siamese Twins.

Both Oz and Gail possessed a wickedly dry sense of humour and we often found ourselves giggling together like naughty school kids at the back of the pack as Christian (and Nancy) forged ahead through the bush in search of new birds. Oz reliably carried the field guide with him, so it was really helpful to be able to double-check what we'd just seen, especially when a flurry of birds all came through at once. Oz was also a keen photographer, though as his style was to stand back and rely on his telephoto lens for close-ups, he was frequently frustrated by others scaring the birds away before he'd had the chance to fire off any shots. By the end of the trip he had a fantastic collection of hat shots, as other people's heads had continually got in the way. A great couple, we've kept in touch with them ever since and would love to go birding with them again.

To complete the American contingent were two more ladies, Mary and Darleen, who, I think it's fair to say, were probably with us by mistake. Their last trip to Africa had been a safari in Kenya and I think they were imagining Ethiopia to be much the same, with comfortable lodges, zebra-striped minibuses, deckchairs by the pool and sundowners over the Great Rift Valley. They were in for a bit of a shock when they found themselves being frog-marched out at dawn and chivvied over rough terrain in pursuit of elusive birds with not a single G&T in sight. At the end of the main trip, before the optional extension to the south, they headed straight for the airport and the first plane out. But fair play to them, they bravely joined in as much as they could, and always made the best of things.

Wondo Genet is a beautiful hilly area, much of which must have been cloaked in forest at some time. Our hotel rooms weren't ready when we arrived so we left the trucks and luggage with Solomon, and following Christian – plus a local villager/bird guide who attached himself to our party – we headed up into the hills towards the forest. Once outside the village, the track wound around large areas of land cleared for agriculture and past huge tree stumps standing like rotten teeth, showing the scale of the original forest. One huge *Hagenia*, or African Redwood, remained isolated in the centre of the fields. In it sat a red blob. We couldn't make it out with the bins so Christian set up the scope. Zooming in to maximum magnification, a handsome bird came into view: deep red throat and belly, black back and tail, bare yellow skin around its eye, a flash of white on the flank, and a chunky ivory bill that appeared to have two teeth along the jagged edge of its upper mandible. This could only be one bird: Double-toothed Barbet.

'Yes,' nodded our self-appointed local guide wisely. 'As I expected, Tooth Double-Barbet!' 'No, no, *Double-toothed* Barbet,' we corrected. 'Yes, exactly,' he confirmed, nodding vigorously, 'Tooth Double-Barbet.' So Tooth Double-Barbet it remained, and duly went on our list.

We carried on up the stony track, constantly stepping to one side to let the local villagers pass back downhill. Without fail, no matter how large or small, young or old, each had a large bundle of firewood on their head. Were there going to be any trees left at the top? At last we reached the retreating forest edge, where stately *Hagenia* trees still stood proud. Christian pointed out one particular tree. This was his Parrot Tree, where in the past he could almost guarantee views of Yellow-fronted Parrot. But today the tree was distinctly parrot-less, and it looked rather vulnerable as it stood in isolation a short distance from the remaining body of the forest, surrounded by the stumps of its fallen brethren. (We stopped off a week later on our return to Addis Ababa and found the tree had been reduced to nothing but a pile of sawn logs and a mound of small branches for charcoal burning, so it's hardly surprising that the wildlife is coming under increasing threat. Luckily for *The Biggest Twitch*, however, we picked up a Yellow-fronted Parrot in a tree further up the hillside, glad not to have let that endemic slip through the net.)

It felt good to walk into the dappled shade cast by these magnificent trees as the leaves shivered and quivered in the slight breeze. Strange non-avian noises had us looking up and we realised we were being watched by a rather serious-faced gang of Black Colobus Monkeys. These handsome black-and-white creatures were lounging around in the sturdier branches, their long shaggy tails hanging down like bell-pulls. They looked as though they had plenty of time on their hands, like a group of old men in some European village square, putting the world to rights over a cigar and a game of chess. Under a black cap, their faces look permanently grumpy, with beetling black eyebrows and a square white beard. Some youngsters cautiously descended a few branches for a better look at their strange furless relatives, while the old captain sat leaning against the trunk, his watchful gaze missing nothing. Our only weapons were binoculars and cameras, however, and we all duly attempted to take the ultimate colobus photograph.

Back at the hotel, the boys had sorted out our luggage and room keys, ably assisted by a large number of Grivet Monkeys, who lived in the hotel's lush grounds. Tall trees cast shade over the coral-pink chalets, while colourful crotons and flaming bougainvillea bushes lined the paths. Grivets had free run of the place and made themselves fully at home. We chased two curious individuals out of our room as we arrived, and then found another curled up on his back underneath the bed and playing with the tassels on the bedspread. Luckily, we'd not opened our bags, or otherwise just imagine the havoc one small monkey might have wreaked.

These monkeys were smart chaps to look at, with a short grey-brown coat, a thin tail, and a dark face bordered with the luxuriant white whiskers of a Victorian grandee and topped by a neat ginger fez. They were great at grandmother's footsteps, tiptoeing along behind us to see what mischief they could find and freezing on the spot whenever we turned around, looking as though butter wouldn't melt in their mouths. Being dextrous opportunists, they made short work of fishing our lunch leftovers from the bin, peeling the blackened bananas and disdainfully discarding the skins. They were totally fearless too, and quite determined to break back into our bedroom for more goodies. At one point, I couldn't resist snapping a photo of Keith, concentrating so hard on digiscoping a bird that he didn't notice a Grivet at his feet, testing its teeth out on the legs of his tripod.

Our next hotel was the Goba Wabe Shabelle, at the foot of the Bale Mountains, where we were grateful to find not only a fully functioning hot shower but also the luxury of internet access. Early the next morning we set off up into the mountains with Wattled Crane in mind. Despite the clear skies and bright sunshine I was wearing two hats: a peaked cap to act as a sunshade and, over it, a fleecy hat for warmth. Climbing to over 4,300m, we could really feel the altitude when we got out the car and continued on foot. By now the lush lowlands were far below us and we found ourselves in the bizarre afromontane habitat of short grass and lichen-encrusted rocks, punctuated by Giant Lobelias sticking up like spiky mutant lollipops.

This alien landscape is home to a very special creature, the rare Ethiopian Wolf, and we soon caught sight of one trotting daintily along a hidden path. The wolf, or Simien Fox, as it is also known, was quite oblivious to us as it went about finding food. 'Fox' seemed to us a more appropriate name, as this animal's rufous coat, pointy face, large ears and bushy tail reminded us strongly of our Red Foxes back home – though it also had distinctive white underparts and four neat white socks. It trotted along in a purposeful manner, possibly following a scent trail through the rocks, until it suddenly stopped and scrabbled intently at the ground with both front paws before seizing something small and brown in its jaws. By now we had the scopes set up and we could make out the little furry body of a Giant Mole Rat. The wolf turned and trotted back the way it had come, the prize swaying from side to side in its jaws. After a short distance, it carefully set down its now-dead cargo in a new scrape. Then it retraced its steps to its original digging site and captured another mole rat, before also carrying this meal back to the new larder. We watched spellbound as the wolf repeated the performance several times more. What was it doing? Was it caching food safely for another day? Did it have pups to feed? In the end we saw no fewer than six Ethiopian Wolves, including a family party. There are no more than 500 of this endemic and highly endangered mammal left in the wild, so we counted ourselves extremely lucky.

Could we be so lucky with our avian target? Higher up the mountain we made a stop and piled out of the vehicles once again. Here the landscape was even more barren, with little but a massive emptiness of lichen-covered rocks and stones. The thin air above us made the clear periwinkle-blue sky shine so brightly it hurt our eyes, and the rocks glowed in contrast against it. Despite the sunshine, though, there was still no warmth in the air and I pulled my double hat firmly over my ears. There was not much oxygen either, as we soon found when we started to move about.

A local guide was waiting for us with good news. He had seen Wattled Cranes only the day before at a lake just over the ridge. Like men possessed, Christian and Keith strode off in the direction he pointed and the rest of us followed. It wasn't long before the altitude began to take its toll, though, and we mere mortals began to fall behind. The group became strung out across the landscape as we struggled to pick an easy path over the unforgiving terrain, our lungs burning as we gasped for oxygen. Alan and I reached the edge of the first ridge and saw no sign of a lake, just Christian, Keith and the local guide striding out towards the next ridge. We must have misheard them, we thought, as we picked our way carefully around the treacherous boulders. Some people were already limping and leaning on each other for support, and the thin air was making it even harder to keep up any kind of pace. Keith and Christian, meanwhile, never seemed to tire – Keith's giraffe legs giving him a natural physical advantage, while Christian just doesn't know when to stop.

We finally caught up with them on the third ridge, only to see them scrambling down the next escarpment. This was hard-going and we didn't feel prepared. Stupidly, we'd not brought any extra food or water, never imagining we were going to find ourselves so far from the vehicles. 'Just over the next ridge,' insisted our local guide, again, but we were wondering how much had been lost in translation. Ken was sent ahead to scout for water but by now some of the group were feeling mutinous about trekking any further. After a stand-off on the ridgeline between guides and clients, Christian proposed a solution: he, the local guide and anyone who wanted to would continue further in search of the lake and the elusive cranes; Keith, and anyone who had had enough, would return to the vehicles where lunch awaited us.

With no water between us, and already feeling worryingly dehydrated and light-headed at this altitude, Alan and I took the safer option and turned back, along with all but Oz and Gail, brave souls. Wattled Cranes would be stupendous birds to see but, for the purposes of our list, one species was only a single tick like any another, and there were others we could add more quickly on our big race. Reluctantly we turned our backs on the cranes and headed back towards the vehicles.

Even so, we still found ourselves with several miles to hike back in the, by now, blazing sunshine. Two hats were now at least one hat too many. Once again, the group found itself stretched out across the plateau as people walked, limped and shuffled back at their own pace. Finding the route wasn't straightforward: there were no clear landmarks, the vehicles were out of sight and all the ridges looked remarkably similar. Then a blurry mirage came into view: a small shimmering lake, with a picnic spread out beside it. To our amazement, we soon discovered this was no mirage. The lake and picnic remained steadfastly real as we approached. Thoughtful Solomon had instructed his drivers to meet us with our lunch part-way, at a lake that we'd somehow failed to notice on our way out. Sadly there were no Wattled Cranes here but, downing several bottles of mineral water in quick succession, we were too busy quenching our thirsts to worry.

Basic needs taken care of, we started to scan our surroundings while we munched our lunch and waited for the others to return. Despite the lack of cranes this spot was not without its rewards. First we saw Ruddy Shelduck on the water, and then someone with very keen eyes picked out a motionless and incredibly well camouflaged Mountain Buzzard perched on a nearby ledge – both new additions to *The Biggest Twitch*.

We were just beginning to doze in the sunshine when Christian, Ken, Oz and Gail returned, looking hot and flushed. Had they been lucky? We didn't really need to ask; their faces said it all. After walking across an extremely hot and dry plateau they had climbed another ridge to see a view of…. you've guessed it, yet *another* ridge. No water, no lake, no cranes. So they had given up and come back, the local guide slipping off somewhere along the way. What a disappointment, especially for Oz and Gail who'd made such a heroic effort.

The next day we experienced the delights of Negele, rather generously described as a 'frontier town'. The Green Hotel, where we checked in, was apparently the best in town. Well, heaven help those who stay in the worst! Being a couple, we had one of their 'upmarket' double rooms. The room was tiny and filthy, the bed little bigger than a single and the bedclothes looked like they'd been in continuous use for a year. What made the room upmarket, apparently, was that it had a door. We had an en-suite bathroom, too, though I use the term 'bathroom' loosely: it contained fittings that may once have worked as a toilet and a washbasin, but both were so dry and grey with grime that clearly no water had flowed this way for a long time. The lack of towels and toilet paper seemed to confirm this.

A knock at the door announced a wizened walnut of a man holding a small bucket of water. This, it turned out, was our supply for the next three nights. What we did with it was up to us. We could drink it, but that was probably not a good idea. We could wash in it, which seemed rather a wasteful luxury given the filthy state of our surroundings, or we could use it to flush the toilet, which given the effects that our diet was having upon our insides seemed like the most sensible option. Floating in the bucket was a small plastic jug, and we quickly became very adept at ladling the water with this to maximum effect. The next few nights were going to be grim, but we were the lucky ones. Some of the others had to share a communal toilet – for which read 'hole in the ground'. To make us feel slightly better, Keith told us the tale of the hotel he and Ken had used in Negele only a short while before. Something very dead had been stuck in the rafters above his room, and the stink of rotting flesh made them both thoroughly sick.

Why were we putting ourselves through this? Birds, of course! And there was one very special species that we were here to see: Prince Ruspoli's Turaco. The history of this bird's discovery is as fascinating as its name is exotic. Prince Ruspoli was an Italian explorer, who collected the bird on an expedition across Ethiopia in 1892. Unfortunately, he was trampled to death by an elephant on his way home. His bag of skins was recovered, but with no notes explaining where or when he had found the bird. Salvadori studied the collection and named the new turaco in honour of Prince Ruspoli. But despite subsequent searches, the bird was not rediscovered until the early 1940s, when several specimens were obtained from roughly the same area. Even then, it was not reported again until relatively recently. It seems almost careless to have lost such a beautiful and charismatic bird not once, but twice. Today Ruspoli's Turaco is classed as an endangered species on the IUCN Red List – though an increase in recent sightings suggests that it may perhaps be slightly more widespread than once realised.

This story was running through our heads as we bounced along the rough, dusty track in our lowly position at the end of the convoy. Suddenly we juddered to a halt and, sticking our heads out of the window, we saw Christian doing an odd victory dance by the side of the road, jumping up and down like a Masai warrior and pumping his fists in the air. He seemed rather pleased about something so we thought we'd better investigate. He pointed up into a large fruiting tree and there, perched solidly on a stout branch and looking straight back down at us, was a turaco. Prince Ruspoli's Turaco, no less.

This was a bird for a paint-box. His head, neck and belly were lime green, his bill was orange and he seemed to have matching orange eyelashes that would make a drag queen proud. Below his eye was a bare yellow patch, on top of his head stood a fluffy white crest and, as he leaned forward to grab a berry, we could see his blue-grey back and flash of red primaries. The bird was clearly as amazing as the story. Despite the inevitable gaggle of youngsters jostling to get our attention, we stayed a long time, soaking up the views of this glorious creature and trying to take photographs that would do it justice. This was worth every second at the Green Hotel.

Well, almost worth it. My tummy situation was deteriorating rapidly and I didn't want to relive my Mexico experience. Having spent a sleepless night in a hot sweaty tangle on our child-sized bed, kept awake by loud music, shouting and all-night roosters, we tried to appeal to Christian's better nature to let us escape Negele early with Ken in our independent vehicle. But Christian was having none of it. He pointed out that if we bailed out now he would have a mutiny on his hands with the others. In my fragile and frustrated state I did what any normal grown-up would do in the circumstances: I burst into tears. (Strike one, Christian! The first Tropical Birding guide to reduce me to tears that year.) But even the sight of a woman weeping didn't melt Christian's heart. "There are still endemics to see round here," he protested, and I knew that these words spelt the end of our escape bid. I dried my eyes and took some more Imodium, then we headed out onto the Liben Plains in search of the Sidamo Lark.

To our eyes, one patch of plain looked very much like another, but the Sidamo Lark must see something we can't, as some 200 birds – that's the total world population – choose to live on a very confined area just a few kilometres square. Now I'm sure Keith, a confirmed lark fanatic, would disagree, but looking at the book, the Sidamo Lark appeared to me much like most larks: streaky-brown, pale supercilium, pinkish legs and a dumpy bill. In short, not a bird to get too excited about. However, the fact that there are so few, and that they live in such a tiny area and are therefore so vulnerable, made even me keen to catch up with it.

Villagers emerged from a nearby village to watch the fun, looking clean, well dressed and cheery. We, by contrast, after just a couple of days without water, were grubby, crumpled and hot. However, we spread out in a line and started to march across the open terrains. In our desire to see the lark, some people were innocently 'stringing' everything (to birders, 'string' means to misidentify a common bird as something far more rare, and is possibly the worst crime you can commit). Wheatears, Plain-backed Pipits and Pectoral-patch Cisticolas were all enthusiastically misidentified as larks, while we marched stolidly onwards, until closer inspection revealed the truth. Once we reached the point where the vegetation changed we turned around, spread out a little further and started to march back – immediately flushing four Temminck's Coursers, which scampered away along the ground with their characteristic bobbing motion.

Then suddenly Stephen spotted what we were all looking for. I think he was more surprised than any of us, as he had very little faith in his eyesight. But sure enough, there sat a Sidamo Lark – a real one – hunkered down against the stony ground. I'd walked within just feet of it without noticing, as it had stayed so still and was so camouflaged, so I swivelled on the spot and remained motionless as the others crept in for a better look. It had quite fine streaking on its head, which broadened out into a rich reddish-brown pattern across its back, and its pale cream supercilium really highlighted the button beadiness of its dark brown eye as it kept a watchful look on us. Not a bad little bird really. For a lark.

Back at the Green Hotel, Alan and I made a stab at cleaning up, as by now we were both a rusty-brown colour from all the dust. We took it in turns to dip the plastic jug into the bucket and pour water over various parts of each other's bodies, while rubbing in vain with a bar of soap. We didn't change colour at all, though the bright pink soap we'd taken from the Ghion Hotel in Addis Ababa quickly turned rusty-brown. Still, the whole exercise was rather academic, as our bags were so full of dust that we didn't have anything clean to change into anyway. Sadly, the dust had also infiltrated the eyepiece of our telescope, and the variable zoom had stopped varying. It was stuck on 60 times magnification, which was fine if you wanted to examine a bird in close-up but made it much harder to pick up the bird in the first place.

The next morning we escaped Negele. Yippee! We'd done so well with our birding that there was nothing new for Alan and me here, so we set off with Ken in our separate vehicle to Yabello, leaving the others behind to scour the plains for more larks. We had another long driving day ahead of us, though we did make a couple of birding stops on the way. We took a break after around 80km at the Dawa River, where we were bemused to see people standing in the flow of water, panning for gold. Here we struck lucky with Salvadori's Seedeater. Reaching town, we checked into the Yabello Motel, the place to break your journey if entering Ethiopia from Kenya, just a little to the south. Masula, our fixer, checked into the motel for us, but came out with a worried look. He was very sorry but there was a problem with the water supply. They could only give us a room with a cold shower. Are you kidding? Cold, running water? What luxury, bring it on!

The next morning we left early, and as the restaurant couldn't serve breakfast before 7am we decided to do without. We drove as far as the filling station next door, as we were out of diesel, but there was nobody there to serve us. Apparently the headman was still at home asleep, so Masula headed into town and eventually reappeared with him, looking rather sleepy. We refuelled and then headed south towards the border with Kenya. Ken wanted to take us to a little village where he and Keith had seen both Foxy and Short-tailed Larks and Shelley's Rufous Sparrow. Here we found the children friendly and curious, but without making a nuisance of themselves. Possibly they recognised Ken from the month before – after all, there can't be many six foot-plus white Americans who pass that way – and they were keen to look at *their* sparrows through the telescope once we'd located them. These kids were really cute, one girl in particular pouting for the camera like a supermodel, with head on one side and hand on hip. Clearly destined to be a handful when she grows up. Further down the track, we added another, Chestnut Sparrow, to our growing list.

Back at the Motel for lunch we ordered chicken soup and chips all round and drank a cola or two while we waited for the food to arrive. The waiting continued, so we birded the trees in the motel garden to pass the time. After an hour or so we chased up our order. Many apologies, but chips were off until tomorrow and there was no mention of the chicken soup. So instead we ordered omelettes. What finally arrived must have been made with Chestnut Sparrows' eggs: a tiny circle of egg lost in the middle of a huge white plate. One bite and they were gone. We ordered a second round, and in the meantime asked for two teas and a coffee. More apologies were offered: the man who worked the tea and coffee machine was on his break and no one knew when he would be back. Maybe tomorrow.

We gave up on refreshment and headed out again, just as the rest of our group pulled into the car park having left Negele a day after us. This time, we visited another slightly different area of savanna. Foraging on the ground beneath a patch of thorn scrub was a Bare-eyed Thrush, its distinctive facial markings showing up in the shadow. Then a high-pitched chatter and squeaking sound led us to a dense bush, where some patient waiting and a spot of pishing brought us face-to-beak with a pair of Scaly Chatterers. This uncommon bird is hard to see, and we had a good view of the scaly throat and breast from which it is named. Very satisfied with our day's birding, we headed back to the Motel and joined the rest of the group, who were just sitting down to their miniature omelettes, having ordered them some two hours earlier.

About 11km north of Yabello was a Government cattle ranch that had been set up in order to improve the stock of the local Brahmin cattle. Despite our written permission to enter, local guards – as we'd earlier found in Addis Ababa – aren't necessarily impressed by such documents, and it took much forceful arguing by our fixer and long phone calls to head-office before he would let us pass. Once inside, we were confused to see striped animals grazing on the grassland. Was the Government breeding striped cattle? Closer inspection with the bins showed them to be a herd of Common Zebra. Our mammal list for the year was coming along nicely, as we'd also added Gerenuk – a long-necked gazelle – and Beisa Oryx to our list in Ethiopia, not to mention our wonderful Ethiopian Wolves. We wandered around the ranch on foot and paused to digiscope the impressive endemic Stresemann's Bush Crows in the shade. This was relaxing birding for a change, but even so, we managed to add new birds to our list. First a pair of Wattled Plovers, which walked slowly away every time we approached for a better view, then a Grey-backed Fiscal, looking similar to the Great Grey Shrike that visits our local Clocaenog Forest back in north Wales, with its grey and white plumage and broad black bandit mask.

But the real fun started when we tried to leave the Government Ranch. Last car in was first car out, so for a change we were in the lead vehicle. Something was obviously wrong as we drew up to the entrance gate and found two stout wooden logs blocking the track. The guard stood in front of them, his feet planted firmly and his gun aiming straight at our windscreen. Clearly, we had seriously upset him on the way in, so he had decided to take his revenge on our way out. He shouted his demands and waved his gun threateningly. Unless we gave him a large wad of money, apparently, he would start firing. The weapon looked pretty old but nonetheless it was still a gun and it was pointing straight at us. Despite the intense heat, my hands were cold and clammy. The world held its breath as we wondered nervously how much cash we had on us and what this guy's idea of a large wad might be.

Thankfully our drivers were made of sterner stuff. Bramo and Masula both went ballistic. This was an affront to their masculinity, not to mention their national pride; they had important Westerners in their care and they meant to defend them, no matter what. With one movement they both jumped out of our truck and rushed the guard, running straight towards him and his gun. They surrounded the man, pushed his gun up so it was pointing harmlessly at the sky, then got out their mobiles to call his boss. The guard knew his game was up. He crumpled instantly, all his bravado disappearing as he begged them not to call, and dragged the logs out of the way to let the vehicles through. Once we were all safely past him and round the corner, Masula got on the phone to his boss anyway; there's probably one ex-guard out there now, stripped of his uniform and scratching a living herding goats. All the same, it was a sticky moment, and we were very glad to buy the boys a beer or two in the evening.

Another dusty drive took us along bone-shaking dirt roads to Arba Minch, with more shouting children lining the road all the way. Here, the local speciality seemed to be break-dancing, and they vied to out-do each other with body-popping moves to impress us. Perhaps they were practising for the tribal dance festival that was soon to be held at Arba Minch.

Ken was sitting in the front seat and, lacking the room to stretch out his long legs straight in front, often rode with his bare feet sticking out the window and his cap pulled down to shield his eyes from the dust. Despite the rough roads, Alan and I used these long drives as time to catch up on precious sleep, and we dozed on the back seat like a pair of nodding donkeys, our heads swaying in time with the potholes.

We were finding our relentless schedule gruelling. After a long, arduous day's birding, we had to be rigorous with writing up our notes and diary every evening without fail. On the one occasion we'd taken the easy option of an early night without doing our homework, and we found it impossibly hard to catch up the next evening. Never again. It was so critical to our quest that we noted every single bird, as well as making copious notes for the blog and book, that we forced ourselves to keep up the routine of note-taking every single night for the whole year. Where we could find internet access, either in our hotel or at internet cafes, we would try to update the blog ourselves as frequently as possible. This was often easier in less-developed countries than in more developed countries, where everyone had their own protected wi-fi systems. For example, we managed to find a fully functioning internet café in a small scruffy frontier town, miles from any other civilisation, deep in the heart of the Peruvian Amazon. By contrast, wealthy California saw us cruising the residential streets at night in desperation, with the computer fired up on my lap as we tried to tap into someone's unprotected home wi-fi. It's a wonder the cops didn't pick us up for acting suspiciously.

We had a back-up team around the world on stand-by, in case we couldn't get access for several days in a row, which we'd ring with a short message and instructions on how to update the blog. My sister Sue, in north Wales, kindly bailed us out a few times. As she is a non-birder, however, we had to spell out all the bird names for her letter by letter to make sure she got it right: Superciliaried Hemispingus can be tricky over a crackly long-distance phone line.

Other back-up options were Sam Wood and Nick Athanas, both Tropical Birding guides based in Ecuador, when they weren't busy guiding elsewhere in the world. At least they were more familiar with the bird names, but calculating the time zone differences wasn't always easy. On one occasion we rang Sam from Africa to ask for his help, not realising it was only 6am on a Saturday morning after he had just returned from guiding a two-week trip to Madagascar a few hours before. He didn't let on until later, and was kind enough to write up the blog anyway. And sometimes we couldn't even get a phone line, so we disappeared off the radar for days at a time, worrying our families and ever-growing loyal band of internet followers that something dreadful had happened.

By now we were down to a smaller group, as Keith had taken Mary and Darleen back to Addis Ababa while the rest of us continued on the southern extension. Keith was guiding a separate group in Ethiopia now, but we still coincided occasionally when both groups checked into the same hotel, and it was a good chance to catch up and compare bird notes.

A long drive the next day – this time, thankfully, mostly on tar – took us to Lake Awassa. We checked into a quaint hotel right beside the lake, where our accommodation was in a series of small cottages scattered throughout the spacious and leafy grounds. As we headed out for a gentle evening's stroll a White-browed Robin-Chat strutted boldly along the path, and Oz and I paused to watch and photograph a troop of Grivet Monkeys treating our vehicles as an adventure playground – climbing over the jerry-cans, admiring their faces in the wing mirrors and trying to figure out how to get at a bag of fruit that they could see through the window. Catching up with the others, we all wandered along the lakeshore. The views were breathtaking in the soft, late-afternoon light. A family of African Jacanas, complete with two gawky chicks, picked delicately across the lily pads, a Malachite Kingfisher zipped past like a flying jewel and a Pied Kingfisher hovered over the reeds. Local fishermen had bound together bundles of reeds to make tubular rafts, and we watched as they expertly punted these unstable craft out through the reeds into deeper water.

It was a great way to unwind after a long day on the road, and we headed into the restaurant for an early supper. As usual, Alan and I stuck to spaghetti. Ken, still feeling more adventurous, went for the *injera* again with the local speciality sauces. He tried in vain to encourage us to taste some, saying it was the best he had tasted. The next morning, we were up early for a visit to the fish market. Or at least, twelve of us were. There was no sign at all of Ken. Christian went back to his cottage to look for him and returned a few minutes later, alone. Apparently the infallible iron gut had a weakness after all: Ken had been sick all night and was still unable to leave his bathroom. In fact, he was stuck there for the rest of the day. So much for the best *injera* of the trip!

If Ken was feeling fragile, it was probably just as well that he didn't come with us to the fish market. This was no place for the faint-hearted or delicate-stomached. Fishing boats were hauled up all along the lakeshore. Young boys worked on the nets – folding them, repairing tears and fixing the floats – while next to them the fishermen crouched at the water's edge sorting their catch into neat piles. With one hand they held the fish, while in the other they used a sharp knife to gut it. Blood dripped everywhere, and the stench of fish and offal was overwhelming.

The guts were tossed into the lake, though I doubt they ever hit the water. Gangs of White Pelicans, Great and Long-tailed Cormorants and Marabou Storks squabbled violently over the scraps. If the first ranks missed anything, hundreds of Black-headed and Grey-headed Gulls, along with a Heuglin's Gull and a Lesser Black-backed Gull, soared and wheeled in the air, swooping down to snatch any tit-bit going. The sound was incredible: the cries of the birds mingled with the babble of the people. Behind the fishermen, the womenfolk laid out the fillets of fish, and fierce trading was going on. Meanwhile Marabou Storks strode around fearlessly, looking for any opportunity to steal something edible. At close quarters you appreciated the huge size of these ugly birds, with their skinhead hair-dos and messy bills. The whole fish market had a party atmosphere, as families picnicked in the shade of the trees, while some hard-working mothers did the family wash in the waters of the lake right next to the blood and guts and fishermen.

Alan and I stood next to Christian in a small patch of shade under an acacia tree to scope some of the gulls sitting on the water further out. In these situations it is always worth looking up first to check where you are standing. Had we done so, we would have realised we were directly under a Marabou Stork who'd just been filling his belly. A large input usually leads to a large output, and the inevitable happened: a load of smelly white guano cascaded down onto Christian's head and scope. Laughing fit to burst, we retreated to a safe distance as he tried to wipe the mess out of his curly hair and off his shirt. He cleaned up pretty well, but for the next few days we were aware of a peculiar smell whenever we used his scope.

We took photograph after photograph, trying to capture the atmosphere of this place: the blood and flash of the sharp gutting knife; the stretching yellow pouches of the pelicans as they scooped up water and fish scraps by the bucket-load; the maraca-like clacking of the Marabou Stork bills, as they turned over the stones on the shore in search of missed scraps; the arrow-like diving of the terns as they plunged headlong into the water. Small boys offered to throw scraps for the storks in exchange for a few coins, but with so much action going on all around us, we hardly needed to entice the birds in closer.

We wandered along the water's edge to a slightly quieter marshy stretch of shoreline, though a gaggle of curious urchins still followed us like the Pied Piper. It was slightly more peaceful here, for birds as well as for birders. We set up our scopes and scanned the area. A curious black umbrella opened over the water, and then folded itself back into a Black Heron as it strode forwards a few paces. Soon it did it again, opening its wings over its head to form a patch of shadow over the water. Was this to stop the glare so it could see underwater clearly, or did the patch of shade it created actually attract fish within reach of its sharp bill? However it worked, this fishing technique was obviously successful in these fertile waters. Not far away a handsome Saddle-billed Stork was also poking around in the water. Its black-and-white body was set off by its enormous colourful bill, red at the tip and base, with a black band around the middle and a bright yellow, saddle-shaped frontal shield over the top. A bright yellow eye completed the picture and confirmed that this was a female. What a place! It is impossible to do justice here to the sights, sounds and smells of Lake Awassa but we will never forget the total assault on the senses.

We'd nearly finished our 25-day tour of Ethiopia, but Ethiopia still hadn't finished surprising us. We broke our journey back to Addis Ababa with another overnight stay at Lake Langano. A few people were laid low with a bad stomach, so it was a smaller group of us than usual that headed out to the nearby Lake Abiata. As we drove along the track to the lake, we became aware of an ever-multiplying swarm of black dots in the sky. Soon they filled the sky from horizon to horizon like an enormous cloud of midges. But checking through the bins, we realised these were not insects but Barn Swallows – more than even Christian had ever seen before in one place. It was as if the whole world's supply of swallows had congregated here. They were swirling like smoke, massing in one place then spreading out to bunch up in a new spot elsewhere, forming clouds and shapes as they swooped and swirled around us, sometimes coming right down to skim the ground before soaring up into the air again.

It was an amazing and unforgettable sight. And there was more to come. We drove closer to the lake and out onto the saltpan, abandoning the vehicles and continuing on foot as the surface became more unstable. The fragile salt crust crackled and crunched under our feet, creating a strange vibrating sensation whenever anyone moved. Not that we paid much attention to our feet, though, as there were much better things to look at. Thousands upon thousands of Greater and Lesser Flamingos strutted their stuff in the water, some stretching their necks and parading while others sifted the water with their bills upside-down, all combining in a shimmering band of pink as far as we could see. Shuffling in the shallows at their feet were thousands of waders: Ruff, Little Stints and Pied Avocets. It was hopeless to try to photograph this view in the heat haze, and hopeless to try to count the numbers, as there were just too many birds coming and going. This was a moment just to stand and marvel at such an awe-inspiring wonder of nature.

We reluctantly tore ourselves away from birding heaven as the light faded. But still the day hadn't quite finished, as we notched up Slender-tailed and Freckled Nightjars flitting around the hotel grounds behind our rooms.

All too soon it was the end of our Ethiopian leg, and we enjoyed our last supper together back at the Ghion Hotel in Addis, where adventure had started. Without saying a word to one another, we girls all had the same idea. From somewhere in the depths of our baggage, we retrieved colourful, feminine clothes, and with clean hair and a dab of make-up we proved that even after 25 tough days in the field, we could still, in Chuck's words, 'scrub up quite well.'

Ethiopia had been an incredible stage in our quest. Nothing had fully prepared us for its sights and sounds, nor the sheer number of birds we would encounter. We recorded a staggering total of 575 species, of which 462 were new for our list. That meant a year total by 26 February of 1,604 species. It had been a tough trip, no denying that, and with hindsight, one of the hardest legs of our quest. But if it's plenty of birds that you want, then Ethiopia certainly delivers. Yes, there is definitely *so* much more to this country than aid appeals.

Christian and Keith had driven us hard – sometimes even to tears – but it was all in the name of birds on the list, which we had managed in spades. It was funny, but no matter how cross we might have felt with them at times – such as when Christian disappeared headlong into the bush in hot pursuit of a bird leaving us to run to catch up with him, or when Keith frogmarched us across the desert in the blazing heat when we'd all rather rest in the shade – the second they got us onto a good bird, we forgot and forgave them instantly. And when they regaled us with their tales over a cold beer in the evening, they would have us in stitches and begging for more the next day. They are men driven; tireless in their pursuit of birds. But to see the miracles of nature in a tough place like Ethiopia, I can't think of two people I'd sooner have by my side than Christian and Keith.

1,604 species

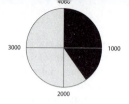

26–27 February, Kenya (Ruth)

Whoever plans a *day* trip to Kenya? After all, with top safaris and sandy beaches, not to mention great birds, it's got the lot. This was not our original plan, of course. We had arranged a few days in the country between our fixed departure tours in Ethiopia and Ghana, and had planned birding around Lake Naivasha and the Gatamaiyu Forest. It was our last opportunity to pile on more East African birds before heading west.

Sadly politics made a mess of our plans. Just as we were confirming our airline tickets, political unrest and outbreaks of violence made Kenya pretty unsafe. The worst violence was exactly where we had planned to visit and, although tourists were not being targeted, there was always the risk of being caught in the wrong place at the wrong time. Furthermore, the Foreign Office was advising against travel. We wanted more birds for *The Biggest Twitch*, but did we want to get killed for them?

Decision made, we needed to change our flights. Back in the UK we'd booked most of our long-haul flights through the travel company Trailfinders, who had done us proud. Steve Alban, especially, was brilliant. Little had he known what would hit him when we first approached his desk at the Manchester office clutching our spread sheet. "Oh!" was all he could manage as he took in the scale of our plans. A true professional, however, Steve managed to untangle our complicated arrangements and made sure that we always had the right tickets in time for our flights. He even personally confirmed our on-going flights for us all year so we never lost our booking. What a star! It was also Steve who got in touch with us to suggest we consider changing our plans for Kenya.

Changing our flights was not going to be straightforward, though. Our African ticket took us from the UK to Ethiopia, down to Kenya, west across Africa to Ghana and then back home again via Ethiopia. Most of this was with my favourite carrier, Ethiopian Airlines. But we had to complete the whole trip as booked. If we didn't turn up for one leg of the journey, we would forfeit the remaining flights. In other words, even had we booked new flights straight from Ethiopia to Ghana without going via Kenya, our original flights back home again would have been cancelled. Such a move would have been prohibitively expensive, so our only option was to keep our tickets but change the dates of our flights out of Kenya to minimise the time spent there. We worked out that we could cut our time down to less than twenty-four hours in Nairobi and fly across to Ghana a few days early, giving ourselves time to relax in Accra before joining Iain Campbell and Sam Woods for our tour. This seemed the best plan, but it was touch-and-go whether Trailfinders could pull it out of the bag in time. We should never have doubted Steve, though, and we were soon on our way with new tickets – and just a day trip to Kenya.

To make sure we avoided trouble at all costs, we booked ourselves into a Nairobi hotel that offered an airport shuttle service, thus avoiding having to run the gauntlet of local taxis. This meant going upmarket for the day, but we took the plunge and booked ourselves into the Nairobi Hilton. A bit steeper than our normal budget, but what price safety?

By the time we arrived in Nairobi the political situation had eased a bit, but we were on Plan B and we couldn't change things again. We were still rather nervous as we looked for our transport, though. The Hilton had arranged for a private taxi to collect us and our driver was Paul Njoroge, an enthusiastic and chatty man, who pointed out the sights as we drove through the capital. He was enterprising, too, and was quick to suggest an afternoon tour of Nairobi National Park where he was confident we'd see plenty of birds. This was only a half-hour drive from our hotel, giving us three hours or so before sunset, so it seemed a pretty safe way to spend the afternoon. The hotel staff were extremely polite and helpful, and very apologetic that our room wasn't ready. To compensate, they upgraded us to a junior suite on the top floor. Now this was the life! A huge bedroom with king-size bed, separate sitting room and two enormous bathrooms. We were still so filthy from our previous trip in Ethiopia that we felt rather like Crocodile Dundee in New York. Should we sleep on the floor to avoid dirtying the sheets? Even taking several showers to clean up, we did our utmost to get full use out of the abundant toiletries, fluffy bathrobes and slippers that were provided. Changing into clean clothes, we went down to the café on the ground floor, with binoculars, field guide and notebook at the ready, to join Paul for our afternoon jaunt.

Unfortunately, it wasn't just our flight that had had to be rearranged for our stay in Kenya. Back in 2007, we'd identified a company called Birdwatching East Africa, which offered short birdwatching packages around the Nairobi area. We had been in contact with a guide called Chege Wa Kariuki who had put together a four-day birding itinerary for us, giving us around 150 species. Of course, our plans had changed and we'd emailed Chege to let him know. He was sad to learn this but emailed us back suggesting that he'd meet us at Nairobi airport and take us out birding for the afternoon. This would have been great, but with no internet access in Ethiopia, unfortunately we didn't get his reply until after we were already in Ghana. However, Chege is a determined man. Even though we hadn't replied to him, he still went to the airport to meet our flight. Of course, because we weren't expecting him and were concentrating on finding the Hilton Hotel shuttle bus, we must have walked right past him. Then, realising that he must have missed us, he drove to our hotel and asked to speak to us. Reception rang our room but by this time we were down in the café having lunch, and so we missed his call. Once again, we must have walked right past Chege as he stood in the hotel lobby, when we followed our taxi driver Paul out to his car. Poor Chege! How persistent – and how unlucky – can one man be?

Back in his Toyota Corolla, Paul chatted away to us about his experience as a wildlife guide. Apparently he visited the National Park frequently and knew it well, so he was sure he could show us the best places for some great birds and mammals. Buffalo, zebra, giraffe, they were all here. And of course there were also his mates, the lions. Well, he was right about how close the park was, and in no time at all we'd filled in the paperwork at the entrance lodge and were driving inside. The main tracks were pretty smooth but there weren't many birds, so we encouraged Paul to head down some of the rougher tracks. At one point, we found ourselves on top of a slight ridge so we could look across the expanse of the park back towards the capital. It seemed so bizarre to scan across the open savanna, dotted with its signature acacia trees, and to see a fringe of high-rise buildings in the distance.

Paul was true to his word on the mammal front. We saw herds of zebras grazing on the short grass, warthogs rolling in their dry dust wallows, elephants swinging their trunks in the shade and giraffes craning up to browse the tops of thorn trees. And all these classic African animals against the backdrop of a teeming capital city; what an incredible place!

The birds, though, were rather trickier. Part of our problem was our field guide. To keep the weight down, we'd left behind our best books on Kenyan birds and just had with us the lightweight, but ancient, Collins *Field Guide to the Birds of East Africa*. Some of the illustrations were pretty ropy and the common names were different from those on our Clements list, so we had to rely on the scientific names. After our success in Ethiopia there weren't many new birds left for us to find and things were pretty quiet until temperatures started to cool down. Being confined to our car because of dangerous wildlife didn't make things any easier. But we still managed to add a few to the list, including Long-tailed Fiscal, Cinnamon-chested Bee-Eater and Little Swift.

Paul drove us down into a gully where, he stated confidently, lions were often seen. Bushes hung low over the narrow track as it crossed a trickling creek. This looked a likely spot for a thirsty lion to drop in so we hung around for a while, but obviously the lions were having a day off. Further on, we came to a designated picnic area where people are allowed out of their cars for a comfort break. After several hours in the car this seemed like a good idea, and as we slowed to a stop I scanned around to make sure there weren't any birds we might flush as we got out. I did a double-take as my bins swept past a large shaggy mane. Could that really be...? Yes, it was: a magnificent male lion tearing away at a kill, his face red with blood.

'A lion!' I squealed. 'A male lion, just over there! Look, he's eating something!'

'Fantastic!' breathed Alan as he picked up the lion in his bins. "Wow! Doesn't he look amazing! Can we get any closer?'

"Oh my God!" gabbled Paul, terrified at meeting nature truly red in tooth and claw. 'We have to go. Right now! Quick, quick, close your windows before he jumps in!'

Clearly Paul had never seen a lion before, never mind a handsome male in the prime of life, dismembering a bloody carcass. He was terrified. So much for his bravado about being an experienced wildlife guide! But we weren't going anywhere: this was our first lion of the year, and a male on a kill, to boot. So we persuaded Paul to stay put as we watched the lion tearing the carcass to pieces. This was some picnic site. Or had we perhaps misread the signs? Maybe we humans were meant to be the picnic rather than the picnickers?

Paul's nerve finally failed and we took off at top speed, not stopping for any more birds until we regained the security of the tarmac road with the entrance lodge in sight. 'We must hurry,' he said. 'There is a huge fine to pay if we're late.' A good excuse for taking the quickest way out.

Once back in the comparative safety of the Nairobi rush hour Paul's Tigger bounce returned. 'Just think of the tale I will tell my family tonight,' he said.

'They'll never believe I have had such an adventure. I must take my daughter to see the lion, she'll love him!' Somehow I doubt his daughter ever saw that lion.

During our half-day in Kenya we saw 12 mammal species but only managed to log a poor seven new birds. This was pretty disappointing. But it took our year list total to 1,611, and every little helped. At least we'd survived the rioters and lions.

The next morning, we tore ourselves reluctantly away from our junior suite, our sponge bag bulging with hotel toiletries. Well, how else were we going to keep clean and fragrant in Ghana? Then it was back to the airport and onto yet another plane as we flew across the widest part of the continent to Accra, and from one climate zone to another. Welcome to Ghana, the sauna of West Africa.

1,611 species

27 February–16 March, Ghana (Alan)

Late afternoon, 27 February, we landed in Ghana's capital, Accra. Here we hoped to give our list a huge boost, as West Africa held many species we could see nowhere else. Stepping out of the cool, air-conditioned plane we were smacked in the face with heat and humidity, and instantly soaked in sweat. The first thing we noticed in the arrivals building was the large, graphic posters that warned against child sex abuse, showing an overweight man grabbing a small boy. Clearly Ghana didn't pull its punches.

Exiting the airport, we looked for a man holding a sign with our name. There were plenty of signs, but none for us. As we sat there, while everyone else was met and headed off into the crazy-looking traffic, we mused on how much – or, in fact, how little – we knew about the country we had just arrived in. With the fast pace of the first two months of *The Biggest Twitch*, we had had no time to swot up on Ghana. Neither of us had been here before, the nearest we had ever got being The Gambia, which we had enjoyed greatly. We had known it would be hot and humid, and we had a vague idea that the slave trade had played a part in the country's history, but that really was it. More worryingly, we had not even looked at the large field guide, though we knew a huge number of new species were possible.

So now what? Well it certainly looked as though our ground agent was not going to pick us up. We spotted an ex-pat type coming into the airport and asked him how much a taxi fare should cost to our hotel. Luckily we had the name of the hotel, though no idea where in Ghana it was. Our new friend, an Aussie working here, knew of the Dutch Hotel and told us the going rate for the ride. So we took a deep breath and stepped out of the tranquillity of the airport into the chaos of Accra.

Immediately we were surrounded by a mob of people all suggesting different ways in which we could part with our cash. We pushed through to the taxi rank and spotted a jolly-looking driver smiling broadly, so asked him for the Dutch Hotel. Yes, he could certainly take us, but it was a long way. Right, so how much? Thankfully he was bang on the price our Aussie mate had suggested, so we shook hands and piled in.

Our friendly driver was keen to point out various landmarks and points of interest as we crawled through the near gridlocked traffic. It was noisy, smelly, hot and humid: an assault on all our senses. The pavements were as crowded as the roads, thronged with people carrying everything from fruit, bamboo poles and bundles of colourful cloth to dead pigs and all manner of unidentifiable stuff.

The traffic began to ease a little as we moved away from the main city, but it was still busy. At last we reached our hotel, a walled plot amongst some empty plots that looked like they were earmarked for development. It looked for all the world like a council block back in the UK. Once we went in, however, we were pleasantly surprised. It was nicely decorated and all the staff were very friendly.

We dumped our bags and headed straight for the bar in search of a long, cold drink. We were looking forward to some recovery time after our crazy, exhausting start to *The Biggest Twitch*. There were still a few days before Iain Campbell and Sam Woods arrived to do their recce tour of Ghana for Tropical Birding. With security problems in other parts of West Africa, they were keen to see whether Ghana could deliver the birds and infrastructure to meet their high standards, and we would be joining them. It was an ideal chance to boost our list with West African birds – and have some fun.

We eventually made contact with the ground agent and it seemed there had been a mix-up over the airport pick-up. Oh well; we'd survived. The good news was that they were able to arrange a local guide for 29 February – our bonus day, what with 2008 being a leap year – and he could show us some nearby birding sites.

One definite plus about Ghana's latitude is that it never gets light too early, so our day did not start until a leisurely 7am. Our young guide, Kalu, arrived on the stroke of seven in a taxi and we set off east from the hotel. Traffic was slow, which gave us the chance to observe more Ghanaian street life. We had noticed several shops selling what appeared to be defunct fairground rides – you know the sort of thing: colourfully painted rabbits, fire engines, planes, dogs and so on, for kids to sit in and spin round. But why were they on sale at the roadside in Ghana? We had not seen a single fairground.

Kalu explained that these were not fairground rides but coffins. We were amazed by the bold variety of colours and shapes for something that in the UK is so plain and sombre. But why the cows, boats, lions and other shapes? These were the choice of the deceased, Kalu explained. They had stipulated in their will what shape of coffin they would like to be buried in. Often it reflected their occupation, so a fisherman might be laid to rest in a fish-shaped coffin, a chicken farmer in a hen-shaped one, and so on. What a great idea: a colourful celebration of a person's life and so much less depressing than in the UK. I suspected we were going to like this country – if only someone would turn on the air-conditioning. Ruth decided that she would like to be buried in a penguin-shaped coffin, though I ventured there might be a problem digging the hole if the penguin was upright.

We also noticed a disproportionately large number of barber-shops. Style must be very important here, as every sixth shop seemed to offer haircuts, or perhaps we were just passing through the barber district of Accra. The shops were little more than shacks, but looked clean and tidy. Ghana is a strongly Christian country and this was reflected in the names of the businesses we saw, such as the 'God Will Provide' grocery store, the 'God helps those who help themselves' self-service corner shop, and the 'Praise be' beautician. You get the idea.

We left our taxi driver to listen to his radio and headed off into an area of scrubby bush. Now we would see how well Kalu knew his birds. His English was very good, though he was very shy and spoke little other than to answer direct questions. The day was growing hotter and more humid by the minute, and we did not seem to be acclimatising at all. But we only had gone a few yards when we encountered our first new species: Double-spurred Francolin. A gang of these partridge-like birds dashed from cover and sprinted down the track ahead of us. Before we'd gone fifty yards, this was followed by a Yellow-billed Shrike, a Yellow-fronted Tinkerbird and, best of all, a Yellow-crowned Gonolek. The last of these was a real stunner: scarlet below, with a black mask and vivid yellow crown.

We left the scrub and headed towards a large shallow lagoon with patches of reeds along the muddy shoreline. This looked good. As we approached the water a pipit-like bird exploded from the grass. Kalu identified it immediately as Yellow-throated Longclaw. Luckily the bird pitched down nearby and soon strode back out into view. Making our European pipits look rather drab, this guy had banana-yellow underparts, a black necklace around the upper breast, a yellow supercilium and – like all his kind – white outer tail feathers.

The lagoon was so packed with birds we hardly knew where to look. All three of us kept calling out new names, each wanting the others' attention as they in turn demanded we look at their find. Slowly we calmed down a little as we realised that most birds were staying put and we had time to slow down and take in the spectacle. For us it was great to see so many familiar species, and we found the tables were turned as we talked Kalu through the finer points of wader identification. Collared Pratincoles, Marsh Sandpipers, Wood Sandpipers, Curlew Sandpipers and Little Stints all vied for attention, all birds we would love to see back in North Wales! The more we looked, the more we saw: flocks of feeding Ruffs; gangs of Spotted Redshanks rushing after small fish; Greenshanks resting in a loose flock; Grey Plovers flashing their black armpits as they flew in. And there were wildfowl too: White-faced Whistling Ducks massed at the far end, while more familiar Pintail and Garganey loafed in the African sun. Black, Common, Sandwich and Gull-billed Terns all roosted on an area of dry mud towards the seaward end, along with African Wattled Plovers, while the shallows were thronged with Little Egrets, plus a handful of Western Reef Herons and African Spoonbills.

Beside the road that separated the lagoon from the sea, we spotted two waders that looked a little different. Surely not? But yes, we were amazed to confirm through the scope not one but *two* Pectoral Sandpipers. These American birds were a very long way from home. We took some photos to prove the record, as this species is a real rarity here in West Africa. We were delighted with our find and, of course, it was a new bird for Kalu, so big smiles all round.

The next morning, we took it easy for one of the few times all year. With Iain and Sam due to arrive in the evening we knew this was our last chance. In fact, we took it a bit *too* easy, as we got sunburnt by the pool. I had forgotten how anti-malaria tablets make you photo-sensitive, so had seriously overdone it on my head and legs. Iain and Sam arrived in time for dinner but Iain was not well, trying to shake off a bout of flu. Ruth was now also feeling rough, as she had picked up cystitis – probably a result of being dehydrated in the incredible humidity. So this was not ideal: with 50% of us unwell and me suffering with sunburn, only Sam was fit.

We met up with Mark Williams, who wasn't what we had expected from a Ghanaian ground agent. For a start he was white, had a cockney accent, and wore a ponytail and glasses. But it was obvious from the start we would get along just fine, as he could take our mickey-taking and fire straight back with a joke of his own. After a couple of beers and lots of laughs, Mark left us and we headed for bed. Ruth was in considerable discomfort with her waterworks and I was on fire with the sunburn, my head throbbing like crazy. Needless to say we did not get a lot of sleep. Luckily Mark had told us we were not setting off until early afternoon, so

Ruth and Iain had an easy morning in the hope they would feel better. That left Sam and me free to go birding (back to the lagoon, where we added two American Golden Plovers to the previous day's haul), and to visit a pharmacy to stock up on drugs and potions for the walking wounded.

Soon it was time to leave the Dutch Hotel and head for Kakum National Park, where we were looking forward to some great forest birding. Luckily our bus was air-conditioned and our driver Steve was very good at avoiding everything that spilled onto the chaotic roads. Steve was a young-looking, slightly overweight chap with a ready smile so typical of the Ghanaians we had met so far. We were also joined by another local guide, Robert, who wore a large black cowboy hat and was Mark's forest bird expert. As we travelled along the coast road we passed the Cape Coast Castle, a grim reminder of the slave trade days. Mark explained that the Ashantis of Ghana traded tens of thousands of slaves with the British and that this castle was used as a holding camp while they awaited deportation.

With the drugs kicking in, both Iain and Ruth were feeling a little livelier – though an unexpected side effect of Ruth's tablets was that she was now peeing bright orange. By early evening we had reached our new hotel: the Hans Cottage Botel. Yes, Botel. That's not a typo.

The next morning found us boarding the bus in the dark, as we headed out before sunrise for Kakum National Forest. Mark, bless him, had been up even earlier and made tea for us all. We reached the park entrance just as dawn was breaking over this protected patch of Upper Guinea forest and began hiking up the hill. Sun or no sun, the heat was already sapping.

Before long we were puzzled to hear Mark announce the canopy walkway. Where was the tower? In fact we were on a steep slope, so the walkway began level with the trail and then headed out over the forest with the ground falling away beneath. This looked like a doddle compared to the huge towers we'd negotiated back in Sacha, Ecuador. But as we stepped out, it felt decidedly unsafe. My knees went to jelly as I took in the homemade-looking ropes that bound it together. Where were the steel hawsers we were used to? With each step the walkway swung wildly. 'Keep moving!' I muttered, through gritted teeth, as Ruth and the others leaned unconcerned over the ropes for a better look at the canopy below. I didn't want to appear a wimp but neither did I want to linger here, suspended over the treetops by a few old ropes.

We reached the first platform, which was small and wooden – another worrying contrast with the secure metal platforms of Sacha. It felt better than being out on the rope walkway, but by no means safe. Looking around, though, it seemed I was the only one worried. The others were birding away contentedly. 'White-crested Hornbill,' called Sam, and we looked round to see this amazing bird perched on the ropes of the walkway we had just crossed, with its huge black bill and white, spiky 'mad professor' crest.

That was just the start. As the day continued to warm up, the action came thick and fast. Everyone was calling birds furiously and we struggled to get onto each one before the next was called. This was birding in the fast lane, with nearly everything new for our list. Malimbes are forest weavers, black and red, and a new family for us, so when Robert called Gray's Malimbe we stayed with it until we got a decent view among the forest tangle. Crested, Red-headed and Red-vented Malimbes quickly followed. Two West African endemics were next up: Sharpe's Apalis and Large-billed Puffback. Roberts's sharp eyes then picked out a small bird far below, and with the bins we could just make out the aptly named Tiny Sunbird.

Looking up from the trees, we watched both Cassin's and Sabine's Spinetails hawking over the canopy, their unusual short-tailed silhouettes looking almost bat-like. As we followed them, Cassin's Hawk-Eagle and Black Sparrowhawk soared past in quick succession. Then another raptor flew by and this time landed in view. Scopes were quickly focused and revealed a Congo Serpent-Eagle, impressive with its striking markings and neat crest. And even then we couldn't linger, as garrulous calls drew our attention to a party of Forest Woodhoopoes clambering around in the branches and showing off their long red bills and iridescent purple and green plumage.

Taking a shaded trail to avoid the sun we soon found more great birds. First up was a cracking Finsch's Flycatcher-Thrush. This was both an endemic and a lifer. Meanwhile a Forest Robin hopped past, giving wonderful views, and a gang of Chestnut-bellied Helmetshrikes moved fast through the forest, and we hurried to keep them in sight long enough for decent views.

There was no doubting the bird of the day though. We had gone off-trail, and it has to be said Ruth and I were not impressed with fighting our way through the tangled undergrowth – especially since we had seen nothing since leaving the trail and, given the impenetrable tangle and limited visibility, seemed unlikely to. But, as it turned out, this was no gratuitous Indiana Jones-style adventure. Robert was heading for a particular clearing deep in the forest. When we got there he asked Sam to play a call – which was immediately answered. And there was a Rufous-sided Broadbill. This stocky bird does not only look good, with its chunky bill and bright orange breast patches, but it can perform too, and we were thrilled to watch the bizarre display, in which it flew up, turned a complete mid-air somersault and landed back on the same perch.

Still buzzing from our broadbill show, we climbed back to the canopy platform and were soon seeing more great birds. Red-fronted Parrots flew through the trees, calling loudly, and were soon followed by African Grey Parrots. It seemed strange to see the latter in the wild, given their depressing abundance in UK pet shops. No time to dwell on it, though, as a shout from Sam out on the walkway alerted us to two massive Black-casqued Hornbills sitting in the top of a huge forest tree. What awesome birds!

It had been a great day, with an incredible 66 new birds for *The Biggest Twitch*. And the next day we turned our sights on a new area, just outside the park. Here logging had opened up the forest, and now the secondary growth was giving a different selection of birds from inside the protected park. And we had acquired another local helper: Mark had taken on Joseph, a young lad from the village, as chief breakfast carrier. He was very proud to be working and walked just behind us with our packed breakfast box on his head. We got him to look through the scopes whenever a bird sat still long enough. Who knows, perhaps he might become a guide in the future.

Not surprisingly, the birding was slower than the day before; no way could we have kept up that whirlwind pace. Nonetheless, additions to the list included Buff-throated Sunbird, Blue-throated Roller and – best of the lot – Black Bee-eater. This bird's name hardly does it justice. OK, so the basic plumage is indeed black, but the throat is scarlet, the eyebrows and under-tail solid blue, and the breast streaked in turquoise. Our cameras went into over-drive as this gorgeous creature posed on a dead snag above us. A sight like this, I realised, is what life is meant to be about. It was only early March and yet we had already seen so many amazing birds. What would the next ten months bring? *The Biggest Twitch* was proving to be the best thing we could ever have done.

The day was not yet over. Next we visited a nearby reservoir in search of African Finfoot, a notoriously elusive, grebe-like bird that lurks in freshwater habitats. We soon spied a female sitting on a dead log, her vivid orange legs and feet seemingly out of all proportion. Then we headed to a coastal grassland with shallow creeks, where we enjoyed wonderful views of a Shining-blue Kingfisher perched low in a tree. And finally, with the light fading into a spectacular sunset, we watched Preuss' Swallows – a scarce bird and one we badly wanted to see – swooping and circling overhead, before they eventually dived down to roost under a bridge. It was a perfect end to another great day's birding.

The next day we were out on the road before dawn and heading back to Kakum, pausing only to tick a Plain Nightjar sitting in the road. We headed straight back up the canopy walkway, where we hoped to mop up a few species we'd missed the day before – notably Chocolate-backed Kingfisher, whose very name was irresistible. New birds were slow in coming, which was hardly surprising given our earlier success. Nonetheless, we'd already scored a flashy Fire-bellied Woodpecker shinning up a tree trunk by the time Mark's 'Get over here now!' rang out from the rickety walkway. We dashed over, followed his directions and there it was it: a stunning Chocolate-backed Kingfisher. It was every bit as tasty as we'd hoped, the chocolate-brown head and back set off by a coral red bill, white breast, and azure wing bars and tail. Wow!

Now it was time for the main event of our visit to Ghana: we were heading off to look for White-necked Rockfowl. This rarity is endemic to West Africa and, until 2003, was known only from countries with major security worries. With recent news of its discovery here in safe and stable Ghana, birders at last had a chance to search for this enigmatic species in safety. The White-necked Rockfowl really is one of the world's weirdest birds, and is one half of an endemic West African family that has no close relatives (the other half being the equally rare Grey-necked Rockfowl). This secretive forest bird not only looks odd but also behaves very strangely. It is a communal nester in caves deep within the Upper Guinea Forest – a habitat dependency that probably explains its rarity. The birds are not particularly shy but they are very rarely seen away from the caves. This was now our chance. Anticipation was high.

When we arrived at a remote forest village everyone came out to greet us. Many of the adults stood back, interested but shy. The children, however, mobbed us as soon as we stepped off the bus. They were really excited at the arrival of visitors and all talked at once – not that we understood a word. We took their photographs and the crowd went wild when we showed them the images on the back of the digital camera. Ruth and I were so busy entertaining the kids we did not notice the others were ready to set off. Sam was worried that any delay might mean we missed the birds; he was also worried about how long the walk would be: did the local guides know exactly where the site was? Sam! Relax!

Mark dragged us away from the waving children to enter the dense forest. Two men from the village were to guide us to the cave. They were muscular, unsmiling characters – a real contrast to the youngsters – and seemed to cover the ground at some speed. (Or perhaps we were just unfit.) At last we reached a cliff face, where we could see the nests above us. These mud structures were plastered beneath an overhang, in the manner of House Martin nests back home. The local guides scrambled up right below the nests and motioned for us to follow. Surely we were too close? They waved us forward and we were soon standing just feet away. We were surprised to see that scientists studying the colony had spray-painted a number in red next to each nest. Surely in this age of digital technology such vandalism was unnecessary. Anyway, the guides pointed to the ledge where they thought we should sit. Unfortunately this left the nests and the surrounding jungle out of sight, so we sat further out on another ledge to give ourselves a better view. The local guys were not happy but at least we'd be better able to see the birds.

We crouched down behind the rocks and waited. It was sweltering and we streamed with sweat. All this liquid attracted sweat bees, which made our vigil hell by crawling around our eyes, up our noses and into our ears. Our legs went numb from the cramped positions we were stuck in, and we began to wish we had brought something to sit on. We watched in total silence. Well, almost. At one point Robert began fiddling with his camera, producing all sorts of whirrs and clicks, but hard stares from the rest of us eventually got through to him and soon all that could be heard was the low buzz of the sweat bees again.

After an hour and a half, which seemed like much longer, there was a movement in the tangle of vines beyond the nest cliff. Could it be? We held our breath and stared, willing the bird to appear. Nothing. Then suddenly it was there on a rock, showing off. And, just as suddenly, it was gone. We looked at each other. Did we all get it? Yes! Phew! The view had been so brief and so shocking it was hard to take in the detail, but we all knew we had just seen one of the best birds on the planet.

Then it was back, in the vines off to the left, and this time there were two. Our hearts beat so loudly we must have been in danger of frightening the birds. Adrenaline overload! Soon we could see at least four, perhaps as many as seven, bouncing in and leaping around on the rocks and among the dense vines. We were spellbound by their extraordinary looks and behaviour. Iain and I attempted to get video footage and photos but it was nearly impossible, they moved so fast and the light was so poor. So we gave up and just watched open-mouthed as these amazing birds did their stuff. This moment alone seemed worth everything we had put into *The Biggest Twitch*.

So how to describe the White-necked Rockfowl? This crow-sized bird has a long tail, long neck and large bill, its largely white plumage set off by grey wings, long blue legs and a bare yellow head. It bounces through the forest from tree to tree or rock to rock in a very un-bird like manner – like a cross between a chicken and a kangaroo, perhaps. We watched, rooted to the spot, for half an hour as the birds came and went, and then reluctantly dragged ourselves away before it was time for the rockfowl to come into roost.

We were on an incredible high as we hiked back to the village, reaching the bus just as darkness fell. All agreed that not only was this the highlight of the trip but one of the best moments of our birding lives. Everyone thanked the villagers for their help, and we waved good-bye to these wonderful people, hoping they would long look after their secret in the forest.

The next day did not start well. Ruth had gone to bed the previous night with a very sore right eye and this morning it was much worse: red, swollen and watering continuously. Anything wrong with an eye is always worrying and Mark decided we should get it checked out. So while Iain, Sam and Robert set off birding, we headed for the hospital. The place was already very busy by the time we arrived, with crowds in the corridors and spilling out onto the front steps, all waiting for treatment. Clearly this was not going to be an in-and-out job. At last, a female doctor had a look and decided Ruth had an infection under her eyelid, possibly picked up when letting some local kids look through the telescope. She prescribed antibiotics, ointment and pain-killers – yet more tablets for poor Ruth, who by now was rattling. But we were very grateful to Mark for helping us sort out this problem so promptly.

Kumasi, Mark's hometown, was our destination for the night. As we neared the town we hit traffic and crawled along at less than walking pace. This did at least give us a chance to witness more lively Ghanaian street life, and as dusk fell we watched tens of thousands of Straw-coloured Fruit-bats taking to the skies. These Herring Gull-sized bats flapped slowly over the town centre, heading off to feed in the surrounding jungle. It was amazing to see so many large animals passing right over this busy urban area. We were also delighted to find Mark had found us a nice modern hotel. As ever, of course, we did not have long to enjoy it. With the late arrival we just had time to grab some food, and then took to bed before another very early departure.

After a very long day's travel north we reached Mole National Park by early evening, and were grateful for a cold beer from the bar. We took our drinks to the edge of the escarpment, with the dry savanna of the park laid out below us. What a view! A waterhole at the base of the escarpment attracted both birds and mammals, and we sat back and enjoyed both the liquid refreshment and the wildlife spectacle. Abyssinian Rollers hawked insects from bush tops and Helmeted Guineafowl scuttled through the brush, as Bruce's Green-Pigeons sat in the taller trees above. Both Kob and Bushbuck came to the waterhole to slake their thirst, while large Nile Crocodiles loafed around the edge and Senegal Thick-knees called into the dusk. As night fell we took our place at the dinner table and met local guide Zack, complete with his trusty, ancient-looking, bolt-action rifle.

The next day we assembled on the terrace before dawn. It was lovely and cool in the dark, and so nice to have left behind the sweltering humidity of the south. Mark passed round mugs of tea to get the day under way. As the sky slowly light-ened, we began to see birds around the edge of the waterhole below. Noisy Hadada Ibises squawked as they flew in from their tree roost. Hamerkops patrolled the shallows, grabbing fish in their hefty bills.

Zack arrived with his gun and rather paramilitary look, but a ready smile. Despite being a little late, he was very keen that we put down our tea and get straight out into the bush. A dripping tap not far from the lodge was a magnet for birds, and the puddles around it heaved with finches and weavers drinking and bathing. We crept closer and carefully checked through the busy flock. Gorgeous Orange-cheeked Waxbills were the undoubted stars and wowed us in the dawn light. Next to these hopped exquisite Black-rumped Waxbills and Red-billed Pytilias. There were Firefinches too, with African, Red-billed and Black-faced all present and showing nicely.

With Zack leading the way, we made our way down the escarpment towards the waterholes. It was great to be birding on foot and walking in the bush with wildlife all around us. We hadn't gone far when a flash of red and purple stopped us in our tracks. A Violet Turaco swept up into a treetop and showed off in the sunshine; this species is confined to the savannas of West Africa and was a great bird for our year list. Red-throated Bee-eaters were all over the place, easy to see as they hawked insects in the rapidly warming air. Lavender Waxbills were lurking in the bushes and, after a little work, gave us good views of their powder-grey plumage, black bill, and red tail and rump. A cool-looking Blue Flycatcher zapped about in a dead tangle.

But one bird that we really wanted still hadn't shown, and we quizzed Zack on our chances of Oriole Warbler. Zack said he knew where it was to be found and, minutes later, announced he had just seen one. The bird was, apparently, deep in a large thorn bush. It has to be said we were a little sceptical: no sooner had we asked about the bird than Zack had seen it – although nobody else had. Was he winding us up? More birds flew into the bush and began to scold, as if they were mobbing something. We moved right up close and peered into the dense branches in the hope of a glimpse. Suddenly Kalu recoiled dramatically, shouting 'Get back! Get back!'. What had he seen? We moved back and joined a shaken-looking Kalu as he pointed into the bush. Wow! A huge snake, at least two metres long, was moving through the bush at about head height. Zack announced that it was a spitting cobra, a deadly animal that can spit venom more than two metres; we had all been well within range.

Our attention was drawn away from the snake as the Oriole Warbler popped up, giving us a brief view of its black hood frosted with fine white scales, its red eye, and its rich yellow and olive-green body plumage. With its long decurved bill and long tail this was certainly one weird warbler.

Other new birds came thick and fast, with highlights including White-shouldered Black Tit, Brown-throated Wattle-eye, both Striped and Grey-headed Kingfisher. A dazzling white-morph male African Paradise-Flycatcher was a real treat. It was not just birds either; we had racked up a good list of mammals this morning, with Yellow-flanked Duiker, Waterbuck, Bushbuck, Kob, Patas Monkey, Vervet Monkey and Olive Baboon.

That evening Zack took us the short distance to a dirt airfield where he reck-oned we had a shot at a very special bird. We waited for the light to disappear and then drove very slowly along the runway, scanning the ground ahead. On the first run we saw nothing except a Togo Hare. On the return sweep, however, we found a nightjar sitting on the runway and in the headlights' glow had a great view. It was the species we had been looking for, but we were disappointed. This Standard-winged Nightjar was a female and so had not a standard in sight. But it went on the list, of course.

Before dawn the next day we were back on the escarpment outside the lodge overlooking the waterholes. A Freckled Nightjar made several low passes over-head as we sipped our tea, then Ruth nearly fell over a large Greyish Eagle-Owl on the path as she nipped back to her room – giving us all a chance to see this formidable-looking bird when it settled a short distance away.

Today we were going back into the park in search of an almost mythical bird – sadly without Iain, who was feeling lousy but managed to wish us luck through gritted teeth. We set off on foot, with 'Zack the gun' leading the way through the bush, striding past elephants as though they were sheep. This was thrilling. We combed small patches of forest around shrinking pools; the lack of water was not a good sign. Zack was sure the bird would fly if it saw us and that given its huge size, we couldn't miss it. Robert was less sure, and thought we would need to check each tree carefully in case we walked past it. So we had two very different approaches from our local guides: Zack striding forward, confident he would see the bird fly; Robert hanging back searching the canopy slowly.

It was Robert who struck gold, and he called us back at the double. We dashed back to find him standing by an almost dry pool staring at a huge tree. There it was, sitting in full view: Pel's Fishing Owl. Huge, with enormous black pools for eyes, its ginger plumage barred with black. We were struck dumb, in awe of this almost-mythical bird. It was another of those 'this is what *The Biggest Twitch* is all about' moments: deep in the African bush, elephants walking past only yards away and one of our all-time most wanted birds perched right in front of us.

In fact, we were so elated that we almost forgot to photograph the owl – and as soon as we remembered it seemed to sense our hurry and flew off. It didn't go far, though landed in denser cover where the light was poor. Still, we weren't complaining. We were watching it and that was all that mattered. Local legend has it that if a Pel's looks at you, it can see into your soul, and with those huge black eyes we could well believe it. We feasted our eyes on this amazing bird for over half an hour. Thank you, Robert. Without you we would have missed it.

Our morning in the bush also added more great birds. It's hard to pick out high-lights, as always, but Blue-breasted Kingfisher was certainly up there, along with Snowy-crowned Robin-chat, Red-billed Hornbill, Senegal Batis and a stunning Sulphur-breasted Bushshrike that, on another occasion, would easily have been bird of the day.

As dusk began to fall, we again headed for the airfield, this time with hopes of male Standard-winged Nightjar. With our luck today, how could we fail? We tried a different tactic and walked about with a powerful torch instead of driving up and down. Soon Zack spotted movement on the ground. What on earth was that? There was something twitching but we could not make it out. Then the penny dropped: we were looking at the standards of a male Standard-winged Nightjar. These elongated flight feathers protrude some 38cm behind the bird, each comprising a long bare shaft tipped with a large black flag – or 'standard'. They trail behind the bird in flight and, when it lands on the ground, stick behind like two separate creatures following the nightjar around. Bizarre! Not for the first time today we stood open-mouthed in wonder at a magnificent bird. At least two males flew around the airfield, occasionally illuminated by our torches and looking quite extraordinary. And we still weren't finished. A low call sent us hurrying to the edge of the airfield, where our torch picked out a pair of orange eyes staring back. Soon we'd got amazing views of a calling Northern White-faced Owl.

It was a nine-hour drive back to Kumasi the next day. We picked up some good birds from the bus, including more looks at Rufous-crowned, Abyssinian and Blue-bellied Rollers, and a fine Giant Kingfisher. Sadly one gorgeous Blue-bellied Roller came a little too close, swooping down right in front of the bus and crashing into the windscreen. Steve was very upset and thought we would be angry. But there was nothing he could have done to avoid it. Very sad, but certainly not Steve's fault.

The day settled into the rhythm of a road trip, scanning for birds, dozing, bursts of conversation and then each of us falling silent into our own thoughts. Sam was poring over the field guide, checking what was still possible – or what we had missed. Iain, meanwhile, was stretched out asleep on the back seat and looking very comfortable. We were surprised to notice he had acquired a large, soft pillow, which looked suspiciously like one from last night's hotel. Mark prodded Iain awake and enquired about the origin of this mystery accessory. It turned out that Iain had taken the pillow onto the bus the morning before – hoping for a little extra comfort on our pre-dawn drive. Unfortunately he had then forgotten to return it to his room. Now he was relishing the extra comfort on this mammoth drive – but Mark was worried he would have to face the anger of the hotel manager next time he stayed there. Surely, we reassured him, they would not miss just one pillow?

We took lunch at a roadside café. We had found that there was not usually much choice at such stops. The menu usually held a selection of local dishes or chicken – which, for Ruth and me, meant chicken. It was usually edible – though with very little meat; Ghanaian chickens certainly don't have much spare flesh. For Iain, a former resident of Ghana, it was a chance to relive his past and experience true local dishes. Iain had long regaled us about his favourite dish in the whole world, fufu. Finally we had found an establishment that served it. Iain bounced around with excitement: fufu was on its way! When it arrived I'm afraid we were under-whelmed: it was an off-white ball of stodge that looked for all the world like sticky plasticine. The lump of fufu sat in a bowl of goat soup, another favourite of Iain's. It is also served with chicken – though what most locals prefer is 'grasscutter', the local name for Greater Cane-Rat, a large rodent that is popular as bushmeat in West Africa.

So now we knew what fufu looked like, but what was it? Iain explained that it is made from pounded yam. It takes two women to prepare it: one to pound the yam with a log while the second turns the bowl to ensure an even consistency. The idea is to fish your ball of fufu from the depths of the soup, pull off a piece and suck it down. Yes, suck. Don't chew, or it will stick your teeth together. Iain tucked in and made loud slurping noises as he sucked down his fufu and spicy goat soup with relish. Ruth was brave enough to delve into the orange liquid, emerging with a lump of pounded yam which she gamely sucked. Her face said it all. I stuck to chicken and chips.

When we at last reached our hotel for the night, there was a message for Mark from a rather angry hotel owner back across country, demanding one stolen pillow to be returned.

The next day began in our by-now established Ghana style, with a welcome cup of tea on the bus as we drove in the pre-dawn dark to our first birding destination. Today this was Bobiri, a butterfly sanctuary in an area of lush forest. Clouds of brilliant butterflies of all colours filled the air. The trees here were so tall that we strained our necks scanning the canopy for movement. The heat and humidity at such an early hour reminded us that we were back in the rainforest belt.

Sam was worried that this was our only real chance of Red-billed Dwarf Hornbill. A look at the field guide explained his concern: this was a cracking bird and one we all wanted badly. The smallest of the hornbills, hence the 'dwarf', this pigeon-sized bird would be a lifer for all of us except Iain. So where was it? We hiked the trails and played tapes of its mournful '*koo, koo, koo*' until finally we got a response. Now we just needed to see the bird. It called again, closer, then appeared on a high branch, giving us a great view in the scopes of its red bill. Perfect!

As the hornbill dropped out of sight a noisy gang of Chestnut-bellied Helmetshrikes came bustling through the canopy. Next we found another gorgeous Blue-breasted Kingfisher sitting out in full view.

Our list was missing some pigeons so we turned our attention to scanning the high canopy. The tactic paid off and we soon added both Bronze-naped and Afep Pigeons. Movement lower down attracted our attention and, after a few tense minutes of brief views, we saw an African Forest-Flycatcher. While watching this new bird along came another: Tit-hylia, a small, rather tit-like species, with a streaky head and breast, olive yellow underparts and green upperparts. It would have been at home in the UK with a colour scheme like that.

Woodpeckers were also on the agenda here and so we set out to track some down. We started at the bottom with a cute little African Piculet, a diminutive woodpecker no bigger than a warbler. Gabon Woodpecker was next, quickly followed by a Melancholy Woodpecker probing for insects buried in the bark of a dead tree. All too soon we were heading back to the bus, very pleased with the great birds we had seen but sad not to have had more time.

En route to our next stop in the Atewa Mountains we reviewed our year list and added the morning's new species. We realised that we were only 19 species away from reaching the halfway point to a new world record, and it was still only 14 March. Could we achieve this milestone before leaving Ghana in just two days time?

We spent the afternoon at the foot of the mountains and quickly found a noisy gang of Vieillot's Weavers. Here this species show the distinctive rufous saddle of the *castaneofuscus* West African subspecies, and we wondered whether it might be a split for the future? The narrow and unassuming strip of grassland at the forest edge proved to hold a surprising number of birds: Black-and-white Mannikins fed on seeding grasses beside the track; flocks of massive-billed Grosbeak Weavers swept overhead; and a Brown-crowned Tchagra skulked in a dense bush, eventually popping out to give us a brief but decent view.

Our next new bird was voted bird of the afternoon: Western Bluebill. This chubby finch has a massive powder-blue bill, jet-black plumage and a crimson chest band, and we gawped at its beauty. Fluty, mournful whistles from the forest betrayed a Fire-crested Alethe but, try as we might, we just could not get a good view. The birding finished with flocks of White-throated Bee-eaters streaming overhead to roost: a wonderful spectacle to end our day. We had added a further six new species; just 13 more needed to reach halfway .

After a night with a thumping head and little sleep – courtesy of spending the day before without a hat – I wasn't sure whether to welcome the morning alarm or curse it. But it was our last day and we had to get moving. As usual, it was a battle to get Ruth upright. She just does not do mornings – not that many people would call 4.30am morning. We drove back to Atewa where we transferred into Mark's Landrover on our final quest for a few extra forest species. A bumpy uphill track took us to 770m, where we found ourselves in one of Ghana's few remaining areas of upland evergreen forest. Despite the increase in altitude it was still very warm and we happily birded in T-shirts.

Progress was slow as we drove up. First we heard a Red-cheeked Wattle-eye calling close to the track. We bailed out quickly but, despite its continued calling, failed to get a glimpse of this sought-after bird. Then we again jumped out, further up, to peer low into the understorey at a pair of Golden Greenbuls – for once, a species of greenbul that we could readily identify. Next we leapt from the vehicle to chase a Yellow-billed Turaco, which flashed red primaries as it swept over the track ahead. This impressive bird didn't go far, and we soon saw him strutting along a mighty bough.

Eventually we reached the ridge top and walked the trail. We soon hit birds: Yellow-spotted and Hairy-breasted Barbets were quickly on the list, followed by Red-rumped and Speckled Tinkerbirds. But there was no time to enjoy these, as Black-capped Apalises popped up just metres away! Meanwhile the calls of both Black Cuckoo and Olive Long-tailed Cuckoo rang through the forest.

We sat down on the track for a break, but a movement in the trees caught our eyes. What was that? We watched and waited and the bird came back to the same spot: a Chestnut Wattle-eye building a nest right next to the track. Rest over, we pushed on. Soon we found an aptly-named Dusky Tit feeding in the same huge tree as the odd rather swallow-like Ussher's Flycatcher that hawked from exposed branches at the top. Copper-tailed Glossy-Starlings called excitedly from the dense forest.

Soon Mark called a halt to our hilltop birding and we reluctantly began to make our way back down. We still managed to pick up more new birds as we descended, with tiny Lemon-bellied Crombecs, Western Black-headed Orioles and a Shining Drongo, the latter giving itself away by calling loudly from the trees as we drove past.

Then it was a long drive back to the Dutch Hotel outside Accra for our last night in Ghana. Where had the time gone? It seemed only a few days since we had first set foot in this sweltering bird paradise. Safely back at the coast, we celebrated our birds with a great meal, Iain of course, tucking into a huge dish of fufu with goat soup.

Our Ghana trip was over. We climbed into a cool, air-conditioned aeroplane with 1,835 species on our list. Now we were over halfway. Just 1,828 left to break the world record.

1,835 species

PART THREE

European springtime

17–18 March, UK (Ruth)

Airline scheduling meant we often returned to Manchester Airport at the end of one trip before heading out again on the next with a fresh set of tickets. It gave us a quick break, with the chance to sleep in our own bed, repack the luggage and gear up for the next stage. Sometimes we even had time to do some birding. These stopovers were usually short and hectic, with so many things to sort out and so many people to see in just a few hours. But this time it was even shorter and more fraught than most.

First, that nightmare all too familiar to the frequent traveller had occurred: our blue bag had gone missing – not in a third-world country, ironically, but on the shuttle between London Heathrow and Manchester Airport. We arranged for it to be delivered home in Llandudno, but with less than twenty-four hours before we set off again, would it arrive in time? In the meantime we unpacked the remaining case and took a huge sack of dirty washing down to the local launderette for a service wash. A bit of a luxury given our time constraints, you might be thinking, but it was the only way to get the job done before the next leg of our trip. Alan dumped the bulging sack in the arms of the proprietor. 'Don't forget we close at 4.30,' he warned, as Alan headed out the door.

The rest of the day was spent in a flurry of essential visits, emails and phone calls to chase our still-missing luggage. In the evening, we headed out to the pub for a birders' get-together. It was great, as ever, to catch up with friends who'd driven from all over North Wales. The drink and conversation flowed as we swapped tales of our experiences in Africa and their news of the UK birding scene.

Suddenly, an unwelcome thought struck me. 'Alan, did you collect the washing from the launderette?'

'Oh heck!' he muttered, the smile evaporating from his face. 'I forgot.'

'Me too. What time does the launderette open?'

'Nine,' he replied. 'And we have to leave for the airport at eight.'

'Oh!'

We both silently contemplated the prospect of heading off on the next two-month leg of our trip with only the clothes we were standing in. 'Oh well, nothing we can do now,' said Alan. 'Want another drink?'

I had to admire Alan's glass half-full attitude. Right on cue, his mobile phone rang: a harassed delivery man wanted to know where to return our missing luggage. We gave him the address of the pub and, when he arrived ten minutes later, bought him a drink for his trouble. Things were looking up. We might not have any clothes to wear but at least we'd have our field guides.

The next morning saw us pacing the street impatiently outside Bubbles launderette. John Roberts, our great friend and unofficial chauffeur, was sitting in his car with the engine running like a getaway driver. Nine o'clock came and went but no sign of the proprietor. We were in danger of missing our flight at this rate. At last he sauntered casually down the road.

'Wondered what happened to you last night,' he smirked as he opened up.

Arizona – Toco, Ruth and Alan on Day 1 of the Biggest Twitch (Moez Ali).

▲ Mexico – Lesser Roadrunner, very welcome after dipping on its Greater cousin in Arizona.

Ecuador – a Masked Flowerpiercer visits a hummingbird feeder at Yanacocha.

▲ *Ethiopia – Ruth and Alan check the dry riverbed for endemics (Oz Pfenninger).*

▼ *Ethiopia – Alan takes identification advice from some young locals.*

▼ *Ghana – Black Bee-eater. What a stunner – a top-ten bird!*

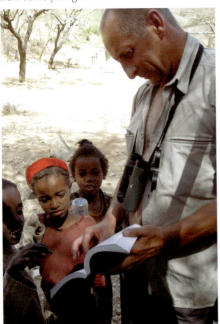

▲ Texas – Roseate Spoonbills. Birds this pink just don't look real.

▲ Spain – Pena Falcon, Monfrague National Park, home of the Griffon Vultures.

▼ Texas – masses of birds at Bolivar Flats, a mind-blowing location.

▲ Panama – male Resplendent Quetzal, a gob-smacking beauty.

▲ California – a Burrowing Owl takes advantage of a wildlife refuge.

▼ Cape May – World Series of Birding, the morning after the big day

Turkey – the mountains of Demirkazik are home to very special birds.

▼ *Turkey – Ali Safak and Owen Roberts celebrate the snowcocks.*

▼ *Turkey – Iraq Babbler lurks in the reeds by the River Euphrates.*

▲ *Finland – Pine Grosbeak. Usually a tough bird to see, but not here!*

▼ *Finland – a juvenile Long-eared Owl peers down at us in downtown Helsinki.*

▼ *Norway – land of the midnight sun, and of twenty-four-hour birding.*

▲ Brazil – our great friend and guide Fernanda Melo adds a touch of glamour.

▲ Brazil – this Spot-backed Puffbird sat and posed for photos.

▼ Brazil – Harpy Eagle, our most-wanted bird of the year!

▼ Brazil – Three-toed Sloth. Lunch for a Harpy Eagle?

▲ *Brazil – Hyacinth Macaws, metre-long bright blue parrots.*

▼ *Brazil – Caimans at Caiman Lodge bask in the sun.*

▲ *Argentina – Lark-like Brushrunner. Funky, bizarre, and on the list.*

▼ *Argentina – Many-coloured Rush-Tyrant, South America's answer to the Firecrest.*

No time for chat. We settled the bill, grabbed the bags and ran. John hit the gas and we tore off like a gang of bank robbers. Would we make it in time?

As we reached Manchester Airport, we leapt out of the car, with barely time to say goodbye to John, and ran all the way to Departures, trailing our clothes in the laundry bags. Much to the bemusement of the check-in staff, we opened up our empty case and threw the laundry straight in. Still gasping for breath, we checked in our luggage – the suitcase now full of freshly-pressed clean clothes – and the blue bag still containing what we'd needed in Africa. We'd had no time to repack it, and over the next few weeks we were to find all sorts of bits and pieces that were utterly useless to us now. (Malaria tablets and mosquito nets in Cyprus?) But who cared? We were at the airport, we had our bags and clean clothes, and we were heading for Cyprus.

Still 1,835 species

19–25 March, Cyprus (Ruth)

'Tremendous!' Owen Roberts' deep, fruity voice broke through the hubbub of meetings and greetings at Pafos airport in southwest Cyprus. 'Look at that, will you?' he boomed to his wife Glynis beside him.

An old friend of Alan's, Owen lost no time in making rude comments about the increasing girth of the 'Biggest Twitchers'. This weight gain had started as a result of the Ethiopian diet, where we found ourselves eating pasta for the twenty-five consecutive days of the trip. The problem was to continue throughout *The Biggest Twitch*, with our combination of poor eating habits, irregular mealtimes and little exercise meaning that we finished the year two clothes sizes bigger than we started.

Continuing our natter about flights and luggage delays, we made our way out to the car park. Girls in the front, boys in the back, Glynis drove us the short distance to their new villa in the village of Tala, overlooking the Pafos headland. We hadn't seen them since they had taken the bold step of selling up in the UK and moving out to Cyprus, so we were excited to hear all about their new life. First we reached the centre of the village, where church, shop, well and taverna were clustered around a tiny square, and Glynis squeezed the jeep down a narrow lane on the far side. She pulled over beside a small olive grove and we all jumped out, staring up at the trees and the velvet starry sky draped over them. We held our breath and listened intently. Soon we heard the unmistakable metronome 'beep, beep, beep' of a European Scops-Owl, our first new bird for Cyprus.

Owen and Alan had become friends through birding in north Wales many years before. Owen is a larger-than-life *bon viveur* who likes nothing better than holding forth with a tall tale. He and his lovely, long-suffering wife Glynis had moved home a number of times in quick succession in pursuit of the perfect birding location, first to north Wales, then Pembrokeshire and finally the Lake District. Throughout this time, Owen and Alan had kept in contact and remained firm friends, while poor Glynis sought to restrain their worst excesses whenever they got together. Their move to Cyprus had happened only a few weeks before we arrived, so we were very grateful they could put us up at such short notice and we were excited to see their new home. And what a home it was! Outside, the swimming pool looked inviting, if cold. Inside, elegant marble steps spiralled up from the beautiful open-plan living area to the bedrooms upstairs.

At dawn the next morning, we could appreciate the expansive view down over farmland to the famous Pafos lighthouse. Small fields of sunshine-yellow wild flowers made a patchwork in between the grey-green dimples of olive groves. In the distance, an ancient tractor trundled across a dry field, a cloud of dust billowing behind. While building is continuing at an alarming rate across Cyprus, for now the view down to the sea was rural and idyllic. We could well understand how Owen and Glynis had managed to tear themselves away from the wet UK.

With no time to lose, we had an early breakfast and drove down to the Pafos headland. Taking a track right to the shoreline just feet from the gently rippling sea, we parked the car and walked, scanning the tidal rocks as we went. We were searching for one particular bird, but our hopes were not high. Until only a few days before a small flock of Greater Sandplovers had been over-wintering at this spot, but with each day that passed more had departed, heading north to their breeding grounds. Would any be left? We all searched hard. Surely, with four pairs of eyes between us, one of us would spot something?

We passed a birder heading in the opposite direction, unmistakeably British in his shorts, white legs, socks and sandals. (How come we Brits always look so uncool in a hot climate?) Had he seen anything? No, not a single wader. On we went. Suddenly Glynis cried out as she caught sight of movement amongst the rocks much further along the shore. There was a moment of panic as we set up the scope and lined up one behind the other to get a quick first look. A single Greater Sandplover pottered amongst the rocks right at the edge of the waves. Panic now over, we carefully moved a little closer for a better look and, while the dapper, sandy-coloured wader fed, preened and then went to sleep on one leg, we digiscoped it at length.

We spent the rest of the morning birding the area of ruins around the Pafos lighthouse in the part of town known as Kato Pafos. This area of crumbling Roman arches and exposed mosaics made an unusual backdrop to our birding and drew a curious mix of visitors: historians on the one hand and birders on the other, frequently British, scouring the columns and archways as much for Spanish Sparrows or Cretzschmar's Buntings as for any historical interest. Crested Larks sang from the dusty paths and tumbledown walls, while Corn Buntings uttered their grating calls from the aromatic bushes on every side, but we had to work a little harder to find any Sardinian and Rüppell's Warblers. Somehow, the picturesque backdrop of fading ruins made these birds all the more special as we added them to our year list. We were now up to 1,852 species.

The next day was bird race day. Back home in north Wales we regularly join in January and May bird races but this was the first time Alan and I had tried it in Cyprus. It seemed a great way to get a quick boost to our list. Before dawn, the four of us headed out to the nearby village of Kallepia to pick up Colin Richardson. Colin had moved to Cyprus in 2007 with his wife Sylvie and was now the official bird recorder for the island. The combination of his and Owen's local knowledge seemed to bode well for a good score. With just one vehicle and one team we had only the clock to beat and the total set the previous year by Owen, Glynis and Colin.

Colin is a slight, softly spoken Scotsman who initially seemed very reserved. As the day wore on, however, we came to realise that he had a sharp wit and a keen eye. Several times he'd catch us out with a dry comment at our expense, ruffling our feathers until we caught the glint in his eye and realised he was pulling our leg. He had put together a plan that maximised the birding opportunities along the southern coast of Greek Cyprus and there was no time to lose.

The weather wasn't in a kind mood as we headed out into the darkness. Even the scops owl that lives beside Colin's house wasn't performing: not a good omen. In the beam of the headlights we could make out the wind whipping the trees about and the mood in the car was subdued as we set off for the renowned reedbeds at Fassouri, near the RAF base at Akrotiri. This relatively compact area of reeds is surrounded on one side by stands of eucalyptus and on the other by exposed sandy stretches. In winter and early spring much of the surrounding area is a water meadow, but as spring advances and the island dries out, it provides an oasis for birds amid the increasingly arid surrounding country. Luckily, though nippy this morning, it was sheltered. We soon started adding birds to our day list: Cetti's, Reed, Sedge and Moustached Warblers; Marsh and Green Sandpipers; Garganey and Teal; Water Rail, Black Francolin, Hoopoe and Marsh Harrier. It was a cracking start to the bird race.

We bumped into a local Cypriot birdwatcher who worked here at Fassouri. He was curious to know why we were all looking for birds in different directions, and we explained the concept of a bird race. He looked quizzical, this idea not being widely known amongst the locals. We talked about the birds he generally saw at this small site and he casually mentioned 26 Demoiselle Cranes he'd seen flying overhead just the day before. Our collective jaws dropped. These gorgeous birds are rare enough migrants in autumn but to encounter them in spring is truly exceptional. Was he absolutely sure? Could they have been the more regular Common Cranes instead? To clinch the matter he invited us into his small thatched shelter beside the water. In the dark shadow inside, he fired up his laptop – advanced portable electronics in a shabby reed hut, how bizarre! – and showed us his photographs. The most fabulous images flashed to life: crystal-clear, dramatic detail, close-ups, action shots – and all, undeniably, Demoiselle Cranes. We were stunned. But there was no time to linger and we had to tear ourselves away from his magnificent slide show.

We dashed off to nearby Zakaki to check out the roadside pool. Lorries on their way to the nearby port thundered by just feet behind us as we lined up along the roadside to scan though the narrow window between the reeds. Behind this curtain lay a tranquil freshwater pool, populated with Greater Flamingos and Black-winged Stilts, quite oblivious to the rumble of the trucks. Somehow we picked out the high-pitched whistle of a Penduline Tit over this din and whirled round just in time to catch sight before it disappeared into the reeds: bird number 50 for the day.

Of course, no bird race is complete without a visit to a sewage works, so off we chased to check out Ayia Napa's. Tucked behind the town, set into a scrub-covered hillside, were several fragrant settling pools, each surrounded with a fringe of low bushes. By now the weather had cleared up beautifully. A blue sky overhead and the sun blazing down meant we had shed our heavy layers and were down to T-shirts and shorts. The glare made us screw up our eyes and shield our faces as we scanned the coarse aromatic bushes covering the slope; a Masked Shrike obligingly perched right out on top and added himself to our list.

A sturdy metal fence surrounded the pools, but by standing right up against it we could focus our bins through the holes and enjoy a feast of birds, including Eastern Orphean Warbler, Cretzschmar's Bunting, Blue Rock Thrush and Rüppell's Warbler. Our day list was shooting up now, but still Colin was worried. He checked his watch and chivvied us on.

Next stop was Cape Greko, the most easterly point we could reach in Greek Cyprus without crossing the border into Turkish Cyprus. We had to content ourselves with the Greek Cypriot equivalent of Land's End, an area of small rocky coves and gentle, scrubby slopes that were very nice but had none of the drama of the original. What it lacked in cliffs, however, it made up for in birds. We were inundated with wheatears: Cyprus Pied, Isabelline, Black-eared and Northern jockeyed for position on the top of every upstanding rock and bush. A fresh arrival of migrants must have happened overnight: Short-toed Larks and Chukar ran over the ground, Alpine Swifts whizzed overhead and Owen picked up an early Woodchat Shrike.

Alan, never one to miss a gull opportunity, had set up the scope to scan the sea. He soon found three adult Mediterranean Gulls and we all lined up and took our turn to admire these chunky, drooping-billed birds. Then, at Kermia Beach, he found no fewer than seven Audouin's Gulls in a row along the sand. But again, there was no time to stop and stare: we had a race to run.

Next we dropped in at Oraklini Pools, which, despite the noisy building works going on all around, lived up to its reputation. Not content with scoping from the bank, however, Alan and Owen wanted to get closer to the action. They shinned over a fence, tottered along a levee and plunged across an area of marshland with total disregard for mud and wet feet – or the risk of losing their boots. Suddenly Owen shouted as he caught a glimpse of a crake on the far bank. Alan spun on his heels in time to catch a tail-end view as it disappeared. But now we had a tricky situation: not only did three of us have to see this bird for it to count on the bird race list but, unless I got onto it, we couldn't count it for *The Biggest Twitch* either. There was nothing for it: I'd have to follow them. With shorter legs I couldn't take their route, but I needed to catch them up quickly and so found a short cut.

Trying to get onto a bird always gives me an adrenalin rush, and my heart pounded as I leaped from tussock to tussock. Of course, the inevitable happened: I teetered on a grassy clump, lost my balance and fell straight into the mud. Still, that wasn't going to stop me. Sloshing along now, I squelched over to Alan and Owen and we all scanned hard. There! Movement! A few metres to our left, a bird popped out again from the reeds: a smart male Little Crake: bird number 85 for the day and another addition to our year list. Funny how a little mud doesn't seem to matter when a good bird's at stake – though Owen did make me clean up before allowing me back into his car.

Time was now ticking away rapidly so Colin spurred us on again, with our next stop a quick drop-in at Larnaka sewage works. This was luxury sewage birding: not only did we have two large lakes to view but a comfy hide from which to view them. Colin, Glynis and Owen picked their way through the Herring-type gulls. These, however, were not recognised on the Clements list and therefore of no interest for *The Biggest Twitch*, so Alan and I amused ourselves finding Slender-billed Gulls and a Black-necked Grebe, both of which we could count.

By now we were well behind Colin's strict schedule, so we roared back westwards on the motorway as fast as the police speed traps would allow. A quick stop at the Aspro Pools produced a couple more species, and then a mad dash around the hills above Pafos, just as the light was fading, produced Serin, Red-throated Pipit and Red-rumped Swallow. With only minutes of daylight left we tore back towards the coast. Close to the airport at a nailed-on site for Eurasian Thick-knee (Stone-curlew) we found a telltale dark lump in a field. Then, and in the last few seconds of daylight, we made out the dark shape of a Short-eared Owl flying low over Mandria Beach: bird number 106 for the day. Was this a new bird race record?

We drove Colin home slumped in a state of exhausted satisfaction. As we pulled up outside his house, his regular neighbourhood European Scops-Owl was calling. The race was still on and energy re-surged. We leapt out of the car, and by the light of the streetlamp could make out not just one but *two* scops-owls on the roadside wire. Bird number 107 for the day. But something was odd about the position of these two birds. Don't birds normally sit side-by-side rather than one on top of the other? Realising what they were up to, and that they might appreciate a little privacy, we discreetly withdrew and went inside for a celebratory cold beer. Colin dug out his notes from the previous year. Good news! They'd scored only 103 species in 2007. We'd beaten their record by four.

As the next round of beers slipped down, Colin's wife Sylvie came home and we took our celebrations to the village taverna. Sylvie immediately took charge of ordering food and it wasn't long before our table was loaded with plate after plate of delicious local fare: hummus and tzatziki, fresh salad, piping hot pitta bread and succulent minted lamb, all washed down with a very robust local red wine. Sylvie also took charge of the seating arrangements, splitting us up around the table and banning the topic of birds. Not a birder herself, she tried to encourage us to talk about children, village life, politics – in fact anything other than birding. But when five of the six of us had shared such a day, it was inevitable that birds dominated the conversation. Sorry Sylvie!

Our breathless bird race had upped our year list to 1,860 species. But there were still a few gaps that Cyprus could fill, so the rest of our time on the island was spent targeting these. Raptors were high among our priorities so we headed inland to check out some likely sites.

Owen took us first to the Episkopi valley. We twisted and turned up narrowing lanes until we reached a tiny picturesque village straight out of a Cyprus Tourist Board brochure. This place was designed for nothing larger or faster than a donkey with panniers, and certainly not a growling 4x4. As old men sat sunning themselves on benches in front of cottages festooned with red geraniums, or put the world to rights over a leisurely game of chess, old women dressed in black from head to toe shuffled home from church down the middle of the road. They had done this since time immemorial and certainly weren't going to change their ways just to make way for a noisy Jeep.

As the road jinked and jived between the buildings, the main route through the village became less and less obvious. Glynis tried to remember: was it the second or third lane on the left that took us back out into the open countryside? Owen is not known for his patience at the best of times and in growing frustration at the time we were wasting he dived up the nearest road. Inevitably it was the wrong one. The vertiginous lane narrowed to a stony goat track and we had to turn round. With precious little room for manoeuvre, Owen tried to reverse back and up into someone's driveway. On either side was an immaculate raised flowerbed, surrounded by a sturdy drystone wall that followed the tight curve of the driveway. Someone obviously took a pride in their garden. The engine revved loudly as we reversed slowly uphill, then Owen turned the wheel at full lock and let the vehicle roll forward. There was a sickening grating noise from underneath and we lurched to an abrupt stop. We tried to reverse: more of that horrible grating noise but no movement. We tried to go forwards: more noise. Alan opened the passenger door and looked down. Somehow we'd got ourselves perched right on top of the flowerbed and that grating noise was the car dismantling those sturdy stone retaining walls!

'What idiot would build a wall in such an obvious turning place?' exploded Owen, already wound up at having taken the wrong turning and further incensed by our giggling.

'Owen!' chided Glynis, in that special way that only she can, which turns her husband instantly into a misbehaving schoolboy caught red-handed by the headmaster. Alan and I chewed the insides of our cheeks to stop ourselves bursting with laughter and making things even worse.

But how could we dislodge the car? Going backwards wasn't an option, so we all bounced up and down in time as Owen edged slowly forward until, with another lurch, we were off the flowerbed and back on the road. Phew! Thank goodness for an off-road vehicle! Looking out of the back window, the damage didn't seem too bad: just a few flattened plants and a pile of rocks in the road, though the owners may have wondered about the tyre tracks right across their prized flowerbed.

We rejoined the main road and headed for the high interior. The road wound up into the Troodos Mountains, and the habitat changed from arid scrub to deciduous woodlands and then coniferous forests as we gained altitude – though the temperature remained a balmy 28°C. Unlikely as it seemed in these temperatures, this was Cyprus' ski resort, home of the Cyprus Ski Federation. In fact, with the right weather conditions, you can spend the morning skiing the pistes before dropping down to sunbathe on the beach in the afternoon. No time for either for us, though, as we had birds to find. There was no sign of our target on arrival, but a walk along a forest trail out of Troodos village added Common Crossbill and the hoped-for Short-toed Treecreeper to our year list.

Driving back downhill, we paused at Platres, a colonial 'hill station' famous for its cherry orchards and singing Nightingales. It ought to be famous for its cakes too, as the apple pie we grabbed here was definitely the best of the year. We rethought our tactics over a cuppa. Owen had another raptor site up his sleeve, so we called in there on our way back down to lower levels. Pulling off into a layby, we scanned the bare hillside off to our left. This was a reliable site for Bonelli's Eagle but access was restricted so we had to content ourselves with scanning by scope from the roadside. No eagle materialised at first – but then we spotted a distant speck in the sky heading towards us. As it came closer it metamorphosed into a raptor. Our hopes were raised that this might be our Bonelli's – it certainly had an eagle-like jizz – but as it cruised closer, we could see quite clearly what it was: a Long-legged Buzzard.

This impressive bird was new for our list so we couldn't be too disappointed, but it wasn't our hoped-for Bonelli's Eagle. We'd tried all the likely sites – and several unlikely ones – with no luck at all. Each country on *The Biggest Twitch* seemed to have its own bogey bird that, try as we might, we couldn't track down. It looked as though Cyprus' would be the Bonelli's. We were disappointed but not totally dismayed, as we still had the chance of finding one in Spain. We kept our fingers crossed.

We continued down the road to the nearby saltpan. This flat, inhospitable area of saline water and sand normally attracts few birds beyond the annual influx of Greater Flamingos. But as we scanned the open expanse, we could pick out the wavering outline of a flock of large grey birds in the centre. At that distance and with the distorting effect of the heat haze, we could not make out any details, but there were definitely twenty-six tall grey birds out there. What's more, they appeared to be dancing: a choreographed pattern of lifting up their wings and legs and jumping into the air. What else could these birds be but cranes? Could they even be the Demoiselle Cranes seen recently at Fassouri? After all, the number of birds was right – as was the size, colour and behaviour. Pretty convinced of our ID, all that remained was a decent view to confirm it.

With hindsight, this would have been a good moment to jump back in the car and continue, having talked ourselves into logging twenty-six definite Demoiselle Cranes out on the saltpan. But our desire for a better look had us picking up our scope and heading out into the shimmering heat. Disregarding the midday sun scorching our heads, we started to make our way out onto the saltpan, telling ourselves that it wasn't far. We tramped out across the crust of grey, dusty soil, picking our way through the sparse straggly bushes that managed to maintain a toehold. Periodically we stopped to set up the scope and examine the birds, but no matter how far we walked, they remained as distant and wavering as ever. I wiped the sweat from my face and tried to ignore the trickle running down between my shoulder blades. Why hadn't we brought some water? We walked and we walked. Not a breath of wind; no sound at all except the scrunch of our feet as we trudged ever onward across the barren landscape.

As we got further towards the centre, even the toughest shoots had given up the struggle for life and by now we were leaving a clear trail of footprints. At last we had to stop: ahead of us the going was becoming treacherously soft. This was as close as we could get. Decision time: were they Common or Demoiselle? Alan set up the scope and took a long look. Still too far for us to decide with just binoculars, we awaited the verdict.

'Er, take a look will you, Owen,' said Alan, non-committally. Owen stooped and peered through the scope.

'Oh,' he said, in a rather deflated tone. By now Glynis and I were bouncing, wanting to know what the problem was. What could they be? '

'Grey Herons!' came the stupefied response. 'We've walked all the way out here just to look at Grey Herons!'

It was all too true. No matter how hard we tried, we couldn't string twenty-six Grey Herons into cranes, either Common or Demoiselle. Tall grey birds, twenty-six of them in a group together, 'dancing' on the drying clay. What kind of cruel coincidence was that? It was certainly unusual to see such a large group of Grey Herons gathered in this unlikely setting and behaving so strangely. Certainly something to ponder – and we had plenty of time for pondering as we trudged back to the car, which now looked a very long way away indeed.

Luckily our Cyprus birding didn't end on this downbeat note. We packed in one last visit to the Pafos headland, where we added a Citrine Wagtail to our list before Owen and Glynis drove us to the airport. We said our farewells on a year total of 1,870 species.

1,870 species

26 March–12 April, Spain (Alan)

After overnighting at a Travelodge near Gatwick Airport, London, we were soon back on a plane taking the relatively short flight down to Madrid, Spain. We were really looking forward to this leg as we both love Spain; Ruth had worked briefly in Madrid for Save the Children and I had birded there many times.

We had decided to do Spain by ourselves, knowing the country so well, and so were enjoying the prospect of birding on our own, without guides. After the whirlwind start to *The Biggest Twitch* we hoped this would also give us a little recovery time, as the number of potential new species was relatively low compared to the other countries we had visited so far. We also know the species and most of the sites very well, so we reckoned it would be easy to rack up the birds.

Our strategy right from the start had been to visit countries that a lot of birders would like to read about, not just where the most birds were to be found. This might sound a little odd for two people who were aiming to break the world year list record. But we had decided that if our book was to have a wide appeal we should bird in areas that many birdwatchers had visited – or had at least thought of visiting. Europe has plenty of birdwatchers, and potential book buyers, so we had planned to spend a good bit of time there. It was a gamble, of course, and by March we had no idea what our total would be by the end of the year. It has to be said that now we were actually on the road doing *The Biggest Twitch*, these were the concerns that preoccupied us. Should we have just gone all out for the highest numbers possible and forget about book sales? We tried not to lose too much sleep over it.

Our plane touched down at Madrid Airport in the warmth of a Spanish spring beneath a cobalt blue sky. We collected our bags and followed the Hertz man to our hire car. Immediately we could see it was damaged: a large dent right in the centre of the bonnet looked as though someone had landed on it in a recent crash. Closer inspection revealed scraped wings, damaged tyres, dented wheels and so on. No way were we taking it out on the Spanish roads in this state. The man on site could not help and suggested we return to the airport.

'We have no more cars,' said the man back at the Hertz desk. 'You'll have to take that one.' But faced with our point-blank refusal he eventually found us another. This one was rather different: an immaculate brand-new BMW 118d. Immediately, though, we saw a problem: no ground clearance. We knew we would be birding along dirt tracks and this car would struggle to make it. But our worries were met with blank looks and we were told it was the BMW or nothing. Reluctant to lose any more time, we resigned ourselves to making the most of our shiny sports car.

Good job we travelled light: the luggage only just fitted in the tiny boot. But then we had to start the thing. No key. How did it work? Eventually we realised that the key-fob slipped into a slot in the dashboard and then we had to push the button labelled 'Start'. As we moved forward we nearly shot across into the parked cars opposite; the clutch was vicious. This was very different to anything

I'd driven before, an animal of a sports car that was straining at the leash. I dipped the clutch and the engine promptly cut out. Great! This was turning into a nightmare. What was wrong? I let the clutch up and the engine kicked in again. Weird! I'd never driven a car like this before.

Nonetheless, we hit the road and headed southwest towards our first destination, Trujillo, in the province of Extremadura. We arrived in good time and headed to our accommodation just south of town, a small family-run place called Casa Rural El Recuerdo in the village of San Clemente. It was lovely, an old farm converted into a beautiful guesthouse, complete with vaulted ceilings and a roaring log fire. Martin and Claudia Kelsey, who run it, welcomed us warmly. It was soon obvious that Martin was a good birder with a wealth of local knowledge.

After a refreshing drink we headed out to find some birds in what little light remained. Even before we were out of the tiny village, we added the spectacular Azure-winged Magpie to our year list. We then headed into Trujillo and made straight for the bull ring – perhaps not the most obvious place to begin our birding but we knew that this was a favourite nest site for Lesser Kestrels, and we only had to wait a minute or so before one flew in and landed on the broken, red-tiled roof. A lovely male with powder-grey head and chestnut mantle, he sat and peered down at us, unafraid, and we soaked up the views.

Raucous calls soon drew our attention to another new bird. A party of Spotless Starlings had landed on nearby television aerials and were calling as more birds flew in to join them. Glossy purple-black in the last of the evening sun, these spiky-crested birds flew onto the roof and climbed inside for the night. We also called it a day and headed back, pausing only to admire a gorgeous Red Kite soaring low over the road, its fox-red tail glowing wonderfully in the dying sunset. This is surely one of the best raptors anywhere and made a fitting end to our long day. We felt we were in for a great time in Spain.

The next morning, 27 March, we drove west from Trujillo in the dark and took a narrow road north. On reaching a dirt track to our right, we parked and waited for the first signs of dawn. It was surprisingly cold and we left the heater running for a while. As the first glimmers of light crept across the eastern horizon, we killed the engine and immediately heard birdsong. Skylarks were belting out sweet music across the vast rolling grass plain. The sound made the hairs stand up on the back of our necks with anticipation of the birding to come. This was a big, wild place, with fields undulating in all directions like a rucked-up carpet. It was full of birds and we had it all to ourselves: just us, the larks, a vast sky and a glorious carpet of wild flowers.

Stepping from our cocoon of warmth, the dawn chill hit us and we wished we had put on more clothes. A bird flew from the ground, flapping fast and rising almost vertically, its black under-wing with white trailing edge revealing it as a Calandra Lark. This big cousin of the familiar Skylarks was new for our list and we watched spellbound as it rose in front of us singing at full volume. As the light improved, we began to see many more flying low over the grassland, then pitching into the flowers, where only an inquisitive head could be seen looking from side to side.

Soon other heads popped up. These weren't larks. Long thin necks and stout bills gave away Little Bustards. Five heads in a row looked back at us, and then, like a flotilla of submarines, lowered their periscopes one-by-one and vanished into the sea of flowers. This was another new bird and we wanted a better look. Our plea was soon answered, as a flock of forty Little Bustards came over the horizon and swept right past us, before dropping down to land in a shallow valley. We walked further along the rutted dirt track, using a low stone wall to shelter from the freezing wind, when two enormous birds came flying towards us. There was only one thing that big in these parts: Great Bustards. It was hard to see how these monsters could get their enormous bulk airborne – and, judging by the effort in those wing beats, they didn't find it easy. What a start to our day: both species of bustard and Calandra Lark on our list and it was only just getting light.

We continued down the track and at the end peeped over the wall to see a flock of 33 Great Bustards strutting around a huge open field. Amazing! We quietly set up the scope and feasted our eyes on these magnificent birds. The males are enormous, like turkeys with long legs and long, thick necks. Their handsome combination of chestnut-brown, white, grey and orange plumage is set off nicely by a bizarre back-combed white moustache and neatly fanned tail. And, even better, at this time of year the males are displaying. You would think that with such finery they would hardly need to do more. But one of the males soon began to puff his feathers out and, right before our eyes, was instantly transformed into a massive white powder-puff – his plumage turned inside-out to show off the snow-white underside. It was a spectacular show, and if we hadn't seen it with our own eyes we would hardly have believed it. We just hoped the female bustards were as impressed as we were, so that these remarkable birds can continue to breed and thrive here.

We crept away, leaving the Great Bustards undisturbed to continue the show. Suddenly first one, then two more, Black-bellied Sandgrouse hurtled across the sky like jet-propelled chickens that were late for a very important date. We made our way back to the car, serenaded all the way by larks, while more Little Bustards peeked from the flowers and Corn Buntings jangled their songs from every wire.

Then we heard a call. At first it was distant and hard to make out, then clearer: '*Gawk, gawk*'. Sandgrouse again, but this time Pin-tailed, a bird we needed. We scanned the sky. The calls were closer now, but where the birds? Suddenly we saw them right above us. Perhaps forty of these scarce nomads swept across the sky at high speed. We willed them to turn and so they did, circling twice and calling loudly as they caught the early morning sun. Sadly, they didn't land in view, but we were left breathless and elated. Sandgrouse are among my favourite birds and we had seen two species in less than an hour.

Some birds were eluding us, including Cirl Bunting, Rock Sparrow and Little Owl, all of which we had found easily in this area on previous visits. But these were soon forgotten as we picked up a large raptor flying directly towards us. This looked interesting, and as it turned and soared, giving us good views of both its upper- and under-sides, we realised we were looking at a Spanish Imperial Eagle – a beautifully marked adult. We were thrilled to see this rare endemic on only our second day in Spain and punched the air in celebration as it slowly drifted out of sight behind a ridge.

Next we headed north into Monfrague National Park. This beautiful area is a mix of habitats: rolling steppe, cork oak woodlands, river valleys and towering rock faces above man-made reservoirs. Not surprisingly, it is a paradise for birds. This was Ruth's first visit and she was amazed at the sight of hundreds of huge Griffon Vultures soaring low over the road near their breeding cliffs. Silently, these almost prehistoric-looking creatures spiralled above us in the rapidly warming air. Red-billed Choughs swooped overhead calling wildly, '*cheaow, cheaow*', just like back home along the cliffs of north Wales. Scanning the huge pale cliff face opposite our roadside viewpoint, we quickly added Black Stork, Egyptian Vulture and Short-toed Eagle to our growing day list.

The triangular rock face that is home to all these birds rises impressively out of a reservoir and towers over the roadside car park opposite. The views of the raptors are wonderful; particularly the Griffon Vultures, which like to come right overhead and eyeball birders. A scan of the cliff reveals lots of ledges, ideal for nesting Griffons, and the odd cave in which you might spot the large, untidy nest of a Black Stork. It is only when you see one of these huge birds standing on the rock that you appreciate just how big the Pena Falcon cliff really is. Time seems to disappear as you gaze at the bird spectacle played out before you. With huge birds coming and going there is always something to see. On this occasion a dark shape drifted in front of the cliff – smaller than a Griffon, but still a good size – and we soon had our second Spanish Imperial Eagle. What a regal bird it was! In the full mid-morning sun, we soaked up every detail through the scope.

But the park had more to offer than just raptors. We walked the road from the viewpoint in both directions, searching for Rock Bunting, Cirl Bunting and Rock Sparrow, all year ticks that were possible here. We quickly found a singing Subalpine Warbler that showed off nicely and a Blue Rock Thrush that dropped down to land near the road, while Black Redstarts were everywhere. None of our target birds were showing at first, but we had time in hand so we stuck at it. On our third walk under the rocky hillside north of the viewpoint our persistence finally paid off, when a handsome male Rock Bunting landed on top of a huge boulder and started singing. As we walked back to the car two more appeared in quick succession. Typical: you spend ages looking for the first one then, like buses, three turn up at once!

With the day almost done, we headed back down the main road to Trujillo in time to add the Lesser Kestrels to our impressive day list. As we returned to our base, we saw a round bird sitting on a roadside wire. The BMW was purring along at a good lick and so we overshot by some distance. But we found it still there after we'd turned back and pulled over: a lovely Little Owl. This was new for *The Biggest Twitch* and a great bird to round off an excellent day.

Next day we headed for the Sierra de Guadalupe in the hope of some lingering winter visitors. After a little trouble finding the start of the road up the mountain, we soon began climbing up via a series of hair-pin bends. The views were impressive, the weather calm and sunny, and we were having fun in our BMW, which relished a road like this, hugging the bends and roaring up the straight stretches. The Spanish military had built an aerial station at the top of the hill, hence the well-maintained road right to the summit, giving great access to this high-elevation birding site. We parked and got our breath back after the fun of the drive then set off to explore the summit area. Now, where were the birds?

Our main target here was Alpine Accentor, with an outside chance of Wallcreeper. Both are winter visitors in small numbers and we were not sure if they would still be here in late March. We quickly discovered Rock Buntings showing well on the towering cliffs around us. Black Redstarts sang from pinnacles and Dartford Warblers were common in the low scrub. Flocks of Red-billed Chough flew over, calling excitedly, while a pair of Peregrines put on an amazing display of stunt flying, stooping and screaming across the skies. Next came five Egyptian Vultures cruising overhead, twisting and turning against the blue sky in surprisingly agile flight.

All great birding, but it wasn't boosting our list so we headed back. Another birder arrived just as we reached our car and, of course, the usual 'Anything about?' conversation ensued. He introduced himself as John Muddeman, the author of a birding site guide for Extremadura. How useful! We explained our quest and lack of success today, and John reassured us that we had done all the right things but that this was a massive area, and accentors and Wallcreepers were few and far between. We chatted, and soon found ourselves spreading the map across the bonnet so he could mark possible sites for other birds we still needed – Bonelli's Eagle being a particular priority. Then we thanked John, swapped mobile numbers and left him in peace.

Not far below the summit we were just tucking into our sandwiches in the warm sunshine when the mobile rang. It was John. He had just found an Alpine Accentor close to where we had been parked. Lunch was forgotten as we dived into the BMW and shot back up the mountain. If we thought our first ascent had been fast, the second time around was even scarier. Screeching to a halt next to John's car, we sprinted over to find him proffering a view through his scope.

What a surprise we got. Not only was there an Alpine Accentor but, just a few feet above it, a Wallcreeper. Amazing: both our target birds in one scope view! We thanked John for saving our morning. As we watched, we realised that there was a small flock of accentors and the Wallcreeper was keeping company with them. The accentors were like small grey mice, scurrying up and down the rock face. The Wallcreeper was also grey, until it opened its wings to reveal a flash of magenta – like the silk lining of a vampire's cape. Its long, decurved bill probed for insects in the crevices. Clearly there was a whole world of food up here, hidden from our eyes.

The next day we took our leave of Martin and Claudia, plus their lively son Patrick and ball-chasing dog Moro, and headed east of Trujillo towards the Belan plain. Our route took us through the narrow, twisting streets of Belan village, where we were as worried about getting wedged as getting lost. Finally emerging on the other side of town, the countryside suddenly opened up into a vast, rolling grassland and we followed a narrow potholed road out into the sea of grass. Birds were everywhere: A Great Spotted Cuckoo flew in front of us, mobbed by Magpies. Corn Buntings were singing from every fence-wire; Calandra and Crested Larks fluttered up from the roadside; and Montagu's Harriers drifted over the grass. Scanning the plain we soon saw a male Great Bustard in full display, a huge white ball slowly walking amongst a group of apparently unimpressed females. Little Bustards flew low and fast, showing off their surprisingly white wings. We also heard their weird calls – which can only accurately be likened to a wet fart. The sound followed us all morning.

We hit the almost empty motorway and made good time, the BMW really coming into its own on these long drives. John Muddeman and Martin Kelsey had both mentioned a possible site for Bonelli's Eagle not far off our route, so we detoured to a picturesque castle perched on a crag overlooking a large reservoir. We found a good vantage point and scanned, but the cool and windy conditions were not promising for raptors. Alpine Swifts swept across the skies and a flock of 150 Lesser Black-backed Gulls drifting slowly north, perhaps headed for British breeding grounds. After two hours with no sign of an eagle, we cut our losses and continued south for Doñana.

We reached El Rocio in the late afternoon and parked by the elegant, white Catholic Church that dominates this beautiful little town. The whole place has a laidback, cowboy feel, with sandy streets and wooden hitching rails for horses outside each building. I love it – and especially because it is in the heart of the famous Coto Doñana National Park, one of Europe's last wildernesses. As a small boy, I had read books about this magical place and always dreamed of visiting it, but never once had I believed these dreams might one day come true. Now here I was, about to embark on my second visit. All the excitement came flooding back.

El Rocio's great lure is its famous lagoon, which laps against the edge of town and is always teeming with birds. You can stand on the promenade just metres from the church and watch flamingos, waders, wildfowl, terns and raptors wheeling over the water. We only had time for a quick scan but immediately scored an addition for *The Biggest Twitch*: Eurasian Spoonbill. Other wonderful birds included Greater Flamingo, Collared Pratincole, Glossy Ibis, Gull-billed Tern and handsome, brick-red Black-tailed Godwits. A familiar call had us looking skywards to find 26 European Bee-eater passing overhead – stunning, paint-box birds – while we also picked up a Black-shouldered Kite hovering over the fields beyond the lagoon. What a place!

With the sun sinking fast we had to drag ourselves away from the bird spectacle and go in search of our campsite. We had booked to stay at Camping Aldea on the north side of El Rocio. Technically, we were not actually camping but staying in a mobile home, which had looked very nice on the internet. What we hadn't appreciated online, however, was its scale: not so much a mobile home as a converted garden shed. I could only just stand up; my hair – and I don't have much – was touching the ceiling. The bed completely filled the bedroom, and it wasn't a big bed. The loo was the same: squashed into a tiny cubicle, it was just possible to sit on it with legs jammed against the door. There was a table in the living room, so that was full, too. The only place to leave our luggage was in the car. It was just like staying in a doll's house. Still, on the plus side, it was cheap, close to the lagoon and we only planned to use it for sleeping,

The next day, we drove south down to the coast at Matalascaña Beach for a dawn sea-watch. Finding a good vantage point near the lighthouse north of the town, we settled down to see what might pass. At first there was little but Lesser Black-backed Gulls slowly heading up the coast, and we began to wonder whether this was the best use of our time. But we kept scanning and – as is so often the case with sea-watching – our patience was rewarded. Seven Audouin's Gulls came and settled on the sea amongst loafing gangs of Lesser Black-backeds. Then a Gannet

110

powered past, a new bird for the year, followed by four Slender-billed Gulls, so close we could clearly see their pale eyes and dark red bills . After more Gannets came a Great Skua, intent on reaching its breeding ground far to the north. Soon eight more Great Skuas followed, all beating out a deep rhythm with their wings, clearly focused on their destination. Three Balearic Shearwaters passed, sweeping gracefully across the sea and making the skuas looked very ungainly in comparison. They provided our third year tick of the morning.

Back at the lagoon later that afternoon we settled at the western end with the sun at our backs. The soft evening light produced perfect conditions to set up the scope and just soak up the atmosphere and the wonderful birds. A flock of over 1,000 waders rose from the islands and swirled over the water, more Collared Pratincoles than we had ever seen in one place before. The birds were very uneasy, however, and would not settle. Other birds were also calling in alarm and soon we saw why: an eagle was drifting slowly over the lagoon, catching the sun beautifully, and being mobbed by a Common Buzzard. At first we were thrown by the striking patterns. Having recently been in Ethiopia our thoughts turned to Steppe Eagle, but this was Spain. We noted as much detail as possible before it moved away out of site.

Back at the campsite, we had some research to do. What was that eagle? With help from the internet and the excellent *Collins Bird Guide* (the only book you need for identifying Europe's birds), we identified our mystery bird as a juvenile Spanish Imperial Eagle, very different from the adults we had seen further north and the juvenile eastern birds we had seen previously. Later we heard from Martin Kelsey at El Recuerdo that this bird had been seen for some weeks around the lagoon, often in the late afternoon. Next we totalled up our list: *The Biggest Twitch* had already reached 1,900. Things were going well.

We left our little shed in pre-dawn darkness and headed for Villamanrique, a small town north of the eastern section of the national park. Here we had arranged to meet four friends from north Wales who had travelled down to Spain especially to be part of *The Biggest Twitch*. We were really looking forward to seeing them after more than three months away.

En route we stopped by a bridge over a stream in a large meadow. The dawn chorus flooded in through our open windows: Cetti's Warblers singing from the streamside vegetation, joined by scratchy Sedge Warblers, throaty Nightingales and the distinctive 'wet my lips' of Common Quail. It was magical just to sit in the still cool air of dawn, listening to nature awakening.

Our route then took us through a huge stone-pine forest and we hadn't gone far when an enormous brown bird swooped across just metres in front of the car. Eurasian Eagle-Owl! This massive predator glided across the flower-filled verge and, with a single powerful flap, melted away into the pines, leaving us stunned. What a start to the day – and it was barely light.

We arrived in Villamanrique to find the guys all there. It was handshakes all round as everyone talked at once; they wanted to hear all about *The Biggest Twitch*, while we were keen to hear news from home. There was Marc Hughes, a headmaster at Craig-y-Don school in Llandudno; Marc's seven-year-old son Aled, a keen birder who was thrilled to hear that we'd already seen a Spanish Imperial Eagle at El Rocio; Mike Duckham, assistant manager at RSPB Conwy

Nature Reserve with whom I had worked for six years; and last but not least, Rob Sandham. Rob is relatively new to birding but is mad keen and gets out every chance he has. He and his partner Emer were renting our flat back in Llandudno, so we were glad to hear there were no problems at home and that they loved living there.

It was time to hit the road and find the visitor centre in the eastern section of Coto Doñana. We found a dirt track that looked vaguely familiar from my previous trip so headed off in anticipation. Progress was slow, as the track was littered with potholes and the BMW's minimal clearance made it tough going. The lads had much better clearance in their hire car and were constantly having to wait for us to catch up. The plus side was that slow progress meant plenty of great birds. At the sound of those familiar 'gawk, gawk' calls we confidently called 'Pin-tailed Sandgrouse!' And there they were, flying fast and low over the fields. A dark raptor drifted over the track ahead and it took us a while to realise this was a melanistic Montagu's Harrier, almost black all over. Purple Herons and Great White Egrets lifted from the ditches alongside the track and Calandra Larks were numerous in the open fields. This was great birding.

As the track became progressively more potholed it was taking much longer to negotiate a safe route for the BMW. At each major pit everyone got out and tried to determine the best way forward. As you can imagine, with five people – including Aled – all offering different advice, it became something of a farce. We were soon reduced to fits of laughter, with progress painfully slow.

By now the grass fields had given way to a drier landscape, almost semi-desert. The herons were gone and we were encountering more larks: both Greater Short-toed and Lesser Short-toed Larks ran in front of the cars, and we stopped to watch the Lesser Short-toed Larks, which were new for the year. It was great to hear them singing, and to compare the two species side by side.

Just as we were thinking the track couldn't get worse, it did. Huge holes appeared and it soon became obvious that no matter how hard we tried, the BMW couldn't continue without sustaining serious damage to its low-slung underside. Reluctantly, we decided to abandon our vehicle and all piled into the other one, which offered much better ground clearance, even with all our weight. Luckily Aled is small and folds up into a tiny space.

We hoped the BMW would be safe beside the track as we slowly picked our way forward, with no idea how far we still had to go. At last we thought we could see the hazy shape of buildings ahead – and yes, there it was: the visitor centre. It was an impressive building, for the middle of nowhere, built with a high thatched roof in the local style. The glass front overlooked a reed-fringed lake that was full of birds. Almost as important, the centre had a café.

Sipping our drinks, we gazed out at the impressive display of birds just a few metres away. Hundreds of Cattle Egrets were crowded into a clump of tamarisk trees, Purple Swamphens stalked along the reed edge, Glossy Ibises probed in the shallows and Black-necked Grebes dived in the deeper water. But the one bird we particularly wanted was missing: Marbled Teal, a bird that we needed for the year and the others for their life list. Plenty of Shovelers swam about amongst the many Coots. That reminded us that the guys also needed Crested Coot. We had seen it in Africa but were still keen to see it again here in Europe.

Mike then spotted a member of the National Park staff arriving and, seeing she was an attractive young lady, wandered over to ask for advice. The news was not great on Marbled Teal: none had been seen recently, though she thought they should be in the area somewhere. She did know of a lake where Crested Coot had been seen, however, and gave us directions. And she explained that the road we had arrived on was not the entrance track; there was, apparently, a much better road, which even the BMW would have had no trouble with.

We dragged Mike away from his new friend and headed back – this time on the correct track – to relocate our car. Luckily the two tracks joined only a mile or so from where we had abandoned it, so we were soon reunited with our gleaming machine and heading for the Crested Coot lake. Luckily we found the spot fairly quickly and were pleased to see about fifty coots on the water. Surely we could find a Crested Coot amongst a flock that size? Within moments we had it. A good tip is that the Crested often holds its back feathers very loosely, giving it a fluffed-up rear end. But you still need to check the forehead for the red knobs above the bill shield.

We headed back to finish the day at the bar overlooking the lagoon at El Rocio. We set up the scopes and scanned the shallow waters for a final boost to our day list. Young Aled was keen to try and speak some Spanish so we thought it would be fun for him to play waiter. After a few rehearsals he had it off pat, and went into the bar to order our drinks. Whatever he said worked, as our drinks duly arrived and we chilled out in the warm evening sunshine. Greater Flamingos strutted across the lagoon, passing Black-winged Stilts and Glossy Ibises. A Squacco Heron landed at the near edge of the water, casting wonderful reflections across the still surface. Wood Sandpipers fed with Black-tailed Godwits and a drake Garganey swam past, with the backdrop of the beautiful church and horses grazing the grasses in the lagoon. Surely this is one of the best birding sites anywhere? Our feelings were underlined when all the Collared Pratincoles lifted in alarm and moments later Aled had his coveted Spanish Imperial Eagle. The great raptor drifted slowly across the lagoon, giving us all a great view and putting the finishing touch to a wonderful day's birding.

Dawn was cold and we shivered on the beach at Matalascañas. The lack of sleep and perhaps a few too many drinks the night before may not have helped. But we were here to see birds and so we set up the scopes and scanned the sea. We soon picked up some good stuff, including Audouin's Gulls, Balearic Shearwaters, Common Scoter and Whimbrel.

We spent the rest of the day birding slowly north from the coast back to El Rocio, visiting the pools and heathland at Acebuche, where we saw similar species to our first visit and added Thekla Lark. Sadly, we missed Western Bonelli's Warbler. Rob found this in some pines near the visitor centre, but we were on the other side of the building and by the time we had dashed back it was gone. What is it with birds named after Bonelli? Be it eagle or warbler they just kept giving us the slip. The Azure-winged Magpies entertained us, though, and Subalpine Warblers showed off in the scrub.

With one morning of birding with the guys left, we looked at what was missing from our list and made plans for the last push together. Everyone agreed that White-headed Duck and Marbled Teal were the top targets. Now all we needed was the site. We had heard that White-headed Ducks could be seen at Laguna de

Marida, a long drive to the east. We decided to check out of our accommodation early that morning so we wouldn't need to return later; the guys could head straight for Sevilla airport and we could head north again.

Early morning saw us meet up on the main road north of El Rocio. Luckily Marc had thought to bring his sat-nav system from home, so we typed in the lake name and were pleasantly surprised to find a route planned for us. We had done a little research ourselves and had been in email contact with John Muddeman, our Wallcreeper finder. John had kindly sent over directions to a site for Marbled Teal and I had noted them down on a piece of paper so we had them to hand rather than having to switch on the computer in the field. Great. We hit the road.

After a long drive we reached Laguna de Merida – the sat-nav had worked perfectly. A short walk took us down to a boardwalk overlooking the large lake and we quickly found our target White-headed Duck: not just one, but about 50 of these rare waterfowl – a new bird for *The Biggest Twitch*. In a field by the lake we enjoyed good views of Eurasian Thick-knee, while one last scan of the lake gave us a bonus bird: a drake Ferruginous Pochard.

We were doing well for ducks so we set off to try and find Marbled Teal. The pools we had been told about were alongside the huge Rio Guadalquivir, a slow-moving body of water that held few birds. We followed our directions but found no pools that looked suitable for Marbled Teal. On and on we drove, and eventually we did find some pools but we were miles away from where our directions had suggested. The area held plenty of birds but hard as we tried, there were no Marbled Teals to be seen. We went back to the area that John had recommended and re-read the directions. They just did not make sense. We fired up the computer and looked at John's original message. Ah, now I could see why there were no pools here, I had missed out a whole vital line of directions. Following the full directions, guess where we ended up? You've got it: right back at the pools we had found earlier. But alas, there were still no Marbled Teal – even when we knew we were in the right spot and looked much harder.

This whole diversion had used up a lot of time, so we had to forgo looking for Little Swifts further south. Marc, Aled, Mike and Rob headed for the airport and life back in north Wales. We turned the BMW north for the next leg of our adventure.

It had been great fun birding with the guys and we had really enjoyed their company. But now we had to focus on our next new bird for *The Biggest Twitch*. We still had not seen a Bonelli's Eagle and if we drove hard there was time for another shot at the site we had tried on the way down, so the BMW was again put to the test on the open road. Boy, did it relish the challenge! After the last few days of dirt tracks and narrow lanes the car fairly ate up the tarmac; in fact, the hard part was holding it back to a reasonably safe speed, so exhilarating was it to drive. We reached the site with a couple of hours of daylight left, but we didn't need them. After just 15 minutes, a Bonelli's Eagle soared over the ruined castle and then dropped down to land on a crag. Distant, but fine by us, another new bird on the list and we were out of there.

We drove hard once more, heading north, then swinging east and back to Trujillo. Early the next morning we tried to tidy up some unfinished business: we still needed Cirl Bunting for our 2008 list and we wanted to find it today. Martin

Kelsey had told us that the buntings are usually found around his house, El Recuerdo, so we tried again, despite having drawn a blank here previously. By chance we met Martin in the village and he was upbeat about our chances. We walked the narrow lane behind his house and soon had our Cirl Bunting: a handsome male sitting on a bush singing away nicely.

As we turned to head back, something caught our eye in a small clump of trees; a shape that seemed out of place. Focusing the binoculars turned the shape into a roosting European Scops-Owl. What a piece of luck to find one of these cryptically marked birds at its daytime roost. We set up the scope and studied its every detail. Then we called in on Martin and Claudia to tell them of our bunting success, and to pass on the owl news in case any of their guests fancied a look.

It was time to move on. Once more we thanked Martin and Claudia for their help and wonderful hospitality, and pointed the BMW back towards Madrid. Our next target was a very special, and rare, bird: the elusive Dupont's Lark. This quest had extra spice, as the bird would be a lifer for both of us; we don't get many of those in Europe these days.

It was a long, hot drive on mostly fast roads to the open semi-desert plain near Belchite, southeast of Zaragoza. We had been told that accommodation would be hard to find near the birding site, so we toured a few towns in the hope of finding a hotel but there was nothing. It looked like we would have to leave the area and then face a long drive back in the small hours to get there well before dawn, which we had been told is the only time the birds sing. We did not relish this prospect, so we asked around at a few bars in our best, very poor, Spanish and eventually found a man who seemed to know of a place down the road. We were pretty unsure about the direction but had not gone far when we came to a petrol station and the sign for a hotel. It didn't look very promising but we needed a place to stay and we were still close to the lark site.

The little group of buildings was called Lecera, and when we asked at the petrol station about the hotel we were greeted with huge smiles and told it had just opened. We were led over a small bridge alongside the garage and there, hidden from the road, was a row of very smart-looking rooms with a garden laid out in front. Inside, our room was lovely – and obviously very new, as everything was immaculate. We loved the place and settled in. The hotel is called Rincon del Cierzo and if you want to try for Dupont's Lark, this is the place to stay.

Next morning we left in pitch darkness and headed for the desert-like Belchite Plains in search of Dupont's Lark. The headlights lit up the dirt track, and we parked a short distance away from the road. We opened the windows and shivered as the cold air poured in. With it came bird song. Larks were in full flow. We listened intently and as our ears adjusted to the orchestra above us, we picked out the distinctive melancholy song of Dupont's Lark. Not just one, but at least four. We jumped out of the car and stood mesmerised by the beauty of the birdsong above us under a crystal clear sky studded with millions of stars. Calandra and Greater and Lesser Short-toed Larks were all filling the air with their voices, along with the Dupont's, even though there was still no sign of dawn. We stood and savoured the moment.

With our hands now numb, we retreated into the car and warmed up as we waited for a sign of dawn – and perhaps just a glimpse of the lark we had come to see. We had heard many tales of birders coming here and hearing this rare and enigmatic bird but never laying eyes on it.

As the light began to flush the eastern horizon we ventured out again and began scanning for a lark high overhead. We could hear them all right but, despite sweeping our bins again and again across the vast skyscape, we just couldn't pick one out. It looked as though we were to follow in the footsteps of all those other birders who had listened to but not seen this special bird. It was becoming light quickly, but the birds still sang – although we had been told they would stop at dawn. We walked down the track a short way, scanning hard and checking each bird that scuttled rodent-like through the parched vegetation. But the birdsong was decreasing and we were beginning to panic.

Then at last we had one: a Dupont's Lark sitting in a tiny low bush and singing from its perch. Through the scope we could clearly see its long, slightly decurved bill. We were ecstatic – and amazed at our good fortune. We even managed a few poor digiscope shots, just to prove these birds can be seen in daylight. Then our bird slipped off his perch and melted into the low scrub, leaving us stunned. Bird number 1,906 for 2008, and a lifer.

Next we headed northwest, where we spent the best part of the next four days birding in the spectacular, high-altitude setting of the Picos de Europa. It has to be said that from a year-listing point of view this did not turn out to be a good return on time. We added just six species to the total and it cost us a lot of money. That's not to say it was not enjoyable: we had a lovely apartment in the tiny village of Basieda, near Potes, where the views were wonderful when the low cloud did not block them out. But the temperature was down to a chilly 4°C. Up here it still felt like late winter.

On our first full day we began birding around the village where we knew Wrynecks ought to be, but weren't. However, we were rewarded for our long search by great views of a Western Bonelli's Warbler. Having missed this species by seconds back at Coto Doñana it was great to get it on our list now.

Next it was time to go up – and up high. We climbed the twisting mountain road to Fuente De, a beautiful valley that ends in a sheer rock wall. Then, leaving the car, we took a cable car up a further 800m in just three stomach-churning minutes to the summit. This is not for the faint-hearted. At the top we found a different world. If we thought it chilly down below, it was the bitter cold of mid-winter up here. Thick snow covered the ground and a chill wind cut straight through us. We instantly added Yellow-billed (Alpine) Chough to the list, though, as these charismatic corvids swooped and tumbled right above the cable car station.

Our main target here was White-winged Snowfinch, and so we set off across the snowfields. At first the path was good, but it soon became clear – as we got further away from the cable car station – that few people came this far. Soon we were wading through thigh-high fresh snow. Birds were non-existent but we kept going, believing that the snowfinches must be here somewhere. Chamois, agile goat-like animals whose pelts have been turned into many a car-polishing cloth, were common and made easy work of the soft snow. As if by magic, a gang of Alpine Accentors appeared right next to us. How had they sneaked up like that? This gave us hope for the finches so on we went. A pair of Golden Eagles displayed over the ridge above us and we watched in awe of these magnificent birds in total control of their harsh environment. Up ahead we could see patches of exposed scree, looking remarkably similar to areas where we had seen snowfinches in the past.

But soon then the weather intervened – as it so often does in the high mountains – and thick cloud descended, virtually blinding us. There was no hope of finding birds in these conditions and a fair chance that we could get lost and step right off the ledge into oblivion. We followed our footprints back to safety and reached the station chilled to the bone, with just the Yellow-billed Chough to add to our list.

The next day, we did a little better and scored Middle Spotted Woodpecker and Wryneck along the footpaths around the pretty village of Tudes, not far from where we were staying. Cirl Bunting was common and we cursed all the time we had spent working to find them down on the plains. Our plan was to try again for snowfinches, but as we drove back up the valley towards the cable car, the heavens opened and it poured with torrential rain. The windscreen wipers couldn't cope and we had to pull over as visibility dropped to zero. Now what? No chance of new birds now. And then we saw the answer to our dilemma: a restaurant.

We had not been eating very well over the last two days. Our attempts at self-catering had been poor, to say the least. Not surprising, perhaps, given our limited Spanish. First we had returned to the apartment with a pizza, only to find that we had no oven. Next we thought we'd keep things simple with a pot of chicken soup, but we had opened it to discover not soup but a thin chicken stock. Starving hungry, we had heated it up and eaten it anyway. So now the thought of decent food on this wet, miserable day was irresistible.

The place was called El Urogallo and looked fine from outside, so we dashed in through the downpour. As we took in our surroundings we wondered whether this was really our kind of place: the walls were festooned with pictures of hunting trophies. But when the owner appeared and explained that the restaurant name meant Capercaillie, we realised – as birders – that we just had to stay and sample the food. Now we also noticed numerous photographs of our host posing with various slaughtered animals. Despite our obvious differences, however, the guy was very friendly and we chatted about birds in the area – mainly the sort you can shoot and eat. Not surprisingly, perhaps, he told us that there were very few Capercaillies left.

When the huge menu and extensive wine list arrived we both decided, given the surroundings, to have the venison. Ruth finally chose a wine while I – mindful of driving back – sipped a coke. The food was just superb: not only the taste but also its presentation on the plate, with even the restaurant name swirled in sauce around the rim. It was a real treat to tuck into such gourmet fare as the rain lashed down outside. Completely full, we now had the rather less pleasant task of asking for the bill. Ouch! It was incredibly expensive. But after the chicken stock we felt we deserved a treat.

The weather remained grim and we were happy to move on from the Picos. We left on 11 April with our year list now standing at 1,913. On our final morning it snowed, making the decision to leave even easier. Perhaps with better weather we could have added those snowfinches. But there was no point in what-ifs. The BMW ate up those mountains bends and we were out of there. Texas awaited.

1,913 species

PART FOUR

Back across the pond

13–16 April, Texas: Part One (Ruth)

There really was only one place in the world for *The Biggest Twitch* to be in April and that was the southern coast of Texas. This was not only the perfect place to boost our year list but also a great chance to catch up with favourite haunts and old friends. So once again we flew back across the Atlantic.

Why is this area so special? Well, it lies bang in the middle of the route taken by migrating birds heading north from their wintering grounds in South and Central America to their breeding grounds in North America. These birds face a stark choice when they reach the Gulf of Mexico: do they head straight out across the water or follow the long shoreline around the edge? Those that take the latter option have the longer journey but can stop to rest and feed whenever necessary. Those, such as most of the warblers, that take the shorter route straight across the Gulf face perhaps the greater peril, as this vast expanse of water is unbroken by any islands, so there's no handy resting point if they get tired or hit a headwind. They launch themselves northwards and fly as fast as they can straight towards the first available patch of dry land.

This land is likely to be High Island. The name 'High Island' is a bit of a misnomer. After all, it is only a few feet higher than the surrounding landscape of flat, grassy fields and marshland sprinkled with 'nodding donkeys' drilling for oil. In fact, the name comes from the large salt dome hidden under the ground, which raises this small patch of land higher than anywhere else on the Gulf coast. This highland is quite well covered in vegetation too, with several tracts of dense wood-land, freshwater pools lined with reeds and rushes, and even the trees and shrubs in people's gardens adding to the variety of habitat. All this adds up to salvation for exhausted migrants, who can rest and feed in order to regain enough energy to carry on their journey northwards.

And that is why, for key weeks in April each year, the urgent northward migration of birds is matched by an equally urgent migration of birders from all over the world, who gather on High Island in their thousands to witness this amazing phenomenon. But since we'd lasted visited in the autumn of 2007, Hurricane Humberto had torn through the area, causing widespread devastation. Now, in April 2008, we were very interested to see what we would find. What had happened to the local community? Would there be any trees left in Boy Scout Woods?

At first glance, things looked much the same. The cheerful Houston Audubon Society volunteers still greeted us near the entrance. The grandstand in front of the water drip was still full of birders waiting for a first sight of the birds coming in to drink. And, most important, birds were passing through in good numbers. All seemed right with the world. But when we continued along the boardwalk to the area known as 'Cathedral' we soon saw what the hurricane had done. Gone were the tall trees that had arched over the footpaths to create a shady, green-filtered nave. Instead, the exposed paths were baking in the sun, and on either side was a tangle of smashed tree trunks, broken branches and low stunted bushes.

Honeysuckle had crept along the twisted branches, covering the tortured wreck of woodland with a mat of white and yellow hanging flowers. The cloying scent hung in the air and filled our nostrils. None of this seemed to bother the birds, though. And life was much easier for birders now that the canopy had been brought down to eye level, with no need to suffer 'warbler neck' from prolonged periods of gazing upwards.

For any British birder, the warblers on show here are mouth-watering. Forget your 'sylvias', 'acros', 'hippos' and 'phylloscs', European families that come mostly in muted tones of brown and green. These American warblers had style and were decked out in colours that hit you between the eyes. Zap! That little striped beauty with a vivid yellow face and black 'necklace' was a Magnolia Warbler. Pow! Up popped a male Yellow Warbler, bright Schweppes yellow all over, with red lines down his belly. Bam! That fiery throat and face showed that at least one Blackburnian had arrived. There was nothing subtle about these warblers; even the monochrome Black-and-white Warbler was a striking little badger of a bird. Meanwhile further colour infusions arrived in the form of Summer and Scarlet Tanagers, plus vireos in Red-eyed, White-eyed and Blue-headed versions, while, at our feet, a Brown Thrasher thrashed and a Wood Thrush did whatever thrushes do.

This was a birding feast and we couldn't wait for the next course. But first we secured the help of Tamie Bulow, of the American Birding Association. We'd originally met Tamie when we guided the ABA Convention in Ecuador in 2006. Between them, Tamie and Brenda Gibb had organised the convention from ABA Headquarters in Colorado Springs and then, on the ground in Quito, had directed the hundreds of American birders onto the right tour bus at the right time with the right packed lunch, morning after morning, and on their happy return in the evening had shepherded them seamlessly into the right dining room to the right table for the right meal.

Tamie's arrival at Boy Scout Woods had brought us immediate good luck in the form of a hitherto elusive Scarlet Tanager. So we decided to borrow her for the afternoon to see how she could boost our birding. I must admit, we were also itching for a ride in her Hummer.

For a change of scene, we drove down to the lowlands of Bolivar Flats, a spit of sand extending out into the sea opposite Galveston. Bolivar is to waders what High Island is to warblers. And they are so confiding here that we could get a much closer look than they would ever allow us in the UK. All the regulars were lined up for our inspection: Sanderling, Dunlin and Red Knot pottering along the strandline, just as they do at home; Semi-Palmated and Western Sandpipers testing our ID skills with their similar plumages. And waders were not the only attraction: Caspian and Royal Terns vied to out-do each other in the red/orange bill stakes; Brown and White Pelicans scooped up water and fish in their expandable pouches; White-winged, Black and Surf Scoters bobbed on the water just offshore; and Least Terns dive-bombed the waves. Faced with such an entertaining spectacle it was easy to forget the fierce sun beating down on us, especially as the stiff breeze kept us pleasantly cool. It was only back in the car that we realised that our hair was standing up on end, rigid with salt (well, those of us with hair, that is!) and our noses were red from the sun.

Our next must-see destination was the fabulous reserve at the Anhuac National Wildlife Refuge, a protected area with a mixture of open water, reed swamp, wet grassland and the occasional clump of scrub. It's home to a myriad of birds as well as numerous lengthy alligators, lurking like discarded tyre treads in the watery ditches beside the track. Our visit necessitated another pre-dawn start but we had a hot date with our great friend Michael Retter, so we didn't mind. We'd last birded with Michael during our madcap tour of Mexico back in January and now he was guiding in Texas for the migration season. It was great to see him again and swap news.

Our date was the only hot thing about the morning though. The pre-dawn air was bitterly cold as we strained our frost-nipped ears to listen for Yellow and Black Rails calling. Unfortunately, the rails had more sense than us and stayed firmly hunkered down in the reeds, refusing to call. As the sun came up, however, so did the birds. Seaside Sparrow chirped on top of a rounded bush. An American Bittern got his bearings wrong and crash-landed onto the open track in front of our vehicle, before recovering his cool and strutting off into the reeds. Fulvous Whistling Ducks and White-faced Ibises left their overnight roosts and flew off across the open skies towards their feeding sites. Stilt Sandpipers and Pectoral Sandpipers wandered through the shallows, while Long-billed Dowitchers probed the deeper water. And a lovely bonus: two River Otters startled us as they suddenly emerged from the shadows of an overhung ditch beside the track and lolloped across the road in a game of tag.

There may be plenty of birding sites around High Island, but there aren't too many good eating places, so most birders descend on Al-T's in Winnie. This Cajun restaurant serves vast quantities of delicious food – crab is always good – at reasonable prices. It's popular with the locals, the men dressed up in their best denims and red-checked shirts; the women usually looking slightly more glamorous, and an intimidating array of enormous status-symbol pick-up trucks is usually lined up in the car park. They're a friendly bunch, too. In fact, one couple on the next table were so friendly that they picked up their plates and invited themselves onto ours just to listen to our 'quaint' accent! Don't knock having a British accent in these parts; it opens doors, makes you new friends and, in this case, even got us a free meal.

Al-T's is equally popular with the visiting birders and in April the khaki will often overwhelm the red-check and denim. We saw many of the same people we had bumped into on the trails, including one particularly wonderful group of *Biggest Twitch* groupies whom we'd met that morning at Boy Scout Woods. Susan, Ann, Joanne and Shirley – whom we quickly dubbed the Golden Girls – were down on a short trip to High Island, having left their non-birding husbands safely at home with the housework back in the Texas hill country. They were having a great time birding and had asked Michael Retter if he knew the whereabouts of the *Biggest Twitchers*, as they'd been following our progress online and knew we were somewhere in the area.

In fact, we were about ten feet away at the time of asking, so Michael had made the introductions. It was exciting to meet real fans; we felt almost famous. The Golden Girls were a lively bunch who thoroughly enjoyed their birds and we had chatted away while watching the warblers at the water drip together. That evening at AI-T's, we found ourselves standing in line with them as we waited to pay our bill. They'd had a very successful day's birding and were full of what they'd seen and where. Somehow we got onto the subject of two very special species that we were particularly keen to find: Golden-cheeked Warbler and Black-capped Vireo. Amazingly, our new friends knew of guaranteed sites for both these species right on their doorstep and, with typical Texan generosity, immediately invited us – two total strangers they'd only met that day – to stay with them so they could show us the birds. Never ones to look a gift bird in the mouth, so to speak, we immediately accepted their invitation and hatched a plan to meet up with them again in a few days' time.

With that, we went our separate ways. At this stage of *The Biggest Twitch* we still had the time and budget to be spontaneous and so we'd booked up a last-minute side trip for a few days. With 1,950 species now under our belt we were about to jump on a plane to a country that would be new to both of us.

1,950 species

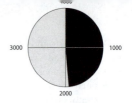

17–21 April, Panama (Alan)

Is that it? Surely it's too small. But my companions assured me that this rather unimpressive length of rusty metal, no more than 18 inches wide and half concealed by leaf-litter, was indeed the very length of pipe to which Panama's famous Pipeline Road owed its name. For years I had read about, heard birders talk about and even watched a DVD about the wonderful birding associated with this place. Only now that I was standing here did it strike me that I had never seen a picture of the actual pipeline. Now I knew why. My mental picture of a mighty miracle of engineering pushing through the jungle was shattered; this looked like little more than a fat hosepipe. Ruth took a picture of me standing on top of it so that other birders would not have to endure the same disappointment.

The Americans had built the pipeline to ensure supplies of crude oil would continue to flow even if the Panama Canal was sabotaged or blocked by a stricken vessel. Luckily, given its clearly inadequate size, it has never been called into service. But the building of the pipeline entailed the construction of a service track running alongside it. And this track provides wonderful access to the pristine jungle that covers the interior of Panama, hence its fame in the birding world.

But I'm getting ahead of myself. What were we doing in Panama when we were supposed to be in Texas? Well, we had actually done rather well for North American passerines during our travels through Mexico and Ecuador in January, which meant that the number of new birds we might find for our list among the returning migrants on the Gulf coast was lower than we had anticipated when originally planning our trip. So the guys at Tropical Birding had come up with a plan and contacted their connections in Panama. A few emails later and we were booked on a hectic, whistle-stop birding tour of this exciting new country.

Arriving on 17 April, we had very little idea of what we were letting ourselves in for and, knowing next to nothing about the country, were a little nervous. As the plane began to descend we got our first views of the Panama Canal far below and the mass of ships out in the bay, waiting their turn to navigate the waterway. Landing in any new country always fills me with apprehension. Would we be met? Would we see enough birds to make it worthwhile?

Our nerves were considerably calmed when we met our guide. Kilo Campos was waiting at Panama City Airport for us with a broad, welcoming smile. Tall and muscular, he was the sort of person you immediately felt at ease with and looked like a man who could take care of himself – and us! Soon we were in his car and heading through the busy city traffic. Kilo explained that he worked for Advantage Tours, a company that had looked after our friends Scott and Erin from TB when they visited Panama. We grabbed a quick lunch at a fast food joint, where the price of around just £5 for the three of us was a promising sign. For good measure, we also added Orange-chinned Parakeet to our list just outside.

Then, to our surprise, it was straight back to the airport. Kilo had booked us onto a one-hour internal flight into the mountains near the town of David, which lies to the north-west of Panama City. We took off over a beautiful area of coral reefs, their blues and greens shimmering in the tropical sun.

Right outside the tiny airport at David was a park-like area with some promising pools, where a Striped Cuckoo sat out in full view for us and a Scaly-breasted Hummingbird eventually perched long enough for a good look. Then Kilo was off again, driving us up into the hills to the hamlet of Volcan, where we checked in at the hotel Dos Rios to spend our first night in Panama. Already, with minimal birding, we had added seventeen new birds to the year list. It was a promising start.

Overnight it poured, and we lay awake listening to the downpour hammering on the tin roof. With dawn just beginning to win the battle with the leaden storm clouds we ventured outside. We did not get far. Despite the poor weather the hotel grounds were full of birds and we simply set up the scopes under the shelter of an awning at reception. A Blue-crowned Motmot hopped around the lawn, while wintering US birds such as Philadelphia Vireo and Rose-breasted Grosbeak entertained us in the bushes. Clay-coloured Robins were everywhere, and our luck was in, as White-crowned Parrots – one of our most wanted species – flew in and fed in the trees right next to the hotel.

Soon it was time to venture further afield and we drove higher into the mountains to Pancho Farm, a favourite birding spot of Kilo's on the edge of the Baru National Park. Luckily the rain had eased to a drizzle and it didn't take us long to discover why Kilo liked the place. He was clearly on high alert as we walked across a field with scattered trees, moving slowly and scanning ahead carefully. "There!" he exclaimed. We followed his directions to an iridescent green bird sitting on a horizontal branch. This lovely creature was a Resplendent Quetzal, a bird that I had ogled countless times in books but had never dreamed I would see in real life.

We were elated but not totally satisfied. Our bird was a female. And while she was certainly gorgeous, what we were really after was the truly mind-blowing male. Suddenly she flew a short distance to her nest hole in a tree and, in a trice, her mate appeared. And what a bird he was! No picture I'd ever seen could do him justice. Even writing this now I get shivers down my spine. We just stood and stared, overwhelmed by the sense of excitement and achievement on seeing this wondrous creature that we had dreamed about for so long.

How to describe a male Resplendent Quetzal? Well the tail, for a start, is ludicrous: no bird needs streamers that are three times the length of its body. Then there are the dazzling colours – iridescent green, with a scarlet belly and golden bill – and that huge black eye that you could lose yourself in.

'Camera!' whispered Ruth, breaking the spell. Fumbling with the scope I managed to fire off a few shots. Poor light and shaking hands weren't conducive to great photography, but at least we had a record. And then he flew, streamers fluttering behind like the tail on an ornamental Chinese dragon kite. By now the poor female was totally forgotten.

Whatever followed was always going to be second-best, but Kilo still managed to produce some wonderful birds. In some nearby woodland we eventually tracked down a gorgeous Golden-browed Chlorophonia, a candidate for bird of the day on any other occasion. An area of coffee plantations at Santa Clara also brought us Turquoise Cotinga, plus a whole gang of aptly named Fiery-billed

Aracaris, flaunting their big toucan-like bills. The sun even came out, illuminating impressive views up across the forested mountain ranges.

Back at the hotel we counted up our day list and found we had already reached an impressive 127 species, of which an amazing 54 were new for the year. The day had been about quantity as well as quality, and in the course of it we had passed another milestone: a gorgeous little hummingbird called White-throated Mountain-gem was species number 2,000 for *The Biggest Twitch*. Sadly, though, it had been overshadowed by a much larger bird in green.

The next morning, still on a high from our quetzal encounter, we headed into the Amastidad National Park. The gates were locked when we arrived, so we walked in along an entrance road that wound through dense forest with plenty of birds. Here the trees were festooned with lichens and mosses, and huge-leaved plants spread across the forest floor like a crop of umbrellas. A movement caught our eyes as a bird darted rodent-like between the umbrella handles. We froze until it popped up again: a tiny, black wren-like bird with a bright orange crown, whose name, Zeledonia, is as funky as its appearance.

All too soon we had to head back to David airport for our return flight to Panama City. Just over an hour later we were back in the capital, where Kilo took us to meet his boss, Guido Berguido, a jolly chap who was keen to hear how *The Biggest Twitch* was getting on in Panama. Guido had very kindly arranged for us to stay at his house, a large three-storey colonial affair with clapperboard walls, and we regaled him long into the night with tales of all the amazing birds that Kilo had helped us find, waxing especially lyrical about the Resplendent Quetzals.

Next morning the alarm had us stumbling downstairs for our 5.30am breakfast. Kilo had planned a bit of a bird race around Panama City and had arranged for some other birders to join us. Ariel, another keen birder, was to be our driver. We were also joined by Michael, a young man who was learning the ropes as a guide and proved to have an amazing facility for imitating bird calls; no need for tapes with this guy around, he just whistles the birds in.

This was the day on which we found ourselves, at last, birding along the famous Pipeline Road. And my disappointment at the size of the pipe soon disappeared, as the birds came thick and fast. Indeed it was difficult to keep track, so quickly did new species appear. The first surprise was a Little Tinamou – normally a secretive bird of the forest floor – that walked calmly across the track right in front of us. We were stunned; you could spend a lifetime in the forest and not get a view like that. Other excellent birds soon added themselves to our list, including a Gray-headed Kite dismembering a lizard, some skulking Spotted Antbirds, a Black-throated Mango, and both Black-throated and Black-tailed Trogons. More colour arrived in the form of Lance-tailed and Red-capped Manakins and Rosy Thrush-Tanagers. This place truly was truly living up to its legend.

As we walked the track alongside the pipeline, we looked up to see Mississippi Kites migrating north overhead. This species was both new for the year and a lifer, but what made the sighting so special was the sheer numbers: thousands and thousands of these elegant raptors swirled across the blue sky, moving from thermal to thermal in search of extra lift. Once again, we just stood open mouthed and stared; it was yet another mind-blowing moment on *The Biggest Twitch*.

Not long after the kite spectacle we went off-trail in search of a calling Pheasant

Cuckoo. Kilo warned us to be careful as the forest here was home to Bullet Ants, whose name gives you some idea of the ferocity of their bite. We were duly cautious and all emerged unscathed, though – having tracked down our bird – we were glad to get back to the safety of the track.

Next we headed for a site called Old Camboa road, now abandoned and alive with birds. Massive bamboo grew alongside the track and small lakes lay either side, creating a great mix of habitats. One of the many delights here was watching the bizarre display of male Golden-collared Manakins, which jumped about and snapped their wings to make a sound like someone clicking their fingers loudly. At the far end of the road were two very sleepy-looking Spectacled Owls; not new for the list, as we had seen them at Sacha Lodge in Ecuador, but a wonderful sight nonetheless.

With the light failing, we called it a day. We had driven only 20km from our base but had recorded an impressive 144 species, of which 31 were new for *The Biggest Twitch*. It had been yet another excellent day's birding.

Our adventure was not quite over. Kilo still had a few more birds to find us *en route* to our airport the following morning. A very early start saw us at another national park, where the highlight was a roosting Great Potoo. This big nightjar-like bird sat motionless on a pale branch, blending in so effectively that you really had to look hard to see where bird ended and branch began; in fact, we'd walked past it twice without noticing it. Next came a quick stop at an Agricultural College, where we enjoyed good views of Short-tailed Hawk.

Approaching the airport we totted up our total list for Panama and reached an amazing 332 species, of which a very satisfying 129 were new for 2008. Moments later we made this 130, with three Cattle Tyrants feeding on the grass outside Arrivals. This summed up Panama nicely: wherever we had been we had added new birds. It had been a great experience and yes, it was yet another country to which we would one day love to return. Huge thanks were due to Kilo and Guido at Advantage Tours: with their help, we were leaving with 2,073 species under our belt.

2,073 species

22–24 April, Texas: Part Two (Ruth)

Back in Texas, it was time to look in on the Golden Girls and catch up with those special birds they'd promised. We'd kept in touch by email from Panama and had been invited by Susan Evans to stay with her and her husband, Carl, in their guest house. Great, we thought, imagining a typical UK guest house bed-and-breakfast arrangement. In fact, we were so confident we'd be paying our way that we had invited our friend Sam Woods from Tropical Birding to come along for the ride, as he needed Golden-cheeked Warbler and Black-capped Vireo for his life list.

Our instructions were to drive to Wimberley, a quaint town in the heart of the Texas Hill Country. Once here, we assumed that we were close to Susan's home so we rang for detailed directions. When it became obvious to Susan that we were getting lost in her lengthy instructions ('close to home' obviously having a different meaning in Texas), she changed tack.

'Stay where you are,' she ordered. 'Carl will come out and meet you. He'll be in a red pick-up.' No surprise there, this was Texas after all.

'Er, we've brought our friend Sam with us,' we confessed. 'You probably met him at High Island; he's another Brit. Is it OK if he stays too?'

Susan didn't miss a beat. 'Of course it is. He's very welcome!' That fabulous Texan hospitality again – and there was still more to come. When Carl arrived at the meeting point he was the real deal: checked shirt, huge red pick-up and a big smile. He told us to follow him, and so we did, along straight roads, down twisty lanes, through villages, over hill and down dale. We'd never have found it by ourselves. At last, Carl drew up at a driveway blocked by a substantial metal gate. Perhaps we're here, we thought. Must be a big garden, we can't even see the house. The gate slid back silently on well-oiled runners and we followed Carl through. It closed firmly behind us and he carried on driving.

It was about now that we started to feel just a touch anxious. After all, we hardly knew these people, we had absolutely no idea where we were going, and no one else in the world had any idea of our whereabouts. We were now on the inside of a high stone wall and a solid metal gate with no way of getting back out again. We'd heard tales about strange cult communities in remote areas of Texas. Perhaps we'd soon be enslaved into a life of kaftans, sandals, lentils, meditation and sharing babies.

Still Carl kept on driving, but now at least we started to pass the occasional house, set well back from the road in a huge private garden. At last he turned off into a driveway and we'd arrived at their ranch. An enthusiastic brown dog bounded out to meet us, barking madly, and Susan followed behind, looking equally pleased to see us. We all said hello properly this time and introduced Sam. Then Susan took us to the 'guest house' and the real meaning of the word became clear. This was no B&B; it was a completely separate house for guests, set a few hundred yards away from their main home, with nine beautifully decorated bedrooms, a computer just waiting to be used and a fully-stocked beer fridge. We felt rather embarrassed at having brought along Sam uninvited, but our hosts didn't seem at all bothered; the more the merrier. We dumped our bags and followed them across to the main home. And what a home it was! This was the first time we'd encountered a house built especially to accommodate the owners' collection of artefacts: fonts and doors from South American churches, weather vanes from old farmhouses, native American arrowheads, carvings, woodwork, pottery, shields, masks ... It was an astonishing collection, amassed on their travels around the world, and we could appreciate Carl's quiet pride as he showed us around. After a hearty supper, we headed back to our guest house for the night, stopping to listen out for Barred Owl, a regular visitor in the garden according to Susan. Sadly on this occasion he was elsewhere.

The next day we were reunited with another of the Golden Girls, Shirley. Together we all drove to the Bamberger Ranch Preserve, a 5,500-acre working ranch established by David Bamberger as the largest habitat restoration project on private land in Texas. It's not normally open to the general public, but thanks to Susan and Shirley's connections, we were not only allowed in but taken directly to the site for our first key bird by Colleen, the Director of Education. She led us to a spot deep in this beautiful rolling landscape, where a Black-capped Vireo had been seen recently. The weather wasn't great, with drizzle fogging our bins and a stiff breeze blowing along the ridge. We stared hard at the low tangle of scrub and for a long while nothing happened. Then Shirley caught sight of movement and a vireo appeared. A moment's disappointment as it was only a White-eyed Vireo, but we should have had faith: a quick burst of call betrayed the presence of a Black-capped Vireo and we soon enjoyed a really good view of this handsome bird, with its black crown and bold white eye patch. One down, one to go.

Colleen had to dash back to her day job at the education centre, but not before she'd directed us to a good warbler hang-out in a more sheltered valley deeper into the ranch. Here we looked and listened hard, but the only bird that seemed to be around was a Summer Tanager. Then Sam's sharp ears made out a faint warbler call, and we plunged into the woodland after it. Scanning the canopy, we were at last rewarded with a flash of gold, black and white as a fine male Golden-cheeked Warbler appeared in his full breeding plumage. He sang from the top of a snag with his beak full of food; no wonder his call had sounded rather muffled. Number two in the bag.

Returning to Susan's backyard in the late afternoon, we heard a by-now familiar call. Scanning the trees we once again saw that telltale black, gold and white pattern – and there was a Golden-cheeked Warbler in full view, just feet from Susan's house. What a bird to have on your garden list!

That evening the other Golden Girls came over with their husbands for a barbecue and we tucked into delicious homemade hamburgers and oatmeal-and-chocolate cookies. It was a riotous evening, with red wine flowing and hilarious conversation as we caught up with Ann and Joanne and shared with them the tales of our Bamberger birding with Susan and Shirley. Luckily, Carl was still on the case, and heard a distant Barred Owl calling as he stood outside grilling burgers. Sam, Alan and I nipped out to listen so we could at least add this to the list as a 'heard'.

Since Susan had been kind enough to lay on some very special new species for us, we invited her to join us the next day on a bit of a bird race on her local patch.

We had some hot gen from our old friend Ken Behrens, who'd taken the record for the biggest day list in the States only a short while before. We had a list of new birds and specific locations but only a few hours in which to see them. Poor Susan! I don't think she'd ever experienced birding quite like it, and at times her feet barely touched the ground. We took her to places she'd never been and showed her birds she'd never seen before, and all within a few miles of her home.

First, a ploughed field gave us Clay-coloured, Vesper and Lark Sparrows, plus a Dickcissel. Next, a stakeout produced Scott's Oriole and a bonus Yellow-billed Cuckoo. Then to the legendary Neal's Lodge, where the cattle guard feeders gave us Pine Siskin and Canyon Wren, and Cabin 61 produced a Long-billed Thrasher in the leaf-litter at our feet and a Hooded Oriole dashing past in a flash of orange. After that, another of Ken's stakeouts took us into a small spinney to locate a haughty Red-shouldered Hawk high up on a branch. And Ken's final tip-off just gave us time to watch a singing, pink-billed Field Sparrow. Then it was time to make tracks, with Sam due back at work on High Island bright and early the next morning.

We handed a rather shell-shocked Susan back to Carl and said our reluctant farewells to these most generous of hosts. Who'd have thought you could make such good friends in such a short time? Susan and Carl Evans, and indeed all our new Texan friends, had shown us lavish hospitality and generously shared with us their home and a magical part of the state we wouldn't otherwise have explored. We delivered Sam back to the Tropical Birding Information Centre at High Island late that night, and early the next morning made our way back to the all-too-familiar Houston Airport. With 2,105 species under our belt, it was time to leave Texas and have ourselves some California dreamin'.

2,105 species

25 April–1 May, California (Alan)

Sharks. That was the only thing anyone wanted to talk about in San Diego, California. We arrived from Texas on 25 April, a day that San Diego will remember for a long time – not because *The Biggest Twitch* had hit town but because the town had just witnessed its first fatal shark attack in 50 years. Everyone was talking about the horrific incident just off the beach. The sea looked very tempting and in the heat of early afternoon a swim would have been great. But, like everybody else that day, we were staying out of the water.

We picked up our hire car and headed cautiously out into the busy downtown traffic. Our plan for the first afternoon was simply to bird the coast north, so finding the route was just a matter of keeping the ocean on our left. At Batiquitos Lagoon we stopped beside some promising habitat to see what we could find. First a California Towhee hopped along the path in front of us, then a pair of California Gnatcatchers danced about feeding in some bushes just below us. Great! Anything with the name California was going to be new – not just for *The Biggest Twitch* but also for our life lists, as neither of us had birded here before.

We then turned our attention to the lagoon, which lay just behind a lovely beach. A sandy island held a gull roost, with three Western Gulls among the California Gulls. Raucous calls drew our attention to a gang of Elegant Terns flying in from the sea, with their drooping orange bills and shaggy crests. They were soon joined by two big Caspian Terns, as Black Skimmers flew overhead and a Western Grebe popped up in front of us and sailed majestically past. An unfamiliar song led us to a male Fox Sparrow sitting atop a small dead tree, and as we watched him, a flashy male Hooded Oriole swept in to land in the sunshine.

With the sun sinking, our thoughts turned to finding a bed for the night. But first we had an important phone call to make – and one that might determine where we stayed. An old friend of mine from north Wales, Hugh Ranson, now lives in Santa Barbara and we had been in regular email contact before our visit. Hugh was not available for the next couple of days – something very dull about 'having to work for a living' – but he had given us the number of another birder. And not just any birder: this was Guy McCaskie, a birding legend!

We knew Guy's name from Kenn Kaufman's wonderful book, *Kingbird Highway*, which tells the story of Kenn's big year in the USA. Kenn dropped out of high school to set a new US year list record on a shoestring budget, becoming a hero for birders everywhere. Though now a long time ago, his epic tale is as great as ever and I have lost count of how many times I have read it. The book describes how, while travelling through California, Kenn meets Guy McCaskie, who takes him under his wing and imparts priceless knowledge.

Not for nothing is Guy known as the 'grandfather of birding' in these parts. Now we had an opportunity to meet the great man himself and perhaps, like Kenn Kaufman, learn from his vast birding experience. All I had to do was phone him.

Deep breath, and I punched the numbers Hugh had given me. After a long, nervous wait Guy himself answered the phone. I hurriedly explained who I was and that we would really appreciate some help in finding a few local specialities.

To say Guy did not sound enthusiastic was an understatement. We had grown used to birders being thrilled to be part of *The Biggest Twitch*, but no thrill was detectable in the great man's rather monotone voice and he was certainly in no mood to chat. He did say, however, that he would meet us early in the morning at La Jolla Cove and we could talk then. The line went dead.

Oh dear. Had I said something out of turn – or worse, dropped Hugh in it by revealing he'd given me Guy's number? I seemed to have severely pissed off California's most revered birder. Well, the damage was done. I could only hope to make amends in the morning.

Meanwhile we needed a bed for the night, and as Guy had suggested La Jolla we thought we might as well try there. A short drive took us to a hotel that did not look too expensive and we wandered in. Then Ruth discreetly drew my attention to the room tariff displayed at reception. Ah! This place may not have looked expensive, but a night here cost mega bucks. The receptionist asked if he could help. Yes, we replied, sheepishly, could he please recommend a cheaper hotel? Following his advice we drove north, quite a way out of trendy La Jolla, and eventually found a small, and considerably cheaper, roadside motel. We would just have to be up extra early to drive back south for our appointment with Guy.

The sea front at La Jolla was already busy when we arrived just after dawn. Joggers, roller-bladers, dog-walkers and fishermen were all up and about. A lone figure was looking out to sea through a telescope and we knew it had to be Guy. We introduced ourselves and soon we were chatting away happily as he enthused about the birds we might see today. His tone was unrecognisable from the man on the phone last night. Had I dreamt it?

Soon birds started to arrive. Brandt's Cormorants flying past close inshore were our first new bird of the day. After a few minutes' scanning we picked up a Sooty Shearwater, soon followed by hundreds more – milling about over the glassy ocean and giving wonderful scope views. Then Guy called a Pink-footed Shearwater, which weaved through the sooties, showing off nicely. It was quickly followed by three Black-vented Shearwaters. This was my kind of sea-watching: standing on a solid surface in warm morning sunlight, without a breath of wind. The more we scanned the more we saw: three Pacific Loons flew low north and a Pomarine Skua circled offshore, looking for a bird to mug for a free breakfast.

Guy called time on the beach and we headed inland to Mission State Park. It did not look like a top birding site: a few trees, a stream and lots of people. We should have known better, of course; we were with a master birder and Guy knew just what he was doing. Our heads soon swam with new birds: Nuttall's Woodpecker, Pacific-slope Flycatcher, Bell's Vireo and Black-headed Grosbeak were just for starters.

Next up was a special site that Guy had only recently heard about himself and, we hoped, a special bird. We drove to a marshy lake and walked around the edge scanning the reeds. Up jumped a black bird. Binoculars focused frantically as we tried to get a clear view of the wing pattern. Guy confirmed it: Tricoloured Blackbird. This new species for us is also a rarity in the US. We enjoyed great views, as our male perched conveniently on top of the reeds, and we even got some reasonable photos.

Then Guy took us to his office and showed us a pair of Cassin's Kingbirds that had nested alongside a pair of Western Kingbirds. What a double act! At this point he phoned home to announce he would not be back tonight as he was on *The Biggest Twitch* and wanted to find us even more birds. This was brilliant news; we had been expecting Guy to make his excuses at any minute and slip away – and we would have been thrilled and grateful for his morning's help. Now we had the master for even longer, and we knew this could only mean more birds.

Guy had really got the bit between his teeth and was going all out to boost our list. At Mission Santa Ysabel we leapt out of the car, almost immediately saw our target – Lawrence's Goldfinch – then jumped straight back in and hit the road. We climbed steeply from the narrow coastal plain into the cool pine forests at 6,000 feet and soon reached the Cleveland National Forest in the Laguna Mountains. Scanning the sky wherever we found a clearing we quickly located small numbers of Violet-green Swallows and picked up Pygmy Nuthatch, Mountain Chickadee, Oak Titmouse and Steller's Jay.

Leaving the trees behind we entered a semi-desert rocky habitat, where we searched for the rare and elusive Gray Vireo. Guy took us to a hillside above a small stream where they had been seen recently. As we scanned, Rock Wrens jumped about on the boulders, a male Lazuli Bunting came to drink, Bullock's Orioles moved through and a Mountain Quail called from cover. Time was ticking away and we discussed moving on, when a movement caught Ruth's eye. She was certain it was something different and, sure enough, out popped a Gray Vireo. Now we could move on happy. As we plotted a route further inland, Guy slammed on the brakes: a California Quail was calling away from the top of a small bush, allowing excellent views in the last of the day's sun. It was a great bird with which to finish a wonderful birding day. Almost. A White-throated Swift swept low overhead to round things off with a flourish.

With the light now just about gone we began the long, winding decent into the desert far inland close to the Mexican border. Our species list had moved onto 2,124 and Guy promised even more amazing birds in the morning, with the excitement of birding the Salton Sea.

It was pitch-black when we left our Motel 6 somewhere in the southern Californian desert. A huge Border Patrol 4WD cruised the street and slowed for a hard look at us, but seemed happy we were not illegals making a dash north and drove on past. Our first stop was a 24-hour diner across the street, where we gulped down hot tea, bacon and scrambled eggs. Feeling much better for that we headed off onto a maze of dirt farm roads in the first grey light of dawn. Despite being hundreds of miles from home, Guy knew this area like his backyard and soon had us overlooking a small lake. A cloud of Yellow-headed Blackbirds lifted from the reeds, leaving their roost to forage in the fields. Nice, but not what we had come for. Scanning the open water we soon had our bird: Clarke's Grebe. It was good to compare this with the similar Western Grebes that shared the lake.

Back out on the farm roads Guy was pretty confident he could rustle up one of our most wanted birds. We were not so sure: we had already searched in vain in Arizona, where we'd been told it was easy to see, and had also tried in Texas, again with no luck. Guy drove slowly and we all scanned the dusty farmland looking for movement. Minutes ticked by. How long should we spend? We had asked ourselves this same question so many times already and would do so many more times before the year was out. It was a constant dilemma: how long to devote to a species that would count just once on our list? We knew many potential new birds lay ahead today; would our time spent now cost us more than one bird later?

'There!' shouted Guy and thrust out an arm pointing at a bend in the road ahead. We just had time to see a bird sprint over the earth bank and dive out of sight behind it before we were out of the car and in hot pursuit. Reaching the top of the bank we had a good vantage point and there below us galloping away was a Greater Roadrunner. 'Beeb-beeb!' Guy caught us up and we had a high-five moment as we celebrated scoring a bogey bird.

The Salton Sea is a huge landlocked body of water below sea-level, so the rivers that feed it never go any further. It is surrounded by desert and lies not far from Mexico; no wonder so many rare and wonderful birds had been seen here.

We headed for the south end and again Guy's local knowledge proved amazing as he guided us down tiny tracks to the water's edge and great viewpoints we would never have found on our own. The shallow waters just heaved with birds. What a spectacle! We quickly realised a good percentage of the waders were Red-necked Phalaropes. Our jaws dropped: we were used to seeing this rare species in the UK one at a time, not like this, in carpets of thousands. Wilson's Phalaropes were here in hundreds, the females just gorgeous in their breeding plumage – illustrating that anomaly of polyandrous species, that it is the colourful female that displays and the dowdier male who takes care of nesting duties. Huge flocks of American Avocets, Long-billed Dowitchers and Western Sandpipers formed a rippling, feathered mass along the shoreline. Stilt Sandpipers, Least Sandpipers, Spotted Sandpipers, Dunlins, Black-bellied Plovers and Semipalmated Plovers all fed just metres from us. Out on the open water the spectacle continued: rafts of loafing wildfowl comprised thousands of Ruddy Ducks, with good numbers of Pintail, Gadwall, Northern Shovelers and Cinnamon Teals. There were even a few Buffleheads and Common Goldeneyes, plus an immature drake Surf Scoter, a long way from the sea where he belonged.

The lake's islands held noisy, breeding colonies of terns: thousands of red-billed Caspian Terns squabbled for space, alongside smaller numbers of Gull-billed and Forster's Terns, which tried to find a spot among their bigger cousins. There were gulls, too, and among the hundreds of California and Ring-billed Gulls, we picked out three diminutive Bonaparte's Gulls and two stunning adult Heermann's Gulls. Just as we were soaking up the latter, Guy pipped them with a Yellow-footed Gull; nowhere near as good-looking, but a real rarity.

For the sheer sense of anticipation – that delicious wondering about what will pop into your scope next – the Salton Sea must go down as one of the most exciting destinations on *The Biggest Twitch*. The numbers were amazing. Sadly, however, it was time to leave. Even sadder, we had to bid farewell to Guy. What a wonderful time he had shown us; and to think how apprehensive we'd been about meeting him on that first morning. We can't thank Guy enough for his time, knowledge, enthusiasm and great company.

After a night in Lancaster we drove across the Mojave Desert towards the snow-capped peaks of Mount Piños. Recent rain here had brought the desert to life, and carpets of flowers made for a beautiful scene. The orange of Californian Poppies stretched ahead for miles, shimmering in the heat, to be replaced suddenly by a carpet of something purple and then just as suddenly switch back to orange. It was like travelling through some psychedelic dream.

We reached the foothills and, leaving the colourful desert below, climbed up narrowing roads through scented pine woods, glimpsing the snowy peaks through gaps in the trees. Soon the snow was at the roadside and the coolness felt good after the heat of yesterday. We stopped frequently to jump out and chase bird calls or a movement in the huge trees – though once we'd learned the calls of Mountain Chickadees, easily the commonest bird here, we stopped less often! Red-breasted Sapsuckers were a real treat, as was a White-headed Woodpecker that swooped across the road in front of us.

At last we reached the end of the road. Now the only way up was on foot. We took a trail and were soon engulfed in the silence of the massive forest. No foot-prints spoilt the virgin snow ahead, while not the slightest breath of wind ruffled the clear blue sky above. We made good progress towards the 8,300-foot summit of Mount Piños, revelling in the solitude and natural splendour. As we heated up from our exertions, we stripped down to T-shirts, which seemed odd when snow lay all around.

Soon a bird flew across the trail, revealing the diagnostic undulating flight and grey plumage of a Clark's Nutcracker – just what we'd been hoping for. We hurried along the path and soon had the bird perfectly in view on top of a pine against the blue sky, its large black bill and beady black eye standing out against the powder-grey plumage. The views from the summit were just awe-inspiring; we could see right back down to the Mojave and even make out the shimmering colours of the floral carpet.

As we turned back towards the car a huge raptor came over the summit. We stared as this hulking black shape, with its distinctive piebald wings, drifted over-head. Only one bird was this big: California Condor. Sadly we could not count this rarity for *The Biggest Twitch*, since the last remaining wild individuals had all been taken into captivity to save the species from extinction. Now a captive breeding scheme is returning young birds to the wild in the hope that a self-supporting population will one day grace the skies of California again. We hoped that our sighting was a sneak preview of that brighter future.

We drove and drove and eventually reached the coast, where we found a motel and crashed out. What a day it had been: from the desert to the high mountains and now back to the coast, California really does have it all. Tomorrow promised one more habitat: the high seas.

It seemed our luck was in when we awoke to a flat, calm dawn. Ventura Harbour was like a millpond and there was not a cloud in the sky. So why did I have an uneasy feeling about the day ahead? The truth is, I hate boat trips on the ocean. I am always ill, and seasickness can be a grim, debilitating experience. Believe me, there have been times when if you had given me a knife I would have slit my wrists rather than endure another minute throwing up over the side.

But surely today would be different. Conditions were perfect and the boat was much bigger than many I have suffered on. We climbed aboard with 50 or so others for the trip out to Santa Cruz Island, where we hoped to see the endemic Island Scrub-Jay and some seabirds *en route*. Even before leaving the harbour we saw great birds, with Black Turnstones feeing on the harbour wall and three species of grebe – Eared, Western and Clark's – loafing on the still waters.

But then we rounded the seawall and headed onto the open sea. The horror began. How could it have been so calm in the harbour when there was such a big swell? The boat pitched and rolled wildly, despite its size, and the two-and-a-half hours crossing time ahead seemed like a life sentence. To make matters worse, the crew seemed to have been equally surprised by the conditions and hastily rearranged people's positions on deck for greater safety. Given the flat calm of the harbour we had opted to stand at the front of the top deck – ideal for spotting seabirds but the worst place in a rough sea. Soon we were hanging on for dear life, as huge waves crashed over the boat.

The crew were in state of panic and seemed unsure what to do. A wind had sprung up from nowhere and the sea was a mass of giant, white-capped rollers bearing down on us. We clung on with white knuckles, but it was not long before the sea-sickness kicked in. Clinging on with both hands, with nowhere to move, I just had to vomit over the side from where I stood. The poor people on the deck below must have loved it. The sickness and the terror was appalling – and we had not seen a single new bird. Somehow Ruth managed to keep birding. I think it was her way of coping: try to shut out the horror by concentrating on the birds. Suddenly she was shouting at me to look left, and I just managed to raise my head long enough to see four Xantus Murrelets pass the boat. Can't say I really cared.

At last we gained the shelter of the island, Cassin's Auklets overtaking us as we passed beneath the cliffs. There are two disembarkation points. The second, Prisoner's Landing, is the one where the Island Scrub-Jay is most likely. But there was no way I was staying on the boat a second longer than absolutely necessary, so off we got at the first stop, Scorpion Landing. I could barely make it to a nearby rock before I collapsed. We had almost certainly blown the scrub-jay and had added just two new seabirds. But at that point all I cared about was that I was off the boat – though I still faced the awful prospect of the return trip.

Ruth, who was feeling fine now that her fear had subsided, went for a walk while I lay in the sun and tried to stop my head spinning and guts churning. She soon came back clutching a map that showed a walking trail heading into the interior of the island. Maybe we could still find a scrub-jay? I did not feel at all like walking, but we had come this far and it was an endemic so this might be our only ever chance to see this bird. We set off very slowly and trudged up through a grassy valley with very few birds. Eventually I had had enough and we sat down to scan the hills around us. The wind was still strong and we saw nothing except a single Loggerhead Shrike. I was swearing never, ever to set foot on a boat again, when suddenly a long-tailed bird landed in the top of a small bush nearby. Island Scrub-Jay! We could hardly believe our luck. The views were a bit distant, but through the scope we could see it just fine. Our horrors had not been in vain.

Mercifully the return trip was uneventful, though I was highly relieved when we slipped back into the sheltered waters of Ventura Harbour. I will never forget Island Scrub-Jay, that's for sure.

But our day was still not done. We had arranged, at last, to meet up with my old friend, Hugh Ranson, with whom I had cut my UK twitching teeth in the late seventies. Hugh emigrated to the USA in the eighties and now resides in Santa Barbara, not far from Ventura Harbour. He and his wife welcomed us warmly, introduced us to their lovely children and sat us down to a wonderful home-cooked meal. Having eaten nothing since breakfast – and having scattered that out across the ocean – I was now starving.

Hugh was keen to go birding the minute our meal was devoured. We were shattered after our traumatic day, but he was buzzing with the prospect of helping *The Biggest Twitch* and was ready to look for owls. We had arranged to meet Peter, a birding pal of Hugh's, high in the hills above town, so jumped in his car and set off uphill. At some 4,000 feet above sea-level, however, the weather had turned cold and windy. Not great for owls. The four of us stood in the cold wind, listening intently, but heard nothing. We drove, stopped, listened, and then drove on again. It was hard-going and began to seem increasingly pointless. But finally we found a sheltered area and at last an owl called. Peter switched on the spot-light and there sat a lovely Western Screech-Owl. Another one for the list. Now it was time for bed.

We picked up Hugh at dawn and set off to explore his favourite birding sites. It was not long before we found another new bird. Just as Hugh was explaining that the land we were passing was part of Michael Jackson's Neverland Ranch, a Yellow-billed Magpie landed on the boundary fence. No sign of the King of Pop though.

Hugh took us high into the pine-clad mountains and we birded a deserted campsite, where we soon added our first Purple Finches, sitting on top of pines against the clear blue sky. It was very cold up here, despite the sun, but Hugh urged us even higher with the temptation of wonderful warblers. We soon found ourselves staring at a stunning Townsend's Warbler, a riot of yellow, green, black and white.

'Hermit Warbler. Get down here quick!' called Hugh next, and we broke away from the Townsend's to find yet another top-drawer new warbler in our binoculars. This was a real beauty: a male, with bright yellow head, neat black chin, white underparts, blue-grey upperparts and clean white wing-bars. With our target mountain birds all in the bag, it was high fives all round and soon we were heading back downhill to the coast.

A California Thrasher was to be our last new bird with Hugh. Once again time had flown by, but it had been wonderful to catch up with our old friend and his family, and share his adopted birds. Back in San Diego we found a motel for the night, ready for our flight north to Canada the following morning. *The Biggest Twitch* now stood at 2,157.

2,157 species

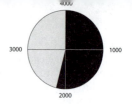

1–6 May, Canada (Ruth)

Maple syrup, pine trees in the snow, beavers and bears, native totem poles, the land where Malcolm the Mountie always gets his man... Once again, given our hectic chase around the world, we were arriving in a new country with little more than a field guide and a set of stereotypes to get us by.

I'd been looking forward to visiting British Colombia and had high hopes of this scenic part of the world. Instead, it will stick in my mind for all the wrong reasons: delays, noisy people, a robbery – and also for being the place where *The Biggest Twitch* partnership came to the brink of separation.

We didn't get off to a good start. Our flight from California to Vancouver was delayed by so long that any hopes we had had of settling into a cosy hotel and starting our Canadian birding went straight out of the window. In the pitch dark and pouring rain in an unfamiliar city, we plumped for the first reputable hotel we came to, just a short drive from the airport.

The next morning we tried our luck in the low cloud and drizzle that blanketed the city. With weather like this, it was clear we wouldn't be enjoying any chocolate-box vistas of pine-clad mountains and sparkling blue seas, with whales spouting merrily just offshore. But a new country is always exciting, so we were fairly optimistic as we headed out into the unknown. We knew two birders who lived in Vancouver and who'd both offered to help us find our target birds during our short visit: Brian, whom we'd guided in Ecuador for the American Birding Association Convention in 2006, and Bonnie, a long-time friend and regular visitor to North Wales. Unfortunately, both were out of town for the same few days we were in town, so we were on our own. We'd laid our hands on the details of a proposed ABA trip to Vancouver, though, complete with a list of sites. We decided to base our birding around that.

First up was a visit to Iona Park. Although right beside the airport, between a sewage works and the runway, this seemed a pretty wild place, with a long, exposed concrete finger of a breakwater that stretched some two-and-a-half miles out into the Strait of Georgia. Alan shouldered the scope and we set off. Some distant, duck-shaped blobs turned into roman-nosed Surf Scoter on closer inspection, and were joined by a pair of Buffleheads, some Lesser Scaups and a few American Wigeons. Despite the stiff breeze, we ploughed on right to the very end of the jetty and it proved a good move. We were able to scope a huge raft of White-winged Scoters on the water, and enjoy fly-pasts from a family party of three Bald Eagles, which cruised the length of the jetty, breaking their journey to perch on various marker posts and glare haughtily down at us. At close quarters, these massive predators send a shiver down your spine, with their fierce glare and cruel, hooked bill. We also scanned the waves for a glimpse of one of Vancouver's famous Orcas, but there was nothing doing today.

Thankfully, the wind was behind us as we began the long trudge back to the car. The breakwater certainly looked all of its two-and-a-half mile length now. The drizzle had stopped but the cloud was still very low and the light cast an eerie wash across the scene. It felt quite a shock after the shiny brightness of California to find ourselves still in the cool grey of winter up here. The eerie call of a Common Loon (that's Great Northern Diver to Brits) floating out of the mist only added to the spooky atmosphere.

We'd intended to pay a quick visit to Starbucks to thaw out around a hot chocolate, but unfortunately someone else had other ideas. With a sickening jolt to the stomach, I noticed that the rear quarter-light window on the car had been smashed. Looking closer, we saw broken glass all over the rear seat and my rucksack in the footwell behind the driver's seat. Funny: I was sure I'd left it out of sight in the boot. When we tried the back door, we found it unlocked. Someone had obviously broken the back window and reached through to open the door. I picked up my rucksack and gingerly shook off the shards of broken glass. It was completely empty. Our spare compact digital camera and my mobile phone had vanished. This was a real blow; I had our main camera safely in my pocket but we had used the back-up one occasionally and now had lost some irreplaceable images. My mobile didn't work in Canada anyway, but with my SIM card missing, all the numbers I'd ever collected from friends and colleagues were also lost.

It got worse. One of the rear seats was pulled forward, exposing the boot and Alan's rucksack hastily stuffed back in. Alan opened it and found it equally empty. His video camera had vanished. This was devastating. In it had been the last tape he'd been using, with all our footage from Ethiopia onwards. This irreplaceable record of a huge chunk of our year to date was now gone for good. We'd hoped to produce a DVD of *The Biggest Twitch* but now we could forget about that. We were gutted.

An envelope fluttered to the ground. This had once held our spare foreign currency. The US dollars left over from California had been taken, as had our emergency Sterling supply, but whoever had broken in had taken the time to sift through the notes and leave us the Ethiopian Birr that we'd been unable to exchange. How thoughtful.

It left a horrid taste in the mouth to know that someone had been watching us, had rifled through our belongings and – for all we knew – was watching us still. At least it wasn't far to the airport rental car desk, where the staff helped us fill out the necessary paperwork and register the theft with the police, then handed us the keys to our replacement vehicle, this time a more rugged, off-road truck. Some sixth sense had made us take out an extra insurance we'd not bothered with before, and months later, even though our travel insurance rejected our claims, the Canadian rental company sent us a small cheque in compensation for our losses. It wasn't enough to replace either the stills or video camera – and, of course, our photographs, video footage and phone number collection were gone for good – but it did go some way to improving our first impression of Canada.

We were in a pretty sour frame of mind when we finally tried to go birding again. This time we paid a visit to the Cyprus Provincial Park in the North Shore Mountains above West Vancouver, apparently a good area for Varied Thrush. Since our hotel was located in Richmond, southeast of downtown Vancouver, we found ourselves gridlocked for hours in traffic as we had to drive right through the centre of the city and out the other side.

Even here, we weren't out of the woods – so to speak. Our Canadian maps seemed to bear little resemblance to reality on the ground, and several times we found ourselves hopelessly lost and heading in completely the opposite direction on a six-lane highway. Alan's stress at steering yet another strange car through heavy traffic in an unfamiliar city was equalled by mine at being completely unable to match landmarks on the ground with the map to get us in the right direction. Harsh words were exchanged, before we descended into frosty silence. Our turning came up and I indicated with a pointed finger that we should leave the highway and head up into the mountains.

Conditions outside the car were just as frosty as inside. Spring was clearly still some way off, and snow piled by snowploughs into huge billowing drifts either side left just a narrow channel down the middle for the winding mountain road. The ranks of pine trees were covered in a thick shawl of snow, which occasionally slid off without warning. We pulled over into a lay-by and, piling on the layers, got out to see what was about. Surprisingly, there were a few birds in this chilly winter wonderland. Some buzzing *zheee* calls overhead betrayed a flock of Pine Siskins in the tree tops. American Robins, smart chaps with white spectacles, grey frock coats and rusty-red waistcoats, investigated the cleared patches of soil beneath the pines. Red-breasted Sapsuckers bounded through the trees, checked the trunks and slipped away again, sometimes as singletons, sometimes in groups of six or more. A flash of blue swooped in, startling against the relentless green-and-white backdrop, and we found ourselves admiring a handsome Steller's Jay.

Birding had thawed the atmosphere between us a little. Normally, we're best of mates, and we both knew that to survive twelve months in close proximity we had to avoid unnecessary arguments, but the stress of the robbery and the tension of the driving had made us both testy. Pointing out birds to each other had at least got us talking, though the tone remained rather prickly. Back in the car, we drove as far up the mountain as we could before snow blocked our path. With skis or snowshoes we could have tried out the trails, but the snow was too soft and deep for our walking boots, so we headed back down again. Clearly, the winter was hanging on a bit longer than we'd expected.

'Look!' cried Alan, suddenly slamming on the brakes. 'Over there, under the trees.'

'Where?'

'Where I said, under the trees,' he retorted. 'Looks like a thrush. Could be Hermit Thrush."

'Where?' I wailed. 'I still can't see it.'

'Where I'm *pointing*!' Alan shouted, sticking out his finger in the vague direction of the bird from the other side of the huge 4WD. But that wasn't much help; he had a different angle to mine and what was obvious to him wasn't at all to me. 'There it is, under the tree,' he insisted. 'Quick, get onto it, it's new!"

'*Where* under the tree? *Which* tree? There are *thousands* of trees out there!' Saying it was a new bird had just added to the pressure. I looked and looked, but still couldn't see where he meant. In fact, the harder I looked, the more I could see only bird-less trees.

'It's *exactly* where I'm pointing! Can't you see it?'

'Well, if I could, I wouldn't be asking, would I?'

By now my blood was boiling. Apart from map reading, I also pride myself on my ability to pick up birds. I'm not as good as Alan at identification, but I get onto birds quickly – sometimes quicker than him. Occasionally, though, you just cannot see a bird. And the harder you look, the more invisible it is. Bird blindness is a terrible thing.

'It's there, where I'm pointing!' Alan persisted. 'Silly cow! Are you blind or something?'

That did it. I exploded. I'm not silly and I'm certainly not blind. There was obviously a good reason why I couldn't see the bird. In pure rage and frustration, I lashed out with my arm and there was a satisfying thud as binoculars connected with ribs. With my other hand I opened the car door, jumped out and slammed it shut again with all my strength. The commotion was enough to startle a freckle-breasted Hermit Thrush out from under a distant pine tree and it flew away down the road. I watched it fly but didn't care. I stomped off down the road, blazing with fury. How dare Alan be so rude, the arrogant sod! If I was so blind, how come I'd seen so many birds this year? I'd shed blood, sweat and tears on this trip; I'd got up at ungodly hours day-in, day-out to go birding; I'd kept going even when I was ill; I'd seen, written about and logged thousands of birds, and this was my reward. Silly cow indeed! Well, if that's what he thought, then he could carry on without me. Let's see how far he'd get.

It's amazing how fast you can walk downhill when you've got a strop on. I'd reached the viewing point about halfway down the mountain before I realised where I was. The trees had been cleared to make a lookout over Vancouver way below. I climbed onto the retaining wall and studied the bleary view with weepy eyes. Behind me, I heard a car pulling into the parking bay, but I didn't look round. The car door opened and closed. Footsteps came towards me but still I didn't look round. I felt two strong arms wrap themselves around me and a cold nose as Alan nuzzled into my neck. I turned round and buried myself into his chest. After all, you can be a drama queen for only so long.

"I'm sorry!" we both said simultaneously, and were instantly being best friends again. Clearly, blowing the safety valve had been long overdue. I don't think Alan ever called me a silly cow again – or, if he did, it was under his breath so I couldn't hear him. We both became a bit more patient in pointing out the birds, and that was the last time I stomped off in a strop.

We celebrated making up in our second-favourite way – by going out for a delicious meal. The shabby-looking Boathouse Restaurant just up the road from our hotel was obviously one of those trendy places where you pay extra for the artfully shabby décor, but the seafood was absolutely out of this world. So was the bill, but luckily making up afterwards in our *most* favourite way came totally free of charge!

The ferry from Tsawwassen over to Swartz Bay on Vancouver Island takes an hour and a half. This roll-on, roll-off boat crosses a fairly major shipping channel and then begins to thread its way between some very attractive pine-clad islands. While most of the locals headed straight for the on-board café, Alan and I took up position by the stern rail and scanned the water. We'd barely left the dock when three Harlequin Ducks flew past: great birds, but a little too distant to appreciate their plumage. Then a hulking Glaucous Gull started slip-streaming right behind the boat. There was an outside chance of an Orca but, hard as we looked, no towering fin broke the surface.

Upon docking, we headed straight south to Victoria and birded our way along the seafront between Ogden Point and Oak Bay. As we parked the car, a superb drake Harlequin Duck bobbed up right in front of us, and then we spied a mixed group of three more handsome males and three rather less showy females following the water's edge. How to describe the drakes? Well, they're not exactly wearing the diamond-patterned clown suits that their name suggests, but their slate grey and bright rufous plumage, patterned precisely with white blobs, stripes and bands, is certainly striking. They were not the only birds around here with evocative names: Marbled Murrelets were suitably blotchy, and the Rhinoceros Auklet had just the horn I was hoping for. I also enjoyed sweet revenge for yesterday's 'silly cow' moment by pointing out to Alan, who was busily scanning the horizon for auks and Orcas, that three yellow-footed Surfbirds were pottering about on the rocks right at his feet.

While Orcas remained elusive, there were other mammals to enjoy. We watched an impressive River Otter from a nearby jetty, so close that we could see it searching for fish under the clear water. It brought its catch to the water's edge, where it crunched away on the bones with obvious relish.

It was bitterly cold at dawn the next day as we checked out Goldstream Provincial Park, reminding us just how far north we had travelled. We had the place all to ourselves when we arrived: an attractive, narrow valley, with a crisp stream tumbling through the dense woodland – all quite reminiscent of north Wales. Our target bird here was American Dipper, but first we had to amuse ourselves with a pair of Goosander, a Song Sparrow, both Orange-crowned and Yellow-rumped Warblers, Brown Creeper, and Chestnut-backed and Black-capped Chickadees. Another River Otter went about its busy morning's work along the edge of the stream; these chunky animals really didn't seem to be bothered by humans. Then suddenly a brown blob shot past low over the water, wings whirring furiously. We followed in hot pursuit and found it perched on a rock in the middle, where it began to feed happily in the tumbling torrent, constantly ducking underwater then popping back up again. American Dipper was on the list. Then we tried again for Varied Thrush, whose handsome features seemed to taunt us from the cover of our *Sibley's Field Guide to the Birds of Western North America*. It was common enough, according to the book, but obviously not where we were.

By now, we were sharing the woods – which had been so peaceful earlier – with a procession of joggers. This was clearly a communal pursuit and they passed us on the trails in groups of three or four at a time, all chattering loudly. Canadians are an active lot, keen on their outdoor pursuits, all of which they seem to carry out at full volume. Perhaps when you have so much open space to share between so few people, you have to make plenty of noise to reach your neighbour. Whatever the reason, it all proved too much disturbance for the wildlife, and us, so we headed back to the car and on to pastures new.

We called in at Whiffen Spit, a low shingle finger that points out into the Strait of Juan de Fuca. The sun was up and the morning was now pleasantly warm, so it made a perfect Sunday stroll for the many dog-walkers who – you've guessed it – were noisily chattering their way out to the lighthouse and back. The birds just offshore didn't seem too bothered though: more Harlequin Ducks, Buffleheads, Surf and White-winged Scoters, Marbled Murrelets and Rhinoceros Auklets all lined up to entertain us against a backdrop of snow-capped mountains and blue-green water. Yet another River Otter was happily devouring a large fish on the beach, completely oblivious to both us and the dog-walkers; the fish stocks around here must really take a pounding! Once again, we looked hard for whales, but obviously we must have been looking in all the wrong places.

The next day we took the ferry back to the mainland. The usual suspects were out on the water – Pigeon Guillemots, Glaucous-winged Gulls, even our daily River Otter – when Alan suddenly shouted out. A flock of seven duck flew past the ferry and landed just offshore: Barrow's Goldeneye, and a new bird for our list.

The Varied Thrush, meanwhile, was proving to be every bit as mythical as the Orcas. Local birders, picking up our blogs on the website, had emailed us with news of their recent sightings but by the time we got there, the bird always seemed to have disappeared. This afternoon was no different. After we had braved the central Vancouver traffic to try Queen Elizabeth's Park, a cast-iron site for the bird, we found plenty of likely habitat but only the ever-reliable Black-capped Chickadee showed up.

On our last morning in Canada, our friend Bonnie returned to Vancouver. We had only hours before our flight to New York when she rang to tempt us out birding to a 'guaranteed' Varied Thrush site. Trouble was, both she and the thrush were northwest of Vancouver, while we and our imminent flight were southeast. Still, this was too good to pass up, so we tackled the rush-hour traffic once again. At least this time we knew where we were going, but sadly the traffic was even worse than expected. We found our rendezvous site but we were late. Still, Bonnie, who should really have been at work, was even later. By the time she arrived, we calculated we had ten whole minutes before we had to head back to catch our flight. We leapt into Bonnie's car and she drove us up into some steep countryside just north of the city. The hillside was being developed, but between the blocks of houses under construction were tracts of forest. These remnants of habitat – pine trees and rocky streams – provided a haven for wildlife amidst the building chaos, and a Varied Thrush had been seen here only the day before. We jumped out the car and scanned in every direction. Five minutes to go and still no bird. Back into the car and we tried a higher spot. Two minutes left and the same result. On for one last try at a more remote part. At three minutes past our deadline it seemed as though all was lost, when a bird flew into a lone pine. We followed with our binoculars and a Townsend's Solitaire came into focus. It wasn't a Varied Thrush, but it was new, it was a lifer and it was bird number 2,173 for the *Biggest Twitch*.

Like something out of *Wacky Races*, we tore back down the hillside, said our hasty goodbyes to Bonnie, and fought our way back across town. We made it to the check-in on time. Just!

So that was Canada. It's official: Varied Thrushes and Orcas don't exist, and neither do beavers, bears, maple syrup or Mounties. But they do a nice line in auks, Surfbirds are pretty cool, and they serve the world's best seafood in deceptively shabby-looking restaurants.

2,173 species

143

7–11 May, Cape May, USA (Alan)

It seemed we had been careless: somewhere between the west coast of Canada and the east coast of the USA we'd lost four hours. This meant our one night in New York was a very brief one, before we headed down the next day to Cape May, New Jersey.

Given our recent experience in Canada, we decided first to check into our motel and dump all non-essential gear before heading off birding at Cape May. The Hyland Motor Inn was *en route* as we drove south. It was clean, if a little tired-looking, and we were given a good-sized room. Less promising was the gang of hairy bikers hanging out in front of the room next door, swilling beer, smoking and guffawing loudly. Luckily they totally ignored us.

A short drive had us at the Cape May Bird Observatory, where we called in to find that the observatory's staff and volunteers were frantically busy. And no wonder: The World Series of Birding was getting under way. This massive, annual 24-hour bird race, which takes place across New Jersey and culminates at Cape May, is the world's premier birding event. What's more, this year was its 25th anniversary.

The World Series of Birding was conceived back in 1983 by local birders swapping tales at their favourite haunt, the C-View Inn, and many great birders have since graced the event over the years. It all began at midnight on 19 May, 1984, when thirteen teams set out to tally as many species of birds by sight or sound in a 24-hour period within the state of New Jersey. Their objective was to raise money for their favourite environmental cause, and to focus attention upon the habitat needs of migratory birds. They succeeded beyond anyone's dreams.

The event is also great fun. Rick Bonney, a founding member of the Cornell Laboratory of Ornithology 'Sapsuckers' team, perhaps expressed it best. 'When I was a kid,' said Rick, 'I used to measure the passage of time by Christmases. Now it's the World Series of Birding.' Since 1984, the World Series – as it is known – has changed the birding landscape and raised over eight million dollars for a wide variety of causes, clubs, and conservation organisations. The New Jersey Audubon Society provides the playing field and the teams simply choose where they want their pledges to go, it is that simple.

Despite being so very busy, Sheila Lego and her staff at the observatory immediately made us very welcome, giving us a mass of leaflets, maps and a checklist. They were excited to hear that *The Biggest Twitch* had arrived at Cape May and promised to do everything possible to help us. Apparently 120 teams were competing in the World Series this year so the area would be crawling with birders; if a migrant arrived, it would be seen. We were blown away by the scale of the event and the wonderful enthusiasm of everyone involved in it.

Anyway, it was time to see what Cape May had in the way of birds. With little daylight left we visited the nearby 'Hidden Valley', a well-known migrant trap. This area of woodland and grassland was busy with birds, and within minutes we

144

were drooling over a male Black-throated Blue Warbler. Drab by comparison, but new for the year, was a drake Black Duck on a small pool.

Then we dashed to the beach, where a scan of the sea revealed Least, Common, Forster's and Royal Terns. None of these was new for *The Biggest Twitch*, but two dark birds moving rapidly north offshore turned out to be Parasitic Jaegers (Arctic Skuas, to UK birders), and these most certainly were. More new birds came in the form of, first, a female Common Eider riding the surf close in, and then, as we headed out to find food, a flock of Fish Crows, which uttered a raucous '*Cah, cah, cah!*' chorus as they flew into the trees to roost.

High winds were battering the Hyland Motor Inn when we woke up the next day. This didn't seem promising for finding small warblers. Down at Cape May Point, our fears were realised and we failed to find any newly arrived birds. Next we tried The Beanery and Higbee Canal, but these two sites proved equally fruitless. Eventually we did find some shelter, though, and with it two Ruby-throated Hummingbirds feeding around a flowering bush. These tiny birds were new to our list and we marvelled that they could have migrated all the way here from Central America, crossing the Gulf of Mexico in the process. This same patch also gave us great views of another Black-throated Blue Warbler, plus a gang of Cedar Waxwings that fell out of the stormy sky.

With the paucity of passerine migrants we changed tactics and hit The Meadows, a wetland reserve just behind the beach not far from the bird observatory. The shallow pools here were teeming with waders, wildfowl and gulls, though none of them were new for 2008. A lone Snow Goose left over from winter would prove a great addition for the World Series teams if it lingered two more days, but we had already seen this species back in January in Arizona. More important though, an excited group of birders came over the dunes to tell us they had just found an Iceland Gull on the beach – a good bird here, and one we needed. We were there in a shot and soon found it roosting among American Herring Gulls.

After the day's birding we had been invited to 'Swap Evening'. This was a new experience for us, and we were a little apprehensive, given the racier connotations of 'swapping' back in the UK. But here at Cape May there were to be no car keys thrown into a bowl; even after nearly five months of being constantly in each other's company we were not ready for entertainment of that type. Swap Evening at Cape May, it turned out, involved a room packed with birders all keen to share sightings with fellow World Series competitors. It was a chance for birders to hear where they might find that tricky species on the big day. We were not sure if such an idea would work in the UK, where birders tend to be a more guarded lot. But here the bird race seemed to bring everybody together. All appreciated that it was first and foremost a fundraising event for conservation, and thus the more birds seen by the more teams, the better.

The evening was presided over by 'Mr World Series', Pete Dunne. Pete has been in from the start and his infectious enthusiasm is a major part of the event's success, ensuring that even after twenty-five years it is still growing. Pete went through the New Jersey list, naming sites where the trickier birds had been seen recently and taking birders' questions about any species their team was struggling to find. He kept good order, and with his ready wit and massive knowledge of the event made it a really great night. It was good to see birders who would soon be arch rivals all exchanging vital information. After the swap, the event turned into a social evening, with plenty of drinking, eating and tales of World Series past. Eventually we headed back to the motel, still together. Despite all the fun, however, we were still a little worried that the day had added just two new birds to our year list.

The morning brought torrential rain – even worse than the previous day's wind. We felt like shutting the door and going back to bed, but with birding having been slow so far we could not possibly ease up. One helpful thing about birding in the USA is that many sites are set up for birding from the car, so at least we could keep going, even in the downpour. We splashed north to Forsythe Wetland Nature Reserve, Brigantine Division, a huge wetland area with a lengthy driving loop, ideal for drive-in, rainy day birding.

Our route took us out onto a raised embankment, with a huge freshwater marsh to our left and even bigger area of saltmarsh to our right. Both were teeming with waders and we hardly knew where to look first. Flocks wheeled and banked one way then the other in an ever-changing kaleidoscope of movement and colour. The vast majority of birds were Short-billed Dowitchers, Least Sandpipers and Dunlins, each of these three species in their thousands. But by working carefully through the flocks we slowly picked out others: breeding-plumaged American Golden Plovers splendid in their gold, black and white finery; spotty Spotted Sandpipers scuttling along the water's edge, rear ends bobbing madly; and hundreds of Lesser Yellowlegs circling the track before landing on the fresh marsh.

Next, a passerine popped up from the sodden grass by the side of the track and flew ahead a short while before ducking back down again. It looked like some kind of sparrow, possibly a new one for the list, so we slowly drove nearer and waited patiently as the windscreen wipers swept rhythmically back and forth. Then suddenly it popped up again, giving us a brief but good view. A quick look at the field guide confirmed it: male Nelson's Sharp-tailed Sparrow. This dapper little chap was new to our list. Then, a few hundred metres further on, a large, dark finchlike bird flushed from the track and flew high up into some reeds; we soon had a clear view of a handsome male Bobolink, our first of the year.

Despite the rain, we saw plenty more great birds, including Black Skimmer, Black Duck, Great White and Snowy Egrets, Glossy Ibis and Osprey. But we had still not found White-rumped Sandpiper, which we had learned at the swap meeting could be seen here if you were prepared to scan the thousands of other waders. We could see that a mass of waders was feeding on mudflats in the distance, but unfortunately we could also see that the tide was rising fast and steadily pushing them off. Panic! We tore along the track and reached the vanishing mudflat with only minutes to spare before the whole area was flooded. Frantically we scanned the mass of birds before us, as thousands of waders were taking to the air and away into the rain-soaked sky. At last we had one: a White-rumped Sandpiper. Then we found another, and another – and then they were gone, along with all the other remaining birds, as the rising waters took over. Phew!

We left Brigantine and headed inland to Belleplain, where the rain was even heavier. Ironically, the first birds we saw were more waders: a Spotted Sandpiper and four confiding Solitary Sandpipers were feeding by a small lake in the forest.

But it was warblers we needed, so we pulled on our waterproofs and braved the downpour. Expectations were low as we trudged along the muddy forest tracks. Every time we attempted to look up into the canopy, huge drops of water exploded into our eyes and drenched our bins. But persistence paid off and a gorgeous male Yellow-throated Warbler, new for the year, fed just above us. Like so many American warblers, you can guess the name once you get a decent view. What was the salient feature of this one? A bright yellow throat, of course! Next up was another classic example: Black-and-white Warbler, living up to its name perfectly. If only all bird names were so intuitive.

Other damp birds we came across in the woods included both Scarlet and Summer Tanagers, Blue-grey Gnatcatcher, Wood Thrush and Northern Flicker – none of them new but all great to see. Then a drab little flycatcher popped up, one of the *Empidonax* genus, which are notoriously difficult to identify in good conditions, let alone a torrential downpour. But we like a challenge, so we stood still and watched carefully as this little chap tried to find food in the downpour. It was good to use a little brainpower, after all those gaudy, easy-to-identify tanagers and the like, and we noted key features on the Dictaphone before heading back to the car. In the dry, we checked our notes against the field guide, where the long broad bill, greenish upperparts, narrow eye-ring, clear wing-bars and long primary projection led us to Acadian Flycatcher. The distribution map confirmed this was very likely, so we were happy with another new bird for our list. Sometimes birding in the rain ain't so bad.

By dawn on 10 May The World Series of Birding 2008 was well under way. The most fanatical teams had kicked off at midnight, searching for owls, nighthawks and any other birds that might hoot, squeak or make any other identifiable sound before it was light enough to see. Hundreds of birders were out there, criss-crossing the state of New Jersey and leaving no bird unseen as they headed for the midnight finish line at the Cape May Bird Observatory. Although we were playing a longer game, we just couldn't help getting swept up in the excitement and trying that bit harder to clock up new birds for our day list.

Meanwhile our main target was the aptly named Saltmarsh Sharp-tailed Sparrow. We headed for the west side of the Cape May peninsula where we knew, from the swap meeting, that we had a chance. Our first stop was a remote boat ramp at Jakes Landing, where there had been some recent sightings, and we hoped our luck would be in. But when we got there and saw how vast the area was, the task seemed daunting: how could we find one small bird out there? Scanning the grasses revealed a few small birds, but each one turned out to be either a Marsh Wren or a Seaside Sparrow. Next we tried East Marsh, where the habitat extended over an even bigger area. Two Eastern Kingbirds flew in, but no sparrow. Our chances were looking slim to non-existent.

Giving up on our sparrow, we headed to the nearby beach where thousands of Laughing Gulls had joined a feeding frenzy along the tide line. The air was full of beating wings and stabbing bills as the birds swooped and dived into the shallows right in front of us. We soon realised they were feeding on the newly laid eggs of Atlantic Horseshoe Crabs. It was a spellbinding spectacle. Among the gulls, waders fought for a share of nature's bounty, while crabs that had become marooned on the beach had themselves become meals for the larger American

Herring Gulls. These weird, prehistoric-looking crustaceans reminded us of squat battle-tanks, with their armoured shells and long cannon-like tails. And, like tanks, they were helpless once on their backs, legs kicking in thin air as the hungry gulls swooped down on them.

Heading back to The Beanery, we drew a blank for new birds yet again, though it is hard to be too disappointed with American Redstart, Blue-headed Vireo, Yellow Warbler and – one of my all-time favourite American birds – a male Prothonotary Warbler. It had been a great day's birding but not a single new species for *The Biggest Twitch*. So, with our list stuck on 2,186, our thoughts turned to all the other birders out there taking part in the World Series. How had they fared? Who had recorded the most species? What rarities had been found? We would have to wait until morning for the answers.

It's not very often we get invited out to breakfast. But this was no ordinary breakfast: it was the post-World Series of Birding Breakfast and Award Ceremony. We did feel a little out of place, as we were not officially competitors, but as soon as we entered the huge ballroom in the Seafront Hotel, we knew we had done the right thing. The place was packed with hundreds of birders, all talking ten-to-the-dozen about their adventures. It was a great atmosphere and we were soon in the thick of it, chatting to people about their best birds and their worst dips. An enormous buffet-style breakfast was laid out and we joined the queue, heaping huge amounts onto our very large plates.

At last Mr World Series of Birding, Pete Dunne, took to the podium to announce the results. The event could almost be subtitled the Pete Dunne Show, as this charismatic figure is both its driving force and figurehead, and obviously loves the limelight. Pete had the room's undivided attention as he ran through a history of the event and introduced the founding members, before moving on to the all-important results. The overall winners were the 'Lagerheads', with an impressive tally of 229 species recorded during the twenty-four hours. The guys received the Urner Stone Cup and vowed to be back to defend their trophy the next year. Almost as impressive was the 'Wild Bird' team, which racked up all its 145 species in a tiny recording area south of the canal near Cape May Point. We were delighted to see so many youth teams involved, each of which enjoyed their moment on the podium.

The World Series of Birding is clearly going from strength to strength, and one year we would love to return and compete in it ourselves. For now, though, we had a flight back to Europe to catch. We headed back to JFK Airport, where we said goodbye to the USA with our year list still stuck on 2,186.

2,186 species

PART FIVE

Europe high and low

12–14 May, North Wales (Ruth)

It was rare that we had a spare moment to catch our breath when we visited the UK, but on this occasion we had two whole days before heading back to the airport. So how did we spend our time? We went birding, of course! This time, back on home turf, we were doing the guiding, showing our very good friends, Richard and Julie Birch, some of the special birds on our doorstep in north Wales.

I had first met Richard in 1996 when he employed me as his marketing manager for the Schweppes brands in Africa. We hit it off immediately: same bad sense of humour, same love of Africa and – though I only discovered it after I'd left the company – the same love of birds. Richard and I remained firm friends after we'd gone our separate business ways. He is heavily involved in the Berkshire, Buckinghamshire and Oxfordshire Wildlife Trust and often showed me his local reserve at College Lake. Now it was our turn to repay the compliment and take him birding on our local patch, as we looked for new birds for our list.

We picked Richard up from his holiday cottage at 4am, in the dark, and took him to the end of the world – literally. World's End is *the* place in North Wales to see our first target bird, Black Grouse. The Berwyn Mountains at Llangollen are a wild place, but on this particular morning they were showing their kindly side. The dawn, though bitterly cold, was beautiful, with clear skies and no wind. Once above the tree line, we could see for miles across the open moorland, and sounds carried through the crisp air. A Grasshopper Warbler began its reeling song from a bush somewhere on the hillside. This was a new bird for the year but not quite what we were after.

We drove further along the single-track lane as it wound between banks of plump, purple, broccoli-topped heather. At the highest point of the moor we pulled over into a lay-by, eased out of the car as silently as possible and then stood and listened. We didn't have long to wait. Over the moor carried the distinctive bubbling sound of several Black Grouse. The coffee-percolator call of the males was interspersed with a weird '*cceerrrek!*' sound as they leapt into the air. We knew they were out there somewhere; all we now had to was see them.

That didn't prove too difficult either. A chunky black bird with red eyebrows, the male Black Grouse has a white bum that shows up for miles when it raises its tail in display. Like miniature black peacocks, a gang of four males with fanned black tails and flashing white rear-ends strutted their stuff in the middle of a clearing, all vying for the attention of the dowdy females, who lurked at the edge of the surrounding heather. And as if Black Grouse weren't enough, a Red Grouse suddenly erupted from cover behind us like an ungainly rocket, cackling 'go-back, go-back!', before crash-landing in a rather undignified fashion into the heather.

When it's on form, World's End offers truly great birding. We watched as a Hen Harrier floated over the heather like a pale grey ghost, a Common Cuckoo flew along the ridge top, Lesser Redpolls flitted around a small conifer plantation and four Common Crossbills shot overhead.

And there was more to come: first a White-throated Dipper (simply 'Dipper' to most UK birders), which swam from rock to rock along the bed of the valley-bottom stream before hopping out for a good preen on a sunlit boulder, and then a gloriously colourful male Mandarin Duck – an unusual record for these parts and new to our list. Six quality new birds, and all before breakfast! Richard was impressed. I'm not sure that Julie was though, as later we regaled her with what she'd missed out on, while all tucking into a slap-up breakfast at the Princes Arms in Trefriw, one of our favourite local eateries.

Next, Alan and I went back to school for a test. To be more precise, we visited the pupils at Craig-y-Don school where we gave a talk about *The Biggest Twitch* and were grilled thoroughly by Marc Hughes, the headmaster – who had joined us in Spain a few weeks earlier – and the members of the wildlife club. The biggest bird we had seen in flight (California Condor), the smallest bird (Ruby-throated Hummingbird), the fattest (probably the Ocellated Turkeys in Mexico on their diet of biscuit crumbs), our favourite bird and our favourite mammal: all came under scrutiny from these young wildlife enthusiasts. They'd even made a huge map of the world, which they pinned on the wall, and marked our crazy, zigzagging progress with Toco Toucan marker pins to show where we'd been.

Back at home, our suitcases awaited us yet again. Ahead was just a short European trip, but one that would include hot temperatures, strong sunshine, deep snow and blizzard conditions. We packed our kit for all extremes, and with our tally standing at 2,192 species, headed back to Manchester airport.

2,192 species

15–28 May, Cyprus and Turkey (Alan)

'Tremendous!' Owen Roberts' deep, fruity voice broke through the hubbub of meetings and greetings at Pafos airport in southwest Cyprus. 'Look at that, will you?' he boomed to his wife Glynis beside him.

OK, so the actual words may not have been identical second time around, but it usually goes something like this whenever we meet Owen and Glynis. Owen is consistent, if nothing else, and loves to take the mickey at any opportunity. He was convinced that I had put on even more weight since our last visit in March. Sadly, he was right.

As always, the conversation and wine were soon flowing. Ruth loves seeing Owen and Glynis, as they always enjoy a good bottle of red. But of course we were here to see birds not just socialise. Most migrants had already headed north, but Owen still thought some new birds would be possible before the four of us left for eastern Turkey. We had been to the same area last May and had enjoyed a wonderful bird-filled week. This time we were trying to compress the week into just four days. It would be hectic, but the rewards might be amazing.

We started on Paphos headland, early the next morning, where we found a fine male Woodchat Shrike and four Spotted Flycatchers. Then we headed inland and quickly found a new bird: a male Black-headed Bunting throwing his head back in exuberant song. We were surprised by how the landscape had changed in the few weeks since our last visit. Gone were many of the lovely wild flowers, and the land already looked dry and dusty. It was only May. What would the next few months be like?

Our musings were interrupted as a flash of electric blue heralded a European Roller beside the road. Owen slammed on the brakes and we leapt out to enjoy this wonderful bird, enjoying great scope views as it landed in a dead tree. We then continued deeper into the hills, following narrow twisting lanes past dry stream beds to an area known as Anarita Park, where a few scruffy goats browsed among the rocks. As we scanned the line of telegraph poles that marched across the small valley, Glynis spotted a small raptor flying almost alongside us that swept up and landed on one of the wires ahead. This was what we were hoping for and we quickly had it in our scopes: an immature male Red-footed Falcon – and another new bird for the year.

Early next morning, we visited the Fassouri reedbed on the Akrotiri peninsula – near the huge RAF base. This is one of the few sites that still has water in late spring and it was busy with birds. Waders were feeding around the shrinking pools at the edge of the huge wall of reeds. Spur-winged Lapwings were getting very agitated about large cows grazing the lush grass, while a fine brick-red Curlew Sandpiper picked away at the surface, along with Wood Sandpipers, Little Stints and four Ruffs. The area was alive with wagtails, with both blue-headed and black-headed races of Yellow Wagtail adding colour to the scene. We scoped a handsome drake Garganey that landed on a nearby pool and, in the process, noticed a male Little Crake – complete with lime-green bill – creeping along the water's edge; a lucky sighting of this notorious skulker.

A Glossy Ibis was next to arrive. But our enjoyment of this iridescent beauty was cut short when I spotted a raptor over the reeds. It was instantly recognisable by its elastic wingbeats and long, twisting tail as an Eleonora's Falcon. This was a new bird for the year and a real beauty, easing gracefully through the warming air to snatch dragonflies on the wing. Next Glynis picked out a male Red-backed Shrike on a small bush nearby. We walked closer and had great views of this second new bird for the list.

No more new birds came our way that day but we did have a real treat when we stopped at Kensington Cliffs on the drive back to Paphos. Standing at the top, enjoying the impressive view, we did not have to wait long before one of the cliff's famous breeding birds floated up to eye-level: another Eleonora's Falcon. We watched as up to six of these raptors stooped, twisted and turned in the up-draughts.

The next day we again headed east across the island, but this time we were making for an airport and a flight to Turkey. There are no flights from the Greek side of Cyprus, where we were, so we had to cross to the northern, Turkish side. Following the Turkish invasion of northern Cyprus in 1974, when much blood was spilt, relations between the two parts of the island remain very frosty.

Owen had arranged to leave his Jeep at a car park in Nicosia, the divided capital of Cyprus. From there we took a short taxi ride to the border crossing. Walking quickly past the Greek Cypriot border post we found ourselves in a weird no-man's-land of derelict buildings, pock-marked with bullet holes. This strip has since been abandoned by both sides and today stands as a chilling reminder of the battles that were once fought here.

A few more questions at the Turkish border point, followed by a close scrutiny of our passports, and then we were through. Another taxi ride took us to Urchan Airport. Our driver did not speak any English but smiled a lot as we passed through a rather rundown landscape along a tired-looking dual carriageway. Gone were the building sites, bright new houses, and teeming shops you would see in most Western counties; a real contrast from the side of the island we had just left behind.

'Look out!' screamed Owen.

The air turned blue as we all saw what Owen had seen: a large Mercedes was hurtling towards us on our side of the dual carriageway, and a head-on, high-speed crash was imminent. Our driver reacted instantly, swinging the wheel to the left, and we swerved violently in front of a large lorry, its horn blaring, somehow missing it by inches. We were all thrown around as our driver fought to regain control. The Mercedes shot past with an elderly gent at the wheel, apparently oblivious to the chaos he had caused. We were all badly shaken and, with the taxi back on the straight and narrow, patted our driver on the back – carefully – for somehow managing to avert a catastrophe.

Arriving at Urchan without further incident, we boarded our flight for Adana in Turkey. Ruth yawned loudly as she took her seat on the plane and was asleep before we even got airborne, staying that way until I woke her up to disembark. By late afternoon we were heading east in our hire car, Owen at the wheel, towards the spectacular mountains of Demirkazik. With the roads almost empty we made good time. The drive was long and roadside birds very few, but as the sun sank, the dusty, rocky scrub began to give way to more mountainous terrain, with steep valleys and rushing rivers. We knew we would not reach our destination before dark so we found a roadside motel, with a Black Stork beside the river opposite, and checked in.

We were out early the next morning, crawling up the twisting mountain roads behind over-laden trucks struggling uphill like huge tortoises. Overtaking opportunities were few, but soon we had turned off the main road onto narrow lanes that were lined with poplar trees and wild flowers. As we reached the Demirkazik Valley, huge mountains towered above us, their snow-capped peaks and massive rock walls gleaming in the May sun. A river tumbled along the bottom of the valley, past flower-filled meadows and olive groves of deep green.

At the foot of the mountains we left the tarmac, heading uphill on a rough dirt track. This was four-wheel drive country but it is amazing how far you can get in a normal hire car if you are reckless enough. Wheels spun, stones flew, and bangs reverberated from the floor pan of the poor Ford Focus as rocks smashed into its underside. When we reached soft mud across the track even Owen had to admit we'd gone far enough. We stepped out onto the hillside and took in the scene. A vast landscape was spread before us, with massive mountains above and villages looking like toy towns in the valley far below. Birdsong floated across the slopes as we drank it all in.

Almost immediately a flash of white wings announced our first White-winged Snowfinch, the bird that had eluded us back in the Picos de Europa. A male landed on a boulder and shivered his wings, showing the Snow Bunting-like pattern. Then three Crimson-winged Finches flew in to land on the scree: chunky birds with large yellow bills, dark caps, and those dark pink wings. As we watched, a group of Twite flew in and landed near the finches.

Then a wheatear flashed by and dropped over a ridge. We were off after it, flushing four Horned (Shore) Larks as we did so. We quickly found our bird and, just as we had hoped, it was a male Finsch's Wheatear, decked out in striking black-and-white livery. Next a gang of six very special little birds landed by a tiny spring and bounced down the rocks to drink: Fire-fronted Serins. These gorgeous finches are also known as Red-fronted Serins, but by any name they are wonderful birds. A deep red cap tops a black head, above a heavily streaked body and buffish-yellow rump and tail.

Our target birds all in the bag, we made our way carefully back down the steep track to the safety of the tarmac. A short drive took us to the mouth of a massive gorge. We walked in, feeling very insignificant as the rock walls closed around us, and soon spied a Golden Eagle sweeping back and forth above the ridge, no doubt looking for its next meal. Next up was a pair of Rock Nuthatches, climbing jauntily up and down the vertical faces inside the gorge.

Very pleased with our wonderful day's birding, we headed off to Pansion Safak, our accommodation for the night. We had stayed here last year, as had Owen the year before that, so we knew what to expect: Ali Safak. Ali is a mountain guide and a real character. A short and wiry man, he greeted us like long-lost family members, with much hugging and shaking of hands. He was dressed, as always, in the local style of black pantaloons that sagged down between his legs. What did he keep down there? There was room for a sack of potatoes, at least!

Hard to say how old Ali is: certainly over sixty and perhaps a good bit more. But he is a bundle of energy, who talks fast and laughs a lot, usually at Owen, with whom he is besotted. Indeed, he laughs uproariously even when Owen has not cracked one of his many jokes. What's more, Ali's English is not quite as good as he thinks it is, and he never lets on if he does not understand something. This often brings a knee-jerk answer of 'Yes, yes, I understand, of course!' to one of our requests, even when he has understood nothing. The result can be confusion all round, but all done with such good humour that we just laugh.

Ali's house is in a stunning location, the view from the veranda offering a jaw-dropping vista of jagged, snow-capped peaks and sheer rock walls stretching to the sky. On this night a full moon rose above the mountains, giving the snow a silver cast, and the night sky was filled with millions of stars as Nightingales sang from the orchard at the bottom of the garden. The magical evening also became a rather late one, as Owen's presents for Ali included a very large bottle of gin, all of which was drunk that night.

Before dawn the next day we were preparing to take on the high mountains of Demirkazik. Yesterday's birding had been great, but today we hoped to go much higher in search of very special birds. Last year, with a bigger group of birders, we had made this trip in a trailer pulled by Ali's tractor. This time, with just the four of us, we could travel up in the luxury of an old, dilapidated Russian 4WD, owned and driven by Ali's cousin.

We took the same track as the previous day and even the 4WD was struggling. How had we got so far in our hire car? As the light slowly came up, we could see we were blessed with another wonderful, clear day. The mountains looked fantastic as the sun crept across the ridges, lighting each one in turn. Slipping and sliding along the track was pretty hair-raising stuff, and a couple of times it felt as though we were going to roll over into the abyss. At last we reached a lofty plateau and the 4WD could go no further. It was bitterly cold, hard frost gripped the ground, but the rising sun brought the promise of warmth. We hiked still higher and found a level area with an amazing view in all directions. Almost immediately we heard the weird, almost curlew-like whistling calls of a male Caspian Snowcock, our main target. But seeing one was a different matter. The place was vast, and we were looking for birds creeping around on scree slopes that mirrored their plumage. It was also very difficult to tell where the calls were coming from, as the sound bounced off the walls of the rock amphitheatre all around us. We scanned and scanned, as the wavering whistles continued to echo off the rock faces, making the hairs stand up on the back of our necks. Then at last we had our birds: two Caspian Snowcocks broke the skyline and we quickly focused the scopes as these large, grouse-like birds crept along the ridge. The views weren't the best, but our main target species was in the bag.

Now we turned our attention to something smaller: Radde's Accentor. This brown bird has a dark head slashed by a bold eye-stripe and is a rare bird in Europe. We quickly found one shuffling around on a steep slope just below us. Meanwhile two Alpine Accentors were feeding on the edge of a boulder field, and we looked up to watch a mighty Lammergeier drift overhead.

Ali's cousin broke out the breakfast, all this mountain air and wonderful birding having given us an appetite. We feasted on boiled eggs, cheese and bread, washed down with steaming mugs of tea, and peeled off our winter layers in the warm sunshine. It was a perfect morning and we did not want to leave this magical place. As we began to pack up, snowcocks called again – this time closer. Where were they? Suddenly we saw two of the big grouse chasing another across the slope above us. One of the chasing birds gave up and flew, fast and powerful, across the hillside. The other two came to a tumbling halt, whereupon the larger bird mounted the smaller. We had just witnessed Caspian Snowcocks mating! How many people have seen that?

Ali was out in the garden to greet us on our return, and he lapped up every word as Owen gave him chapter and verse on each bird we had seen. After our meal that evening, things went downhill, courtesy of another large bottle of gin and some traditional Turkish folk music. Ali was keen we should celebrate our success in style, and before long he and Owen were dancing around the dining room 'singing' loudly, with Owen attempting to learn the loud finger snapping that came with the dance. It was not a pretty sight.

Everyone was looking very tired over breakfast the next morning – even Owen being uncharacteristically subdued. There was only one solution: time to go birding. We thanked Ali for another wonderful stay, took a last lingering look at the mountains and headed out – pausing briefly in a forest area on the way down to jam in on a calling pair of Krüper's Nuthatches.

It was a long drive east to the River Euphrates and the bustling town of Birecik. Our first stop was in town, at a tea garden beside the river. The locals sat playing chequers in the shade. They knew from our binoculars and craning necks exactly why we were here, and the owner soon came over to show us frame-filling photos of Pallid Scops-Owl, taken at this very spot, normally a regular roosting site. Sadly he had not seen the bird for some days. This was bad news, as last year we had struck lucky before we had even finished our first cuppa. A few of the men broke off their game and wandered around to see if they could see the bird, but in vain. Syrian Woodpeckers were feeding young in a hole just above us and Eastern Olivaceous Warblers were as common as Chiffchaffs back home. But the owl was not at home.

Time was ticking and we were not seeing new birds, so we moved on. We re-crossed the river and headed down to the old gravel pits just west of the bridge. This was a pretty grim-looking place, with rundown buildings, mangy dogs and huge trucks rumbling past, throwing up a smokescreen of dust. Down by the river itself, however, we were out of the dust and among the sparse reedbeds that lined the shallow pools, and Owen soon found our bird: an Iraq Babbler. This was a mega bird to see outside of Iraq, a country that definitely wasn't on *The Biggest Twitch* itinerary, and had been discovered in Turkey only recently by friends of ours, Neil Donaghy and Steve Cale. We could make out its fawn plumage and long tail as it jumped around at the base of the reeds, though it did not emerge well enough for a clear photograph.

Although this area didn't look very promising, it was a fine example of how, in birding terms at least, appearances can be deceptive, and we quickly picked up Ménétriés's Warbler and Dead Sea Sparrow. An even more impressive bird was showing well, but sadly we could not count Bald Ibis for *The Biggest Twitch*. These odd-looking, charismatic birds roam feral around town but are taken into captivity in winter to ensure they are not shot during their migration south. Thanks to this intensive conservation effort, however, their tiny population is slowly expanding.

Back among pistachio nut groves on the north side we soon found Yellow-throated Sparrow, a rather plain bird with a tiny yellow throat patch. Then, as dusk fell, we headed back to the tea gardens, hoping we might get lucky second time round. Unfortunately we arrived to find a festival in full swing, with drummers, fireworks and dancing in the street. Our Pallid Scops-Owl, unsurprisingly, was keeping its head down.

At dawn the next day we stood beside the road just north of Birecik, scanning some arid fields where last year we had seen See-see Partridge. It was not the most peaceful place to look for birds: passing drivers, bemused by our scopes, waved, shouted and blasted their horns, while a band of drummers began a thumping beat on the other side. So we drove alongside the river west of town where we knew of another site for this species. The river's mirror-like waters reflected the blue sky and yellow cliffs, while Pygmy Cormorants stood on the bank and Little Swifts tore through the air above. We parked by the Bald Ibis Centre, where the ibis were coming and going at their cliff nest site inside the fenced-off compound, and followed a narrow wadi inland, scanning the steep slopes on either side. Soon Glynis spotted movement and Owen quickly confirmed what we'd hoped: a pair of rare See-see Partridges was slowly creeping up the side of the wadi. They were trying hard not to be seen, but too late: they were on the list.

We felt we had earned a cup of tea and, of course, there was only one place for that. We headed back to the tea garden and again searched for the owl. The shade was lovely and the tea very refreshing but our bird still failed to show. Having scrutinised every tree in the garden, we were now convinced it was no longer there. After all, no locals had seen it for days. Fed up at having missed this rare and lovely bird, we went back out into the heat in search of other targets.

A long drive through a parched landscape of dusty fields and rocky, more mountainous areas took us to Halfeti. On a hillside above the river we quickly found a vocal pair of Eastern Rock Nuthatches. We then headed northeast through dry farmland in hope of a Desert Finch, which we had seen here in 2007. It was very hot and few birds were moving. We drove slowly, scanning hard, and then a small brown bird flew across the road and landed on a rock. Not a Desert Finch but something even better: a Pale Rockfinch. This rather subtle, pale fawn finch was a new bird and a lifer for all of us. It showed off, singing its bizarre cicada-like song loudly and even staying around long enough for us to capture some reasonable digiscoped photos.

Further along the same road we reached a small cemetery, with a few cypress trees around the graves. Trees are always worth a look in this open landscape so we stopped for a scan. A small bird flew up and landed on top of one of the trees, and we had our Desert Finch.

Though well pleased with our day, we headed back to the tea garden where we still had unfinished business. This time we searched a wider area, stopping just short of a children's playground, where it was very busy and the trees were much more open: hardly a place for an owl to get a good day's sleep. Once again we drew a blank, but at least we were popular with the café owner and were boosting the local economy with our tea-drinking.

That evening, however, our luck changed. French bird guide Fabrice Schmitt, who now lives in Chile, was staying at our hotel. Fabrice had amazing news: he and his group had seen the Pallid Scops-Owl. Having heard our tale of woe they had tried further from the tea garden and found the bird roosting in – guess where! – the children's playground. Armed with Fabrice's sketch map, we rushed back and quickly found our bird asleep in an open tree close to the swings and roundabouts. Once we had the right tree it was obvious, and we took plenty of photos.

The next day we left Birecik and drove west, breaking our long drive to bird the upland area around the remote village of Durnelik. Fabrice had been here a few days earlier and had given us some good tips on where to look. We walked slowly along a rough dirt track through the olive groves, scanning a boulder-covered hillside on our left, and soon heard the weird tooting calls of our target bird. Soon we saw the makers: a pair of Trumpeter Finches. The area also produced Cinereous Buntings, White-throated Robins and more Pale Rockfinches. We would have loved to stay longer, but with a hard drive ahead we had to hit the road.

It was early evening when we finally reached the Goksu Delta. We checked in at the Lades Motel, where we had stayed last year, and were greeted like old friends by the owner, Nurular. There was just time for a quick peek before dark so we headed out to climb the rickety observation tower overlooking the vast shallow waters and surrounding reedbeds. It was very windy and we felt the tower might just keel over at any moment. Nonetheless, the birding was good: a Dalmatian Pelican flew in and landed on the water, keeping apart from the White Pelicans; Ruddy Shelducks were all over the place; and two Little Gulls picked food from the surface amongst Gull-billed and Common Terns. But we could not find a single Marbled Teal, a species that we still needed after our fruitless search in Spain.

Dawn found us heading straight back to the delta. This time the wind had fallen and it was a calm, warm morning. En route, a White-throated Kingfisher flashed past along a canal and Black Francolins called from the scrub in the grounds of a disused factory, one male perching on a mound to give us great views. We drove to the far end, where some shallow, muddy pools bordering the main body of water were alive with birds. Soon we had our Marbled Teal. And having seen one we soon saw plenty, of course, with ample time to appreciate their subtle, mottled plumage and dark eye masks.

Our Turkish adventure was over. We headed back to the airport for our short flight back to Northern Cyprus. It was early evening by the time we landed at Urchan. We took a taxi to the border crossing and again walked through no-mans-land, feeling a shiver down our spine as we passed among the deserted, bullet-holed buildings in the gathering dusk.

Back on the Greek side, however, we had a problem: no taxis at the border. Owen was not impressed and stormed off in search of a ride. Eventually we all walked down to a busy road and soon managed to flag down a taxi. But by now Owen was fuming – and worse was to come. The taxi dropped us off outside the car park where we had left Owen's Jeep, but there was no sign of his vehicle among the cars in the enclosure. A young man was just locking up the building, but knew nothing about Owen's car. He jumped in his own vehicle and drove away before we could find out more.

If Owen had been annoyed before, now he was hopping mad. 'How could this have happened?' he raved. 'What a rubbish place Cyprus is! I hate living here.' On and on he went, deaf to Glynis's efforts to calm him down.

I was bored with this and decided to look around for help. At the back of the car park I came across a man feeding some dogs and chatted to him. It turned out he was the brother of the car park owner and happily agreed to telephone his brother. Now we were getting somewhere. A quick conversation and all became clear. His brother had not known when Owen was coming to collect the Jeep and had expected a phone call prior to Owen's arrival. In the meantime he had parked it at his own home, thinking it safer there. Seemed reasonable enough to me. Unfortunately he was out on business, and would not be back for about an hour and a half. His helpful brother suggested we could go to the restaurant next door and have a meal while we waited.

We walked back round to where Owen, Glynis and Ruth were waiting, with Owen still muttering about car park owners and Cyprus in general. I explained the situation and suggested that as we were all starving, a bite to eat while we waited for the Jeep to be delivered would be ideal. My new friend Milton was shocked that Owen was so angry; he was, after all, only trying to help us. But by now the red mist had well and truly set in, and Owen was not going anywhere until he had his Jeep back. We tried reasoning with him but it was hopeless.

Ruth, Milton and I headed next door while Glynis loyally stayed in the cold dark car park with Owen, who was still swearing and stomping around. The food was excellent and we feasted on lamb, washed down with wine for Ruth and tea for me. Over dinner, Milton gave us his full life-history in minute detail: his family had fled northern Cyprus when the Turks had invaded. At first they worked in the tourist industry on Corfu, then Milton sailed to Albania, where he befriended a shepherd who taught him the importance of being rich in the heart rather than the pocket. Now he is a painter and decorator in Nicosia, and seems happy – and very talkative!

By the time the Jeep arrived Owen had calmed down somewhat, so we were soon on the road. We got back to Paphos around midnight after what had been a very long day. Our trip had recorded 170 species, of which 35 were new to *The Biggest Twitch*. Earlier successes in Ethiopia had pre-empted some of the new birds we had originally planned to find on this leg, but nonetheless we were very happy with our haul, and our time with Owen and Glynis had been as entertaining as ever.

2,230 species

30 May–12 June:
Finland, Estonia and Norway (Ruth)

The paparazzi were waiting. The flash bulbs sparked and microphones were thrust into our face for a sound bite. OK, maybe a slight exaggeration, but we were greeted at Helsinki airport not only by Pekka, our guide and an old friend of Alan's, as expected, but also by two journalists. Eva and Peter were from a Finnish radio station and newspaper respectively, and had a cameraman in tow. There was no time to lose, so the press gang came along for the ride as Pekka took us birding on the outskirts of Helsinki.

We didn't have to walk far before we found ourselves gazing into not one, not two, but five pairs of amber eyes, which stared back at us from a row of fluffy bundles lined up along a branch. With that marvellously curious way they have of extending their necks and twisting their heads sideways, five Long-eared Owl chicks peered down at us in as much fascination as we stared up at them. Cameras, both professional and amateur, clicked away merrily as the Scandinavian leg of *The Biggest Twitch* got off to a cracking start.

But there was no time to stand and stare, as Pekka herded us on to our next site. Pekka Saiko (not Pecker Psycho, as I'd imagined from hearing his name on the phone) was a man of a few words. Perhaps that's not quite fair: by Finnish standards he's positively loquacious, and would chuckle away at a good joke. But still we found ourselves travelling in companionable silence for hours on end as we drove through the beautiful, if repetitive, Finnish landscape of pine forest, lake, pine forest, lake and pine forest.

It wasn't long before he had us onto our next new bird, Blyth's Reed Warbler, which sat up and sang in full view in a tiny scrubby area beside some wooded parkland. Then on again to a shallow lake with muddy margins, where we logged an exceptional sixty-seven Broad-billed Sandpipers, several Red-necked Phalaropes, a flock of Barnacle Geese and a singing male Common Rosefinch. As we drove away from the lake, a Black Woodpecker swooped low over the road in front of us and vanished into the woodland. This was a pretty good start and the tour wasn't even officially underway yet.

While we'd flown from Manchester into Helsinki, the other participants on this Scandinavian tour arranged by great friend Owen Roberts had flown from all over the UK into Tampere airport further north. The next morning, as our numbers had increased, we needed three separate vehicles to get about. Alan and I stayed in the front vehicle, driven by Pekka One, with the second minibus driven by Pekka Pouttu (or Pekka Two as he became known), and Owen bringing up the rear in an estate car.

Finland is *the* place for owls, and over the next couple of days the two Pekkas lined up quite a beauty parade of these creatures. First up was a family party of Ural Owls. The chick was easy enough to find: just spot the large wooden nest box fixed high up on a pine tree and wait. Attracted by the strange noises outside, a head soon popped out of the substantial hole in the front to see what was going on.

It looked impossibly dishevelled and endearing, with its bright button-brown eyes and hooked yellow bill rather incongruous amid the fluff. Nothing harmless about the adults though, who were watching us very intently from a short distance.

Tengmalm's Owl was next, waiting at a bus stop. This seemed an unlikely place for such a resolutely nocturnal bird but there it was, in all its brown, spotted glory. Perhaps it was waiting for a night bus.

In the *Collins Bird Guide*, Great Grey Owl is described as looking in profile like a 'steamship flue funnel'. This I really wanted to see. We drew up at a good site and scanned for a long time. Nothing. Then, just as we thought we'd drawn a blank, someone noticed a huge Great Grey Owl perched in a tree behind us, looking silently down at us with apparent disdain in its beautiful yellow eyes. The pale concentric circles on its facial disk resembled the age rings on a tree and added a regal haughtiness to its appeal. It truly was 'Great', and it knew it. We must have been close to a nest site, because having seen one we then saw another – otherwise unusual for these highly territorial birds. This second adult had clearly read the guide and perched at just the right 'steamship flue funnel' angle. Perfect!

From there, we descended from the sublime to the ridiculous, though the diminutive Pygmy Owl may not appreciate the description. This tiny predator is ferocious for its size and happy to tackle prey as large as itself, including other birds, which mob it in noisy alarm if they detect its presence.

With four new owls in the bag – all seen during daylight – we caught a ferry from Helsinki across to Tallinn in Estonia, a completely new country for us. Luckily for Alan, the sea was like a millpond and so he was able to enjoy the stirring spectacle of Brent Geese migrating in their tens of thousands as they flew in skeins high overhead, or even low over the sea in front of us.

Back in the vehicles, we threaded our way through Tallinn, which seemed packed with interesting and historic buildings. There was no time to play the tourist, though, as our convoy headed out into the Estonian countryside. Pekka Two had now been replaced by local birding expert Mica, who was a bit of a hit with the ladies: that toned and tanned body, clad in tight-fitting shorts and T-Shirt, could turn a girl's head after weeks on the road.

Estonia seemed a land of extremes. On the one hand, it was like travelling back in time, with empty rural roads, traditional farm machinery and old clapperboard farmhouses dotted about. By contrast, buildings dating from the communist era were a mess of crumbling concrete. And there was also plenty of new money around, judging by the number of bright, shiny Audis, BMWs and Mercedes in the towns.

Luckily for us, traditional farming means plenty of good birds. We started our Estonian bird quest by standing at dusk in a large damp meadow. We waited, our binoculars poised, and pretty soon we could make out the strange clicking noise of Great Snipe displaying. This sound is almost impossible to convey, though experts have described it as 'accelerated clicking, like bouncing table tennis balls' or alternatively 'chinking ice-sticks' or 'wooden bill-clattering'. However you write it, it was a thrilling sound. But we wanted more. Stoically ignoring the mosquitoes that were gorging themselves on this unexpected feast of British blood, we continued to wait – until our bloody sacrifice was finally rewarded with two Great Snipe calling away in full view. We watched this spectacle for an hour, also enjoying a Corncrake – another new bird for our list – and a male Red-backed Shrike.

The treat continued early the next morning with a rash of warblers at a marshy area close to our hotel: River, Marsh, Grasshopper, Great Reed, Savi's and Sedge Warblers all poured out their melodies, while Citrine Wagtails added a splash of colour. Even better for us was the Grey Partridge strutting about on the frosty ground just round the corner. This was a bird we could easily have missed on *The Biggest Twitch*, as it can be hard to pin down to a specific site.

On we continued, with White-tailed Eagle a bit further down the road, and the day was warming up by the time we reached a forested area, where Pekka heard the call of a Red-breasted Flycatcher even before he'd switched off the engine. We leapt out after the bird and followed the song in hot pursuit. However, the song stopped, and so did we. We held our breath but there was only silence. We walked back to the vehicles and the song started up again. We walked back amongst the trees and the song stopped. The wretched bird kept up this game of hide-and-seek for half an hour, before it finally relented and revealed itself.

By now, our birding party was beginning to divide itself into two groups. The first group, let's call them the Young Guns, comprised Mike Duckham, a long-time friend and birder from North Wales who'd joined us with some other friends in Spain, plus Alan and myself. We tried to squeeze in as much birding time as possible in search of every available bird for our list. The others, Maureen and Morris, Beryl and AT, Jan and Jeff, Marion and John, Judith, Rosetta, Byron and Jonathan, were all friends of Owen and had been on many trips that he'd arranged. Their priorities seemed a little different: first, to have a good time; second, to enjoy some good birds along the way. But we all got along famously. The Young Guns would get up very early to squeeze in a few hours' birding before returning to the hotel to join the others at breakfast. After birding all day together, we'd be happy to go our separate ways after dinner, the Young Guns to have an early night before the next morning's early start, while the others enjoyed the hospitality of the bar, singing songs and telling tales, with Owen often acting as chief raconteur.

Back in Finland the next day, our pre-breakfast trip had a particularly juicy target bird, Parrot Crossbill, so this time there were more takers for the early start. It was already light as we headed out at 5am, but the scenery was incredibly atmospheric as the mist floated over the damp green meadows carved out of the pine forests. Round a bend in the twisty lane, we came face-to-face with a gangly young Elk in the middle of the road. It was hard to tell who was more surprised. He sprang off the road with a lurch, but then stopped to look back at us over his shoulder as we took his photo.

Our destination at the end of the lane was a lookout point on the coast, where the conifers gave way to a ledge of exposed rocks from which we could scan the shoreline in the perfect early morning light. Skeins of Cormorants flew past, an Arctic Skua powered by, and a crèche of young Eider chicks bobbed and bounced along the water's edge under the guidance of an adult female, providing the perfect Kodak moment. The scene offered such a beautiful combination of scenery, light and wildlife that Judith became quite emotional. She's a wonderful friend, a retired schoolteacher and a local birder, who leaves her non-birding husband behind to come on Owen's trips. She's also one of those people who never complains and always sees the positive in everything. A scene like this, complete with adorable Eider chicks, was guaranteed to bring tears to her eyes.

Pekka then demonstrated the Finnish way of attracting a bird using taped calls: turn on the tape, place it at the bottom of a likely tree or bush, and then retreat a reasonable distance. The bird, with luck, hears the call and responds by coming into the tree, where it is not disturbed by the watching birders. It worked well with a Greenish Warbler, but the Parrot Crossbills weren't playing ball that morning.

Later we headed to the airport, where much chaos ensued with taxis mixing up people and their luggage, but at last we were all assembled and we checked in for our flights north to Rovaniemi. We were now at the Arctic Circle, according to the signpost, so all lined up for the obligatory team photo, with our mascot, Toco the Toucan – surely the most northerly toucan ever. Multiply the shot by the number of cameras we had between us and you can imagine how long all this photography took. Poor Pekka must have wanted to disown us in embarrassment. Santa also had his grotto here. It was only June, so we weren't allowed to pay him a visit. But if we didn't tell him now, we worried, how would he know where to deliver the *Biggest Twitch* Christmas presents come December? Perhaps that's why Christmas Day 2008 passed uncelebrated in southern Ecuador!

The good, and bad, news about birding so far north is that summer means almost endless daylight. This means you can go birding pretty much all day if you want but it also means that you don't get much sleep. Dawn is ridiculously early – or rather, there isn't much of a dawn because there isn't much of a sunset the night before. Those with the stamina can go birding twenty-four hours a day.

Next day we headed into the woods to look for Hawk Owl. Pekka knew of a sure-fire site, but finding it proved a little tricky as all the forest tracks looked the same. A few phone calls and several three-point turns later we were on the right track, literally. The nest boxes we passed were all unoccupied, but further along the track a lone Siberian Tit shot across in front of us. We jumped out of the van in hot pursuit and were just in time to see it disappear into a hole in a tree trunk. No artificial housing for this family, thank you!

Trouble was, we'd now lost the other vehicles. Where were they? We waited and waited, worried that they'd miss the bird. Eventually they appeared and all ticked off the Siberian Tit as it headed out on another feeding sortie. But what had held them up? It turned out they'd also had a bird in a hole, though theirs had been rather larger. In fact, three juvenile Hawk Owls were dotted around various trees in one particular spot, while a gorgeous adult perched high up, looking after them. This was a beautiful bird, with striking black markings around the face, fierce yellow eyes under beetling brows and a beautifully barred body. Even when it turned its back it was still astonishing to look at, with the pattern on the back of its head replicating the markings on the front and creating a 'false face'. This bird really did have eyes in the back of its head!

Pekka still had another treat up his sleeve. We called in at a café at Kaamanen, which has become almost legendary with birders. Apart from the excellent hot chocolate, the owner has a series of feeders all around, which attract Mealy and Arctic Redpolls, and – best of all – Pine Grosbeaks. These are tough birds to see under any circumstances and are not even entirely reliable here – we met one man who'd spent three unsuccessful hours here the previous day – but we didn't mind, as we filled our boots with close-up views of the feeding redpolls. The best feeder was attached with suckers to the window, so that while you could view it from outside, you could see equally well from indoors and keep warm at the same time.

Alan and I were both inside, refuelling the inner birder with hot chocolate and discussing the finer points of Arctic versus Mealy Redpoll differentiation, when suddenly Rosetta gave a squeal of excitement. A gorgeous red male Pine Grosbeak was on the window feeder. We all rushed over to take a look. He was so close that binoculars weren't needed. Soon the orangey-brown female arrived for comparison. These chunky birds chased off the smaller ones and dominated the feeders, as they took their fill of the seeds and peanuts, giving us the chance to take some great photos. And while their backs were turned, an opportunist Siberian Tit nipped in, just in case we hadn't had good enough views earlier.

Pekka really did have to drag us away this time, but we had a welcome surprise when another Hawk Owl was seen flying over the road. Piling out of the van to follow it, we tracked it through the trees to another cluster of juvenile owls just a few yards in from the road. This new site was a real find. All in all, it had been a pretty good day – and not bad for one that Owen had completely missed off the printed tour itinerary.

We could now tell we were above the Arctic Circle by the temperature as well as the amount of daylight. It was hard to move around quickly when we were as padded as the Michelin Man, with six layers of clothing plus two pairs of socks and gloves.

We could also tell by the wildlife. Reindeer were everywhere, and although these domesticated animals weren't really wild they roamed freely enough. Not programmed to deal with road traffic, they would look placidly at you as they blocked the road, or would dash from the safety of the verge right out in front of your vehicle. And they were substantial beasts; you wouldn't want to hit one. Their bodies were covered in a dense brown or cream coat, their antlers were wrapped in soft brown velvet, they had chocolate brown noses, and their feet looked a little too big for them – as though they were wearing those quaint old-fashioned zip-up slippers. In all, we found them adorable, though I'm not sure Pekka shared our views. We also saw Arctic Hares in a variety of pelts, ranging from pure white to brown and all shades in between, depending upon whether they thought they were best camouflaged against snow or soil.

Pekka took us to a craggy cliff overlooking a river, where a Gyr Falcon was known to have a nest. It was a long escarpment, so it was hard to know which section to concentrate on first, but our luck was in: the bird, which had been away hunting, flew back to the nest. We felt we were a bit too close and backed off a little so as not to disturb it. The views through the grey mist weren't great, but we were satisfied with scoping the adult from a distance and watching as it preened.

Next came a new country, as we crossed a bridge into Norway. There was little to acknowledge the border, apart from a locked hut, so we continued without stopping. Dropping down from the highlands we came to the wide expanse of Varangerfjord, Norway's most easterly fjord. Tiny fishing hamlets clung to the shoreline, their wooden drying racks lined with fish like a row of clothes pegs. Life here looked simple but harsh, and being north of the treeline there was nothing to stop the bitter wind as it whistled across the tundra.

We stopped by a church, which perched on a promontory jutting into the fjord. Through the scope Alan picked out our first Steller's Eiders, one lucky male revelling in his harem of fourteen females. Scanning further out we could see some peculiar black shapes breaking the water and then disappearing again. Soon these revealed themselves as the tall dorsal fins of Orcas. At last! After missing these exciting animals in Canada, we were thrilled to see them here. You could just make out the black-and-white patterns as a pod breached, blew and dived again. It was a fantastic sight and – luckily for Alan – we were enjoying it from dry land.

Further along the point we saw some handsome female Red-necked Phalaropes in a small pool. Dotterels were pottering about among the low heather, and approached us to within a couple of metres when we sat down and stayed still. A Puffin flew past – distant, but clear enough to add it to the list. Then Pekka got a call from our old friend Hannu Jannes, leading another tour group in the area, who told us that a White-billed Diver was in the next bay. We rushed up the hill as fast as we could to get a better view. Another phone call brought another bay and another bird, this time a King Eider. We jumped in the vehicles and moved on again with military efficiency – all except Owen, who had to turn back for the scope he'd left standing on the ground beside the car as he drove off. But he soon caught up with the rest of us and we all enjoyed another new bird. This was a great place, once you got used to the cold. And to think it was midsummer!

Vardø was our destination for the next few nights. Something looked very odd about this town as we drove towards it, and it took us a while to register that it was in fact on an island about a mile from the mainland. We were barrelling along the road at a good speed – Pekka doesn't hang about – and between us and our destination was a strip of rough water. How were we going to get across? What we hadn't spotted, though, was the tunnel beneath the channel that linked the island to the mainland. Amazing! We passed the Vardøhus Festning, a fortress, which had two small Sorbus trees – yes trees! – outside the front door. These two precious plants have to be artificially protected in winter so they can withstand the cold. Being the only trees for hundreds of miles they must be extremely popular with the local dogs.

Our hotel overlooked Vardø harbour, Norway's most northerly ice-free port, thanks to the warming currents of the Gulf Stream. OK, so there weren't any icebergs floating about but it still looked pretty cold to me. What it lacked in ice, however, it made up for in birds: without even leaving the warmth of our cosy bedroom, we could scope the Brünnich's Guillemots in the harbour.

Despite the deteriorating weather, we all decided to carry on birding and headed out in convoy as usual. However, just as we were leaving town I realised I'd left my bins in our room – crisis! – so we had to turn around and go back. Because we were leading the convoy, everyone else turned around and followed us back too. Then, while I was fetching my bins, Mike slipped into the supermarket to buy a snack. The others took this as their cue to go shopping and all piled into the supermarket too. Jan had cut her finger and wanted a plaster, so she approached the assistant at the pharmacy counter and, as her Norwegian wasn't too fluent, tried to express what she required by holding out her finger and rubbing it up and down with her other hand. After watching intently, the assistant nodded in understanding, picked up something from under the counter and – smiling broadly at Jan – handed her a packet of condoms.

Some twenty minutes later order had been restored and we set off again. We made a number of birding stops around the area, seeing some great birds, though adding nothing new to our list. Each time we stopped it seemed to take longer for everyone to round up all their stray hats, gloves, scarves, binoculars and other gear in order to step out of the vehicle. Owen stayed in the car, refusing point blank to get out or even look through his binoculars, preferring to chat through the window to anyone nearby about such critical issues as *Holby City*, the difference between northern and southern accents, and how warm he was in the car. It was birding like we'd never experienced before – and it took even longer to cram everyone back into the vehicles again. Poor Pekka, we must have sorely tried his patience. Perhaps that was why he always disappeared so promptly after dinner.

If Vardø seemed remote, that was nothing compared with the tiny hamlet of Hamningberg, which was right at the very end of a long and winding road around the coast. The drive was amazing, with a wild landscape of exposed tundra and craggy cliffs on the one side, and the cruel sea whipped up into white frothy peaks on the other. If you liked open space and unspoiled nature, this was the place to come. The few dwellings were clustered together and painted in bright, jolly colours to liven up the scene, all constructed on stilts rather than built directly on the unstable permafrost. It was a close community in the middle of nowhere – a stirring place to visit, but I'm not sure I'd want to live there.

We tramped for miles over the rocky hillside in search of Ptarmigan. With such a huge expanse to cover, we spread out to maximise our chances. Pekka headed off in one direction, playing the call on tape. Mike, Alan and I headed off in another. It was strange terrain underfoot: one minute rocky, the next mossy, then a springy mat of dwarf bushes, and occasionally a hidden bog waiting to trap the unwary. The three of us were fairly spread out but we all stopped in our tracks when we heard the distinctive bubbling call of a Ptarmigan. Oh, it must be Pekka, we thought at first, dismissing it, but then realised that Pekka was nowhere near us and that we must have been listening to the real thing. Retracing our steps we searched high and low, but there was no sign of the bird itself and we had to make do with a 'heard only' record.

Checking a small stream as it passed under a bridge, I pointed out a Temminck's Stint to Alan as it stood alone on a tiny patch of mud. We called the others over to look and, as we stood there, a flash of bright blue announced the arrival of a beautiful male Bluethroat. This bird really does live up to its name, and just like the fishermen's cottages, its bright throat added an incongruous splash of colour to Norway's muted tones.

Our Scandinavian tour ended in Finland, where on the final morning Alan and I made a last-ditch attempt with Pekka to track down Ptarmigan. Although it was fine when we left the hotel, just a short way up the road we encountered snow. As we continued up the hill so the snow became deeper, and by the time we'd reached the site for the bird, the grey clouds had descended to ground level. Despite carrying his wooden tripod and heavy scope, Pekka strode off at top speed along the wooden boardwalk and soon disappeared from sight. We followed as best we could, with our boots slipping on the wooden steps and snow flurries stinging our eyes. How could we hope to see a white bird like a Ptarmigan in this? By now I was dripping with sweat from the exertion, having piled on all my layers to keep warm. Alan had decided the weather wasn't too bad and had only come out in T-shirt and fleece so by now he was equally dripping wet, but in his case from the snow and hail – and his walking boots now chose this moment to spring a leak. We slogged up the hill for several miles without a single Ptarmigan, though bizarrely we did encounter a Northern Wheatear.

At last, even Pekka gave up the chase and we turned to go back downhill. But if going up was hard, going down was even harder. Three times Alan slipped over on the lethal footpath and landed flat on his back – which was entertaining for me but less so for him, as his last dry bits also became wet through. I ploughed through the undergrowth beside the boardwalk, which was less slippery but had hidden snow-drifts. A hole suddenly opened up and, without warning, I disappeared up to my middle.

We arrived back at the hotel, wet, soggy and disappointed. We were late, too, and just had time for a rapid shower and very quick breakfast before we had to drive back to Rovaniemi airport. Back in Helsinki we all went our separate ways: Pekka returned to his family, where he was probably glad to escape us and enjoy some peace and quiet; Alan and I returned to Manchester for another lightning-quick turnaround before we climbed on yet another plane and headed for a complete contrast of climate in hot and steamy Brazil. We'd seen 214 superb species on our Finland/Estonia/Norway leg thanks to the brilliant Pekka Saiko, Pekka Pouttu, Mica and Hannu Jannes. This upped our grand total to 2,285 species for the year so far; pretty impressive for the halfway mark. If we could only keep this up, that world record was ours.

2,285 species

PART SIX

Latin reprise

14–30 June, Brazil: Part One (Alan)

Just days ago we had been wading through a blizzard in Finland, failing to see Ptarmigan. So it was quite a shock setting foot into the hot, humid night of Sao Paulo, Brazil. We were tired, dehydrated and hungry after the uncomfortable trans-Atlantic flight, and had slept very little. The 24-hour daylight during our Scandinavian leg had made for a relentless pace, and now we were feeling it. It was nearly the halfway mark of *The Biggest Twitch* and we felt exhausted. Could we survive another six-and-a-half months? The good news was that our bird total stood at a very healthy 2,285. A good score here in Brazil would put us on track to break the world record of 3,662; we were more than halfway there, with less than half of the year gone.

Inside the airport we found a chaotic, seething mass of humanity, with everyone pushing to get somewhere and going nowhere. How we would find the right desk for our onward flight towards Campo Grande? We had already been travelling for over twenty hours and were not in the mood for this. But this was South America and we were hardly surprised, so with a shrug of resignation we waded into the fray and pushed with the best of them. Somehow we retrieved our luggage and fought our way to the Tam Airlines counter, where we checked in for our next flight.

After over four hours of queues and hassle it was a relief to climb above the sprawling city of Sao Paulo, with its endless slums and millions of people. Now we could start to look forward to what lay ahead: the vast wetland wilderness of western Brazil known as the Pantanal. Our flight west took us across a huge chunk of this enormous country, heading over tracts of land once forested but now given over to cattle or soya bean production.

At last our little plane touched down, rather unsteadily, at Campo Grande, a city known as the gateway to the southern Pantanal, and we were delighted to see our friend and guide Fernanda Melo smiling warmly at the arrivals gate. Thankfully she realised that we were pretty shattered, and whisked us away to a nearby hotel to dump our bags and have a quick wash. It's amazing what a little hot water and soap can do – and even more so when it's followed by lunch.

Suitably refreshed, we hit the local park. The great thing about the first day in a new country is that just about every bird you see is new, and we were soon ticking off plenty of wonderful birds. Although we had known Fernanda a while from the British Birdwatching Fair (BirdFair) this was the first time we had been birding together. It was quickly apparent that she knew her stuff, calling new species thick and fast by sight and sound, and soon she announced one of our most wanted birds for *The Biggest Twitch*: a Toco Toucan. This spectacular bird – our mascot species – did not disappoint, as it landed on a dead branch in bright sunshine, flaunting its outrageous banana of a bill.

Altogether we added eighteen new birds in a few hours, and although nothing could knock our Toco Toucan off his bird-of-the-day perch, the runner-up was definitely Helmeted Manakin. This jet-black, sparrow-sized bird sported a crimson crown and nape, and the feathers above his tiny bill were modified to form a protruding horn like a miniature rhino. We finished the day on 2,304 species.

Fernanda may be female, pretty and great fun, but she had been trained by Tropical Birding in Ecuador, so we had a very early start on day two. Dawn found us parked on a dual carriageway on the outskirts of Campo Grande spellbound by a group of spectacular Blue-and-yellow Macaws. And the day continued in a similar vein, as we amassed forty-four new birds en route to our next destination. Highlights included Frilled Coquette, a tiny hummingbird with orange crest and iridescent plumage, Streamer-tailed Tyrants displaying over a marsh and a gang of noisy Curl-crested Jays that worked from post to post across a wooded field.

As we crossed an open plain we saw Greater Rhea, Brazil's answer to the Ostrich, and Red-legged Seriema, a long-legged cross between a bustard and a stone-curlew. But a mammal stole the show here, as we had our first encounter with a Giant Anteater. This extraordinary creature, with its long snout and hairy tail, walked with its enormous claws curled back off the ground, keeping them sharp enough to hack into termite mounds.

Finally, after a long drive over-loaded with wildlife, we approached our destination: the famous Caiman Lodge, about which Fernanda had told us so much. But progress along the entrance track was almost impossible, as the place was heaving with birds. A flock of two hundred Nacunda Nighthawks lifted into the air and swirled over the car, while Plumbeous and Bare-faced Ibises fed in roadside ditches, Whistling Herons waded through shallow pools and – best of all – metre-long, royal blue Hyacinth Macaws swept overhead. Had we died and gone to heaven?

With dusk approaching we finally made it to the lodge. And we were delighted when we saw the place: this was five-star luxury, with our beautiful room over-looking a large lake and friendly staff attending to our every need. The food, when it came, was equally impressive, both in quality and quantity. Clearly we were going to be spoilt rotten.

Wildlife was everywhere – and not always as expected. The next day we headed out in search of a roosting Common Potoo and came back having seen Great Rufous Woodcreeper and Chotoy Spinetail. As we drove back towards the lodge a Crab-eating Fox appeared ahead of us, and we soon realised he was watching something at the forest edge. We waited patiently and an Ocelot appeared. This beautiful small cat, with markings a little like a Jaguar, walked calmly out of the trees and strolled across the track in front of us.

The following day we treated ourselves to lunch at the lodge. Our meal was twice interrupted by the guides sitting on the deck, who found us first a Black-bellied Water Tyrant sitting in a small bush, then a Scarlet-headed Blackbird in a distant clump of reeds. The afternoon was very hot and birding was slow but still we added Common Thornbird and Rusty-backed Antwren. Coming back after dark we tried a little spotlighting, hoping for a Jaguar, and found a Common Potoo, his orange eyes giving him away.

With many of our wanted birds already on the list, we could now plan to target those that we had missed. Of course Fernanda knew just where to look: in a garden over at the staff quarters we collected Swallow-tailed Hummingbird, and enjoyed amazing close-up views of Hyacinth Macaws feeding on the ground.

Then we visited a particular dead tree where a Great Black Hawk sat, just as predicted. Next came an area of tall grass, where we crept in and played a tape. It took a while, and cramp was setting in, but eventually our call was answered and a Small-billed Tinamou stepped briefly into the clearing. A quick glance confirmed that we had all seen it: this was a tough bird to get.

The afternoon was hot and humid and there were no additions for the list. But we still saw plenty of birds. A pair of massive Jabiru Storks tended their young in an untidy nest in the fork of a dead tree, Capped Herons speared fish in roadside pools, and Black-crowned Tityras sat out on a snag to give us great scope-filling views. We also came across two more Giant Anteaters bumbling around the grasslands. They reminded Ruth of vacuum cleaners, with their long nose the nozzle at the front and their huge brush-like tails the dust-bag at the back. By the end of the day we had reached exactly 2,400 species.

It was time to move on from the fantastic Caiman Lodge, which had proved one of the very best birding locations of *The Biggest Twitch* to date. But we still had the company of Fernanda for a little longer. We headed for a patch of woodland where Fernanda was hoping to add another new bird to our lists and, for once, to her own. Chequered Woodpecker had recently been discovered in the area and this was her first chance to look for it. The woodland was bordered by a railway line, which made a good access route, so we left the car at a level crossing and walked down the tracks to scan the trees. It was now very hot and there was little bird activity. A movement caught our eyes – not a woodpecker, but a Green-backed Becard, soon followed by a Crested Becard. Both were good birds but neither was what we were looking for.

We were just discussing how much more time we could afford when a woodpecker swooped across the tracks and landed a few trees away from us. We crept slowly forward peering up into the branches – and suddenly it shuffled up into view on a sunlit branch: Chequered Woodpecker. We had wonderful views of its piebald plumage and red cap, and were delighted to share a lifer with Fernanda after she had found us such a bucket-full of new birds.

As we turned away from the woodpecker we noticed a gang of horsemen just where we had left the car. Through the binoculars we could see they were armed, and a right rough-looking bunch – just like baddies from a western. These desperados all turned to stare intently as we approached. What did they want? Were we about to be robbed, or worse? They did not look the sort to take on in a fight.

One guy was older and, from the glances of his companions, seemed to be in charge. He leaned forward and theatrically spat a long stream of phlegm onto the ground in front of us. Fernanda was not fazed and greeted the gang cheerily in Portuguese. Surprisingly they broke into toothless grins, and the tension immediately broke; it seemed we were not to be murdered. They were curious to know what gringos were doing walking down a railway line in the middle of nowhere, and chuckled darkly as they learned we were looking for birds. Now that the mood had lightened we asked whether we could take their photo. 'Hang it on the wall', said the leader. 'It will keep away the cockroaches!' We bade the gang farewell and thanked our lucky stars we had escaped unscathed.

Sadly we could not smuggle Fernanda on to our flight out of Campo Grande, and we waved her good-bye as we boarded the Tam Air flight. Tam Air, I'm sad to say, won the prize of most frustrating airline of *The Biggest Twitch* by a mile. They seemed to us to be operating like some sort of ramshackle bus company, not an airline, with an amazingly casual attitude to schedules and punctuality. It was very frustrating for passengers like ourselves, used to a more European-style service, to wait for our flight to depart believing that we could not possibly make our connection on time. The staff seemed completely unconcerned and were clearly hardened to complaints.

Finally we got airborne and flew north on the first of two leapfrog flights towards Alta Floresta in the southern Amazon. We flew over vast plains of farmland with no visible natural habitat. As the plane began its descent into a small airfield in the soybean desert we knew we had missed our onward flight by over half an hour. Would there be another flight today? Would there be anywhere to stay in this one-horse town – and would it have anything other than soya beans to eat?

We trudged off the plane in a bad mood, knowing this enforced delay could cost us birds. But good old Tam Air had news for us; we had not missed the connection, as the onward flight had also been delayed, but it was revving its engines on the tarmac and about to take off. We ran as fast as we could out onto the runway, leapt up the steps and collapsed, sweating, into our seats. Then we remembered our bags. Oh well, there was nothing we could do. At least we had our bins and scope in the hand luggage. Off we went again and eventually reached our destination. We waited nervously for the bags to be manhandled off the plane – no fancy conveyor belts here – and, by some miracle, there they were. We ventured out into the heat and sweltering humidity of the Amazon.

Our friend Brad Davies was waiting for us. Brad was to help us on this leg of the journey and we knew we were in good hands. We had kept in touch since birding with him in Ecuador and now, living and working in Alta Floresta, he was just the man to help boost our list.

Alta Floresta, on the edge of the vast Amazon wilderness, has a real frontier town feel to it: bustling but run-down at the same time. Luckily, the Amazonica hotel was only minutes from the airfield, so we soon dumped our gear and went birding. Brad's tiny Fiat bumped along the rutted dirt roads to a small marsh on the edge of the forest. Our target was Gray-breasted Crake but we drew a blank and Brad was really apologetic. We assured him that after eight months of non-stop birding we knew some birds would not show. Luckily, the next marsh – Brad's plan B – soon produced the crake and Brad visibly relaxed. I guess he was very fired up for our arrival and was determined to get us a huge number of birds, so to start by missing the very first one must have hurt.

The light was failing but Brad was not done. We drove to a patch of forest and stood listening and watching. Soon the distinctive calls of parrots came our way, and four Red-fanned Parrots alighted on dead branches, giving us a great view through the scope and a fitting way to end our day.

Back at the hotel Brad told us that the following day we would have a chance – just a chance – of a very special bird; one that was engrained deep in my psyche.

When I was a schoolboy, even then passionate about birds, I had always looked forward to the long summer holidays when we set out on a family trip in our camper van. Sadly my older brother, Richard, and I were trapped in a confined space with almost constantly warring parents. But we each received some extra holiday pocket money for the trip, and while Richard spent his on a daily fix of comics and sweets, all mine went towards a new bird book. My parents and Richard could never understand it, but I knew that money was short in our house and there was no chance of an extra handout once this holiday cash had gone. So each summer I added to my small, but precious, collection of bird books. And one year, aged about nine, I had spotted a book that I wanted more badly than any before: *The Hamlyn Guide to Birds of Prey*. On the front cover was an eye-catchingly gruesome image of a huge raptor tearing apart a monkey, just the sort of thing to appeal to a budding nine-year-old birder. The raptor was a Harpy Eagle. And though I read the book from cover to cover it was that image that I always returned to and that has stayed with me ever since. Not once did I dream that I would ever lay eyes on the bird itself.

Forty years later and here I was in the forests of Brazil about to set out in search of a Harpy Eagle. Good things come to those who wait, I prayed. And Brad was the man to make it happen: he had studied a pair of these awesome birds here at Alta Floresta in a patch of forest right behind our hotel. The bad news was that the single massive chick had recently fledged and had not been seen for some days.

At dawn we headed for the huge tree where the eagles had nested. Strangely, once the youngster had left the nest the adults had completely dismantled it. We stood and gazed up at the mighty tree and Brad explained where the nest had been. Not one twig remained. Weird: I had never heard of any large eagle doing this before. We scanned and scanned, but nothing. While we were waiting, of course, plenty of other new birds appeared, including one of the world's smallest passerines: Short-tailed Pygmy-Tyrant. This bird's name was bigger than it was. It made our Goldcrest back home look positively beefy.

We trudged back to the hotel for a break in the now very hot mid-day sun. Despite having seen some good birds in an impressive forest we did not feel like celebrating. Harpy Eagle would have been, for me, the bird of the year. It was the answer I had given to every journalist or fellow birder who had asked which bird I most wanted to see on *The Biggest Twitch*. And we had just missed it.

Brad had suggested some ideas for the afternoon session. But for once the lure of another bag-full of new species was not enough. All we wanted to do was return to search for the Harpy – and so we did, spending a long, hot, frustrating afternoon in the forest. At one point Brad suddenly froze and put a finger to his lips. We waited stock-still and silent, until we too heard the thin, high-pitched call of the juvenile Harpy Eagle. But where was it? We peered up into the dense canopy, but it was hard to see anything through the leaves. And moving off the trail was impossible to do silently – the last thing we wanted was to disturb the bird and have it slip away unseen. We scanned until our necks ached – but you could have hidden an army of eagles up there. As dusk fell we had to admit defeat. We had been so close to our Holy Grail bird but denied even a glimpse. We were gutted. Not even a Blackish Nightjar on an out-house roof back at the hotel could lift our spirits. Brad really felt for us, and vowed that we would try again in the morning.

At dawn we were back near the nest site and again straining our necks to the canopy. A movement caught our eye, and we watched as a tiny Rose-breasted Chat caught flies above us and showed off in the early morning sun. It was lovely, but only a minor distraction from the job in hand. We waited and scanned.

Then at last we heard it again: the thin, rather plaintive call of the juvenile. And this time it sounded closer than yesterday. The tension was electric: could we find it this time? Luckily it was calling regularly, perhaps hungry and hoping for a parent to bring breakfast. We went for a more pro-active approach, splitting up and making our way slowly through the dense jungle towards the sound. I stepped over a fallen log into a tiny clearing where a little more of the canopy was visible and raised my binoculars to the tangle of greenery, and there it was: a huge pale grey and white eagle sat looking down at me. What a beast!

Now what to do? I could not shout and risk scaring the bird. I hissed as loudly as I could and, luckily, both Ruth and Brad were only metres away. Soon all three of us were gazing up at this awesome bird. I managed to set up the scope and find an angle. Now every detail was visible: the massive meat-hook bill, designed to tear monkeys apart; the disproportionally thick legs, strong enough to pluck a sloth from a branch in flight. Its head look enormous, the fanned crest giving the face an almost owl-like expression. A Harpy Eagle at last! It was another of those magic moments when time stands still. The eagle looked down on us and, happy we were no threat, soon lost interest and continued to look around and call for food. We blasted off dozens of photos, then finally crept away, leaving the bird to his forest. We were thrilled.

It was time for our next adventure: Cristalino Jungle Lodge. A large four-wheel drive collected us from the hotel. Brad had explained that the road would be pretty rough, and boy, was he right! We bounced along the orange dirt track past first cattle pastures and then jungle, and eventually reached a large, slow-moving river. Here we transferred to a motorised canoe and sped upstream over the brown waters with forest pressing in on both sides. Twenty minutes later we were at the lodge. After our experience at Sacha Lodge in Ecuador and more recently at Caiman Lodge in the Pantanal it has to said that Cristalino seemed a little basic. But lunch awaited us – and it was delicious.

That afternoon we were soon out on the lodge's excellent network of well-maintained trails. Forest birding is always tough, as the birds are usually either skulking in the gloom of the forest floor or way up out of sight in the canopy. But Brad worked hard and came up with some top-drawer birds. Amazonian Royal Flycatcher was especially impressive: a nondescript-looking brown bird, until it spread its amazing fan-shaped crest of red and yellow. Occasionally a gap in the canopy would reveal a small patch of blue sky, and we jammed in on fly-over Red-throated Caracara and a screeching gang of Kawall's Amazon parrots. Such was our concentration that we lost track of time and ended up finding our way back by torchlight. It was lucky that Brad had one.

It was still dark when we were back on the trails next morning, heading – by torchlight again – for a 50m-high canopy tower. Brad was keen we should get there early, as the tower was exposed and we would be baked by the sun once the day warmed up. But he had not reckoned on the number of new birds we would encounter *en route*. As soon as it was light we just kept seeing new species and, of course, stopping to admire them: a tiny Helmeted Pygmy-Tyrant sat out for us; a Gray Antbird crept past low down; and two more hummers – White-chinned Sapphire and Gray-breasted Sabrewing – buzzed around red flowers in the gloom of the awakening forest.

As we reached the base of the tower the temperature was already rising. The metal structure looked pretty solid – but it sure looked high. In fact we could not see the top, as it was lost in the lofty canopy above. The narrow stairs made progress slow, as I was carrying scope, tripod and backpack, and as we got higher and the tower began to sway, it was a real effort to suppress my fear of heights. We climbed on and up for what seemed like ages and then suddenly burst out at the top above the canopy.

What a view! A sea of green treetops stretched all around us. Within moments wonderful birds were coming thick and fast. White-browed Purpletufts, Gould's Toucanets, Yellow-shouldered Grosbeak, both Flame-eared and Yellow-backed Tanagers: all moved through the canopy at or below eye-level. It was a real treat not to be straining our necks for once, as Scarlet Macaws flapped slowly below the tower, giving spectacular views, while Bare-faced Fruitcrows and Wood Storks also passed very close. An obliging pair of Striolated Puffbirds popped up in a nearby treetop, allowing us to snap dozens of shots of these large-billed, rather kingfisher-like birds. But Brad had been right about the sun, and soon it was far too hot to be out in the full glare. Down we climbed, well pleased with our high-level birding.

We spent the next morning birding another trail behind the lodge, which led through stands of towering bamboo. At least the birds here tended to feed low down, so there was no neck-aching peering into the canopy. Brad's knowledge of calls helped hugely: we knew what to wait for and what we could move on past. Blue-cheeked Jacamar was my favourite: not only was it beautiful, but also one of the few new birds that sat and showed off – even allowing us some reasonable photos, despite the poor light. Bar-breasted Piculet was another super bird, a tiny-billed woodpecker that was smaller than a sparrow.

Brad had warned us that the day would become very hot later and he was right. As the mist burnt off, the sun beat down from a cloudless sky sending the temperatures soaring into the high thirties. Sweating our way back towards the lodge we heard a loud 'thonk!' We assumed it was workmen, though the lodge was still a good way off, but the thonks continued and we soon realised that they were coming from right above us. A troop of Black-striped Capuchin Monkeys was attempting to open Brazil nuts. Sitting astride a branch, one animal took a two-handed grip on the large nut and brought it crashing down on to the limb. Two more of the troop were working, while many others looked on – just like a typical UK building site! Below the tree lay a good number of empty nut cases, which had been bitten open and the nuts removed. Clearly the hard work paid off.

The second half of the day was spent birding another area of forest upriver, but it was a hard slog. We added just three new birds: a handsome Bronzy Jacamar, a Buff-throated Foliage-gleaner and a heard-only Variegated Tinamou. Some very weird trees grew in this part of the forest, their bark covered in large thorns, like an outsized rose bush. It was dark by the time we trudged back to the riverbank for the boat ride home, tired, sweaty and badly bitten by mosquitoes.

This was the rhythm for the next four days: up early birding the forest trails, a break around noon to hide from the searing sun, then back out on another trail or boat trip as the heat subsided. We encountered some wonderful birds. One morning brought us a lovely Agami Heron seen at dawn on the river bank, while another produced three gorgeous manakins – White-capped, Snow-capped and Flame-crested – all on the same stretch of trail.

Perhaps most impressive was when we encountered a swarm of army ants. This mass of black bodies moved like one organism, pouring so fast across the forest floor that we had a shock at one point when, having been looking up at birds overhead, we found them swarming over our boots. We jumped away hurriedly, brushing off any that remained; the massive jaws of these insects can deliver a very nasty bite. Still, it was fascinating to watch the columns surging forward – especially because we knew that these ant swarms attracted special birds, drawn to the countless insects and other small creatures that tried to flee them. Soon we were enjoying amazing views of Bare-eyed Antbird, Black-spotted Bare-eye, White-backed Fire-eye and Scale-backed Antbird, all dropping down to grab morsels from right in front of the advancing ants. Then a sudden commotion announced a Cryptic Forest Falcon that dived in and tried to grab an antbird. This rare raptor perched briefly, allowing us a great view, before it melted away into the forest.

An early morning boat ride upriver to the Doctor Hoff trail paid off when Brad's meandering whistle brought an instant response from a Nightingale Wren. This elusive bird shot past us at high speed a couple of times, then finally perched in full view, singing away beautifully. We also, finally, saw a Musician Wren, a bird we had missed at Sacha Lodge in Ecuador. And, after climbing a steep forested ridge, eventually tracked down the rare Guianan Gnatcatcher.

A return trip up the canopy tower brought Black-girdled Barbet – like all barbets, a real cool character – plus gangs of Curl-crested Aracaris, which boasted striking Tom Jones perms. We also found a very smart White-browed Hawk, which sat on a bare branch sporting a highwayman mask above its pure white breast.

Of course there is more to Cristalino than just its wonderful birds. This huge, pristine area of the southern Amazon forms a vital link in a network of conservation projects determined to stop deforestation and ensure that the wilderness survives for future generations. And we had certainly had a very productive time here, with a hatful of new birds for the list.

Brad had done us proud. We had much enjoyed birding with him, and had appreciated his rare combination of passion and knowledge with a great sense of fun. On our journey back to Alta Floresta he had one more surprise in store: we stopped by a patch of palm trees, where he played a tape, and in came a Point-tailed Palmcreeper. This can be a tough species to find, and we were thrilled to enjoy excellent views.

Back in town we went for a celebration meal, where we were joined by Brad's lovely Brazilian wife Jessica. The food was good, the company excellent and our list was coming along nicely. We were now halfway through the year and had already recorded 2,595 species. With the world record at 3,662, we were certainly well on course. So far, though, we had been lucky: we'd suffered no serious health problems and had no major travel disruptions. Would our luck hold?

2,595 species

1–7 July, Argentina (Ruth)

The hot, dark night was thick with danger, passion and sex. He bent her backwards over his arm and leaned low to kiss her pale, exposed cleavage. She arched further back and gasped with pleasure, running her fishnet-stockinged leg up the length of his thigh. Her stiletto heels glinted wickedly in the candlelight.

No, don't adjust your set. *The Biggest Twitch* was always more than just a bird race – and here we were, in the middle of one heck of an experience, Tango-style.

I looked across at Alan. All trace of his birder's cynicism had vanished. His eyes were glued to those long, shapely legs and heaving bosom as the dancer wound herself around her partner and writhed sinuously to the urgent tango rhythm. And the pleasure wasn't all Alan's: a tall, handsome Argentinian man in a sharp suit can easily turn a girl's head after months ogling nothing sexier than shapeless khaki and walking boots.

But what on earth were we doing at a tango dinner-dance? Where were the birds, for heaven's sake? I suppose the clue should have been in the name, The Complete Tango Hotel. But when I had searched the internet for somewhere cheap to stay in downtown Buenos Aires, Latin dancing had been the last thing on my mind. The fact that it was affordable and – even more importantly – close to a nature reserve was all I had noticed, as I booked us in for a couple of nights.

On arrival we had drawn up beside a solid wooden door. Two men in heavy overcoats stood guard outside, their collars turned up against the cold and the glowing tip of a cigarette adding a spot of colour to the dark Buenos Aires night. One storey up, light flooded out of a big studio window and the sound of a live tango band blared into the night. Could this really be a hotel? One of the bouncers opened the door onto a narrow spiral staircase with an ornate wrought iron railing. Not the ideal entrance, when you're loaded with suitcases, rucksacks and telescopes. Upstairs, the music was even louder, the pulsating rhythms punctuated with rounds of applause.

'Welcome to the Complete Tango Hotel!' the young receptionist had said, as we found ourselves entering an office. Reality was beginning to register, as he offered us a seat and confirmed that we were booked in for two nights for bed and breakfast. 'Would you like to sign up for our special evening entertainment?' he continued. 'Three-course dinner and a live tango show – it even includes a free tango lesson.'

By now it had gone 11pm and we were exhausted birders. All we wanted was to sleep, so we had declined the offer and he had shown us to our room, up more spiral stairs and then along a narrow corridor. Chinks of light glowed through shuttered windows on our left, and the sound of the band and audience were even louder. We walked round two sides of the auditorium, as the show continued behind the wall, feeling as though at any second we'd step through the velvet curtains into the spotlight.

At the very last door on the right, our host stopped and ushered us through into what I can only describe as a museum piece. We were back in the 1940s. The furniture, lighting, bed, wallpaper, curtains and pictures on the wall had all been artfully chosen to transport us back to the tango's heyday. Vinyl records and their sleeves were arranged in a glass cabinet, along with porcelain figurines of dancers. On a small wooden table beside the shuttered window sat a period manual type-writer, forever silenced in mid-sentence. Lace tablecloths protected the bedside tables, on which sat – our every need anticipated – two steaming cups of tea. Between them, an inviting bed was piled high with pillows and blankets.

'Your breakfast will be just outside in the morning,' said our host, and with that he left us. Opening a small door, we stepped back into the twenty-first century in the form of a tiny but beautifully appointed en suite bathroom. By now it was nearly midnight. Too dog-tired even to shower, we collapsed straight into bed. Outside our room the music finally drew to a close, but not even the rapturous applause could keep us awake.

The next morning, we awoke to silence. We jumped into our clothes and peered cautiously around the bedroom door. It was as though last night had been an illu-sion: there was no one about – no music, no dancers, no candlelight. But there *was* breakfast, laid out on a small balcony overlooking the dance hall. And below us were the stage, the bar and the dining area, all looking strangely diminished in the daylight. We hurried through our breakfast, grabbed our kit, thundered down the spiral staircase in our walking boots and pulled open the heavy wooden front door.

Winter smacked us soundly in the face. The sky was a seamless grey and the air was so cold it chilled your lungs. This was a shock. So far, ours had been a year of perpetual spring. In Texas and southern Europe we had been chasing bird migra-tion and so we had also chased spring, with its warm weather, new blossom and unfurling leaves. In between these strategic birding locations, we had sandwiched equatorial countries with a constant hot climate, where birds were plentiful all year round. We had tasted winter in northern Europe but hoped we had seen the last of it.

We pulled our fleece hats down firmly over our ears and headed out into Buenos Aires. Our destination: the nature reserve of Costanera Sur. This protected wetland is right on the edge of the city, squeezed between a trendy development – much like the London Docklands – and the broad River Plata, where it meets the Atlantic. Skyscrapers fringed the edge of wild lagoons and pools like a row of uneven teeth. Apparently there had been plans to build housing and a football stadium here but, luckily for wildlife, funds had run out, so it had remained a nature reserve, sandwiched between city and sea. Alan had visited here many years before and had been enthusing about this fantastic nature reserve right on the edge of the city: freshwater pools, reed-fringed lagoons and a myriad of waders and waterfowl to delight the birder. He told a good tale and I was quite keen to see this watery wonderland.

However, a sorry sight met our eyes: no pools, no lagoons and not a duck in sight. Buenos Aires seemed to be experiencing a drought and the wetland had dried up, the pools first becoming mud-scrapes and then covered by grass. Raised footpaths criss-crossed areas that should have been covered in water but had now turned into a well-established grassland, with patches of shorter grass among the clumps of tall, waving Pampas Grass. Clearly there was little chance of adding any water birds to our list, but that didn't stop us trying for some new grassland species.

This was one of the few times we had been birding by ourselves in an unfamiliar area, even though Alan had visited Argentina on a bird tour years before. It made us concentrate even harder on the birds, as we could not afford to miss a thing. In *Birds of Argentina and Uruguay* by Tito Narosky and Dario Yzurieta, the rather sketchy illustrations made many of the birds appear to be variations on a theme of brown, so we looked extra carefully for any distinguishing features.

First up was Black-and-rufous Warbling Finch. Initially we caught only glimpses as a pair flicked through the leafy branches: a black bandit mask here, a stripe of white there, a rufous throat next. But at last our persistence was rewarded as one of these striking little birds appeared in all its glory, the black mask edged above and below by a thin white stripe, which stood out against the russet throat and waistcoat. The tones may have been muted after the paint box colours of Brazil, but these were handsome birds nonetheless.

Next we were entertained by a fearless Spectacled Tyrant, which ran about on the short lawn beside the path. Head down, he would charge towards us, then stop suddenly, pause with his head cocked on one side, change direction and charge away again. He also lived up to his name: black all over, with a striking flash of white in his wings when he flew, and a cream ring around his eye that gave him a rather odd appearance, as if he was wearing thick, bottle-bottomed spectacles. I tried to photograph him with our little camera, but he never stayed still for more than a second or two, so I was left with plenty of shots of something black and blurry – or just the tip of his tail as he exited stage left.

It seemed that Argentinian birds also had some excellent names. We were delighted to add White-tipped Plantcutter to our list for the name alone, and we were just as pleased to pick out Freckle-breasted Thornbird and Black-capped Warbling-Finch in the scrub beside the path.

Soon the light began to fade and the winter wind nipped harder at our finger-tips. I pulled my gloves on and thrust my hands down into my pockets. It was time to return to the hotel and thaw out around another steaming hot cup of tea, as we updated our bird list on the computer.

Back at reception we were asked once again whether we wanted to join the tango dinner-dance. This time we felt a little more adventurous. After all, we would have to listen to the music all night anyway, and the alternative meant braving the dark, sleety streets in search of somewhere else to eat. We took the plunge and signed up for the evening entertainment.

At the appointed time, and dressed in our cleanest T-shirts, jeans and trainers (a change from walking boots, at least), we made our way down to the auditorium. We were rather alarmed to be shown to a table that was literally right in front of the stage. Food and wine soon arrived, however, and we tucked in.

Halfway through the main course, the lights dimmed and the orchestra struck up. Then began three hours of amazing entertainment. The cast took us through the history of the tango, from its origins in the competitive footwork of men from opposing street gangs vying to outdo each other, to the introduction of female dance partners and the high-kicking moves we associate with the dance today.

As the girls demonstrated how the tango had evolved through the ages, their outfits became skimpier, their stiletto heels higher and their moves ever more suggestive. (How did they get their legs up that high?) Alan stopped eating and gave the floorshow his full attention, as lace and fishnets flashed past our table just inches from his face.

Then came what we'd been dreading: audience participation. All around us people jumped up from their tables, eager to try out the steps they'd just learned and to dance with a real Argentinian tango expert. Alan and I clung on to the table as two very determined dancers tried to prise us out of our seats. Why didn't we want to dance? They just didn't understand. But there was no way we were going to undergo total humiliation, what with our four left feet and completely inappropriate shoes. At last we agreed on a compromise, and reluctantly had our photos taken as we posed in the arms of our respective dance partners, attempting forlornly to point our trainer-clad toes. Then we let the experts entertain us with more dances and songs, while we finished up our food and wine. At last we staggered to our bedroom way after midnight with our ears still ringing to the rhythms of the tango. What a way to finish our first Argentinian birding day!

We awoke the next morning nursing one of our few hangovers on *The Biggest Twitch*. Today was going to be tough, given our slightly fragile state. And first we had to pick up our hire car, which meant finding our way to the Thrifty office right in the heart of town, and then navigating our way out of the city in a strange vehicle.

Buenos Aires traffic has a fearsome reputation – and, believe me, it is entirely justified. No wonder the rental company required such a high deposit. We loaded up the car, said a few Hail Marys and plunged into the fray. It was just like the dodgems but without the big rubber bumper. Forget mirror, signal, manoeuvre: mirrors are for checking your hair, signals are for wimps, and the only manoeuvres are violent swings of the wheel as you swerve between cars at maximum speed. As for lane discipline: what are lanes?

Somehow, more by luck than judgement, we found ourselves past the city centre and heading out of town in the right direction: south. A few road signs later and we found we were even on the right road; those Hail Marys had obviously done the trick. According to the road map of Argentina that we'd bought from the rental company we were looking to drive about three inches south along the Atlantic coast to the seaside resort of San Clemente de Tuyu. We'd be there by lunchtime, we thought.

As we drove south, leaving the urban sprawl behind, the fog lifted and the sun came out. Argentina suddenly looked like a different country. We crossed a vast flat expanse of open grassland, the pampas, stretching as far as we could see. This enormous prairie was dotted with small, reed-fringed pools and dumpy, wind-twisted trees. It was prime cattle territory, and we passed herd after herd of strong and fit-looking animals. Getting a good steak supper would clearly be a doddle.

Spotting some pools beside the road we pulled over to see what birds they held. Most obvious were the Chilean Flamingos. These pink, haughty-looking creatures also sported crimson knees and feet – not that we could see the latter underwater, as they performed their military slow march forward, sluicing their bills from side to side through the water to feed. A pair of swans with black necks cruised by: these were unmistakably Black-necked Swans. Others that were white all over apart from a red bill were Coscoroba Swans. Among several species of duck were Ringed and Speckled Teal, Red Shoveler and Lake Duck – the latter with a sticky-up tail like its relative, the Ruddy Duck. Not a bad haul for a roadside pool, we thought.

Three inches turned out to be a very long drive. It was evening when we turned off the main north-south 'Pan-American' highway and reached our destination of San Clemente. But we still had to find our accommodation. At first San Clemente felt a little like El Rocio in Spain, with its higgledy-piggledy maze of sandy streets. But there the similarity ended. While El Rocio is bustling, San Clemente was a ghost town. Everywhere was boarded up. Granted, we had arrived off-season, but the whole place had an eastern bloc atmosphere: concrete buildings slowly crumbling, ancient vehicles held together by string and a prayer, and the few open shops offering just one or two staple items. This was a world away from the glitz and glamour of Buenos Aires.

We were in a mood for steak, having passed so many cattle *en route*, but finding a restaurant open for business proved quite a challenge. By the time we had tracked down somewhere with lights on and tables set, we were ready to eat anything – which was probably just as well. The waiter recommended lasagne, so lasagne we ordered. Well, it may have been lasagne, Jim, but not as we knew it. Here's the recipe: open your kitchen cupboard and ignore any pasta, minced beef, cheese or tomatoes. Instead, whip up some thick spongy pancakes and stack these in a dry pile in the middle of a large plate. In a fresh pan, make a ham and mushroom sauce. Take the two separately to the table, pour the sauce ceremoniously over the pile of pancakes in front of the diners, *et voilá!* Argentine lasagne was a whole new experience. Obviously all those prime cuts of beef we'd seen grazing the fields must have been destined for the bright lights of Buenos Aires.

First thing the next morning we headed out into the cold grey dawn. Our directions were pretty sketchy and we had trouble even finding our way out of town, but eventually we were on the right sandy track heading for Punta Rasa. This low peninsula jutted out into the ocean, and as we drove out along it the pampas gave way to scrub, criss-crossed with muddy creeks and canals that linked small saline pools. Bubbles popped slowly in the silky grey water and pocket-sized crabs pottered about on the banks.

As we neared the coast, the bushes gave way first to dunes and then a wide sandy beach. On the one side we had the estuary of the Rio Plata and on the other the Atlantic Ocean, but on both we were exposed to the full force of the wind as it whipped up the white-capped waves. This was a bleak spot, not that it bothered a pair of Two-banded Plovers that pottered along the shoreline – new birds for our list, and unmistakable with their two blackish breast bands. The scopes revealed a pair of Olrog's Gulls on the shoreline. Sounding like a character from *The Lord of the Rings*, these good-sized, black-backed gulls had a black-and-red tip to their strong yellow bill, and were another good one for the list.

Just offshore, Snowy-crowned Terns were diving for fish, their deeply forked tails showing up well in the scope as they plunged repeatedly into the water. As Alan watched, a massive seabird passed rapidly through his field of view. He began to gibber incoherently as he swung the telescope violently to the right.

This had to be something good – but could we pick it up again? Seconds later, as the bird swept past once more, I matched his gibbering. It was a Black-browed Albatross.

This was amazing: a huge ocean-going wanderer cruising effortlessly over the water and we hadn't even gone to sea. It was my first ever albatross and I was unbelievably excited. This regal white bird seemed to glide past on its colossal two-metre wingspan with barely a movement of those long black wings. It was so close to shore and moving so fast that we could barely keep up. But we needn't have panicked: within minutes another one cruised past. And then another.

For the rest of our time standing on the point Black-browed Albatrosses continued to pass by, close enough to watch even with our binoculars. By way of comparison, we watched an Antarctic Giant Petrel. Much the same size, it lacked the albatross's grace and seemed to have to flap harder to make the same progress. By further contrast, a Brown Skua, an aggressive mugger of other seabirds, lumbered over the breakers like a Hercules cargo plane to the albatrosses' Concorde.

It was hard to tear ourselves away from this awe-inspiring spectacle, but we had so little time in this country and so many other sites to try that we had to move on. As we drove back down the sandy track towards San Clemente, a dumpy brown bird without a tail strolled across the road from one side to the other in a very leisurely fashion. Its body was mostly mottled in brown, with a creamy ochre belly and a bright white patch on the throat. Thumbing through the field guide, we discovered that this bizarre bird was a Spotted Nothura, a member of the tinamou family that looked rather like an oversized quail. 'Crosses roads (unhurriedly),' said the field guide, helpfully.

Unfortunately, after our brilliantly successful morning, the afternoon saw us fight a losing battle with the weather. The wind had dropped but the fog had closed in so that we could soon see only a few metres in front of us. We called it a day and crawled back to San Clemente with our headlights on, pulling over at frequent intervals to avoid collisions with the locals who weren't about to let impenetrable fog get in the way of their speeding. Still, at least the enforced early stop gave us the chance to get our bird notes up to date.

The fog had disappeared the next morning and so had the bitter wind. Unfortunately the seabirds had also gone. Back at Punta Rasa we drew a complete blank on sea watching. But before leaving we spotted a flash of movement in a small clump of grasses, where flitting amongst the stalks was one of the handsomest birds we had seen in Argentina: a Many-coloured Rush-tyrant. This diminutive jewel certainly lived up to its name: olive back, yellow breast and belly, white bib, black crown – split by a red stripe – and a striking triangle of royal blue around each eye. This kaleidoscopic little bird proved almost impossible to photograph as it flitted amongst the stems and leaves. Nonetheless, it was definitely bird of the day. We headed back to Buenos Aires that afternoon happy, and prepared ourselves for a big birding day ahead.

The next morning, Alec Earnshaw, an Argentinian birder, guide and photographer, picked us up from our hotel. He'd heard bad weather forecast on the radio, but when the torrential rain showed no sign of materialising we jumped in his car and headed north towards Ceibas. Alec, as we soon found out, was not afraid to change his plans on a whim to find birds. He had been following our progress on our website, and we'd got in touch when we'd arrived in Argentina hoping he'd show us some of his best local sites. This also meant we didn't have to risk driving again. As Alec drove us towards Ceibas in typically madcap Argentinian style he chatted enthusiastically about his life and birding. His English boarding school education had given him an excellent command of the language.

We passed a sign for Otamendi Nature Reserve. Perhaps we should stop here, Alec wondered, although he'd had great birds further north recently. After a moment's dithering, we carried on for Ceibas, which held an area of remnant forest and some pretty special birds. Even before we turned off the main road, we started adding to our list, as Giant Woodrails strutted about on the roadside verges, far bolder than their skulking smaller cousins.

Turning onto a dirt side road we began birding in earnest. First up, two flycatchers arrived in the trees above us, and Alec identified them as Suiriri Flycatcher and White-crested Tyrannulet. Then back into the car to drive a few yards down the road, and Alec jumped out again with his iPod to play the call of Little Thornbird. A few seconds burst brought no response, so we jumped back in again. But no, we should give it a bit longer, according to Alec, so we jumped back out. We were half-in and half-out when Alec changed his mind a third time and jumped in to reverse back to where we'd started. Then out we all jumped again. Should we try the tape on the right or the left side of the road? Which call should we try – Little Thornbird, or how about Short-billed Canastero? Or should we get back in the car and drive a bit further? By now, Little Thornbird had appeared, obviously as confused by the snatches of call playing from different stretches of road as we were.

Alec dashed from one side of the road to the other; he ran backwards and forwards along the same short stretch; he jumped in and out of the car. He couldn't decide where was best to bird, what bird to concentrate on and which calls to play on his tape. Alan and I struggled to keep up: were we driving or walking, looking to the left or the right, and just what call were we playing this time? We were also struggling to keep a straight face, and didn't dare catch each other's eye for fear we'd burst out laughing. Poor Alec. We'd lost time because of the misleading weather report, so he was desperate for us to see every single bird possible. But his indecisiveness didn't really matter, as new birds came thick and fast: Spot-winged Pigeon, Short-billed Canastero, Stripe-crowned Spinetail, Tufted Tit-Spinetail, Green-barred Woodpecker, Brown Cachalote. Wherever we looked along this short stretch of dirt road, something new popped up.

Next we stayed in the car for slightly longer as Alec drove us to a new area. We walked through some woodland and then out into an open area where once there had been a lagoon. Unfortunately the drought had clearly afflicted this place too, and there was no sign of water or wetland birds; climbing up onto a stone wall, all we could see was dry grassland in every direction. However, a little gang of birds was hopping along the fence ahead, stopping to stand upright on the fence posts and check all round. With their funky crests and bright orange legs and feet, they were rather charming – and had the odd name of Lark-like Brushrunner. Unlike so many birds, they were kind enough to sit still for a photograph. Further down the road, we encountered the bizarrely named Firewood-Gatherers, so named for their huge stick nests, which are totally out of proportion to the small birds themselves. Sadly we didn't see these birds actually gathering any firewood, but their nests were pretty impressive all the same.

Another promised wetland area held little more than a patch of mud, and Alec debated what to do. Should we stay or should we go? It was already mid-afternoon, and though we'd done well so far, where would be the most fruitful place to try next? We suggested heading south to Otamendi, which would not only take us to a new birding area but would also start us back in the right direction for Buenos Aires.

By the time we arrived, an hour later, the light was beginning to fail and there were a few spots of rain. We drove up the road cautiously, crossed a railway line – tipping a few coins to the scruffy lad who manned the level crossing gates – and then drove down a dirt track beside the reserve. Unfortunately a fire had devastated a huge swathe of land, so we birded yet another dirt track that ran alongside it. This was hardly peaceful, as quad bikes and speed junkies raced by, and all the time the light was disappearing. But the water-filled gullies on both sides of the road, plus the variety of bushes and trees, all promised birds. In quick succession we added Curve-billed Reedhaunter, such an evocative name and a good bird to see, Wren-like Rushbird, Chicli Spinetail, Cream-bellied Thrush, Rufous-capped Antshrike, Straight-billed Reedhaunter and Grassland Yellow Finch – the last bird in the very dying embers of daylight.

We drove back to Buenos Aires, and were soon back at our hotel and saying our grateful goodbyes to the wonderful, charismatic Alec. It had been a memorable, entertaining day's birding.

By now we'd spent a whole week in Argentina and seen an awful lot of cattle, but hadn't had so much as a sniff of a steak. So there was only one thing we wanted for supper. Although our hotel was in the business district, we found an excellent steak restaurant just two blocks down the road. Right at the entrance was an *asador*, an open fire of glowing coals, around which a number of spits holding various joints of meat were slowly rotating. This was no place for a vegetarian, but the smell was divine and we started to drool. The menu offered big steaks, huge steaks, enormous steaks and half a cow. We both opted for the smallest rump steak on the menu.

Needless to day, the cuts of meat, when they arrived, were colossal, but mouth-wateringly tender and utterly delicious. As hard as I tried, I could only manage half of mine, and the piece I left was still larger than anything you would be served in the UK. On the next table was a party of macho Texans, who had all ordered the largest steak possible. Even they had to admit defeat in the end and ask for a doggy bag.

We were still feeling full when we headed to the airport the next morning, and a two-hour delay gave us plenty of time to reflect on our Argentina experience. Water shortages notwithstanding, we'd had a great time. Argentina had been a gamble, but we felt it had paid off. In just three birding days, we'd picked up 74 new species out of a total 136 recorded in the country, and seen some amazing birds at both extremes of the scale, notably the Black-browed Albatrosses and the Many-coloured Rush-tyrant. We'd had great fun, learned some dance moves, and certainly enjoyed our day out with Alec Earnshaw. Now, just over halfway through our big year, our grand total stood at 2,665 species. We had some tough, but bird-rich countries still ahead, and needed around 1,000 more species to break the world record. All in all, things were looking pretty positive as we headed back to Brazil.

2,665 species

9–14 July, Brazil: Part Two (Alan)

We woke up to a lovely sunlit morning in the Luxor Hotel at Rio de Janeiro airport. This is how airports should be: peaceful, organised and with spectacular views of green mountains. What a contrast to the madness of Sao Paulo just down the coast. Our only concern was whether anyone would arrive to pick us up and take us to Guapi Assu Bird Lodge, part of the REGUA project in the Atlantic rainforest? We had arranged our visit a long time ago but had received no confirmation of the transfer details, despite our emails. But we needn't have worried. Bang on time a man arrived and asked for Alan and Ruth. We were off.

It is a long drive from the airport north to REGUA but there was plenty to keep us amused en route. As we left Rio we could see the Christ statue on Corcovado towering over the city. It would have been nice to visit, but not this year. There were birds to see. In fact birds were everywhere – none of them new, but it was encouraging to see so much life in an area crammed with people and development.

Our driver, Alcenir, was a chatty soul. Luckily for me he directed most of his chit-chat at Ruth, allowing me to scan for birds out of the window. Our new friend was keen that we should learn a little Portuguese, and helpfully taught Ruth the word for 'car'. Then 'car seat', 'steering wheel' and so on, naming – over the next hour – every car part he could think of.

'That's enough for today,' ventured Ruth. 'We won't remember them all!" But he was undeterred. Brake, accelerator, exhaust ... You think of a car part, he gave us it in Portuguese. We later heard that other guests had enjoyed the same treatment, but with farm animals.

Finally we reached REGUA and the lovely lodge, which perched on a small hill overlooking a beautiful wetland, with forested mountains looming beyond. Ruth was very impressed with the standard of everything inside. But nobody was about, so we set off for a walk.

The place was teeming with birds and we quickly picked up five new ones, starting with a shocking scarlet Brazilian Tanager before we had even left the lodge garden. The tall trees at the start of the trail held Yellow-lored Tody-Flycatcher. At the edge of the marsh a dapper little White-headed Marsh-Tyrant popped up on a reed-stem. And on the far side of the wetland we found Black-capped Becard and Azure-shouldered Tanager from a track that ran along the forest edge.

Back at the lodge, other guests had returned from their various activities. We met Kelly Jacobs from the World Land Trust who was here to research a potential project, while another girl was here researching eco-friendly sources for supermarket vegetables. Perhaps less surprising were two Dutch birders, Roy and Anja de Haas, whom we quickly realised were very experienced and widely travelled. Soon we were chatting away like old friends and comparing our birding adventures from around the world.

Dinner was served around a large table and the conversation flowed. We were joined by Nicholas, who manages the reserve and farm at REGUA. He is a real character, educated in an English public school, with a huge general knowledge, a zest for life, and an infectious enthusiasm for everything he is involved in. REGUA is his life and he is passionate about driving the project forward. The only problem for Nicholas is that there is only one of him; his job clearly demands several people, and our fear was that he would explode right in front of us.

The next day Roy and Anja were heading out birding early. We joined them and local guide Leo on a trip to Caledonian Mountain for some high forest species. It was a fairly long drive along twisting mountain roads. With Roy driving, it was Anja's responsibility to ensure the safety of his huge camera lens – and she did this by sitting in the middle of the back seat with the lens sticking out from between her legs between the front seats. It looked rather odd, and distinctly phallic, but at least the gear was safe.

As we climbed, I began to recognise this road from my previous trip and smiled broadly. Ruth asked what I was looking so pleased about.

'Wait and see,' I replied. 'Should be a few more bends before they start.'

Ruth, Roy and Anja looked blank but I just sat back waited. Round a bend we came and there was the first one, just as I had remembered: a huge, full-colour bill-board featuring a beautiful girl clad in the skimpiest underwear imaginable. What a great road! This was the first of a series, each one with another sexy girl model-ling lingerie. The small mountain town we passed through specialised in lingerie shops, dozens of them. It was very strange indeed, each shop window crammed with basques, bras and knickers. And all this up in the mountains, miles from anywhere. Weird, but rather wonderful.

Trying to banish all thoughts of sexy underwear I forced myself to focus on the birding. At 1,300m we parked and set out on a contour trail, with great views of the forested mountains. We quickly picked up great birds: White-throated Hummingbird and Brassy-breasted Tanager just sat there, waiting to be ticked. Every few metres brought another wonderful new species, with Brazilian Ruby hummingbird, White-shouldered Fire-eye, Dusky-tailed Antbird and Ruby-crowned Tanager all thrilling us.

Two species of spinetail took a little more work, but we eventually nailed them as Grey-bellied and Rufous-capped. Mottle-cheeked Tyrannulet and Ochre-faced Tody-Flycatcher were next up. Then came a hummingbird that was a strong contender for bird of the day: a exquisite bottle-green Plovercrest, with its amazing lapwing-like crest – though a few metres further on a beautiful Bay-chested Warbling-Finch had us rethinking the award. As we headed back towards the car we could hardly believe that a whole morning had gone by; this had been first-class birding. Even the path back brought two new species: Rufous Gnatcatcher and Diademed Tanager.

We enjoyed our picnic lunch in warm sunshine, with a handsome Aplomado Falcon overhead, before we climbed even higher in search of Gray-winged Cotinga. The road here was so steep at times that our wheels were spinning, straining for a grip. Sadly the cotinga was nowhere to be seen, but we did enjoy stunning views of both Black-and-gold Cotinga and the aptly named Large-tailed Antshrike.

Roy and Anja headed south the next day, though not until we had all enjoyed fine views of the beautiful – and elusive – Shrike-like Cotinga. This left us one last day at REGUA, and Nicholas had arranged a day out for us. Jerry Bertrand from the World Land Trust had suggested this, as he was hoping to add some much-wanted life birds to his considerable list. Nicholas explained that we would join Jerry, picking up his friends Bill and Marsha Gette en route, for a full day cleaning up some very special birds – including the highly prized Three-toed Jacamar. How could we say no?

After a long slow drive we finally reached the Gette's hotel. They were not happy – and not surprisingly, as they had understood a transfer to REGUA would pick them up early morning and it was now past eleven. What's more, they had planned to drive straight to the lodge; there'd been no mention of a birding trip. Now we were being blamed for 'high-jacking the transfer'. Hang on a minute, we thought, this trip hadn't been our idea. By now Jerry had gone very quiet.

We reached a sort of compromise: first do a little birding, then head for the lodge earlier than planned. Not ideal, as all we had done so far was drive. Trouble is, we couldn't find the first birding site. Our target bird, the very sexy-looking White-bearded Antshrike, was reputed to occur at Pousada Paraiso Lodge – if only we could find the place. Our driver was reduced to stopping and asking people in the street. Eventually we found a man who seemed to know and, after much arm waving and pointing, we were off again. By now poor Marsha was feeling travel sick and Bill was not happy at all. 'Soon be at the site,' said Jerry, trying to soothe the situation, 'Then we can find the bird and head back.'

Unfortunately it didn't quite work out like that. We did reach the lodge, only to learn that the bird was at the end of a long hike up a mountain. No way were Bill and Marsha going to stand for that, and by now the atmosphere had turned a tad tense. Cue another compromise: we would bird a shorter trail around the lodge and then head back. In truth this pleased no one, as we missed our most wanted birds and the journey back was delayed. It was not a happy little group that eventually arrived back at REGUA, with just one new bird for our list, none for Jerry's, Bill fuming and Marsha feeling sick.

The mood had lifted by the next morning, but sadly we had to bid farewell to Nicholas and all at the lodge. As ever, we would have loved to have stayed longer: there was so much more to discover about the amazing conservation and habitat restoration work at this fabulous place. But soon our transport pulled up and Alcenir's familiar face was smiling broadly behind the wheel.

'Good morning,' came the warm greeting. 'Now, the Portuguese for arm is *braço*.'

It was body parts all the way back to the airport. We smiled weakly and slid deeper into our seats.

2,747 species

15 July–10 August, Peru (Ruth)

Our hopes for the Peru stage of our trip had been high. Peru has around 1,850 bird species spread across a great spectrum of habitats, and we had allowed over three weeks in which to find them. What's more, one of Peru's best known and most experienced bird tour operators was lined up to help us. What could go wrong?

Back in November 2007, when we were still in the UK planning our trip, it had all looked so promising. We'd contacted Barry Walker, a British birder who'd moved out to Peru some years ago and had set up Manu Expeditions, providing guided birding tours along the Manu Road and accommodation at the Manu Wildlife Centre. Barry was well known in birding circles and seemed just the man for the job. We'd explained to him all about *The Biggest Twitch* and asked if he'd be able to help, knowing that his contribution could prove invaluable. Barry's reply had been prompt and generous. He thought that our expedition sounded exciting, and it appealed to his lifelong twitching instincts. He had offered the support of Manu Expeditions as exclusive Peruvian sponsors and outlined some areas he thought we needed to visit. He himself would be joining us for much of our time. This all sounded perfect, so we had mentally parked Peru and turned our attention to arranging the next country on our tour.

Barry had warned us that, as a busy tour guide, he was offline in remote areas for long stretches at a time, so we weren't unduly worried when we set off on *The Biggest Twitch* in January that we hadn't been able to finalise the details of our Peru itinerary. After all, Peru was in July and that was months away. But when we still hadn't been able to reach him by May alarm bells began ringing. Finally we received a one-liner from Manu Expeditions. Gone was the offer of a tailor-made tour with Barry as our personal guide. Instead, we were offered places on a fixed departure tour that he had since arranged for some other clients. But this didn't match our dates: it started ten days after we arrived in Lima and continued for almost a week after we were scheduled to be back in the UK, to talk at the British Birdwatching Fair. It just wasn't possible for us to join this tour. And even if we had been able to, the accommodation in some places was already fully booked, so we'd need to pitch a tent in the garden.

This was a disaster! Why had Barry decided not to support *The Biggest Twitch*? And why had he left it so late to tell us? We didn't have time to worry about his reasons; we were now under pressure and had to salvage something from this critical country if we were to stay on track. If anything, in fact, this latest setback just made us all the more determined to succeed. We really had put everything we had into this once-in-a-lifetime adventure; we'd sold the house and had both given up good jobs. Failure wasn't an option.

By now, however, we were back on the road again, so we had to organise our Peru trip on the hoof. First we had to plan how most productively to spend our time, which we did using *Where to Watch Birds in Peru* by Thomas Valqui. Then we needed to find local tour operators who could help. Availability at key destinations was limited, at such short notice, and we found we had to pay top dollar to get there. We booked internal flights, arranged hire cars, found local guides and reserved accommodation, all with limited Spanish and an intermittent internet connection. And it was just our luck, of course, to coincide with a national festival, so flights were unduly full and hotels in many destinations were already booked up.

We arrived in Lima worried and frustrated, and with most of our plans for Peru still very much up in the air. In keeping with our luck, the National rental car we'd arranged wasn't available due to an administrative error on their part. Since they couldn't help us we tried the next rental desk in line. Luckily, Budget did have a vehicle, and once we'd got the two flat tyres replaced we tried our luck with the Lima traffic.

According to our book there were good birds to be had along the coastline here, so we joined the Pan-American highway and headed south. This road – Peru's most important national artery – was a two-lane highway riddled with potholes and crawling with overloaded lorries. At one point we had to swerve around a workman digging at a hole with a pickaxe in the middle of the road, protected by just a single traffic cone. To our right were small villages and gated entrances to protected beach areas – presumably weekend boltholes for the more affluent of Lima. To our left was open desert, with huge grey sand dunes marching across the otherwise empty landscape. It was a bizarre contrast.

We were heading for the little fishing village of Pucusana, a few miles south of Lima. Here we found a quayside bustling with boats nosing their way into the jetty to offload their catch, and women with baskets waiting to buy the pick of it. The sweeping cove was full of brightly painted little rowing boats, a counterpoint of colour to the grey dunes that slipped right into the sea. The smooth lines of these little boats were broken with birds that lined up along the gunwales waiting for scraps. Without moving from the one spot, we amassed an impressive list: Peruvian Pelicans, Belcher's Gulls, Guanay Cormorants, Red-legged Cormorants, Peruvian Boobies and – the stars of the show – Inca Terns. The latter were handsome, lead-grey birds that had coral-coloured bills with matching legs and feet, and sported white Poirot-style moustaches that fluttered in the breeze. All these birds swooped in the air, plunged into the water and squabbled viciously over scraps and cast-offs.

We wanted to find some height in order to scan further out to sea. Above us, we could see what looked like a restaurant at the top of the cliff, but couldn't work out a way up through the maze of lanes and footpaths. A tuk-tuk proved to be the answer. These miniature three-wheeled taxis buzzed about everywhere. The cab had a windscreen, motorbike handlebars and a central seat for the driver. The back part had a bench seat just wide enough to take two birders and their kit. We climbed aboard, and it felt as though we'd just got into a fairground ride – a giant teacup perhaps, or the waltzer. The motor buzzed like an angry wasp as we negotiated the narrow alleyways, dogs barking manically at our wheels.

Unfortunately the restaurant at the top, El Mirador, was firmly locked up. Still, we set up our scope on a hummock and – with lots of waving and gesticulation to overcome the language barrier – arranged for our taxi driver to pick us up in a while. Now we could look down into the next bay along the coastline. We could see the distinctive large outlines of Peruvian Pelicans, some on the water and some flapping languorously over towards the feeding frenzy by the fishing dock. But there was also another bird down there: dark, short-headed, its long body low in the water. I gave a squeal of excitement: could it be? It dived, and – after an eternity – popped back up again and into our scope. Yes, as we'd hoped, it was a Humboldt Penguin. Not the greatest of views, at that distance, but my first wild penguin. How exciting!

We'd not been able to find accommodation in Pucusana on the internet and now we could see this tiny little village for ourselves, we realised why. There were a couple of places advertising rooms, however, and we plumped for one of them at the equivalent of a princely £7 a night. Given how basic it was this must have been the tourist rate. At night, with the lights twinkling away merrily, the harbour looked almost romantic as we sat out on the terrace eating our fish supper. Darkness hid much of the squalor and poverty.

We continued further south, making a few birding stops on the way. One weird area of dried clay soil was known to be a hangout for Amazilia Hummingbird. The soil had dried into a pavement of hexagonal clay tiles, leaving wide, treacherous gaps in between. In effect we were walking on a series on narrow, fragile columns. If we didn't watch where we put our feet we risked twisting an ankle or worse, yet if we didn't look up at the scrubby bushes we risked missing the bird. Standing still seemed the best option. Sure enough, we soon spotted not one, not two, but a myriad of Amazilia Hummers buzzing from bush to bush.

Reaching Paracas, we tried to find our hotel, which apparently had good birding in the grounds. But true to our current luck, the hotel was closed for the whole of 2008 for total refurbishment. Luckily the Hotel Mirador provided a good alternative hotel, and must have been enjoying the boom time in extra visitors. We dumped our cases and headed straight out to look for more birds.

Beyond the town was the Paracas National Park. Bizarrely, this also holds the region's huge port, so heavy goods trucks thundered along the tarred highway through the dunes – an unlikely set-up in a nature reserve. Once we turned off onto a side road, however, calm descended. There was a circular route through the dunes. It looked appealing on the map, but as they were recommending 4WD vehicles only we decided not to attempt it in our dinky Renault Clio. Instead, we stuck to the tarred road in a straight line to the shore. The scenery was pretty dramatic: huge curving dunes swept in military lines towards the sea, ending abruptly in a sheer cliff above the foaming waves. The cloudless sky, blue water and white rollers, combined with the almost salmon-coloured cliffs and dunes here, made for some spectacular photography. We got some good close-ups of Peruvian Pelicans fishing, too, but no new birds for our list.

We decided to try our luck elsewhere, so drove back along the Pan-American Highway looking for likely patches of vegetation. It wasn't particularly pleasant birding, as huge lorries thundered past at regular intervals, many piled high with rubble. We'd noticed over the past few days a constant succession of these lorries driving out to the coast and dumping mountains of rubble – broken concrete, brick and twisted metal – along the shore. It all seemed very strange, and created an unsightly mess along what was otherwise a beautiful coastline. We'd also passed extensive areas of flat sand covered in row upon row of tiny shelters, now mostly empty and beginning to fall apart. They reminded us of empty refugee

▲ *Peru – birding the Abra Malaga Pass, the highest point on The Biggest Twitch.*

▼ *Peru – Festive Coquette. This beauty fed in the garden of our cabin.*

▲ *Peru – this Peruvian Thick-knee was found on a rubbish dump.*

▼ *Peru – the infamous Manu Road, where feeding flocks move faster than the trucks.*

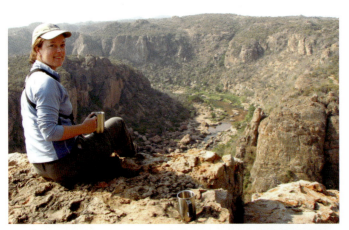

◀ *South Africa – Ruth takes a tea break in Kruger.*

◀ *South Africa – charged by a young bull elephant in Kruger.*

◀ *Zambia – birds, bins and a brew. Does it get any better?*

▲ *South Africa – a Crested Barbet looks for a mate.*

▼ *South Africa – Cape Town pelagic. Heaven or hell?*

◀ *Australia – Bluebonnet, the world record-breaking bird!*

◀ *Australia – a champagne moment for Alan, Iain Campbell and Ruth as they set a new world record (Jackie McClellan).*

◀ *Australia – it's very important to be with the right tour group …*

Australia – Blue-faced Honeyeater joined ...s for a burger.

Australia – just one of the 196 Koala ...hotos taken by Ruth!

▲ *Malaysia – Ruth models her leech socks, essential kit when you're birding here.*

India – Birding on elephant-back in Kaziranga National Park (Peter Lobo).

▲ *India – birding the Sela Pass; literally breathtaking.*

▼ *India – Slender-billed Scimitar-Babbler. What a weird-looking bird (Peter Lobo).*

▼ *India – Black-throated Parrotbill popped up and wowed us (Peter Lobo).*

▲ *India – Lama Camp in Eaglenest Sanctuary, home of the Bugun Liocichla.*

▼ *India – our great friend and guide Peter Lobo, enjoying the forest birding.*

▲ *India – breakfast in style beside the Brahmaputra.*

India – scanning for Ibisbill as we float downstream (Peter Lobo).

▼ *Southern Ecuador – a Jocotoco Antpitta feeds at our feet.*

▲ *India – Blue-bearded Bee-eater, our 4000th bird. We never imagined we'd get that many.*

▼ *Southern Ecuador – Tumbes Tyrant, a new species for Ecuador, found by us! (Nick Athanas).*

camps – and, in fact, that's just what they were. We'd forgotten that on 15 August 2007 Peru had suffered a severe earthquake, which had destroyed nearly 80% of the city of Pisco and had been felt as far away as Lima. It wasn't until later, when we were safely home again in the UK, that we were reminded about this natural disaster and its immense human impact. The penny dropped. The mounds of rubble, the rows of dilapidated shelters, the surly attitude of the locals: all this was immediately understandable. Life had been cruel to the Peruvians and just one year later many still had little to smile about.

Perhaps that's why some families chose to eke out a living in the desert. Far from any falling debris, they were trying to farm by pouring water onto the sand. How long such a lifestyle would be sustainable wasn't clear. The few rivers that existed were being sucked dry, as farmers watered small patches of land to grow crops. These bizarre oases stood out for miles, each a small square of emerald green in a sea of sand. Not surprisingly, they were pretty obvious to the birds as well, who congregated here to take advantage of the water, plants and insect life. Small passerines chased each other through the bushes: Slender-billed Finch, a uniformly grey bird with orange bill and legs; Yellow-billed Tit-Tyrant, a black-and-white striped humbug of a bird with a black crest and a yellow-and-black bill; and Parrot-billed Seedeater, the male with a luminous yellow bill that wouldn't look out of place on a scaled-down parrot. But star of the show was a flock of some fourteen Tawny-throated Dotterels. These elegant birds trotted along the furrows of the cultivated fields but were too nervous to allow a close approach. We watched them for ages, soaking up their graceful demeanour and their eye-catching tawny throats.

All too soon, our time exploring the coast was over. For the next leg of our Peruvian adventure, we were going to be based in Cusco. This is a popular jumping-off point for the rainforest, the ancient Inca ruins and the Andes. If we were to have any chance of seeing enough birds in this country, we had to visit the Manu Road. But getting there was a financial and logistical nightmare. We knew where we needed to stay, but we couldn't just jump in a hire car or hop on a bus as the lodges were too remote and the driving conditions too rough. We needed to find a tour operator and we needed more money. It was going to cost us thousands of pounds, but having come this far we didn't want to give up now. We still had a few days in hand, however, as first we had planned to do some birding around Cusco itself.

Having spent our first few days at sea level, just walking along the street in Cusco at an altitude of over 3,300m was an effort. Arriving by aeroplane had given us no time to acclimatise. While neither of us felt ill, exactly, we were both short of breath and slightly light-headed. It was like having a hangover, but without the fun bit beforehand. We'd read about drinking coca tea for overcoming altitude sickness, so we tried a cup, pouring the water onto the leaves and bruising them slightly before drinking the pale green liquid. The amount of actual cocaine in the tea is minuscule, apparently, but it definitely helped with the altitude and we downed a few more cups to help our exploration.

After the squalor and dirt of the coast, Cusco was beautiful. The central square, the Plaza de Armas, was paved with cobblestones, so the cars rattled as they drove around the ornate gardens, beneath the grandiose cathedral. On two sides of the square were rows of small shops on the ground floor, all with balconied cafes above. This was *the* place to sit and enjoy a hot chocolate, soaking up the atmosphere, watching the world go by – and quietly gasping for breath.

It was here at a local café that we met up with our friend Fabrice Schmitt. Meeting Fabrice had been one of those fabulous chance encounters that happened so many times on *The Biggest Twitch*. We had bumped into one another earlier in the year in eastern Turkey, where we had found ourselves sharing the same hotel in Birecik. Every evening we had swapped notes and stories, and had all got along famously. Fabrice had offered his help in Peru later in the year and, luckily, we'd kept in touch by email, as now we needed all the help we could get. With Fabrice, though, we had really fallen on our feet. He was entertaining, charming and certainly knew where to find good birds around Cusco.

First Fabrice took us to Huacarpay Lake, about half an hour's taxi ride from Cusco. A gentle level walk around this placid lake was about all Alan and I could manage as we still struggled with the altitude, but luckily our loud panting didn't put off the birds. It was a beautiful and peaceful spot: reeds surrounded the edge of the water, which was so still that the mountains and clear blue sky were perfectly reflected. While Andean Gulls flew low over the surface, a pair of Puna Teals floated by and Andean Lapwings posed on the bank.

Turning our attention to the hills behind us, we picked out a Giant Humming-bird buzzing round some small bushes, a species we'd looked for but missed in Ecuador. Then Fabrice called out excitedly that he had found a Bearded Mountaineer. We rushed over to get a look at this beautiful, uncommon hummingbird as it flitted around the montane scrub. It had a deeply forked black-and-white tail and a white belly, but its 'beard' was truly staggering: a narrow 'gorgette' of iridescent green and purple that glittered as it caught the sun.

Rusty-fronted Canastero, Chiguanco Thrush, and Rufous-naped and Spot-billed Ground-Tyrants soon added themselves to our list. Then, as we wandered further round the lake, we caught sight of a Puna Snipe, a secretive brown striped bird with a long tapering bill, skulking among the reeds. While we were watching this, a handsome male Andean Negrito – a sooty-grey bird wearing a rust-coloured cape – popped up at the lake edge. Finally, as we downed a well-earned drink at the restaurant beside the lake, a Green-tailed Trainbearer, another hummingbird for our list, shot past, flaunting its shimmering green tail.

We returned to Cusco around mid-afternoon to finalise our plans for the next two weeks, and to prepare ourselves for the following day. Tomorrow would be possibly one of the toughest – and certainly the highest – but ultimately one of the best days of the whole year.

Not that it felt so good at 4.30am as we bounced up into the snow-covered mountains in a car with no heating. We were aiming for the Abra Malaga Pass at around 4,300m and the pre-dawn air was icy. It had been a long drive from Cusco, first to Ollantaytambo, then up into the mountains on a hairpin road that doubled back on itself again and again as we gained height. By now our feet, hands and noses were numb with cold.

We continued to a huddle of huts at the very top of the pass. If there was civilisation, perhaps there was the chance of some hot coca tea. Sure enough, despite the early hour, an elderly lady was up and about. She already had a fire burning merrily and soon had coca tea on the go. Around her feet scuttled a family of guinea pigs of various sizes. These weren't pets on the loose, but nutritious meals-in-waiting: a traditional Peruvian dish that we'd seen on a few menus but hadn't tried for ourselves as we were rather put off by the preparation. The guinea pigs were first flattened with a heavy stone and then baked in the oven until the skin was crisp. Finally they were served on the plate in a flat guinea-pig shape. I still held fond memories of Sammy and Sandy, our school pets, and it didn't seem quite right. At least these ones had a happy life, roaming freely around the house until that fateful moment when the large rock fell from the sky. Splat!

We paid for our tea and bought tickets to enter the nature reserve, which contained the area's last remaining patches of Polylepis forest. Then we said goodbye to our driver – who we'd arranged to meet many hours later at the foot of the mountain – and shouldered our packs for the hike.

We started slowly, Fabrice leading the way. The plan was to climb the ridge in front of us and then walk down the valley to join up with our driver at the bottom, some 15km away. At this altitude, walking uphill was a struggle. By now we were over 4,450m high and the air was incredibly thin. Every breath left us gasping for oxygen, and the even the slightest incline was a struggle. Fabrice was far more acclimatised than we were, but even he was taking things very gently. Step, step, gasp. Step, step, gasp. At least we could use the search for birds as a pretext for resting every few strides.

The sun was coming up and the mist that had cloaked the mountaintops was beginning to rise, but we were still in shadow and our breath steamed like a trio of manic dragons. We hadn't gone far before a group of five Gray-breasted Seedsnipe flew in and immediately vanished amongst the rocks, so cryptic was their plumage, but we soon found them again and enjoyed wonderful views. Then a gang of larger animals loomed eerily out of the mist: a motley collection of vari-coloured Alpacas domesticated beasts who were left to roam wild. The Alpacas seemed better dressed for the climate than us, with a thick coat over their stocky bodies, and somehow they were finding something to nibble on the stony ground. We took the obligatory photographs, with snow-covered mountains as a back-drop.

Slow but steady progress took us to the top of the ridge, where we stood gasping. It wasn't just the lack of oxygen that made us catch our breath: we were on the edge of the most stunning landscape we'd ever seen. The thinness of the air added to the clarity of the view as the sun burned off the last of the mist and the mountains were fully exposed. Under a cloudless cobalt blue sky, the snow-covered peaks shimmered with a glare that hurt your eyes. We were at the head of a huge bowl, or corrie: an immense basin at the head of a glaciated hanging valley, which had been carved out by ice. To our right was a sheer cliff face of jagged grey rock. Ahead of us stretched a mountain range covered in snow, as thick and smooth as perfect Christmas cake icing. Curving and snaking away to our left was the valley we were going to walk down, covered in pale spiky grass. Nobody said a word, as we stood and drank it all in.

We picked our way cautiously over tussocks of grass and treacherous rocks; to slip here would mean a rapid descent of several hundred feet to the bottom of the valley. Suddenly Fabrice stopped in his tracks as he caught sight of a bird ahead of him. We crept up behind him and peered over his shoulder. A tiny Puna Tapaculo, a dumpy little grey bird, was creeping through the grasses. As we stood there, a flight of green Mitred Parakeets shot overhead, looking very out of place in this high Andean landscape.

A few metres lower and we entered a patch of Polylepis forest. It felt strange to be walking through a forest where we were often taller than the trees themselves, but these trees were specially adapted to the harsh environment, with their stunted, contorted branches and tiny leaves. In the misty conditions, threads of lichen hung from the branches while mosses gathered in the nooks and crannies. Under the trees, the grass grew green and damp.

Our main target bird here was the Royal Cinclodes, an endangered species of which only around two hundred pairs remain in the world. One or two pairs were resident here at Abra Malaga, but sadly our chances of happening upon them in this huge landscape were quite slim. Nonetheless, a jaunty White-browed Tit-Spinetail did pop up into view, a stick-and-ball bird with a small round body and a long jagged-tipped tail. Then a Streak-throated Canastero suddenly hopped out into the grass in front of us, showing small white streaks against its brown throat. While we were still looking at this first bird, another similar but slightly different one hopped into view. It was obviously a member of the same family, and the darker colouring and orange patch under the chin showed it to be a Junin Canastero – also found at high altitude, but much less common than its Streak-throated relative. What a stroke of luck: two for the price of one!

Ironically, as we were now descending quite rapidly to the valley floor, Alan was beginning to feel the effects of the extreme altitude. At first he went rather quiet and didn't seem to show much interest in the birds – always a bad sign. Then he developed a thumping headache and felt dizzy whenever he moved his head. We paused for a moment to catch our breath and drink some water; it's easy to become dehydrated at high altitude. But, however heartless it may have seemed, we couldn't stop. Going back wasn't an option – that would have meant climbing back up a near-vertical cliff to reach the road, and in any case our driver had long since driven off. No, we had to carry on, though at least we were gradually losing height all the time.

The lower we descended, though, the worse Alan became. This was getting serious. Nausea followed next, and then his vision started blurring. At first he thought he'd knocked his binoculars and damaged them somehow. This would have been a disaster. He tried using mine – and found they suffered from the same defect: double vision. Where Fabrice and I both saw one Ash-breasted Tit-Tyrant, Alan saw two, and where we had one Tawny Tit-Spinetail, Alan saw a pair.

Meanwhile the birds kept coming. Three Stripe-headed Antpittas (or was that six?) fed on a patch of open short grass, and then as we made our way through another patch of damp moss-laden Polylepis, a White-winged Diuca-Finch sat on a low branch. Apparently this was also the preferred habitat of the Royal Cinclodes, which particularly liked the damper patches of the forest under the trees. But it seemed as though we didn't meet with royal approval that day – and as we had to get Alan down to lower altitude as quickly as possible, and this was the last patch of Polylepis we would go though, our last chance was gone.

Alan was really suffering by now and had become pretty wobbly on his feet. I carried the rucksack and scope and we picked our way downhill as swiftly as we could, under the circumstances. On either side of us, the mountains rose up like a cradle, while yet more peaks came into view ahead of us. As we lost altitude, so the temperatures rose, with the sun now much higher in the cloudless blue sky. We knocked back the water and piled on sunscreen as we peeled off more layers of clothing.

Altitude sickness is a strange thing. It is hard to anticipate whom it will strike and when, and it can be extremely serious if not addressed quickly. If you lose altitude soon enough, however, the symptoms can stop equally rapidly. By the time we had descended far enough to see the road in the distance, Alan's vision had returned to normal and his queasiness and headache had improved – though, oddly, he still seemed happy for me to carry the rucksack and scope. We encountered more herds of Llama and Alpaca, and even a small area of ploughed fields; carving these out of this stony terrain must have been back-breaking work. The footpath wound through a collection of huts and we said hello to a woman doing her washing, with her little daughter playing beside her. Both were wearing the traditional dress of a full skirt over many layered petticoats, a felt jacket and a bowler hat.

Losing another thirty metres or so, we rejoined the road as it snaked through the hills, and there was our car and driver. He'd been waiting so long he was fast asleep, head thrown back and snoring like a steam train. It felt fantastic to quench our thirst with the cool water he had stashed in the boot and we climbed wearily into the back seat. Not for long, though. We stopped to check the bushes on the bends on the way down and, at this intermediate altitude, encountered a whole new range of birds. These included Andean Hillstar, a smart hummingbird with a white belly and an iridescent green throat; White-tufted Sunbeam, another hummer with purple in its wings, which flashed as it caught the sun; and Black-throated Flowerpiercer, who is as partial to nectar as any hummingbird, but who – using lateral thinking – cheats by boring sideways through the flower to reach the sweet reward. A handsome Golden-billed Saltator also flicked around the montane scrub, while a gorgeous Creamy-crested Spinetail showed off its rufous coloured tail and bushy magnolia headdress.

Descending into the Sacred Valley, we stopped off in Ollantaytambo for a drink and a snack. By now, the town was buzzing with tourists who'd come to explore the Inca terraces that towered over the town and the curio market that had sprouted to tempt them with original artisan items. Savouring a hot chocolate, and enjoying that pleasant weariness of the limbs that comes after a long and satisfying walk, we gazed up at Andean Swifts scything through the clear azure sky. I think we probably snoozed on the long drive back to Cusco, which took us along the Sacred Valley and up over a high pass before dropping down steeply into the town. Checking into our second hotel, we said our farewells to Fabrice and thanked him for an unforgettable day. After fifteen kilometres of thrilling scenery, twenty-one new species (possibly forty-two in Alan's case!) and a hugely enjoyable time, we were sad to say goodbye – and hoped our paths would cross again before we left Peru.

Our next big adventure took us back into the mountains, but this time by train and in search of culture. Now, as may have been mentioned a few times before,

Alan isn't exactly what you'd call a culture-vulture. But even he had to agree to taking a few hours out to visit Machu Picchu, since we were close by, in Peruvian terms – and there were also plenty of potential new birds in the area, so he didn't take too much persuading. By now, we'd tracked down a local tour operator called InkaNatura to put together a few days' package: they had arranged the train tickets, the transfers, accommodation in Aguas Calientes – the nearest town to the ruins – and entry tickets to the ruins themselves. All we needed to do was show up.

We'd heard rumours of it being a bit of a bunfight to catch the train to Aguas Calientes but, thanks to the efficiency of InkaNatura's team, everything went like clockwork. We drove to Ollantaytambo once more and jumped on board, to find our designated seats awaiting us. The blue and yellow train chugged its way very slowly up the winding valley, with the torrential Rio Urubamba on one side and sheer cliffs on the other. In fact, it chugged so slowly that we were able to watch Torrent Ducks on the river below. At Aguas Calientes, we were met by the local representative and taken to our hotel, a small family-run establishment in the centre of the little town. It was a very touristy location, with just about every building being dedicated to removing money from visitors' pockets, but there was a buzz about the place, and it was attractively situated in a narrow gorge with a turbulent stream leaping over boulders right through the centre. As its name suggests, there were even natural hot springs just above the town for those with time to spare. Once again this went on the list of swimming pools we never tried out, as we had more important things to do: we went birding.

First of all, though, we played Postman. InkaNatura had given us a letter to deliver to the Machu Picchu Pueblo Hotel. This lovely hotel was set in exotic gardens complete with hummingbird feeders. It would have been the ideal birding accommodation for us, were it not for our budget. Now, however, we had the perfect excuse to visit and, having delivered the letter, we wandered into the grounds to check the feeders. The endemic Green-and-white Hummingbird immediately visited the feeding station right beside us. We added it to our list and nipped off to check out the rest of the gardens before the management realised we hadn't left the premises. Soon we disappeared out of sight along the maze of little footpaths as the formal grounds gave way to natural forest. Walking along silently, we watched a White-throated Quail-Dove delicately pick its way through the tangled undergrowth, totally unaware of us.

Back in the town, we downed another hot chocolate and planned our attack. The traditional thing to do at Machu Picchu is climb the mountain before dawn and watch the sun rise over the ruins. We, however, decided to watch the sun rise over the railway lines back down in the valley. Given that the ruins would still be there in the afternoon, whereas the birds might not, we'd reached a happy compromise that we'd go birding first thing when the temperature was low and the birds were at their most active. Then, when it became too hot for the birds, we'd play the tourist and visit Machu Picchu. You might be thinking that culture drew the short straw here, but knowing Alan as well as I do, I was confident that once we'd spent the most productive part of the day birding, he'd be happy to spend as much time as I wanted visiting the ruins.

And so we found ourselves walking along the railway tracks beside the

Urubamba River first thing the next morning. The altitude here was slightly lower than at Cusco, so walking beside a level railway was very pleasant. As the humid forest came down to the railway tracks it gave way to bushier vegetation along the banks of the tumbling river, and this marginal habitat held a great variety of colourful birds: a Rust-and-yellow Tanager showed off his rust-coloured head and yellow belly; a male Silver-backed Tanager did have a silvery back, but his mate was definitely more green than silver; a Speckle-faced Parrot crashed around in some branches directly overhanging the railway line, its reddish face conspicuous against the greenery; and a Rusty Flowerpiercer searched out suitable flowers to tap for the sweet nectar hidden within. Our perseverance with two flighty birds hidden deep in a bush was rewarded when a pair of Bluish-slate Antshrikes finally hopped into view, the male a deep grey-blue all over, the female similar but with a russet belly.

It was time to return to the town, but there was one last surprise in store for us. Looking up, we were gob-smacked to see a huge bird soaring over the cliffs above. It was unmistakable: Andean Condor! This wasn't new for our list but it was nonetheless exciting to see so close – and in such a perfect location. Cue the Indian panpipes! And then, as if one bird wasn't enough, a second – this time a juvenile – followed the first, and together they spiralled effortlessly over the cliffs, making several circuits over the town before disappearing out of view.

Then it was culture time, and so we jumped on board a minibus to take us up to the entrance of Machu Picchu. This ancient site, shrouded in myth and mystery, was founded around 1642 during the heyday of the Inca Empire but abandoned again only a hundred years or so later. Ever since its 'discovery' by an American historian named Hiram Bingham in 1911, tourists have flocked here. To be honest, we were worried that it might turn out to be a bit of a let down. After all, who hasn't seen the familiar pictures of the ruins set against their backdrop of lozenge-shaped forested mountains? Could the real thing really inspire us when the image had become such a cliché?

Well, quite simply, yes it could. We quickly found ourselves on the ledge where *that* photo is taken, the one that shows the full extent of the site, with its terraces cascading down the hillside, the rows of stone cottages, the sacred buildings built on the central plateau and the peak of Huayna Picchu in the background. Below us the Rio Urubamba snaked through the depths of the valley. It was mesmerising – and of course, like every good tourist, we had to have our snaps taken to prove we had really been really there.

I think it was the sheer scale that surprised me the most, as I hadn't really appreciated the full extent of these ruins. Although there must have been thousands of visitors, many of them Peruvian as well as from further afield, it was easy to find a quiet corner all to yourself. At the most popular sacred sites, such as the Hitching Post of the Sun and the Room of Three Windows, the tour groups moved through in waves, following their guide's brightly coloured flag, umbrella or other distinguishing feature, but once these groups had passed on, the peace resumed.

The site had been constructed using the famous Inca dry stone walling, where each piece of stone was carefully carved to fit exactly the ones it abutted, leaving barely enough room to slide a sheet of paper between. Despite being in an earthquake zone, there was only one wall that showed any ill effects, with a single jagged crack from top to bottom. The sheer scale of this settlement, and the incredible skill and labour of its construction, was mind-blowing. Even Alan had to admit that it wasn't bad 'for a pile of old rocks'. High praise indeed.

Sadly, we missed the one new bird that Machu Picchu might have produced, the Inca Wren, but that was a small price to pay for the haul of new birds we'd logged down by the railway track in the early morning. In fact the railway tracks were so good that we went back again at dawn the next day, and were rewarded with a riot of colour in the shape of Blue-necked, Beryl-spangled, Rust-and-yellow, Silver-backed and Blue-capped Tanagers, Orange-bellied Euphonia, and Blue Dacnis – all sparrow-sized birds in paint box colours. Making our way back to Aguas Calientes in time to catch the train, we caught sight of one more new bird for our list: a tiny little 10cm-long White-bellied Hummingbird, which buzzed around the blooms just above our heads.

That night, back in Cusco, we had an important meeting. InkaNatura had arranged a nine-day trip for us along the Manu Road and into the lowland areas of Peru, due to start early the next morning. We had paid a premium to hire a dedicated bird guide familiar with the birds of this region. Her name was Marlene. She was tiny, and seemed very young – and quite nervous.

Unfortunately the meeting didn't start well.

'I don't know the flycatchers or tyrannulets,' announced Marlene.

Alan and I looked at each other in dismay. Just a glance at the Peru field guide will show you that the various flycatcher, tyrant and tyrannulet species take up a large chunk of the book, and that many of the illustrations look worryingly similar. There are an awful lot of these birds along the Manu Road, and we were going to need all the help we could get to identify them. And it got worse.

'I don't have any of the bird calls.'

This was another blow. In the dense vegetation along the Manu Road, playing calls would be essential to encourage the birds close enough for us to see them. Without them, birding the Manu Road would be seriously tough. We explained to Marlene, as gently as we could, what we were about and what we were hoping to achieve. So there was a lot at stake when she arrived at 6.30am the next morning with a cheery smile, a driver and a minibus.

It wasn't long before we left the tarmac behind, and now we could see why our journey to Cock-of-the Rock Lodge was going to take all day. The Manu Road is a legend. Starting in Cusco in the central Andes, this rough, single track weaves its way down the eastern slope of the mountains all the way to the Amazonian lowlands, passing an amazing variety of landscapes en route. We started by winding up more hairpin bends through the mountains. We looked out across broad valleys at a patchwork of terraced fields in shades of green and brown, with tiny communities dotted across the hillside. The sun shone and the track was in pretty good condition, although our wheels left a stifling cloud of dust behind. As we gained height, we began to reach the clouds and soon the road was enveloped in mist, which wafted across the road. The temperature fell, and things felt decidedly cool and damp. We reached the pass at 3,400m and climbed out to take a look, but the mist here was too thick to see anything and the place was crowded with other minibuses all making a pit stop, so we pressed on further. Ironically, we saw two

Manu Expeditions vehicles parked at the top, but we waved to them all and just kept going.

As we started to descend on the other side of the mountain, the habitat changed dramatically. Here the lush cloud forest brought a palette of vivid greens, with ferns, palms and big-leaved secropia. Immediately we started to see birds. Every so often we hopped out of the vehicle to take a walk along the road. Birds passed through in waves, the mixed feeding flocks offering the different species greater collective security against predators. We would hear them first, the excited calls and fluttering of wings, then see them as they picked off the ripe fruits or teased insects from the undersides of leaves: first one bird, then two, and soon many different birds all hopping through the branches, before there was a rippling sigh from the foliage as they filtered away to the next bush.

Catching a mixed flock like this was exciting and nerve-wracking in equal measure. We both had to see each bird for it to count on our list and so we'd frantically call out what we were looking at and where to make sure that we were both seeing the same species before it disappeared.

'There's a Black-faced Brush-Finch.'

'Got it!' Then, 'I've got a Cinnamon Flycatcher here.'

'Yep. But what's that dark bird above it with a white moustache and rusty colour under the tail?'

'Moustached Flowerpiercer, I think. But did you see that...' And so it continued.

Meanwhile the road itself also became more interesting. On one side might be a vertical cliff, and on the other a sheer drop to a tumbling river far, far below. Meanwhile the surface became increasingly rough: in some places, thick with gooey mud where mountain streams flowed over the road; in others covered in loose scree. We'd turn a corner to find the road had been partially washed away by a landslide, which had tumbled fully grown trees like matchsticks, or was undercut and held up by nothing more than tangled roots and inertia.

And we weren't alone on the road, either. Apart from a few other bird tour minibuses, there was a procession of trucks, piled high with bamboo poles or sacks of produce, often with people hitching a lift perched on top. These cumbersome lorries growled their way up or down the road, transporting goods and people in and out of the Amazon and back to Cusco. Whenever they met it was a game of brinkmanship as to who had the bigger vehicle and the right of way. Originally the rule had been that you could drive in one direction only on Mondays, Wednesdays and Fridays, and in the other direction on Tuesdays, Thursdays and Saturdays, while Sunday was presumably a religious day of rest. The older truck drivers still upheld this tradition, but many of the younger drivers took no notice, and so the two trucks would try to squeeze past each other, with a sheer drop just inches from their wheels.

What with the birding stops, the terrain and the roadblocks, it took us ten bone-shaking hours to reach Cock-of-the-Rock Lodge. We were welcomed with open arms and shown our cosy little wooden chalet on stilts. There was just time to enjoy a hot candlelit shower (no electricity here) before supper and bed.

The next morning, we awoke to torrential rain. But we couldn't worry about the weather, we had a date with a very bizarre orange bird and we couldn't be late.

As we walked up the road we could hear a series of strange noises coming from the forest: grunts, snorts, chuckles, even a miaowing sound, all emanating from one particular spot on the other side of a high fence. Reaching a gate in the fence, we crept through silently and found ourselves almost face-to-beak with a bright orange bird. It was a male Cock-of-the-Rock. And he wasn't alone: there must have been half a dozen of them, shrieking, grunting, hopping, jumping, swinging and generally making a real spectacle of themselves – not a new bird for our list, but a sight we just couldn't miss.

These pigeon-sized birds don't hide their light under a bushel. They are bright orange all over, apart from a small grey patch on their backs and black wings and tail, and sport a bulbous orange crest that extends from crown to bill. Every morning at 6am they came to this same display ground – or lek – and put on their show to attract a mate. The more noise and effort they put into it, the more attractive they were to the ladies. As we watched, a couple of rather dowdy brown females arrived, and the males promptly ratcheted up the performance a level. But despite their best efforts, one female had clearly seen better things and flew off in a rather haughty fashion. For a moment the nearest males seemed rather deflated, but then, undeterred, they remembered that there was at least one other female in the area and so they cranked up the orange merry-go-round again. This crazy spectacle went on for about an hour or so until the females finally lost interest and the males wound themselves down. Only to do it all over again at the same time the next day. And the next.

All that day we bounced our way further down the Manu Road, one minute riding in the bus, the next walking on ahead and ticking off new species. All the birds had exotic plumage and names to match: Bluish-fronted Jacamar, Paradise Tanager, Versicoloured Barbet, Orange-cheeked Tanager, Plum-throated Cotinga. We came to a rough-looking settlement, where the locals eyed us suspiciously, but amazingly it had an internet café, so we stopped off to check our emails and update our blog. Who knew when we would next reach civilisation?

More bumpy road, more birding and then we reached the tiny riverside town of Atalaya, where we swapped the minibus for a motorised canoe. The river here was wide but shallow, as the current rippled over a series of rapids, and it took a sharp push with a pole to get us over the rocks. Luckily we were travelling light, having left the bulk of our luggage back in Cusco. We didn't have long to enjoy the ride though, before we pulled into a rickety wooden jetty. We hopped ashore and offloaded the bags, and then followed Marlene along a footpath into the forest.

'Be careful,' she said, as we reached a crossroads in the paths. 'There's been a huge snake here in the past.' We had a good look, but saw nothing serpentine, so carried on to Amazonia Lodge. This was on a former tea plantation and the guest accommodation was in an attractive, ochre-coloured low wooden building with a veranda along the front. Below it was an ornamental garden, and a large bird table covered with fruit that was attracting a steady stream of tanagers. We checked into our rooms, which were simple but adequate, and then made our way over to the dining area. The food was plentiful and tasty, though we were amused to see that all the meat was flattened out into thin escalopes; perhaps it wasn't just guinea pigs that received the large rock treatment.

The next few days took on a regular birding routine: up and out at dawn to walk the various forest trails while it was still reasonably cool; back for lunch and a rest in the shade of the veranda watching the hummingbirds on the feeders during the fiercest heat of the day; and then back out again on the trails in the late afternoon until dusk, when we returned for supper, the bird list and bed. Steadily we added new lowland birds to our list: Rufous-crested Coquette, a gorgeous little hummingbird, with a red crest that flared whenever it perched or fed; Sungrebe, an aquatic bird with a striped head that looked part duck and part grebe but was in reality neither, and disappeared out of sight upstream with a flurry and a squawk once it knew it was being watched; and Horned Screamer, an enormous unicorn bird, with a 'horn' on his head and a call to match his name.

One day we took a trail through an area of bamboo and added a collection of specialist Ant-thingumyjigs who resided there: Great Antshrike, Spot-winged Antbird, Rufous-tailed Antwren, Goeldi's Antbird, Amazonia Antpitta, Bamboo Antshrike, all of them living in the stands of bamboo and requiring us to contort ourselves into peculiar postures to get a good look – not to mention contort our brains over the bird list in the evening to make sure we logged the right ones. Was it Rufous-capped Antthrush, or Rufous-tailed Antwren we'd seen earlier?

Down in this lowland area, surrounded by lush forest and streams, the humidity was incredibly high, and it was only in the blissful pre-dawn cool that we could walk about without breaking into a sweat. Once the sun came up, we were permanently bathed in perspiration. This seemed to be an invitation to dinner for all the starving mosquitos in the area, which quickly developed a taste for British blood. But all this insect life meant an abundance of other wildlife too. Everywhere you looked you were confronted by nature: from the umbrella-sized secropia leaves, which dripped rainwater down the back of your neck, to the industrious leaf ants, which cleared broad tracks through the undergrowth as they cut up leaves and transported the sections all the way back to their nests – like a trail of Green Shield Stamps marching through the forest. Then there were the spiders that we never saw, but which each night would cunningly spin their web across the trails at head height to ensnare us in the morning. And, of course, the warty green toad who lived under the dining hut.

Best of all, there were birds everywhere. Glittering hummingbirds, like Gould's Jewelfront, Fork-tailed Woodnymph, Many-spotted Brilliant and Blue-tailed Emerald, whose feathers glistened with iridescence in the sunshine. Fruit-eating species, which foraged through the trees bearing ripe fruit, like colour swatches from a paint chart: Scarlet-hooded Barbet, White-winged Shrike Tanager, Emerald Toucanet, Chestnut-eared Aracari, Olive Tanager and Purple-throated Fruitcrow. There were skulking birds, which picked their way delicately through the shadows but occasionally gave themselves away as they broke for cover in a dash across the trail: Razorbilled Curassow, and Cinereous and Black-capped Tinamous. And, despite having told us that she didn't know the flycatchers and Tyrannulets, Marlene, along with the excellent *Helm Field Guide to the Birds of Peru*, helped us add a few of these confusing species to our list, including Mottle-backed Elaenia and Johannes's Tody-Tyrant. As it happened, not having the bird calls on tape wasn't too much of a hindrance. The tapes had been played so much in the area by visiting bird guides that, apparently, the birds had become accustomed to hearing them and were not responding. In fact, what often proved more effective was to record the actual bird singing and then play its own call back. You could almost see the quizzical looks on their faces ('Hey, that sounds just like me!') as they burst out of a bush to see who was making all the noise.

There were interesting mammals too, such as the very cute Saddle-backed Tamarin, a monkey the size of a large squirrel that wore a black cowl over its head and shoulders, and had a black face with greyish eyebrows and muzzle. He peered down at us as we gazed up at him, but he clearly wasn't impressed with what he saw, judging by the scowl on his face.

We weren't the only visitors to Amazonia Lodge. One day, Rose Anne Rowlett led in a group from the American bird tour company Field Guides, and having to share the rather restricted bathroom facilities with a much larger number of guests was a small price to pay for the privilege of meeting one of our birding heroes. We'd read about Rose Anne in Kenn Kaufman's book, *Kingbird Highway*, which had helped spark our enthusiasm for this world trip. Now here we were, sitting right next to one of the people he'd birded with and written about. At dinner, we sat at the table next to their group, and our ears were out on stalks as we tried to eavesdrop on Rose Anne's tales of birding legends Kenn Kaufman and Ted Parker.

Rose Anne herself was a charming lady and a great birder. We had the chance to chat to her on several occasions, and she was so graciously enthusiastic about our adventure that we felt truly humbled. She had a good sense of humour, too. 'Note the distinguishing slim feet of this bird,' she said in a serious voice, as she called us over to look at a Slender-footed Tyrannulet that was close to the ground under a nearby shrub. It was only the wicked glint in her eye that revealed she was pulling our legs.

Our last morning at Amazonia Lodge, and we walked down to the wooden jetty, casting one last unsuccessful look for the snake at the crossroads. Then our bags were thrown onto the motorised canoe tied up beside the jetty and we followed suit. After all the extra rain we'd had over the previous 24 hours, we'd imagined the river would be a raging torrent. But no, it looked no deeper than on the day we'd arrived – and, sure enough, when we reached the rapids the boat became stuck. The helmsman tried pushing with a pole, but we didn't budge. His assistant jumped off and tried pulling from the front, but still we didn't budge.

What was the heaviest thing on board that we could jettison? We looked around and all our eyes fell on Alan. He bowed to the inevitable, taking off his boots, rolling up his trousers and climbing cautiously over the side of the boat. Once his bare feet had got a firm enough hold on the stony riverbed, he bent his back into pushing the boat forwards. At first the three men's actions were pretty uncoordinated, but finally, with much puffing and grunting, they managed to heave in time and the boat slid forward over the rocks. Marlene and I giggled our heads off, and did our bit to help by taking photographs of Alan working up a sweat.

It didn't take long before we were tying up in Atalaya once more, to find our driver and minibus waiting for us. We retraced our steps along the bumpy Manu Road, still jumping out and chasing birds whenever we caught sight or sound of a feeding flock. In the one-horse town we stopped again at the internet café, with just time for a blog update, to check our emails and take a quick peek at the year list totals on the Surfbirds website. We had a shock.

Surfbirds is *the* website for the worldwide birding community, and one of its many features is an updated year list for both various geographical regions and for the whole world. In addition to posting our total on our own website, we'd also posted it on Surfbirds every time we'd left a country. Up until now we had been way out in front of everybody else, but suddenly it seemed we had competition. OK, we were still top of the leader board with 2,918 species recorded so far. But out of the blue, David Shackleford, a professional bird guide, had just posted a total of 2,200 species. This was a real worry: where had he come from? Why hadn't he posted his list before? Where was he going next? It looked as though he hadn't been birding much in Latin America, so he could easily ramp up his total. We were worried.

We cheered up somewhat when we reached the Cock-of-the-Rock Lodge and found that this time we had been upgraded to the delightful honeymoon suite, with its huge four-poster bed and beautiful en suite bathroom. Not that we had much time to enjoy the facilities before trotting out again to try our luck on the trails around the lodge, but the rain came on very heavily again, so we gave up the unequal struggle and contented ourselves with drinking tea on the veranda and watching the hummingbirds around the feeders. Rainfall always has the hummingbirds zapping around and chasing each other with more agitation. And even as we drank our tea, we added a new bird to our list: a jaunty little Peruvian Piedtail zipped in amongst the other hummers to enjoy the sugar water.

We were up at 5am again the next morning for the Cock-of-the-Rock lek, and the show was as good as before, with the bright orange birds throwing themselves around enthusiastically. Overhead a family party of Woolly Monkeys swung through the branches on long, dark brown arms, including one mum with a baby wrapped round her back like a brown furry rucksack. I tried in vain to take a photograph but they were moving too quickly.

We checked out of the lodge and birded our way back up the Manu Road, jumping out at likely corners to walk for a stretch before the minibus caught us up again. On one bend, out of the corner of my eye I caught a glimpse of something red down amongst the lush vegetation below. It was a car! A red VW Beetle, about 50m below the road, pointing back up at us. Judging by the dented roof and broken windscreen it looked as though it had slipped off the road, possibly in the previous day's rainstorm, and had rolled over before coming to a rest against a large tree. It was lucky that tree was there, as the next stop would have been the river bed another 150m or so lower. Just looking at it made the hairs on the back of my neck stand up. It looked as though someone had climbed down quite recently, but we couldn't see anyone still down there so we hoped they'd been rescued by now.

We hadn't gone much further when a little old lady flagged us down. She had a gnarled walnut face and was carrying a huge sack of coca leaves. Had we seen any policemen, she wanted to know. Well, yes, we had passed a group of three policemen walking up the Manu Road just a few bends back, our driver told her. They'd been searching all the vehicles going up and down the road, and had been checking the bushes along the roadside. She squealed and scurried back up the road a short way before disappearing straight over the edge. Catching up, we found her burying her sack of coca leaves under a bush and covering it with extra dead branches and leaves. People are allowed to collect coca leaves in small quantities for their own consumption, but the police were cracking down on large-scale smugglers using the Manu Road to get their product into Cusco. We had to admit, however, that she seemed a pretty unlikely drug dealer.

Over the top and down the other side into lower altitude again, we drove through a town where the entire population seemed to have taken to the streets. It was football night, we found out. Apparently the ladies' teams are a real hit, as the women charge up and down the pitch on their little legs, still wearing their traditional full skirts, which go flying whenever they dive for the ball – much to the delight of the male spectators. It was such a shame that we didn't have time to stop and enjoy the fun too, but there was still several hours' driving ahead of us before Cusco. We finally made it back to the hotel, thanked Marlene and our driver, and crashed wearily into our bed.

There was slight confusion in the morning when we tried to check out of the hotel to go to the airport. Somehow we'd got our days mixed up and weren't due to leave until the next day, so we returned to our room and unpacked our overnight things again. With extra time on our hands now but no birds within easy reach, we fired up the computer and worked on our presentation for the British Birdwatching Fair. After several hours of this, however, we started to get cabin fever and went for a walk around Cusco.

Alan had decided he needed a haircut, so we wandered the streets looking for a barber. Suddenly Yoda stepped out of a doorway and said 'Haircut you want?' Actually, we're not sure what he said, as it was all in rapid Spanish, but before you could say Star Wars, Alan was sitting in the barber's chair enjoying a '*Numero dos*' from a very short barber with a broad bald head and decidedly pointy ears. Anyway, if that's what a Jedi Master does in another life, he certainly makes a very good job of it.

Successfully checking out of the hotel a second time, we jumped in a taxi down to Cusco airport, and then began our marathon haul back to the UK: Cusco to Lima, Lima to Madrid, Madrid to Heathrow and Heathrow to Manchester – about two days later. Amazingly, our luggage made it too.

Peru had been much tougher than we'd anticipated, but we'd added 183 new species to our list and left with a grand total of 2,930 species under our belt. The 3,000 landmark wasn't far off.

2,930 species

12–25 August, UK:
BirdFair and the Banker (Ruth)

It felt very strange to be back home in August for two whole weeks. Not that we sat around and put our feet up. First, we made time for some admin. We checked our website statistics and were thrilled to see how our visitor numbers had grown around the world. Most important, however, we were here for the British Birdwatching Fair – or BirdFair, as it's more familiarly known. We, and thousands of other birders, make the annual pilgrimage to Rutland Water, east of Leicester in the UK Midlands, to be part of this annual Glastonbury Festival for birders. OK, so there aren't too many rock bands here, but at least the muddy wellies are the same. BirdFair is a Mecca for anyone with even the vaguest connection with birds and birding. Under a collection of huge marquees you'll find tour operators, bird art and photography, outdoor clothing, bird books, bird food and feeders, optics demonstrations and sales, conservation charities, rustic craftsmen, guided walks, talks and quizzes.

We go every year to help out on the Tropical Birding stand, although I'm not sure whether we're more of a help or a hindrance, as many of our friends drop by for a good chinwag rather than to book up one of the tours. This year was a little different though. Apart from showing our appreciation of all that the guys had done for us so far – by buying them coffees during the day and beers in the evening, at least – we were here as guest speakers. We were booked to give a half-hour talk on *The Biggest Twitch* in the Events Marquee: a privilege this, as most mere mortals are given twenty-minute slots in the smaller lecture marquees. Had we achieved celebrity status?

Now, we're both old hands at giving talks, but it was still a little daunting to stand up in front of a large audience, including many of our friends grinning away at us from the front rows. But we certainly weren't short of material for our half-hour whistle stop tour around the first half of *The Biggest Twitch*, as we shared some of our best photos and funniest anecdotes to give the audience a flavour of our adventures so far.

And what a fantastic audience! They laughed in all the right places and gave us a rapturous applause at the end. For the rest of BirdFair, people visited us on the TB stand, or stopped us as we walked around to tell us how much they'd enjoyed it. Brian Bland of Sunbird was even kind enough to say it was the best talk he'd ever seen, which was high praise indeed.

We dropped by our sponsors to thank them for their support. Swarovski Optik had given us each a pair of binoculars and a telescope, which were still working well despite everything they'd had to endure. So the least we could do was drop by and thank Christine Percy for their support. Next, we visited Maria on the Country Innovation stand to prove that the fleeces she'd donated were still in full working order too.

We also made one of the most important contacts of our big year, or at least for the follow up to *The Biggest Twitch*, when Keith Barnes introduced us to

207

Nigel Redman of A&C Black publishers, who are well known for their excellent Helm field guides, among many other bird books. Nigel immediately saw the potential of a *Biggest Twitch* book that would bridge the birding/adventure travel gap. He encouraged us to contact him with a synopsis and some potential chapter headings. And now here you are, holding the book in your hands and reading the results of that very conversation. Thank you Nigel, for having such foresight!

We even managed to add a UK bird to our list at BirdFair, based on some hot gen from US visitor, Don Doolittle, who was working on Debi Shearwater's stand opposite us. Somehow the fact that we still needed Tawny Owl had come up in conversation, and Don told us where he'd seen one the previous night as he drove down a narrow lane to his hotel. That evening, we cruised slowly along said lane and, sure enough, a dark shape swept low across in front of us. Not the greatest view, perhaps, but we're both familiar enough with Tawny Owls to be confident, and another bird was added to the list.

If the days at BirdFair are long and hard, then the nights can be even longer. A lot of networking takes place around the bars and restaurants of Oakham, the nearest town, with vast quantities of beer and wine consumed to seal the deals. Even though we'd spent all day with them on the TB stand, we still wanted to go out in the evening with Iain, Keith and Christian, to catch up on what they were up to and to talk about our itinerary for the rest of the year. They now knew that we had run out of money at this critical stage; we had enough funds for the remaining flights, but no money left over to eat or stay anywhere. Alternatively we had enough money to eat for the rest of the year if we stayed in the UK and didn't travel – but we wouldn't see enough new birds. We needed a Plan B.

The most expensive part of our year so far had been the flights, since fuel costs had caused ticket prices to rocket. Ahead of us lay some big, bird-rich countries where day-to-day living was pretty cheap once you'd actually got there. So we got out the big red pen and slashed our itinerary. Out went the short visits to several side countries, nice though their endemic birds might be. Instead, we focused on three main countries that would give us plenty of birds without too many costly international flights. Thus New Zealand, Thailand and Borneo were ditched; they were just too expensive. Instead we planned to spend a month each in southern Africa, Australia and India, where the birds were excellent and the living was easy. We kept the last two weeks of the year free. If we had enough money left, or needed a final boost to our list, we might be able to make it across to southern Ecuador, back on Tropical Birding territory, where we could finish with a flourish and not break the bank.

Suddenly our challenge seemed do-able again. With a sweep of the red pen, the TB guys had made the impossible possible, and had given us hope that all our efforts so far hadn't been in vain. We still had a budget shortfall to find a way around, but at least now we had a firm plan that would give us the bird numbers we needed and a good idea of how much money was necessary to achieve it. Now all we needed was the money itself. Simple.

We'd already put everything we owned into *The Biggest Twitch*, so now there was just one person we could turn to for help. It was time to visit my mother. Although Mum is more of a garden birdwatcher than a global twitcher, and though she may have privately thought me totally mad, she was very supportive of *The Biggest Twitch* and proud of what we'd achieved so far. She also understood our dilemma: if we stopped now, we wouldn't bankrupt ourselves but we wouldn't have achieved anything either. We'd be two people who'd tried to break a world record and failed – and who would be interested in that? But if we went for broke and managed to succeed, we could be world record-breakers. Who knows what this might lead to? Fame in the birding world, bird guiding commissions, perhaps even more book deals.

I showed Plan B to Mum and explained how much money we needed to complete the year, including both the cost of flights and food until 31 December. Mum took a deep breath – and then reached for the chequebook. Hey presto: we were solvent again. Aren't mothers the most marvellous people! The *Biggest Twitch* wouldn't have been completed had it not been for Mum's amazing generosity. This book is for her, and if it takes every single royalty payment we ever receive, we'll pay back every penny. So go on, dear reader: buy yourself another copy. It's all in a very good cause!

I also got the chance to see my sister, Sue Kenwell. Sue had been kind enough to run *The Biggest Twitch* 'Base Camp', looking after all the admin at home for us while we'd been on the road, fielding enquiries, paying bills, sweet-talking the bank manager. It wasn't a very glamorous role, but it was absolutely crucial to our success. Ewan McGregor and Charlie Boorman on *The Long Way Down* had a whole team of Sues to sort things out for them – we had just the one, but we couldn't have done it without her.

By now Alan and I had been apart for five whole days, with me visiting the family bank and my friends in southern England, while Alan looked after the Tropical Birding guys in Wales before they had to fly back to Ecuador and South Africa. However, refinanced and reunited, it was time to pack up and get going again. *The Biggest Twitch* total had been stuck on 2,931 species for too long. We had to get back on the road.

2,931 species

PART SEVEN

Back to Africa

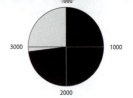

3000

1000

2000

26 August–10 September, South Africa: Part One (Alan)

'We can really boost your score on this leg if we go hard and fast,' declared Keith, as he greeted us with a smile at Johannesburg airport.

We liked his style. We have known Keith Barnes, from Tropical Birding, for many years and have shared some great birds and great fun – including our February trip to Ethiopia – so we were really looking forward to this African adventure.

First, though, there was some important admin. We needed visas for our trip to India in November, so had to present our passports at the British Embassy in Jo'burg. As we did not want to lose any birding time, Keith had arranged for a man to handle the visas for us. We felt more than a little uneasy handing over our precious passports and a wad of cash to Claude.

'No problem,' said Keith confidently. 'Claude will sort it all out. He'll have your visas back before you are due to leave.'

Easy for him to say, it was not his passport that was now disappearing into the crowded streets of one of the meanest cities in the world with a man we had met only minutes earlier. What if we never saw him again? How much time would we lose then? With the world record so close, we could not afford any setbacks.

But Keith was already striding on his very long legs towards the hire car collection point. We hurried after him. To lose passports would be bad; to lose passports and bird guide would be a disaster!

We were soon out of the city and heading for the rolling grasslands of Wakkerstroom, with the promise of lots of new birds. Our progress, as ever, was slow; Keith slammed on the brakes and leapt out of the car at regular intervals, frantically pointing out additions to our list. A bizarre and wonderful Long-tailed Widowbird flapped over a field of tall grass, with jerky wing beats and its ludicrously long tail flowing behind. South African Cliff Swallows, always good to pick up, hawked over an area of bare ground.

After a long drive we reached Wakkerstroom and met our local bird guide, Lucky. We hoped he would live up to his name. He was rather tubby, had a ready smile and spoke good English. As we headed off into the open grasslands in search of larks, Keith quickly briefed Lucky about our quest and warned that we had to move fast. Lucky got it straight away and was soon hurrying us along if we lingered on a bird. No sooner were Red-capped and Pink-billed Larks on our list than we were on our way again.

The next lark was a tough one: Rudd's Lark. Lucky called in at what he said was *the* place. It looked identical to the miles of grassland we had just driven through, but the man knew his patch. We spread out and began to walk slowly forward, scanning for movement ahead. We soon found Rufous-naped and Eastern Clapper Larks both new for us. And then Keith heard the Rudd's. What Keith does not know about larks is not worth knowing: the man is a walking lark encyclopaedia.

But where was the bird? We retraced our steps and there it was. How had we missed it? No time to dwell on the question, we were off again.

Larks are fine, and of course these were new for our list, but it has to be said we did not quite share Keith's passion for these rather subtle little brown birds. We perked up, however, when Lucky announced our next target bird: Blue Crane. Some distant shapes two fields away were transformed in the scopes into South Africa's elegant national birds, striding across the stubble, with their trailing elongated wing feathers looking like a Victorian lady's bustle.

It had been a nice afternoon out on the grasslands, mild and calm, but suddenly a cold wind sprang up from nowhere. It was amazing how quickly the temperature plummeted. This wind was coming from Antarctica, apparently, and we could well believe it. We hurried to don extra layers, hats and gloves. Birds vanished from the open plains as they sought shelter from the icy blast from the south.

Out of the wind, thankfully, we explored our self-catering house at Wakkerstroom. Suddenly, just as we were wandering around bagging bedrooms and checking out the facilities, the air was filled with an ear-splitting high-pitched scream. What on earth was happening? We all met in the kitchen covering our ears against the appalling noise. Ruth was looking guilty and pointed to a button on the wall. She had pressed it to see if it was a light switch.

'That's not a light switch,' bellowed Keith. 'It's a panic alarm!"

How could we stop it? We searched frantically for an instruction book, thinking that any second now a crack police swat team would burst in. Luckily we managed to turn it off and peace was restored. No police arrived, anyway, so just as well it was only a false alarm.

Dawn found us overlooking the wetland just outside Wakkerstrom. Jesus, it was cold! But the shallow pools and marshes were teeming with life and we were adding new birds fast. They all had a similar theme: African Rail, African Snipe and African Marsh Harrier.

We collected Lucky again and headed out into the sea of grass around the town, this time taking the Utrecht road. The bitter wind was making it tough to find birds, but we eventually picked up a lovely Buff-streaked Chat (looking to us more like a wheatear) and a handsome male Sentinel Rock-Thrush.

Taking our leave of Lucky we set off on our long drive southeast to Mkuze Game Reserve, taking the bad weather with us. We arrived too late to enter the reserve, so had to be content with birding around the periphery. Here we found Brown-headed Kingfisher, Burnt-necked Eremomola and White-throated Robin-Chat, before a spectacular thunderstorm hit, complete with frightening lightening bolts crashing to earth. This was particularly cruel timing, as we were right on the verge of a major milestone, with just one more species needed to reach 3,000. It was not going to be today, in this downpour, but Keith promised a pre-dawn start. We retreated to our rooms at the Ghost Mountain Inn with high hopes for the morning.

The next thing we knew, Keith was hammering on our bedroom door. Damn! The alarm had not gone off. We shot out of bed and scrambled to get ready, bird number 3,000 awaited!

Once in the park we entered real safari country, heading on dirt roads into thick thorn bush, where Keith instructed us to look out for rhinos. We drew up in a parking area, hopped out and set off on foot towards a nearby hide. Now we were out on foot, the idea of rhinos took on a whole new significance. Adrenalin was pumping as we crept through the bush, half-expecting to bump into a huge beast at any moment.

We reached the hide and settled down to watch the almost-dry waterhole. In swooped a chicken-sized bird dressed in a riot of colour. Purple-crested Turaco. What a bird for number 3,000! High fives all round. We fired off a few record shots, despite the bird being on the far side of the pools. It was a very special bird.

Then, something very large appeared, moving towards us: the massive bulk of a White Rhinoceros. This ancient-looking creature, like something evolution had overlooked, came lumbering down the slope and into the mud just a few yards from the hide. It was amazing to be this close to such a huge wild animal. We could see its eyelashes and hear it breathing. When it finally moved away, we thought it safe to return to the car. But on very high alert.

As we reached the vehicle Keith came to a sudden stop. Had he seen another rhino? No, this time it was a small bird moving about in the bushes on the edge of the parking area. At first we could not get a clear view. Then it hopped up, revealing itself as a female Pink-spotted Twinspot. This delightful little finch was high on our wanted list here. Typically, we were still not satisfied and wanted a male. We didn't have to wait long: a stunning spotty male jumped up and joined the female. Perfect!

Deeper into the park, Keith heard a call and leapt from the car. We followed him into the bush, walking several hundred yards from the track, but the call had stopped. We stood quietly waiting for it to return.

'Rhinos!' bellowed Keith, suddenly. 'Run!'

Ruth and I high-tailed it out of there at full pelt towards the car. We had gone about fifty yards before we realised: no Keith! We looked back, half expecting to see him being trampled by a huge rhino. But no, he was doubled over with laughter. No rhinos, just Keith's rather sick sense of humour.

'Gee, you guys can run fast, eh?' he managed to say, through his laughter. Hm, we thought, revenge will be sweet – and served cold.

Meanwhile we kept picking up new birds, with highlights including Neergaard's Sunbird, African Penduline-Tit, Senegal Lapwing and Black-backed Puffback. A stop by a lake brought us Pink-backed Pelican and Water Thick-knee, while both Open-billed and Yellow-billed Storks were feeding next to loafing hippos and crocodiles. Only in Africa would you get a combo like this. We were loving it.

A long drive that evening took us east towards the coast and St Lucia wetlands, our next birding destination. It was very late when we found a bed and breakfast for the night and the owners were less than pleased to have guests arrive at that hour, but we charmed them into letting us stay.

Down at Richard's Bay the next day we eventually found a wetland reserve surrounded by industrial complexes. It was a grim place, the hide littered with fast food junk and graffiti, reminding us of the UK. But, as is so often the case, the grottier the place, the better the birds. We scored with Lesser Jacana and then two African Yellow Warblers.

As we left here on a very rutted and bumpy track, the boot of the car suddenly popped open. The catch had sheared and now it would not shut. This wasn't good, as we had all our kit inside and wanted to be able to leave the car when we went off birding. Nothing for it: we tied it down with rope as best we could, and would have to keep the car in sight at all times.

Stopping to scan a roadside lake paid off, with better views of Lesser Jacana and three White-backed Ducks, new for the year. Then we reached St Lucia, where woodland just behind the beach was very productive. We tracked down a gang of impressive Trumpeter Hornbills, along with Crested Flycatcher and Woodward's Batis. Our luck ran out that evening when we drew a blank on owls and nightjars, but we did enjoy the beautiful stars in the crystal clear sky. And when we totted up the list before we collapsed into bed, we had reached 3,040 species for the year. We were getting there.

The last day of August 2008 will always live in our memories – and nightmares. The day started in fine form, as we added Wattled Crane to our list. This was a huge relief for me as it was a bogey bird. Back in 2000 we had looked hard for this species but had failed to find it – despite meeting other birders who had seen them only two days before we arrived – and then earlier this year we'd failed to find them in Ethiopia. On this occasion it was easy: we scanned some distant fields with a scope and there they were: two magnificent Wattled Cranes. We drove closer and enjoyed a much better look at these stately birds. In fact, the morning went very well indeed. We picked up the scarce Red-winged Francolin, and went on to see Cape Rock-Thrush and Cape Robin-Chat before screeching to a stop to watch Cape Vulture soaring overhead.

It had been a 4am departure from St Lucia, so by early afternoon we were flagging a little and needed to find a lunch stop. The wind had been picking up all morning and was now blowing hard, but it was still very hot. In the distance, we could see several huge fires blazing out of control, eating up the grasslands apace. Eventually, driving between Bulwa and Underberg, we found a roadside café and thankfully pulled in for a break. On the ridge in the distance was another fire.

'We can watch the fire while we eat,' I joked.

The car boot had still been giving us trouble, so Ruth and I tried to retie the ropes yet again while Keith walked up the long flight of stone steps to order lunch. I am not sure how long we fiddled about, not long, that's for sure; but when we turned to follow Keith we had the shock of our lives: the fire was racing down the hill towards us. We couldn't comprehend how it had covered the ground so quickly. The huge flames, higher than a house, were coming at us like a steam train. Shit! We ran towards the café, shouting for Keith to get out and run for the car.

'Too late!' Keith yelled back from the doorway. 'Get in the building now!'

There was no time to argue the point. We could already feel the intense heat on our skin. We dived inside and slammed the door. Several other people were inside, and all looked petrified as they saw the wall of fire advancing on us. Keith grabbed the owner and fired a question.

'What's this roof made of?'

The answer came back that it was corrugated iron.

'Then we stay put.' It was a statement, not an invitation for debate. Ruth clung to me and everyone just stood and stared, wide-eyed, as the roar of the blaze swept towards us. Time stood still.

'We're going to die, aren't we?' whispered Ruth.

'No, shouldn't think so,' I said, though thinking yes, very likely!

The room quickly filled with acrid, choking smoke, stinging our eyes and burning our lungs. We pulled our T-shirts up over our noses and mouths to try and filter out the worst of it. Then the flames came, licking the windows on all four sides of the tiny building. The temperature rocketed and I looked around for any water supply to douse ourselves in when the flames burst through.

Then it was gone. Silence. A woman began to cry, and we realised the flames had passed us by. We stood in silence, taking in the smoke-filled room, the tables and floor covered in ash and soot. We open the door and gulped in fresher air.

Then we remembered the car, with all our gear inside. We ran down to the car park and were astonished to see it standing as we had left it. Luckily we had abandoned it well away from the edges of the large parking area, so the fire had swept around it rather than through it. The force of the wind had pushed the fire so fast that it didn't really take hold for long in any one spot. We had been incredibly lucky. As we reached the car we saw that we did have a small problem; the ash and smoke had been sucked through the opening in the boot. The car was full of soot and ash, and of course it stank and would do so for days. But we still felt very fortunate.

Had it not been for Keith's quick thinking to stay put rather than try to outrun the fire, it may have been a very different story. The local paper the next morning reported the tragic deaths of fourteen people in the very fire that had engulfed our lunch spot, and it sent a shiver down our spines to read the awful story. There but for the grace of God …

Putting the fire behind us, we headed for the spectacular Drakensberg Mountains in Lesotho for high-altitude birds. A long drive took us to Underberg, where we confirmed our booking for the next day's 4WD adventure up the Sani Pass into the heart of the Drakensberg. Everything was looking good – a driver in a 4WD would pick us up early at our hotel for our highland adventure – until the question of passports arose. Of course we didn't have ours, Claude had them back in Jo'burg, but we'd need them to get beyond the South African border post at the foot of the pass. This was a problem. The border post is at the bottom of the long, twisting mountain road that winds up the pass, while the Lesotho border post is perched on the edge of the escarpment at the top. The no-mans-land in between is where our birds were!

Keith was not confident we would get past the guards in the morning, but all we could do was try. We checked into the rather expensive Sani Pass Hotel; there was little choice in this area, as we needed to be close for an early start in the morning.

After dinner that night we counted up the new species for the day. We were on 3,055 birds for 2008. This meant we needed just over 300 more to break the record, with just eight months gone.

At dawn we were out in the bitter cold. It was already clear that we had climbed in altitude – and we were set to go a lot higher. Thankfully the gale-force winds had gone, and it was a beautiful clear, early spring morning. Our vehicle duly arrived with driver Mondli, and we set off towards the Sani Pass. The road became rougher, and we soon realised why Keith had booked a 4WD and local driver. As it deteriorated, though, the scenery got better, with steep cliffs and spectacular waterfalls.

At the South African border post we went to speak to the guard. His answer was simple and blunt: 'You must go back and fetch your passports.'

'We can't go back and get them,' I told him. 'They are in Jo'burg. We just want to see the birds; we won't go into Lesotho.'

'You must go back,' he retorted.

'We want to see the birds!' I persisted.

And so it continued, until – to our surprise – the guard suddenly conceded, with a weak 'Oh, go on then.'

We thanked him, dashed for the car and sped past the border post before he had time to change his mind. We were elated. Now, where were the birds? As we progressed further up the pass the scenery became even more dramatic – and all beneath a cobalt blue sky. We soon picked up our first great new bird, as raucous calls drew our attention to a family party of Ground Woodpeckers. They came swooping down the valley from rock to rock and ended up perched on a boulder right next to us, posing for photos. Next up was Gurney's Sugarbird, sitting out sunning himself. Higher up, near the top of the escarpment, we scored our most wanted Sani speciality: Orange-breasted Rockjumper. What a bird! And living up to its name perfectly, jumping around on rocks in the sun. Lifting our eyes from the birds, we had the whole of the Sani Pass falling away below us and rock walls all around, with views across the mountains as far as we could see: another magic *Biggest Twitch* moment to savour.

Driving up over the top of the escarpment we were almost in Lesotho, and in danger of needing our passports again, so we kept a healthy distance from the border post. Here we added a new mammal to our list: the cute and enchanting Sloggett's Ice-Rat. These small, rather gerbil-like animals somehow managed to survive up here, despite the bitter cold at night. They were obviously tougher than they looked.

We were very reluctant to leave this awe-inspiring place, with its weird and wonderful wildlife, so we savoured every second of the return journey and took hundreds of photos of the gob-smackingly beautiful scenery.

The afternoon was spent exploring an area of forest that was new to Keith but about which he had received good reports. After a little confusion over the directions, we noticed a signpost with parrots on. That looked promising. We followed, and it led us to the forest. We had quite a long shopping-list of species that we needed here, but one topped it: Cape Parrot. And no sooner had we entered the forest than we heard a telltale squawking overhead!

'Run!' yelled Keith.

And we did, out of the wood and into the open, scanning the skies. But we'd missed it. Damn! There are only some five hundred Cape Parrots in the world, so if we missed it here, we missed it for good. Keith was sure of the call, but we had heard only one brief squawk. Although the Clements taxonomic list hasn't yet split this species from Brown-headed Parrot, it is a likely contender for the future so we wanted to see these birds for ourselves. Not that we doubted Keith, of course, though he gave us a look that suggested we ought to believe him.

So now we had a decision to make: go back into the forest, where we knew we had a good chance of plenty of new birds, or stay out in the open and hope for more fly-over parrots. The decision was made for us. Twenty-two squawking

Cape Parrots swept overhead! It got even better: the flock wheeled around and landed in the top of a dead tree in the sun against a blue sky. Now Keith was smiling broadly. The flock took flight and circled again, and was joined by more birds. We now had sixty-one birds – over ten percent of the world population – in view. It was a sobering thought.

Back onto the forest trail and it turned into one of those magical birding experiences when everything just drops in your lap. Not only had we found the parrots quickly but each time Keith mentioned a bird we should look for, out it popped right in front of us. It was outrageous good luck: new bird followed new bird. A Bush Blackcap erupted in song just feet from our faces; Forest Canary flew in at the merest hint of our tape; Orange Thrush just hopped onto the path; Red-necked Francolin scuttled through the undergrowth and, best of all, a stunning green and white Knysna Turaco paraded along a thick branch above us.

As the light began to fail, we left this amazing place, where the birds had been so good to us and headed for Creighton and Button Birding. Our destination for the night was the B&B run by friends of Keith's, Malcolm and Gail Gemmell. Malcolm also runs a birdwatching tour company called Button Birding, and we were hoping he could help us with some potentially tricky species. Despite our late arrival, we were greeted warmly and ushered in to join a family meal. What lovely people!

Our daily log confirmed we'd added a pleasing thirty new species, inching up *The Biggest Twitch* total to 3,085. It was now less than 600 from the world record. We could do this!

The next morning, out in the pre-dawn cold, Malcolm was buzzing with excitement at the prospect of the day ahead. This may have been because of *The Biggest Twitch*, but in fact he'd been exactly the same when I first met him nine years earlier: a bundle of energy and enthusiasm, and ever eager to share the next bird with his companions. We scanned open farm fields and quickly found huge Denham's Bustards, the males strutting about turning their feathers inside out in display, reminiscent of the Great Bustards we had watched in Spain. Was that really only this year? It seemed so long ago already; we had done so much and seen so much since.

We upgraded our 'heard only' Red-winged Francolins into 'seens', as a male called out in the open in a nearby field. The same spot gave us another mammal: a pretty Oribi antelope, which Malcolm told us has adapted well to farmland living. We drove a network of dirt farm roads, with numerous stops each time Malcolm leapt out to point out another bird.

Sadly, mindful of our long drive ahead, Keith had to call a halt to our Button Birding experience. But Malcolm insisted that he first did us one more favour, and he made a professional job of tying down our boot lid. Our only worry now was whether we would ever get our bags out again. We said our thank-yous and promised to return. (How often had we spoken those words this year? And each time we'd meant it.)

Our route now took us via Jo'burg, where we swapped our broken-booted car for one that locked without ropes. Keith headed back to Cape Town. We were to bird on alone towards Kruger National Park, where we hoped to ease off just a little and have some recovery time before we went hard at it again.

Our destination for the night was the beautiful forest reserve of Kurisa Moya

Nature Lodge in Northern Limpopo Province. We arrived late and apologised to our hosts Ben and Lisa de Boer. This lovely couple ran the lodge and were key players in the conservation of this wonderful area. Once again we were humbled by what Ben and Lisa were achieving here with limited resources, another recurring theme during *The Biggest Twitch*.

At first light the following morning Ben led us into the wonderful forest around the lodge. Our most-wanted target bird soon appeared: Black-fronted Bush-shrike, a range-restricted species. But the highlight was still to come. We drove to another area of forest where a pair of Bat Hawks had built their nest on the edge of a clearing and Ben knew just where it was. At first we could see nothing. But I really wanted these raptors, so Ben said we would stay a little longer. We all redoubled our efforts and suddenly Ben had one. No, two! These mega birds were sitting in a dead tree not far from the nest, but you needed to get the angle just right to see them through the trees. A great spot by Ben. The telescopes gave us wonderful views of these crepuscular hunters, which – surprise, surprise! – feed almost exclusively on bats.

Another morning had just whizzed by and we realised that we must leave if we were to reach the Kruger. We thanked Ben and Lisa for their wonderful hospitality and great birds, and headed east.

Ben had very kindly phoned ahead and booked us into a lodge at the northern end of this vast park. We entered by the Punda Maria gate and drove towards the Mozambique border crossing, where Ben had told us we would find the lodge close by. It had all sounded so easy. Well, we found the border crossing all right, but there was no lodge to be seen. The light was fading and we knew there was a driving curfew in the park: you have to be in camp by 6pm or the gates are locked. Anyone caught outside after this runs the gauntlet of the lions roaming around or pays a huge penalty to be let into the locked lodge. Time was running out fast. We didn't want to pay a heavy fine, nor did we fancy driving around lion-filled Kruger in the dark! Then we saw a 4WD parked by a river and we drew up alongside the group of four, rather shifty-looking white men, who seemed unconcerned about the imminent curfew. They reassured us that the lodge was only minutes away and gave us directions. We breathed a huge sigh of relief and headed straight there, arriving at one minute to six. How's that for timing?

Walking in, we were struck by what an amazingly beautiful place this was: more luxury hotel than bush camp. A member of staff approached us rather timidly and asked if we had a reservation.

'Oh yes! Ben from Kurisa Moya rang earlier to make the booking.'

This brought a blank look. 'I will go and enquire.'

He was soon back with an attractive white woman who introduced herself as the manager. 'Are you *sure* you have a reservation?' she enquired.

Less sure now, I told her about the phone call, but the manager explained that she had no record of the booking and that the lodge had been fully booked for weeks. Now what were we going to do? It was well past curfew and now pitch black. Clearly we had come to the wrong place, but there was no chance now of finding the right one.

'Take a seat and have a drink,' the manager told us. 'I'll see what can be done.' With that, she vanished into the African night. We ordered stiff drinks and crossed our fingers that a bed would appear. Didn't fancy sleeping in our little hire car.

Soon she was back and smiling. 'We can offer you a room, but it's just been painted, so please be careful,' she explained. 'Also, we have new guests arriving in the morning so you'll need to be out by 10am. Would that be all right?'

We were delighted, of course, until Ruth – ever practical – asked the price. Our faces must have fallen when she told us the usual fee: 1,700 rand per person per night. This was a fortune, by our standards, nearby two weeks' budget for just one night. But she kindly offered us a generous discount on the basis that we had missed the afternoon game drive and would be leaving before noon.

Mumbling our gratitude, we were shown to our 'room'. It was a tent, but no ordinary tent. And having got over the shock of the cost, we decided we might as well enjoy it. The centre piece was a giant four-poster bed. Beyond were his and hers bathrooms with both indoor and outdoor showers. It seemed luxurious beyond belief for a safari camp in the middle of nowhere.

We were very tempted by the huge bed, but as dinner was included and all we had eaten today was a few biscuits, food for once took priority over sleep. In deference to our surroundings, we showered and put on clean T-shirts before heading down to the dining area overlooking the floodlit river.

Well, we thought we had made an effort, but boy, did we feel out of place! Our fellow diners were dressed up to the nines. The waiter greeted us with a rather embarrassed smile and showed us to a table in a dark corner well away from the other guests. The food was in keeping with everything else here at Pafuri Camp: we feasted like kings and drank fine wine, while listening to the noises from the surrounding bush. Afterwards, very full, we walked slowly back to our tent gazing at the magical sky above, littered with millions of stars. We collapsed into the wonderful bed and wished time could stand still so we could stay here a while. As we lay there, a lion roared close by.

All too soon the alarm shattered our night of bliss and we were up and out, ready for the morning game drive. It was still dark as we made our way down to the veranda overlooking the river, and we received steaming mugs of hot chocolate and croissants, with the promise of a real breakfast later. Together with the other guests we piled into two large, open safari vehicles and set off in search of wildlife. It was quickly obvious that our guide and driver both knew their stuff, and they were soon explaining all about the wildlife, plants, geology and history of Kruger. It was fascinating to be out in the bush with people so knowledgeable and passionate.

We stopped to climb up on a rock summit that overlooked a vast river gorge and just sat and stared at the view. Walter our guide produced tea and biscuits, our second of three breakfasts. This was how birding should be. OK, it would have been nice to add a few new birds, but for once we were not complaining; the elephants wandering right past our vehicle were a pretty good alternative.

Back at camp, a delicious breakfast buffet was laid before us and we tucked in with gusto. As we ate, we watched the river below us. A young elephant came down to drink – so close we could hear the water gurgling up his trunk. Then, a moment of panic as a plover flew in and landed out of sight. We leapt up and scanned the river. Where had it gone? We dashed over to our tent, which also overlooked the river, and there it was, just ten metres away: the bizarre and beautiful White-headed Lapwing, one of our most wanted birds here in Kruger. Those long, yellow facial wattles gave this new wader extra appeal.

A polite cough from behind us announced the arrival of Edward, our room attendant, who sadly informed us that it was time for us to leave.

It felt a little odd to be driving through the park in our pocket-sized hire car, just the two of us, no armed guards or big 4WD. But we soon got used to it and began picking up more wonderful new birds: a loop road that swung by the river produced Bat-like Spinetails overhead, their flittering flight living up to their name; a bit of patient stalking at a picnic site gave us Eastern Nicator, like an over-sized cross between a warbler and a shrike; and then we first heard then saw a gang of Brown-headed Parrots. Nice to have the chance to compare them with the Cape Parrots we'd seen earlier.

Heading south, our next destination was the Punda Maria Rest Camp and this time we did not want to leave finding it to the last minute. It seemed very odd driving steadily through the bush, without stopping for the elephants and giraffes we saw by the roadside, but in Kruger you would not get very far if you stopped for every single animal, however amazing.

At Punda Maria we booked a night drive, in the hope of some owls or nightjars. At the appointed time we waited at reception but there was nobody in sight. Then we saw an open safari truck approaching, complete with spotlights, It turned out there was no one else; we had the drive to ourselves. This meant we had a spotlight each and could scan for eye shine and shout 'Stop!' as often as we liked.

First to show was an African Civet, a new mammal for us. Then an elephant loomed out of the night right next to the track, looking even bigger than normal in the dark. Meanwhile Springhares bounced around, more like kangaroos than hares.

Suddenly the brakes went on hard. Oh my god! We had come to a halt just a few metres from a pride of lions. These huge cats were lounging beside the road and taking no notice of us whatsoever. Our hearts pounded: one bound and they could easily have jumped straight into the open truck. How amazing to be this close to these beautiful creatures, and just the three of us in the black of an African night. Yes, another of those *Biggest Twitch* memories that will live forever.

Birds? Oh, yes, we did see some of those, too, managing to notch up African Scops Owl, and Square-tailed and Fiery-necked Nightjars. Almost as we were back at the camp three Spotted Hyenas slouched past and ran into the bush.

Safely back in our room, Ruth decided to phone home to wish her mum a happy birthday. She'd left her mobile phone in the car so decided to use mine. Ruth's mum had a strange tale of her own to tell: earlier that day she had taken a call from someone in South Africa asking if her son Alan had lost his mobile phone. This was pretty weird, as Ruth only has a sister, but the South African connection was too much of a coincidence. Checking the car, we soon realised it was Ruth's phone that was lost. But how had the caller known my name and, more importantly, where was the phone now? It looked as though it would stay lost, as no contact number or name had been left with Ruth's mum.

The next morning, we were out searching for birds but a strong wind had sprung up and birding from the car, as you must do in most of Kruger, was proving tough. We had stopped to watch a fine bull Greater Kudu when another vehicle passed us very slowly, stopped just beyond us and reversed back.

'Are you Alan Davies?' asked the driver, winding down his window.

We were stunned. Here we were, driving around the middle of Kruger looking for birds. How would anyone know who or where we were? Surely we weren't that famous? Then the penny dropped.

'We think we found your phone yesterday,' confirmed the driver.

These kind people had had the presence of mind, on finding the phone, to look at the address book then phone 'Mum', before looking at the photos in the memory and recognising a few of me. What were the chances? Where they had found the phone was over one hundred miles away, but they'd even handed it in at the Punda Maria Rest Camp, so we were soon able to return and collect it.

A six-hour, stop-start drive south to Satara Rest Camp then followed, progress slow due to the sheer amount of wildlife demanding a look every few yards. Bird highlights included a gang of restless Retz's Helmet-shrikes, Groundscraper Thrush, Purple Roller, Red-crested Korhaan and giant Kori Bustards. Accommodation was in lovely round bungalows with thatched roofs complete with nesting Little Swifts.

The next morning we found a massive male lion striding through the bush. As we watched him, a Lappet-faced Vulture soared low overhead. It was just like a scene from a wildlife documentary – where was David Attenborough?

South again, and we came across a pride of lions devouring a recently killed Cape Buffalo. It was a gruesome but fascinating sight. The lions were covered in blood and soon a traffic jam built up as more cars stopped to view Africa in the raw. Ruth thought the cubs were just the cutest things – even though they were covered in blood and gore!

Then came the birding highlight of the day: three massive Southern Ground-Hornbills came marching down the road straight towards us. Huge black birds with bare scarlet facial skin and powerful black bills; they looked a mean bunch. We stopped and watched quietly. The birds came closer and closer, and looked as if they might walk over the car. At the last second they split, two passing the driver's door and one the passenger side just inches from us.

We reached Lower Sabie Rest Camp in the early evening and found we had hippos for neighbours, so the sound effects were interesting as they grunted, farted and bellowed just fifty metres away. Their toilet manners are interesting: they flick their tails rapidly from side to side, while dropping their load, like a homemade muck-spreader. Fascinating, but it certainly does nothing for your appetite watching this just before dinner.

Our last day in Kruger dawned all too soon, and we took a game drive out from Sabie and enjoyed wonderful close up views of elephant families, some with very small young – even cuter than lion cubs, apparently. We also oohed and aahed at the baby hippos and giraffes we saw. Our driver told us the elephant population in Kruger was reaching capacity and a cull was being considered. It seemed very sad, but perhaps better than them starving to death and destroying their own habitat.

We left the park en route for our next quest: to find the very rare Taita Falcon. It was midday by the time we reached the Strijdom road tunnel at Abel Erasmus Pass, where this bird was said to live. We had received precise instructions to drive 1.3km south of the tunnel and park by the craft stall. This we did. Now we needed to find a large rock with the words 'Place of the Bird' painted on it. Easy, right by the road opposite the stall. Then we looked up. A giant rock-face towered above us, stretching up into the blue sky and baking sun. How could we spot a small falcon up there? We'd received another tip for this, too. We walked over to the craft stall and the lady immediately knew why we were here. She came back with us to the rock and all three of us squinted up against the bright sun trying to find a small bird on a vast cliff face.

Then, 'I see it! I see it!' Our new friend had found it. Great news, but now we needed to see it too. The problem was that the cliff was huge and with so many ledges and cracks, it was hard to give directions. A very frustrating few minutes followed as the lady tried repeatedly to direct us to the spot. Then I had it, flying against the cliff. Luckily it soon landed and we got it in the scope. All three of us enjoyed good, if a little hazy views of this miniature Peregrine: such a dinky raptor. Sadly the haze meant our attempts at digi-scoping were very poor, but what a great bird for *The Biggest Twitch*. And a lifer, too.

In this rocky landscape, we also picked up Black Swift and Yellow-streaked Greenbul – a notoriously skulking species – as well as more Cape Rock-Thrushes. The drive on to Long Tom Pass and the Misty Mountain Hotel was scenic but produced no new birds.

Opening the curtains the next morning, our lovely vista of the night before had been replaced by thick fog; guess the hotel name should have been a clue. A very slow drive through the mist and drizzle was no fun and of course there were no birds. We were heading back to Johannesburg Airport for a flight to Zambia, so the fog was particularly unwelcome. We finally escaped the fog but then hit road-works, slowing us again, and then roadworks in fog. Great! Stress levels were rising as we began to think we would miss our flight. Finally we hit clear roads and bombed along, arriving at the airport just in time.

Reaching the airport was a relief, but an even bigger one was seeing Claude waiting for us. He had our passports, complete with their shiny new Indian visas ready for later in the year. So we were free to head for check-in and look for Ken Behrens, who was coming with us to Zambia, our next destination.

As we left South Africa, our year list stood at 3,123. That world record was getting ever closer.

3,123 species

11–29 September, Zambia and Malawi (Alan)

We touched down at dusk in Lusaka. It was a very small airport, for a capital city, and there were few people about. Ken phoned his hire car contact and we took a taxi to a compound to collect our very large, rugged 4WD and hand over a lot of money. Hans, the Dutchman who owned the car was very helpful, if expensive, and he gave us his mobile number as back-up. Did he know something?

It was only a short drive to our accommodation at Pioneer Camp on the outskirts of Lusaka, but it was pitch black by the time we rolled up at our large cottage. We wandered over for a pre-dinner drink, chatting about our trip to the characters leaning on the bar. A couple of beers and one chap bade us farewell and headed off into the night. He was soon back.

'As you guys are into birds,' he said, 'you might want to come and look at this weird bird by the light.'

Intrigued, we hurried outside. At first we saw nothing. Then a bird swooped in and hawked around the light. Jaws hit the floor: a Pennant-winged Nightjar! What's more, it was a male, with full trailing pennants behind each wing – weird and wonderful in equal measure. These elongated wing feathers make it look as though someone has attached a streamer to each wing. If this is what Zambian birding is like, we thought, then we should do just fine.

The next morning, however, our enthusiasm for this new country took a hefty knock. All we wanted to do was get our hands on some Zambian cash: Kwacha. We were in the capital city with plenty of ATM machines about, but not one would accept any of our cards and none of the banks was open. We knew credit cards are not accepted in much of Zambia, and we were heading for remote rural areas where cash would be our only option. Then we remembered Hans and his offer of help. Bet he hadn't imagined we would be phoning him on day one. Hans loaned us some ready cash against Ruth arranging a wire-transfer from the UK into his account. What a nice man!

Much later than we had planned, we headed south out of the city and drove to Masuku Lodge. This lovely place was part of a large farm, where guest cottages had been built in the grounds. It was run by an English couple, Sue and Bill, now retired from the Foreign Office in Lusaka. Before dinner we just had time for a little birding, and picked up Racket-tailed Rollers, Miombo Tit and, best of all, White-headed Black-Chat nesting in the chimney of the main house. Sue produced a lovely home-cooked meal, as Bill entertained us with tales of his adventures in the Foreign Office.

Next morning, with the help of local guide Ruston, we set off in search of Zambia's only endemic bird. Ruston had seen a nesting pair at a neighbouring farm. A dead tree had a promising hole and, sure enough, a head soon popped out and we had our Chaplin's Barbet. Mostly white with red eyebrows this was a striking bird. Soon a second bird flew in and landed in an adjacent tree, showing off in the morning sun. Loud calls broke out and a nest changeover took place, with the sitting bird leaving while her mate climbed in to take over.

Time to hit the road again. But first we had a very nasty shock: fuel here was even more expensive than in the UK, and way more than we had just been paying in South Africa and once more our budget was taking a hit. This could be a pain, especially with problems getting cash. Still worrying about this, we set off for Lochinvar National Park, which sounded more Scottish than African. The directions were vague and, even in our big 4WD, the road was becoming rougher and rougher. We knew we had to take a right turn somewhere but had not seen any turns at all. Then we saw two men sitting on a bench by the road.

'Which way to Lochinvar National Park?' we asked.

One man rose slowly from the bench and came over to the truck. 'The road to Lochinvar is buggered,' he announced, slowly and carefully, rubbing his chin in contemplation.

Not what we wanted to hear. Our new friend breathed alcohol fumes into my face and told us that we should not turn right but keep straight on and ask again in the next village. We continued straight ahead and, maybe predictably, the road rapidly deteriorated into a succession of potholes, each one deeper than its predecessor. Progress dwindled to a painful, boneshaking crawl. Just which road had been 'buggered'?

Mid-afternoon we finally found the entrance gate, but any thoughts of birding were soon dashed. The park warden did not see many visitors, so he was going to make the most of this opportunity. He produced a large entrance form and took great pride, and a very long time, in filling it in, asking all sorts of pointless questions.

Having enjoyed his moment of glory, the warden raised the barrier and allowed us to enter. Now the road became even worse and there were no birds to be seen. We pushed on, but it was another bone-shaking 17.5km before we finally reached the vast lake. By now Ruth was in real pain, as her back had been badly jarred on these impossible roads. This had always been a big risk on *The Biggest Twitch*, as a few years ago she had had major spinal surgery.

While Ruth tried to find some respite in a position that relieved the pain, Ken and I set up the scopes to scan the very distant birds. Typical of our luck this day, the water level was very low. The flocks were distant, and between them and us lay an expanse of gooey mud that made a closer approach impossible. Through the scopes all we could see were hazy shapes. All that effort and discomfort for this!

We drove along the shore of the lake to the Lodge, or – as it was now – a ruin. We had been told that the lodge was not in use, but that there was now a tented camp on the site. Oh no there wasn't! There was nothing here except a few ruined buildings. No chance of staying here the night: we would have to drive all the way out again. Ruth looked gutted; the prospect of that back-shattering drive all over again filled her with dread. And we still had not added a single new bird.

With what little time remained, we drove beside the lakeshore and scanned as best we could. Finally a new bird, and it has to be said it was a top quality one: African Skimmer. A whole flock of these large tern-like birds with their mismatched mandibles rose from a sandbank, circled and landed again. Just for a moment we were elated by this much wanted tick. Then it was back to reality, and the dreaded drive back to the main road in the hope of finding accommodation.

The return journey was every bit as bad as we had feared, with Ruth's back now a major concern.

At least the day ended with a little good fortune. Back on the tarred road – well, more pot-hole than tar – we quickly found a reasonable hotel, The Golden Pillow, with clean rooms. We collapsed, exhausted. But it was not a peaceful night: Ken had to endure a major building project in the room next to his, which went on into the early hours. We, meanwhile, were near a very loud generator that cut in and out all night. What with this and Ruth's back in agony, none of us got much sleep.

Back in the capital Lusaka, we had hoped to end our money problems but, as with everything we had so far experienced in Zambia, it was not easy. After several emails between us and Keith Barnes' wife Yvonne, we thought we had a plan: Yvonne would wire money to Western Union and we would collect it. Easy. We toured the streets of the capital and spotted a Western Union. We duly queued up and finally got to the window.

'We can't help you,' came the response.

'Why not?' we asked, puzzled.

'We don't do wire transfers at this office.'

'Is there an office that does?'

'Yes.'

'Where?' This was painful.

Finally we were given directions. So off we went and queued up again at another identical window.

'We can find no trace of this transaction,' came the discouraging answer.

'Please look again, it was made yesterday.'

'We can find no trace of this transaction.'

Back on the street, we telephoned Yvonne. It turned out that she had not been able to wire the money to a Western Union office, hence 'We can find no trace of this transaction.' Instead, the money had gone to a Moneygram office, so off we went again.

Once we had found a Moneygram office, Ken went in while we looked after the truck. It was a rather dodgy-looking part of town, with far too many people staring intently at us and peering in through the windows. Well, they should have waited a little while longer for the real show: Ken came staggering out of the bank with 13,000,000 Kwacha. Yes, that's thirteen million. We were multi-millionaires!

Now it was time to get out of there. Ken gunned the Toyota's huge engine into life, while Ruth and I broke the 'wad', as it became known, into more manageable chunks and hid them all over the truck: under the seats, under the carpet, behind the door panels, anywhere we could find a space. If we were to be robbed, the bastards would have to work hard to steal it all! Nonetheless, we felt very vulnerable: here we were driving around Zambia with a king's ransom in used notes. We kept checking to see if we were being followed, worried that someone had seen us emerging from the bank. Now at last we could set off into rural Zambia, where we hoped we could add more than the odd bird to our stalled list. Thank you, Yvonne.

It was a hot, dusty and mostly birdless six-hour drive to Kasanka National Park, and we rolled into the camp as dusk was falling. After our Lochinvar experience, we were glad that there was a camp at all. The thatched bungalows overlooked a shallow lake and marsh. We stumbled out of the truck and finally raised our bins on some good-looking habitat – and even some birds. A Dickinson's Kestrel was new for us and a bizarre, low, deep call gave away a handsome Coppery-tailed Coucal sitting up in the reeds. This was more like it. Hippos splashed around in the shallows as crocs lay in wait for unsuspecting prey, and the sunset painted the sky a flaming orange and scarlet.

We sat around a campfire overlooking the lake and chatted to Frank Willems, the resident bird guide. Frank, a Dutchman, had been here for seven months, with his wife Kim and their two children. It was great to hear him reel off the birds he had seen in the park and he promised us much the following day. Food arrived and it tasted so good. At last we were starting to enjoy Zambia. We headed back to our room taking care not to bump into any hippos wandering the edge of the marsh.

The next day, 16 September, was Ruth's birthday. But no lie-in was allowed. We were woken before dawn and Frank was fired up to show us the birds of his new local patch. A quick cup of tea passed for breakfast, then we went out exploring the trails. Kasanka's good variety of habitats – marsh, miombo forest and grassland – meant we quickly saw a lot of birds.

The first major highlight was Ross's Turaco, which – like all its kind – was a stunner. Cabanis' Greenbul and Bocage's Akalat, both forest dwellers, led us a merry dance, before good views were had by all. Boehm's Bee-eaters, posing beautifully in the sunshine, were definitely bird of the day. Mammals also featured well, with both Puku and the elusive Sitatunga being new antelope for us.

It was a long day: over twelve hours in the field. And having had no breakfast, and nothing except emergency biscuits and raisins on the trail, we were starving when we returned to camp at 6.30pm. Water was heated over the fire and welcome showers taken, as the camp staff prepared an overdue meal. We reviewed our sightings for the day and found we had added twenty-one new birds. At last Zambia was beginning to pay its way, and even Ruth agreed that, despite the lack of food, Kasanka was a pretty cool place to spend a birthday.

The next morning we thanked Frank and his staff for their help, and headed off to the much-anticipated Shoebill Lodge. It was another long, dusty drive: six hours, mostly on dirt roads, before finally we found ourselves overlooking a huge, open panorama. In the wet season this would be a shallow lake but now it was an endless expanse of dusty, short-grassed plain: Bangwuelu Swamp. Somewhere out there lay Shoebill Island Camp. All we had to do was find it. As we set off across the flat land, kicking up a cloud of dust in our wake, we encountered herds of Black Lechwe, a handsome antelope endemic to this part of Zambia, while a flock of Caspian Plovers flew ahead of us.

At last we saw a raised area with a gateway and some derelict buildings beyond. Oh no, we thought, not another abandoned camp. But the track continued, and so did we. The next raised area had a few trees. We headed for that and found the tents and shacks of Shoebill Island Camp.

We were shown to our tents, which were rather grubby and tired-looking, then dumped our gear and scanned the adjacent wetlands. It was heaving with birds, which was great, and mosquitoes, which was not so great. A Painted Snipe flew in and began to feed at the water's edge. Fishermen, meanwhile, were all over the place, dragging nets through the shallows, paddling canoes and squabbling with their wives and children. We had expected a wilderness, not a fish market.

As we ate dinner that night in a shack near the tents, the camp manager came to tell us he had exciting news. We had known not to expect Shoebill here at this time of year, as they move deeper into swamps when the waters recede. But now a fisherman had come into camp with the fantastic story that he had found a Shoebill nest and would take us there in the morning. What amazing luck! We couldn't sleep with excitement: the Shoebill is one of nature's freaks, a huge, heron-like bird with a Dutch clog for a beak. It uses this massive appendage to capture lungfish deep in the swamps of central Africa, where it is highly elusive – a must-see bird for birdwatchers, but few ever get the chance. Were we about to join those lucky few?

At dawn, we assembled on the edge of the wetlands: the three of us, plus two guides from the lodge and the nest-finding fisherman. We all climbed into a large canoe and the guides expertly punted us down a maze of tiny channels through the swamp. The atmosphere was electric: we were about to see a once-in-a-lifetime dream bird.

The setting was idyllic: carpets of purple water-lily floated on the surface and herds of Black Lechwe were everywhere. Malachite Kingfishers darted about, Marsh Widowbirds displayed all over, and Greater Swamp-Warblers sang from papyrus beds. Perfect. As the water became too shallow for the canoe we splashed through the wet grassland on foot, towards another huge block of papyrus where the nest was, apparently, located. One guide and the fisherman continued on into the papyrus to scout the route while we waited on the edge. We were not happy about this. What if they flushed the Shoebill and it flew without us seeing it? But they insisted we wait until they had checked out the terrain to make sure it was safe for us. Meanwhile a wader called and we spun around to see three Long-toed Lapwings dropping down onto the wet grass not far away. These were sumptuous waders and we were thrilled at another new bird.

Time was ticking. Where were the two health and safety inspectors? Had they sunk without trace in the swamp? Or had the Shoebill attacked? At last, two muddy, wet figures struggled out of the huge reeds. Their faces told the story: we were not going to see our bird. The fisherman had not been able to show the guide any nest, let alone that of a Shoebill. The guide was now convinced the man had lied from the outset in the hope of some easy cash. I felt like punching him. What an idiot! It was a very sombre trip back to the lodge; barely a word was spoken as we gave the man murderous looks.

Our last morning at Shoebill Island Camp was spent out on a canoe gliding silently through the myriad of channels, watching thousands of birds. This was just such a wonderful way to enjoy wildlife. We passed within metres of a feeding Lesser Sandplover, which allowed great photos. A Lesser Moorhen stalked along the edge of a reedbed as flocks of Garganey and Comb Ducks swirled around.

Back in the Toyota, it was another long, bone-shaking drive on awful tracks – this time south. But Ken handled the 4WD superbly, somehow maintaining a good speed despite the rutted surface. We were all shattered when we finally reached our next destination: Mutinondo Wilderness Lodge. Here we were due to camp but the owners mentioned they had bungalows for a little more cash, so Ruth and I readily upgraded. Ken was not impressed by our wimping out, but the saggy beds at Shoebill had been very uncomfortable and Ruth's back was still giving her pain.

At least that was our excuse, and we were sticking to it. The bungalows were open-plan to the extent that one wall was missing, so we enjoyed a lovely view from the comfy bed, and showers with endless hot water. Luxury!

The scenery here was very different again, with huge granite rock formations, known as whale-backs, rising abruptly from the dense carpet of miombo wood-land. Around the lodge we added Miombo Sunbird to our list. We also watched another sunbird, similar to the Miombo, which some observers believe to be a new species – though the jury remains out on that for now, so we will have to wait and see whether we can add it to our list retropectively.

We spent the next two days birding around Mutinondo Wilderness Lodge, walking the trails through the woodlands and grasslands. On day one we finally caught up with the pretty Rufous-bellied Tit, tracked down Striped Pipit and, in a wet grassland area, spent a long time pinning down a calling Broad-tailed Grassbird – which looks a bit like a giant Grasshopper Warbler, from back in the UK. Next morning we went after the localised Bar-winged Weaver. And, though we failed to find one, we did jam in on a Whyte's Barbet, which gave us one new bird for the day.

It was time to move on. We left Mutinondo before dawn and began the mega drive towards Malawi. Ken had planned a 4.30am start and the three of us were at the truck and packed ready to go. Sadly, the lodge staff were nowhere to be seen. We had been told an early breakfast would be ready for us. More impor-tantly, there was no sign of the diesel that we were due to collect. We had very little fuel and it was unlikely we would find many garages open at this hour.

Ken was fuming. He knew we had a tough driving day ahead and wanted to make good time, so he leapt in the truck and tore off down the track to the staff quarters, where he banged on doors and made a massive commotion. Bleary-eyed staff eventually appeared with drums of diesel, and we filled up our tank and spare jerry cans. Breakfast was not on offer, as we were now late, so off we went into the dark, Ken still steaming.

We drove and drove, heading steadily northeast, stopping only to change drivers and have a roadside pee. Early afternoon we found a garage and pulled in to top up, as we had no idea how easy fuel would be to find over the border in Malawi. As the attendant pumped the diesel, calls overhead drew our attention to a colourful flock of Madagascar Bee-eaters. These birds were migrating back to Madagascar and we would have loved to follow them. At one point we had consid-ered adding this weird island to *The Biggest Twitch* itinerary, but sadly our finances had said no. Definitely one for the future, though.

We had planned to cross the border near Nyika National Park, which actually straddles the Zambia–Malawi border and was our destination for the next few days. The park entrance lies in Malawi, hence our need to cross over. Unfortunately Ruth and I had another passport problem. When we had entered Zambia it had been on a single-entry visa. This visa let us in once and out once. Having left Zambia, we would technically need another new visa to re-enter. This might prove tricky.

The good thing was, however, that we were about to make the border crossing at a very remote point. We hoped security here would be minimal. The dirt track that ran towards the crossing certainly didn't look well used. We took a deep breath and drove on. Ken, however, was still a worried man. He was thinking about getting the Toyota across the border and back. We had heard tales of border guards charging huge bribes to take a hire car across borders in Africa. Our friend Hans, the Dutchman, had supplied us with all the correct paperwork, but that might not stop a guard adding some extra 'regulations' that would need to be paid for.

The Zambia border post was a derelict shed, with no sign of life, so we drove straight past. So far so good! A few hundred metres further, and we reached a barrier across the road and the Malawi border. Here a tidy office was obviously in use. Damn! We still had to wander about and find the border guard, though, who seemed to have been asleep in the house behind the office.

The guard was a cheery chap and we learnt it was his second day in the job. This could go either way, we thought. Would he be a total 'jobs-worth', determined to do everything by the book, or would he be keen to please his first border-crossing visitors?

Luckily, it was the latter, and he scarcely looked at our passports and documents, happily stamping them in all the right places and waving us good-bye enthusiastically. We prayed the same guy would be here on the way back, as we felt we had a good chance of avoiding the awkward subject of entry visas.

At the entrance gate to Nyika National Park, however, we hit another problem. Entrance fees were due and the lady on the gate would not take Zambian Kwacha. We had nothing else. We explained that we had just arrived in Malawi and had not yet seen a bank to change money. A long delay followed as the lady telephoned somewhere but eventually she came back with good news. As we were staying in the park she would let us in, but we must pay the bill before we leave.

At last we were in the park and heading for our base, still a further 60km up a rough dirt track. The scenery seemed almost more Scottish than African, with small patches of forest clinging to open rolling grassland on high hills. Mammals were numerous, and we had good views of Common Duiker, Roan Antelope and Side-striped Jackal. By now, the light was disappearing fast and we arrived at our cottage by a small lake with pine trees around – it really *was* Scotland – well after dark.

Inside we found a room attendant, who had already got a roaring fire going; and we needed it: the temperature had really dropped as darkness had fallen. He immediately set about cooking us a great meal from the supplies we had bought during our long drive. Food demolished, we headed for bed. It had been a tough day.

Soon it was 5am and we headed out to explore this very European-looking landscape. What with bracken everywhere, the pine trees and lake, it was hard to believe this was Africa. It was hardly surprising the dawn was cold, as we were now at 2,500 metres above sea-level. We walked the area around the cottage and then explored the tracks in the Toyota. Two new species of cisticolas were singing at the bottom of our garden, Churring and Black-lored. Out in the grasslands we also found Buff-shouldered Widowbird, Scarce Swift and Malachite Sunbird: all new.

We spent the whole of the next day exploring the park, this time trying for forest birds. It was very hard going. Patches of forest were few, and those we did find were impenetrable. Birds were elusive: we saw Moustached Tinkerbird and Fuelleborn's Boubou, and heard Bar-tailed Trogon. But it was a lot of effort for comparatively little return. Mammal ticks included Gentle Monkey and Eastern Sun Squirrel. Luckily the day ended with two good birds back near the cottage: a Mountain Yellow Warbler sang from a patch of scrub, and at dusk we had good views of a hunting Montane Nightjar.

Ken went to see the park manager to enquire about changing money and was told it would not be a problem. The nearest town, Rumphi, about 60km beyond the park gate, had a bank where we could exchange our Zambian for Malawi Kwacha, so that was the plan for the next day.

A pre-dawn start saw us at the gatehouse before the staff were on duty. Eventually the woman who had let us in appeared, but she was not letting us out! We explained that we were on the way to the bank for the very job of changing money so that we could pay our bill. She wasn't having any of it: we had to pay before we left in case we didn't come back. But we couldn't pay until we left and found a bank. Stalemate!

Eventually we led her to the truck and showed her that it was empty. We had left nearly all our gear back at the cottage deep in the park, so we *had* to come back. This did the trick and finally the barrier was lifted and we set off for the bank.

As we drove, we realised that our fuel gauge was nearly in the red and all the jerry cans were empty. No problem, we thought. We were heading for a town with a bank, so surely they would have a garage and some diesel?

The town turned out to be busy and rather rough, though we were met by smiling faces. We pulled up outside the bank, where and Ken and I extracted several bundles of the wad and headed inside to make the exchange, leaving Ruth in charge of the truck. A long queue was at every position so we sweated and waited. At last our turn came and we explained what we wanted.

'We cannot change Zambian into Malawian Kwacha,' came the answer.

'We were told you could,' we replied. 'This is the only money we have.'

'We cannot change Zambian into Malawian Kwacha.'

'What can we do?'

'We cannot change Zambian into Malawian Kwacha.'

Ken decided we should see the manager. Surely they should be able to change money from a neighbouring country. Another long wait, then at last we were ushered into the manager's office. He was a very polite man.

'I am very sorry,' he confirmed. 'We cannot change Zambian into Malawian Kwacha.'

But at least he did have an idea. He told us of a much larger town, some three hours' drive away, that had more and larger banks. He was sure one of these would be able to help us. But we had a problem: no fuel and no money to buy any more.

'There is no fuel in this town,' the manager told us. 'We have a shortage in Malawi. But wait outside. I might know someone who can help.'

We sat in the truck, a minor tourist attraction here in Rumphi, and sweated while we waited to see if the bank manager knew people. Two young men approached and, looking very shifty, asked whether we needed fuel.

We explained that we did, but that we had no money. However, Ken showed them his very fancy-looking mobile phone, which he was happy to exchange for fuel. Desperate times required desperate measures. Soon we had enough diesel to reach the big town and the banks that would change our money. But we had lost a mobile phone.

Mzuzu turned out to be a big town, with plenty of banks, but all had the same, now familiar, message: 'We cannot change Zambian into Malawian Kwacha.'

This was becoming serious. We had no money and of course we were now just about out of fuel again. And all the ATMs rejected all our cards. There was, however, one last bank to try. And this time, as we turned away from the counter after another rejection, a man approached us and very quietly asked whether we wanted to change some money.

We most certainly did and would happily take any lifeline offered us. 'Then go to Z's Hardware Store,' our new friend told us. 'He can help you.'

A hardware store? This didn't sound the sort of place to change money, but our options were very limited, so off we went in search of Z's. It turned out to be a large shop selling all sorts of stuff, from shovels and ropes to knives and glue, but there was no sign of a *bureau de change*. An Arab gentleman sat behind a desk, punching a calculator. This presumably was Z.

'Hi,' said Ken. 'We were told you might be able to exchange some money for us. Would that be possible?'

'What are you talking about?' came the vehement response. 'This is a hardware shop! I don't know where you got that idea from?' Z's expression was one of confusion and disbelief. It looked as though we had been sold a dummy by our friend at the bank. No doubt he was having a good laugh now.

Back out on the street, we pondered what to do next. We noticed a FedEx office across the square and in desperation we went over there. 'Do you know anyone who could change some money for us?' I asked.

The young woman looked thoughtful and then asked us to take a seat while she slipped out into the busy street. She was soon back and looking puzzled. 'Apparently you have already been there,' she said. 'Z's?'

What was going on here? Time for another visit to the hardware store. This time, though, it was totally different. Z was in the mood to trade. Yes, he could change money but would need to check the rate before making a deal. We sat outside for over an hour before eventually being called back in by one of Z's henchmen. He had the rate, but what a rip off: the guy was giving us one quarter of what we had expected. But Z was a canny businessman and knew we were desperate.

So we at last had money, if not as much as we had hoped, and luckily this town had diesel too, so we filled the tank and set off for the long drive back to Nyika. We stopped off in Rumphi to buy back Ken's mobile phone, which the guys were happy to sell as Ken had cleverly removed the SIM card before handing it over.

It was dark by the time we reached the park gates and as we drove along the dirt track back to our base we nearly ran into the back of an unlit lorry that was reloading its shed stack of wood. We eventually got past and it was now nearly midnight. But we were rewarded for our late return when a large leopard bounded across the track in the headlights. It was a dramatic end to a very tough day.

Despite our late return we were up again at 5am and breakfasting on stale scones and orange juice, all that was left of our supplies. With all the hassle yesterday we had forgotten to stock up on food. We birded some new forest areas, picking up Red-faced Crimsonwing and Olive-flanked Robin-Chat and, at last, had great views of a gorgeous Bar-tailed Trogon. The long route back to camp after a full day's forest birding crossed a vast plain with not a tree to be seen. At a small lake, we watched Blue Swallows hawking over the water; these mega-rare birds were beautiful in the late afternoon sun.

For a change we got up even earlier the next day, a 4am start, and feasted on even staler scones and the last of the orange juice. It was a good job we were moving on. Our early departure was made a little less painful by having headlight views of a Montane Nightjar on the track. We reached the park gate before 6am and had to wait to be let out – after paying our fees, of course!

Back at the border, our friendly guard welcomed us like old friends, and we passed back into Zambia without the slightest problem – even though we had no valid entry visas. We left Malawi on 3,211 species.

It took us most of the day on rutted roads to reach Kapishya Hot Springs Lodge, an expensive place but worth every penny after the basic Nyika set-up. There was just enough daylight to find Green-headed Sunbird in the garden. Then we showered in hot water and stretched out on large, clean, comfy beds. Bliss!

Our time in Zambia was coming to an end, and we still had the huge drive back to the capital, so we couldn't spend long at Kapishya. Over-sleeping did not help: we were all shattered and slept through the alarms. But still we managed to add White-tailed Blue-Flycatcher before we reluctantly hit the road again – driving and birding our way to Forest Lodge, where we arrived late and crashed out.

The following morning we headed straight for the airport, leaving Ken to spend a few more days exploring the area around Forest Lodge for more great birds. As we approached the capital, we realised that we were low on diesel. We weren't too worried, assuming that the main road into the city would have a garage. But there was none to be seen, and as we watched the needle drop and the fuel light come on, we started to panic. We had a flight to catch and didn't want to be stranded. On we went. Down went the needle. Now it was on the stopper and could go no lower. Then, just as we waited for the engine to die of thirst, salvation! A garage came into view and somehow the Toyota found enough fumes to carry us to the pumps.

We returned the truck to Hans and told him our tales of money and fuel problems over a very welcome cup of tea. Then his son drove us to the airport for our flight back to South Africa. We were very anxious as we approached passport control. Would they notice we had crossed over into Malawi and re-entered Zambia without a visa? The border guard barely glanced at our documents, and we were out of there.

3,221 species

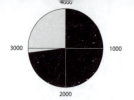

29 September–4 October,
South Africa: Part Two (Alan)

We arrived in Cape Town late evening, 29 September, and were met by our great friend Christian Boix, from Tropical Birding, and Kayla, his lively daughter. Kayla insisted on travelling with us in our hire car as we followed Christian back home, and Ruth was instructed to read a fairy-story in Spanish as we drove through the dark streets. Hard going when you don't speak much Spanish.

Christian and his partner, Lucy, had very kindly invited us to stay with them at the start of another whistle-stop leg of *The Biggest Twitch*. Christian was fired up and ready to bird hard and fast. We were worried: the man had energy to burn, and seemed to have no need for sleep or food. We, by contrast, had just returned from our gruelling tour of Zambia and Malawi with the tireless Ken. But still, Christian's enthusiasm was infectious, and he had promised some mouth-watering new birds over the next few days.

We set out the next morning at the very civilised hour of 7am, heading north-west from Cape Town. The journey produced some great birds: Cape Bulbul, Cape Sugarbird, Cape Gannet, Southern (Cape) Penduline-Tit, Karoo Scrub-Robin, Sickle-winged Chat and South African Shelduck among them, and we ended the day at Klein Cederberg on the edge of the great Karoo desert.

The next day we were out of our lodge before dawn and listening to the weird song flight of the Cape Clapper Lark, which rises up, whirring its wings with a rather wooden sound, before falling to earth with a low buzz-bomb whine. Then, after a hearty breakfast, we headed out to spend the rest of the day birding the arid Karoo scrublands, which recent rains had carpeted with flowers. It was bitterly cold at first, but heated up rapidly as the sun rose in the cloudless sky. Excellent birds matched the wonderful scenery, with Rufous-eared Warbler, Black-headed Canary, Kopje Warbler, Karoo Lark, Karoo Eremomola and Black-eared Sparrow-Larks.

We spent the night at Brandvlei, a ghost town, complete with tumbleweed rolling down the empty streets. The only hotel was rather run-down, but we had little choice. The owner told us he had spent the last twelve months doing renovations, but sadly these were not immediately apparent. Skinny cats had the run of the place.

The only food we could order was fish omelette, which was odd, but edible. Perhaps it was popular with the cats. As we tucked in, some locals arrived for a drink at the bar. Huge Afrikaner farmers, they had legs wider than Ruth's waist and each literally needed two chairs to sit at the bar. We turned in, hoping for a shower before bed, but the water sprayed out in every direction except down.

Another cold dawn, another lark. This time our target was Ferruginous (Red) Lark and it came very easily. 'Drive out into the desert and stop by the second windmill,' Christian had said. Sure enough, there it was.

Climbing out of the desert, we crossed the spectacular Swartberg Pass, where the rock formations looked as though they had been created by some enraged devil. The top of the pass was enshrouded in mist, giving it a very eerie feel. And out of the mist came a top-drawer bird: Cape Rockjumper. These charismatic creatures hopped around just metres away – though, sadly, the mist did not allow any decent photos. On the way back down the pass we also managed to find Victorin's Scrub-Warbler.

Christian called for a pre-dawn start, as we had a long drive ahead of us. So no breakfast, just up and in the car, stopping only for fuel and a welcome cup of tea. Driving east along the coast, we soon reached De Hoop Nature Reserve, where we picked up Knysna Woodpecker and Southern Tchagra, then continued on to Betty's Bay, arriving late afternoon. Here we enjoyed the bizarre spectacle of penguins on an African beach. Jackass Penguins, of course. Ruth loved it: hundreds of these comical birds were waddling around just metres away in the warm sunshine – and their tuxedos. A whole penguin soap opera was playing out right in front of us: squabbling neighbours, marital strife, misbehaving young-sters and meal time disputes. Just to add to the scene, huge Southern Right Whales breached offshore and Shy Albatross cruised over the waves.

There was time for one more stop as the sun sank over False Bay, just east of Cape Town, and we managed to add Orange-breasted Sunbird and Cape Siskin to the list – species we really should have seen by now. We finished a very long but rewarding day with our tally on 3,280.

Christian had some very bad news for me when we reached his house. Despite our strict instructions to the contrary, he had gone ahead and booked us on a pelagic trip the next morning. As you know by now, I do not do boats, and the thought of braving the mountainous seas off the Cape sent shivers down my spine. I felt ill already and we were still on dry land. The news got even worse when we heard the weather forecast and learned that the our departure had been brought forward to try and beat an approaching storm. Great! When we laid eyes on the small and rather frail-looking boat, we were severely tempted to chicken out.

At 4am the next morning, however, there was no going back. The boat slipped its moorings and we chugged out under the still dark skies on a sea that was decep-tively calm – though we knew it couldn't last. Our companions were a cheerful bunch and bombarded us with questions about *The Biggest Twitch*. I left Ruth to field most of these; I was in no mood for chitchat. I slid down into my corner of the boat, pulled my hat down over my eyes and pretended I was somewhere else.

Ruth was having a fine time as dawn came creeping across the ocean, watching the Southern Right Whales and Cape Fur Seals which, at times, came right along-side the boat. I lifted my hat for a second, saw them, then retreated back beneath the wool. That familiar queasiness was beginning to grow in the pit of my stomach. As we got further from the coast the swell increased, and over the side went my breakfast. It had only been a matter of time. Yuck! I felt awful.

'Trawlers ahead!' went up the cry.

I risked a sneaky look, and way off on the horizon were trawlers hauling in their nets. Even at this range we could see the cloud of birds swarming around them. Ill though I was, even I felt a tiny bit of excitement.

Our trusty boat, the *Zest II*, reached the trawlers and the seabird fest began. Ruth and the others were whooping with excitement at this amazing spectacle. Yellow-nosed Albatrosses were here in their hundreds, and both Shy and Black-browed Albatrosses were all around us. Wilson's and Black-bellied Storm-Petrels buzzed around the trawlers like a swarm of angry flies. Ruth was now squealing with delight, lifting my head and insisting that I look at each new wonder on offer. But I could hardly bear to open my eyes. A quick glance to tick it off, then I slumped back for more stomach heaving, feeling like death.

Then came a shout that even I had to respond to.

'Wanderer!'

I hauled myself groggily to my feet, lifted my hat and raised my bins for the longest time all day. There it was, sitting on the sea looking enormous amongst a gang of Black-browed Albatrosses: a huge Wandering Albatross! As we watched, it unfolded its gigantic wings like some monstrous pterodactyl and managed to find enough lift to lumber into the air. Now it was a very different creature: no longer a lumbering hulk, but a majestic master of the air. We gazed in awe: it was another magical *Biggest Twitch* moment, and undoubtedly bird of the day.

Back on dry land, I felt well enough to thank the guys and Ruth for looking after me and ensuring I did not miss any species we needed for the year. We were also very grateful to Trevor Hardaker, who had organised our pelagic trip but had been unable to come due to family commitments.

Then it was back to Christian's house, where we had a day to recover and catch up on admin, before packing our bags for the next stop. Namibia.

3,288 species

5–7 October, Namibia (Alan)

It felt liberating to be heading for an airport carrying hand luggage only. Namibia was to be our last African destination before we headed for Australia, and we were hoping for some great new birds before we finally left the continent behind.

Our reason for travelling light came down to airline bureaucracy. Our round-the-world ticket stipulated that we had to follow a route from Cape Town via Johannesburg before heading on to Perth. This meant that, although we were flying back from Namibia into Johannesburg anyway, we still had to fly down to Cape Town then straight back up again in order to stick to the exact schedule on our ticket. Crazy, but the upside was that we could leave most of our gear at Christian's place in Cape Town while we were in Namibia, to collect on our way back.

At Cape Town airport, we boarded the tiny plane that would take us north to Walvis Bay, at the southern end of Namibia's Skeleton Coast. As we neared our destination, the clouds melted away and we could look down on the famous red sand dunes that stretch along this desolate and forbidding coastline. Soon our little aircraft was bumping down on the tarmac and we were taxiing right up to the small chalet-style arrivals building; if only all international travel was like this. Our hire car was waiting outside, and within minutes we were on our way to the shallow lagoons at Walvis Bay.

This was our second visit here and we had really loved the first one back in November 2006. Arriving at the seafront, however, we were a little disappointed to see that the tide was a long way out. It had never occurred to us that this might be a problem. Our last visit had been at an easy pace, with time to wait for the tide to come back in. No such luxury this year; we had a tight schedule to follow. We bombed south along the coast road, scanning as we drove. And soon we saw our target bird: two Damara Terns hovering over a creek that crossed the vast mudflats. Similar in size and build to our Little Terns back in the UK, these dinky seabirds have all-black bills and a solid black cap. There were also plenty of distant waders tempting us to explore further, but we had no time for these. We were off north again, fast.

At Swakopmund we turned inland, leaving the dunes behind, and took the Kalahari Highway east. After a long, hot drive we eventually hit a gravel road north and slowed in order to look for birds. We quickly picked up a pair of Rüppell's Korhaans, our main target bird along this stretch. By late afternoon we had reached the rather drab-looking town of Usakos, where we rocked up at the Bahnhof Hotel, the only place we could find a bed for the night. It didn't look very inviting at first, but turned out to be rather better on the inside than out, and we had a comfortable night's sleep.

The best thing about the hotel, however, was its proximity to our next destination, Spitzkoppe. Dawn saw us exploring the spectacular rock formations that punched straight up from the flat gravel plain of this famous site. As the sun crept up, the towering rocks took on an orange glow, which slowly faded as the sky brightened behind them. Soon it would be very, very hot. Bradfield's Swifts left their roost on the sun-warmed cliffs and spiralled high into the cobalt blue.

We needed to find our birds and quickly, but hard though we looked there was no sign of the endemic Herero Chat. This was a bitter blow, as we had missed the species on our previous visit and had hoped to correct things this time around. As we trudged around the thorn scrub at the base of the rocks, however, we did find a lovely family party of White-tailed Shrikes, which bounced around from boulder to boulder, showing off their piebald plumage and yellow eyes.

Next we headed for Orongo Wilderness Lodge, a wonderful place, hidden on the far side of a steep rocky ridge. We had fallen in love with it during our last visit and arranged to call in again this time round. Our little hired Toyota Corolla was not up to the rough entrance track, so we were collected by a 4WD truck and driven the last mile or so.

It was still baking hot when we arrived, so we sat in the shade of the restaurant overlooking the water drip. Our previous visit had shown us that this tactic could pay off in the heat of the day, and we didn't have to wait long. A gang of gorgeous Rosy-faced Lovebirds, endearing little parrots, soon flew in and drank greedily. They were new to the list, as was the flock of Black-throated Canaries that came next.

Once the temperature began to drop, we ventured out to search around the lovely chalets scattered across this boulder-strewn moonscape. We soon found a pair of Ashy Tits feeding on caterpillars in the thorn trees above the path. Then, after an hour's careful searching, we caught sight of a Damara Rockjumper. This Namibian endemic, also known as Rockrunner, showed off its orange breast and streaky back as as it leapt about the boulders, vanishing before our eyes only to pop up again, like some magic act.

After returning to the nearby town of Omaruru to find a bed for the night – the lodge being fully booked – we were back at Orongo at dawn. But now we had a problem: the entrance gate was firmly padlocked. Luckily we had a plan B: Christian had told of us of a dry riverbed beyond the entrance, which we had planned to bird later. Why not try it now? We soon found the spot and quickly heard the sound we'd been hoping for: Southern Pied Babblers. A roving band of these cool birds, with their striking black and white plumage, was moving restlessly through the trees, calling to each other constantly. Target bird in the bag, we headed back to Orongo.

The gate was open now but there was no one in sight, so we set off walking up to the lodge. This proved to be a very good move. Not far up the slope we had great views of more Damara Rockjumpers just a few metres away. Then a movement in the scrub above us revealed a Hartlaub's Francolin creeping surreptitiously up the hillside. As we reached the crest of the hill, we tried playing a tape for Barred Wren-Warbler. Instant success: a male popped up and showed off from the top of a small thorn bush. This was already a great morning.

Finally we reached the lodge, with just Short-toed Rock-Thrush left on our shopping list. As we neared the restaurant we heard voices that sounded strangely familiar. Surely not? But yes, our ears were not deceiving us: Chuck and Nancy Bell, whom we'd met in Ethiopia back in February, were sitting there having breakfast. It was very strange to bump into people we knew all so far from home. And it was especially painful to have Chuck regale us with his Herero Chat sighting at Spitzkoppe the previous day. How had we missed it?

But it wasn't all bad news. Chuck and Nancy had seen the rock-thrush only that morning, and Chuck led us to the very spot. Sure enough, there was the male Short-toed Rock-Thrush singing away on a pinnacle in the morning sun. Shopping done, we gave Chuck our birding notes from Christian, as we now had to head for the airport. We wished them good luck in their search for the babblers.

All we now had to do was drive back to Windhoek for our return flight to Cape Town. But just as we were nearing the city, we saw a police road-block ahead. We didn't like the look of this, given our experience of Namibian police.

I should explain. On our previous trip to Namibia, we had packed our bags ready for our flight home then set out for a nearby lake for one final bit of birding. We had come round a corner to find a police road-block, where an officer had asked for our passports and driving licences – and was not satisfied with our explanation that we had left them at the hotel.

'Oh!' the policeman had said. 'This is a very serious offence in Namibia. You must come with me to the police station back in town.'

Well, we didn't want to do that. We could see ourselves having no time left for birding and, even worse, maybe miss our flight.

'Is there a way around this situation?' I had asked.

'Step into my office,' had come the reply. And here, out of earshot of the other policemen and Ruth, the officer had an idea. 'If we come to an agreement,' he suggested, 'this agreement would be between you and me. This agreement would not involve the Namibian Government.'

'How much would this agreement cost?' I had replied. 'That is, the agreement between you and me and not involving the Namibian Government.'

A broad grin had spread across the officer's face. 'The agreement between you and me would cost three hundred Namibian dollars.'

At the time I had just wanted to get going, so we had paid the 'agreement' fee and were waved through the road-block. After birding a nearby reservoir we had headed back into Windhoek, whereupon the same policeman had flagged us down again, only to express his hope that we had enjoyed our stay in his wonderful country and would return soon. Bastard!

Now in 2008, the officer at this same road-block waved us on. Phew! we thought. But just as we passed him, he changed his mind and shouted for us to stop.

'What's the problem?' we asked, backing up a few feet.

'You failed to stop when I asked you!' he snapped.

Talk about déjà vu. I could see where this was going and I was in no mood for it. 'You waved us through!' I protested. 'We have a flight to catch and we are late!' This seemed to take him aback and, grudgingly, he let us go.

At the airport we had another brush with the authorities. We had bought a bottle of champagne for Christian and Lucy, who were about to be married. The airport staff, showing no sense of romance, wanted us to leave it behind at the x-ray machines. Buoyed by our success at the roadblock we simply insisted we were taking it through. The tactic worked as we managed to get our way once again. We were liking this new assertive approach.

Back in Cape Town, we went for a great meal with Trevor Hardaker, who had organised our pelagic trip, and his lovely wife, Margaret. It was one of those occasions when you just click with people, and the evening simply flew by as we talked and talked.

As we took our leave of Africa for the second time, our year list stood at 3,310 species. Australia was next, with the world record looking very close. We couldn't wait.

3,310 species

PART EIGHT

End game

9 October–6 November, Australia (Ruth)

Iain Campbell from Tropical Birding is always a force to be reckoned with. But once back Down Under, in the land where he grew up, he was like a man possessed. He wanted more birds, he wanted them now, and he wasn't going to let the fact that he couldn't find the nature reserve get in his way. We spun round the round-about once more and tried driving back down the same road again. Perhaps things would look different the third time around.

'That building wasn't there last time,' roared Iain in frustration, as we drove past a large, well-established DIY outlet. 'They must have just built it!' He pulled over and grabbed the map, turning it first one way up and then the other.

'This map's wrong too!' he thundered, flinging it into the back of the minibus. Everyone looked at one another nervously, apart from Alan and me, who were used to Iain losing the plot from time to time. In fact, from the safety of the back seat, we found it all very funny.

Third time lucky. This time we spotted a narrow entrance to the Peter Murrell Reserve in Hobart and pulled into the car park. We muffled up against the cold wind and piled out of the minibus, scattering a gaggle of Tasmanian Native-hens, swamphen-sized rails, which scurried around the grass beside the reed-fringed pool. Walking round the edge of the pool towards the trees, we watched a flock of Green Rosella parrots feeding in the treetops, soon joined by some Yellow-throated Honeyeaters.

The key bird at this reserve was the Forty-spotted Pardalote, a small, olive-green bird with white spots on its dark wings and tail. It took a while to find, and though it didn't stay still long enough for us to check the number of spots, the views were good enough for a positive ID. We dashed back to the warmth of the minibus, and sped off for our next birding destination.

Our birding month in Australia had started peacefully enough. Alan and I landed in Perth, Western Australia, after a long flight from Johannesburg and had a few days in which to bird this side of the country by ourselves. Even here, though, Iain had reached out through cyberspace to direct our birding. 'Don't forget the Porungorup National Park on your way down,' he had emailed. 'And you'll need to be out in the field by 4.30am to get Western Bristlebird'. But we were up for any advice: Australia was an entirely new continent to us both, so everything was new and exciting, and many of the birds – indeed, entire bird families – lay completely outside our usual frame of reference.

Mind you, we were lucky to be allowed in. Australia is paranoid about visitors to its shores bringing contaminated soil on their boots and strange foodstuff in their baggage, and here we were arriving with our boots still caked with the accumulated mud of southern Africa and our emergency supplies of Twinings English Breakfast teabags and Marmite. But we smiled sweetly at the authorities and were whisked down the fast track lane and out into warm Australian sunshine. We picked up our pocket-sized hire car, squeezed in our luggage and headed southeast towards Albany on the south coast. On the road atlas it didn't look very far, but we quickly learned that everything in Australia is a very long way from everything else.

As per Iain's instructions, we dutifully called in at Porungorup National Park. Initially, it was tough actually seeing the birds: we could hear several calling but not much was showing. But with persistence we gradually dug them out and, without exception, they were all lookers: Scarlet Robin, self-explanatory; White-tailed Black-Cockatoo, you can probably picture it; Western Rosella, a handsome red-and-green parrot. With miles still to go, we couldn't hang around for long. Even so, it was dark by the time we reached the caravan park at Cheyne Beach, where we were staying in a cosy mobile home for the next couple of nights.

We were woken before dawn by the din of a new bird calling right outside our window. In the pitch darkness we had no idea what it was, but it sounded pretty distinctive. After gulping down a hasty breakfast we headed out to explore. With the waves crashing in on the nearby beach, the campsite itself provided a sheltered haven of cover for birds. First up were New Holland Honeyeaters. All new birds are exciting, and these handsome creatures, with their bright yellow wing patches, were no exception – though we soon found ourselves tripping over them all around our cabin. Honeyeaters were an entirely new family for us, and Australia has 67 species, which have adapted to various habitats across the country. These birds collect sticky nectar and honeydew using a long tongue that is tipped with a brush for this purpose. They don't hang around either: apparently they can drain a flower of its nectar in less than a second, so quickly do they lap it up. This might explain why they didn't wait to be photographed, though we finally managed to get a reasonable shot or two.

We left the campsite to follow a coastal footpath, checking all the bushes thoroughly. One tiny bird gave us the run-around, popping up first on one side of the bush, then the other, each time disappearing before we had the chance to nail it. We surrounded the bush – well, we stood on either side of it – and finally the bird submitted and hopped up on top. It was a Red-winged Fairywren, and this was our first encounter with one of Australia's most charming bird families. About the size of our UK Wren, this cute little bird had a pale blue cap and ear coverts, a dark purplish-blue throat, and a long, sticky-up tail.

Back at the campsite, we chatted with the owners and explained our quest. They promptly set about helping us to find as many of the local birds as possible, by giving us a file of the local gen. In it were maps of the immediate area marked up with where and when birders had seen key species. This was invaluable. They also lent us a CD of bird calls, which we played on the car stereo. Now we knew who our early morning alarm call was: Western Whipbird, one of our target species for this area.

Armed with this new information, we went back into the field. New birds came thick and fast: Blue-breasted Fairywren, similar to Red-winged but with darker blue patches; Western Spinebill, a dapper bird with a chestnut collar and throat, and a black and white 'mayor's chain' chest-band; and White-cheeked Honeyeater, very like our New Holland Honeyeaters earlier, but with larger white cheek patches.

We didn't realize just how lucky we were to find Noisy Scrub-bird, until some local birders emailed us later to let us know. Using the car as a mobile hide and playing the call on the stereo, we encouraged the bird to make its way slowly, slowly forward, until it was right in the bush next to us. Even then, we didn't actually see it until the tiniest movement gave it away. Red-eared Firetail was an interesting bird too: its barred olive plumage sported a large black patch around the eye, as though the bird had been the loser in a fistfight.

The next morning the wind was so strong that we could hardly stand upright, so we decided to head back north towards Perth to try our luck inland, hoping it might be more sheltered. We drove and drove, seeing few birds, and eventually reached a small town where a rusty petrol pump stood outside a dilapidated general store. The check-shirted owner seemed pretty reluctant to serve strangers, but eventually we persuaded him to part with some petrol and a dusty packet of biscuits. As we drove away I could swear I heard the sound of distant banjos.

More driving followed, and then we saw a sign that got me very excited: '2 miles: Giant Ram and the Woolorama'. Now there was a sign to conjure with. I'd read in Bill Bryson's brilliant book on Australia, '*Down Under*', how the Aussies liked to create giant 'things' in out-of-the-way places with not much else going for them. These acted as tourist magnets, drawing in people from miles around, who had little else to look at and were just bursting to spend their money on a cup of tea or an ice cream. Here was my chance to see one for myself.

Needless to say, Alan didn't quite share my excitement. But believe me, the Giant Ram of Wagin didn't disappoint. It was huge, measuring nine metres high by thirteen metres long and six metres wide, and weighing four tonnes. Being a male, it was suitably endowed with testicles as big as wrecking balls. Of course I had to have my photo taken standing next to it. Sadly the Woolorama only took place in March, so I was left to imagine just how exciting that would have been.

Yet more driving, and we finally reached the Dryandra Forest, as per Iain's instructions. Unfortunately large areas of this woodland were temporarily out of bounds to visitors because of an infestation of dieback fungus, which could be spread by car tyres and walking boots. This meant we wouldn't see some of the creatures found here, with such mouthwatering local names as Mernine (Banded Hare-wallaby), Marl (Western Barred Bandicoot), Boodie (Burrowing Bettong), Wurrup (Rufous Hare-wallaby) and Dalgyte (Bilby), not to mention the endangered Numbat. We did manage to explore a small area around the Old Dam, and did track down four new species, but nothing like the bird list Iain had provided for this area.

Driving back towards the main road, we found the way blocked by a posse of Western Grey Kangaroos. As children, we'd been brought up on *Skippy the Bush Kangaroo*, but seeing these bizarre mammals up close in the wild, they seemed so much more – well – kangaroo-like! That delicate face and slender muzzle; those funny little forearms that seemed useful only for scratching their tummies; the handy front pocket for keeping things in; those two long, flat feet; and that thick, strong tail that stuck out behind like a tiller when they bounced. And how they bounced! Once in top gear, they really covered the ground and could clear a fence more easily than an Olympic hurdler.

Having seen our first kangaroo, of course, we soon started to see plenty more.

They never failed to bring a smile of delight to our faces. Well, apart from when we nearly hit them in the road in the middle of the Outback at night, but that's another story.

For now though, we had to leave Skippy and his mates and head back to Perth, where we were booked into a motel on the outskirts of town. As part of a 'Pioneer Village', the local pub was called Ye Olde Narrogin Inne. Inside, though, it was authentic 1970s throughout: purple flock wallpaper, paisley pattern carpet, Chicken Kiev on the menu and Lionel Ritchie on the sound system. All that was missing was the Black Forest Gateau on the dessert trolley. Obviously it was in the contracts of all staff to wear perms that Kevin Keegan in his heyday would have envied, but presumably they kept their medallions safely under their uniforms for health and safety reasons.

The next day we flew to Ayers Rock airport, where we soon found ourselves queuing up at yet another rental car desk. Ahead of us was the slowest couple in the world, and by the time they had finally resolved all their rental problems, everyone else on our flight had long since departed and all the staff gone home. The airport was silent and even the lights had been turned off. The Avis girl hustled us through the paperwork and handed us the keys before jumping into her own car and heading off into the Outback at top speed. We were now entirely alone.

This time we were picking up two vehicles, which were going to be the transport for a Tropical Birding tour we were joining at Alice Springs in a couple of days' time. Alan's huge silver 4x4 looked the part, but I had a brand new estate car: top spec, very comfy and extremely fast, but so low to the ground that I hoped we wouldn't be doing much off-roading. Driving in our separate cars, this was the first time Alan and I had been apart by more than a few inches for a very long time. It felt strange. No, I'll be honest, it felt great, as I pressed the accelerator flat to the floor and left Alan as a tiny silver speck in my rear-view mirror.

We had hoped to reach our overnight stop before dark, but thanks to Mr and Mrs Picky back at the Avis queue, it wasn't long before darkness began to fall. The sunset was spectacular, bruised purple clouds outlined in orange and highlighted in crimson, but all too soon it was dark. I mean really, really dark. There is surely nowhere in the UK where you can get as far from artificial light as we were here.

This was the cue for kangaroos to metamorphose from entertaining TV characters into lethal mankillers, intent on running cars off the road. As the temperatures dropped, Red Kangaroos – the big, chunky ones that stand about six feet tall – appeared from wherever they'd been hiding by day. Perhaps they like the warm surface, or perhaps they don't like sand between their toes, but for whatever reason, these roos love to gather in the middle of the road – preferably with their backs to the oncoming traffic so that you can't even see the warning eye-shine. It was alarming to come round a bend to find several large lumps of kangaroo right in front of you. As Sean Dooley wrote in *The Big Twitch*, 'You can forget your venomous snakes, poisonous killer jellyfish and funnel-web spiders; the most dangerous thing out here is driving at night in the Outback'. Flashing the headlights and honking the horn didn't encourage the roos to move, nor did the threat of an imminent flattening, so I found myself swerving wildly around them and clearing a path for Alan following behind.

We had planned to stop at the first roadhouse we came to but hadn't quite grasped the scale of things in the Outback. It wasn't until I'd driven at least ten minutes past a building and a couple of electric lights that I began to wonder whether that might have been our stop. I pulled over and Alan drew up alongside. After a quick confab and look at the map, we decided to press on to Mount Ebenezer. We needed to continue in this direction tomorrow anyway so there was little point in going back on our tracks. On again for another hour or so into the darkness, and then I spotted a light ahead. I slowed down. I wasn't going to miss another roadhouse in a hurry. One light turned into several, and a building materialised: Mount Ebenezer Roadhouse. I parked at the side of the road and switched off the engine with a sigh of relief. We needed food and sleep, and we had found just the right place for both.

What the roadhouse may have lacked in luxury, it certainly made up for in its warm welcome. The people running it were so incredibly friendly that it was hard to believe we'd never met them before. In fact, they were both expats who'd settled out here to have a bit more space and had never looked back. They wanted to hear all about home and our crazy adventure, but they seemed almost more Australian than the Aussies, talking about 'going inland' to mean branching off the tarred road and venturing into the hinterland, as if you could get any more inland than the centre of this vast continent. Basic tables and wooden chairs, a well-stocked bar, pool table, toilets, television, gallery of Aboriginal art, fridge full of soft drinks, huge plates of sustaining food and hot tea on tap: what more could you possibly want? We staggered to our room to collapse in bed and dream of kangaroos overturning cars.

The Mount Ebenezer area was surprisingly birdy first thing the next morning, given the hot and windy conditions and desolate terrain. First we searched the scrub around the buildings, where we added Spiny-cheeked Honeyeater to our honeyeater collection. Look closely, and you could admire the bristling white feathers, which ran like spines from its bill to its cheeks. We drove a short distance to another clump of mulga acacia scrub, and were rewarded with wonderful close-up views of Variegated Fairywren. Like the other fairywrens we'd already seen, this little character was a patchwork of colours, including blue, purple, black and russet, with an upright steel-blue tail, tipped in white. We would spend our whole month in Australia almost but not quite succeeding in photographing these birds, as they never stopped moving for an instant.

Next stop was Alice Springs. On the outskirts of town the local landfill site and sewage works offered an oasis of birds – if a pretty pungent one in the midday heat. Views were tricky, as most of the birds were on the distant settling pools. Nevertheless, we set up the scope and added some new waterbirds to our list, including Black Swan, Pacific Black Duck, White-eyed Duck, Masked Lapwing and Red-necked Avocet.

We'd been tasked with stocking up on breakfast stuff for the whole group for the next few days, so when we reached the centre of town, we parked the cars and tracked down a supermarket. We looked at the shopping list we'd had from Iain: six packets of breakfast cereal, ten litres of long-life milk, forty plastic bowls and spoons, six litres of long-life orange juice and forty plastic beakers: enough to keep nine birders going until lunchtime for four days. Just.

At the airport, we met Iain and the rest of the group: Ken, and Mary and

Norman from the USA; Ray from Canada; and Neil and Julie from the UK. We shoehorned birders and luggage into the vehicles and drove for a couple of hours to Glen Helen, where we stayed for the night, arriving in the pitch dark with little idea of our surroundings.

It was still dark when we left at 5.30am the next morning to go to the nearby Ormiston Gorge. This was a deep canyon of red rock cliffs, but we were here for the particular habitat: spinifex grass. It might sound quite nice, but don't be fooled: this spiky plant is among the most vicious we encountered during our whole year. It grows in hummocks about a foot high, and its sharp edges will slice straight through your clothes – or your skin, if you're foolish enough to go bare-legged. True spinifex is found on the coast, where it holds the sand-dunes in place, but the genus found in the arid Outback is also called *Spinifex*, and gives its name to the two specialist birds that manage to eke out a living here: Spinifex Pigeon and Spinifexbird. These were our targets for the day.

We snacked briefly on cereal out of the back of the car then started walking up the trail, which wound its way up onto the hilltops, out of the shade of the valley and into the full glare of the sun. Progress was slow. People were unsteady on the stony paths, even with the help of walking sticks, and although the hour was early, the temperature was rising fast, so frequent water stops were necessary. It was dry here, even by Outback standards, and the birding was pretty slow. There was no sign at all of our Spinifex Pigeon or Spinifexbird, though we did add to our mammal list, with a pair of Black-footed Rock Wallabies.

Iain wasn't impressed by the dry conditions here, so we returned to the cars. Further down the road, we tried our luck again at another area of spinifex, spreading out across the plain as we picked our way around the tussocks. Iain was playing the tape for Spinifexbird, a nice little warbling call, when suddenly the real McCoy replied and hopped up in plain view. As fast as we could, without ripping our legs to shreds on the vicious grass, we homed in on our target. This large warbler has brown back and pale front, with a rusty-coloured cap. Not particularly exciting to look at perhaps, but still a good bird to add to our list. We had to admit defeat with the Spinifex Pigeon, but the conditions in the centre of Australia were particularly dry this year, with even less rainfall than normal, and the birdlife had suffered.

The midday heat was unbearable for birds and birders alike, so we headed back to the hotel. Daylight revealed its fantastic setting, with a backdrop of a long terracotta cliff being carved away by the river at its foot. While some of the guests disappeared for a siesta, and Neil and Julie went exploring, Iain sat us down to interrogate us on what species we'd seen so far. But it wasn't long before he was up and off again into the Outback. He had some 'hot gen' about a new site, so we parked up beside the dirt road and walked a short way along a dry riverbed, before stopping a safe distance from a particular tree. About ten feet up was a large hole, and as we stood and watched, a pink head popped out to survey us. This was the nest site of a Pink Cockatoo, or Major Mitchell's Cockatoo, if you prefer the more macho name. This glorious bird had a candy-pink head and belly, and contrasting white wings and back. As we watched, he flexed his red-and-yellow striped crest, looking like a native American Chief in his war headdress. We digiscoped him as best we could, but the light was too bright to do him justice.

Iain's next bright idea was a 4am departure in the morning, to return to Alice Springs. We were going to visit the Sewage Works again. No one could understand why we had to leave quite so early to visit this area that had been teeming with birds at midday, but there was no changing Iain's mind. Even Jim and Barbara at the Sewage Works were persuaded to open the gate for us at 6am, and this time we were able to view the settling ponds from close up. We worked our way through the flocks of waders. Most were Sharp-tailed Sandpipers, but we also picked out a single Latham's Snipe lurking on the edge of a clump of reeds – a good local record.

The bushes surrounding the pools also held birds, and we all enjoyed close views of White-winged Fairywren. Little Grassbird was harder for the whole group to get onto. Our ten months of daily practice meant that Alan and I had become pretty good at locating elusive birds quickly, but luckily this one popped up again and flew to some bushes so that everyone had at least flight views.

Next we headed back down the Stuart Highway towards Ayres Rock but had to keep stopping and piling out of the cars to catch up with raptors overhead. In this way we succeeded in adding most of Australia's inland bird of prey to our list, including the impressively large Wedge-tailed Eagle.

After another night at Mount Ebenezer, where Alan and I were greeted like old friends, Iain led us out before dawn to the spot of mulga woodland where Alan and I had birded a few days previously. Since our last visit, one of the hardy local cows had given up the struggle to survive, so our birding was accompanied by a revolting stench. That didn't seem to bother the birds though. We watched the males of both Splendid and Variegated Fairywrens having a stand-off, just feet away from us. Then two emerald-green Mulga Parrots were joined in their tall tree by a salmon-pink Bourke's Parrot, a welcome addition to our list. Two particular birds gave us the run-around – we could hear them calling but we never seemed to get any closer as they moved from bush to bush. 'Tootsie cheer!' would call one, and 'Ee cheer!' would reply the other. Finally they allowed us a better look: Chirruping Wedgebills, living up to their name. As we made our way back to the cars we added a handsome Red-capped Robin to the list.

Two hours further down the road we checked into the Ayers Rock Resort, a busy complex close to the famous rock – now known by its Aboriginal name of Uluru. As it was too hot to do much birding beyond the well-watered grounds, with temperatures in the mid-40s, we lingered in the shade near the bar and caught up on more computer work. Once we'd passed the hottest part of the day, however, we jumped back in the cars and headed towards Uluru. We paid our entry fee for the Uluru-Kata Tjuta National Park, but instead of making straight for the rock itself drove a short distance to the second large outcrop, Kata Tjuta or Mount Olga. Unfortunately, a large number of other people had also thought they'd avoid the crowds that way, and so we piled back into the vehicles and drove on to a second car park and another footpath.

This site was only slightly less busy, as buses were lined up in rows and a steady stream of sweaty people came striding along the path, obviously following a circuit around the rock. Kata Tjuta looked quite different to Uluru, comprising a collection of individual rounded lumps rather than one single mass. The rocks were a rich terracotta colour and resembled balls of unbaked clay all rolled together. Two dead trees in the foreground stretched their bare arms up to the impossibly bright blue sky and made for a perfect photograph.

These hot, dry and busy conditions didn't seem ideal for birding, but we gave it our best shot, scanning the rocks over and over again, and checking every brave tree that tried to survive here. Iain played calls on his iPod to try to entice any birds a little closer, but succeeded only in attracting the attention of a Frenchman, who stopped dead in his tracks and stared in amazement as the call of a honeyeater floated up from this strange group of khaki-clad birders.

Then Iain checked his watch and shepherded us back to the vehicles in order to make it back to Uluru for sunset. Was he going soft on us? Surely we should still be thrashing about in the desert after birds rather than watching the sun go down on Uluru? But no, it appeared that Iain did have a tiny streak of romance in his soul. Or perhaps he just bowed to the inevitable, realising that he'd have a mutiny on his hands if he didn't let us enjoy one of the greatest spectacles on the planet. Either way, we drove to the viewing point, and stood in line to watch the magical colour display across the rock as the sun slowly dipped below the horizon. The ridges, cracks and fissures seemed to deepen and spread as the surface turned from terracotta to deep maroon, then purple and finally blue as the sun's rays shone on it for one last time that day.

It was an unforgettable moment, even though we were sharing it with around five hundred other picture-snapping tourists. Unfortunately, all five hundred of them seemed to be staying at our hotel too, so we drove in a very slow crocodile back across the desert, which sorely tested Iain's newfound poetic sensibilities.

We returned to Uluru at 5.45am the next day to try our luck in the cool of the morning, and followed a trail that led right up to the rock. Seen this close, it was hugely impressive: a single enormous mass of sandstone which, like an iceberg, had more out of sight below ground than showing above. The surface was scaly, as though suffering from a skin complaint, and hidden deep within a shady crevasse was a pool of cool water: a sacred watering hole. It was easy to appreciate why fresh water would be revered as sacred in such unforgiving territory.

This marked the end of the Tropical Birding Outback tour, and most of the group were leaving us here. We dropped off Ray, Mary, Norman, Neil and Julie at Ayers Rock airport for their flights home. We were heading for the east coast, where more birding adventures awaited us.

Cairns hit us in the face like a warm, wet sponge. OK, we did arrive in a thunderstorm, but even so, we weren't prepared for the heat and the humidity when we stepped off the plane. The roads swished wetly as we made our way the short distance to the Fig Tree Hotel in downtown Cairns. Apparently the forecast was for unsettled weather over the next few days, and some really bad stuff was scheduled to hit eastern Australia later. This all seemed very strange after the oven of the Outback.

Officially we were between tours: the Outback Tour was over and the Eastern Australia Top-to-Bottom Tour didn't start until the next afternoon, so we had a relaxing few hours to do our laundry and catch up on emails. It felt like the lull before the storm, when everything seems to hold its breath but you know the clouds are gathering.

I'll admit I was a bit apprehensive. Even Sam Woods of Tropical Birding, who will bird until he drops, had said that the Top-to-Bottom Tour was hard work and that Iain would drive you like a maniac. Or was it that he would drive like a maniac? Either way, it was going to be tough. We'd been on the road now for ten months and we were pretty tired. Iain had already proved that he liked to get his tours under way early in the morning, and I knew better than to suggest that we needed some down time; nothing would have been more likely to make him schedule a ludicrously early start.

But we were getting close to that world record now. In fact, we were starting to count down how many birds we needed, with the magic number of 3,663 in our sights. Iain was just as hungry for that number as we were – after all, it was Iain who'd persuaded us to up the ante from spending a gentle year birding around the world to a year-long race after the world record, so I knew he had our best birding interests at heart.

Soon Iain tracked us down, and we went into town with him to pick up the hire car. This time it was a minibus, and big enough for all of us. Iain was bouncing, clearly in a good mood – perhaps in anticipation of the exciting new birds he'd be taking us to see. After a quick but delicious laksa in a downtown noodle bar, we picked up the rest of the new group. First there was Ken, who'd been with us at Ayers Rock. Then there was Jackie, a lively American lady whom Alan and I had guided in Ecuador at an ABA Conference a few years before, and who'd left her husband behind to concentrate on his writing. And then there were Len and Linda, also from America. Linda, who was rather short, was the birding half of the partnership and wanted to see all the birds possible. Len, who was rather tall, was not as keen on birding as his wife, but enjoyed seeing wildlife in general.

First stop was Centennial Park, where we enjoyed the botanical gardens, lakes and pools, and strolled along a boardwalk through an area of rainforest. To our vegetation-starved eyes, this all looked amazingly lush and verdant, and it wasn't long before we were totting up good numbers of new birds.

They came in all shapes, sizes and colours. First up were Orange-footed Scrubfowl and Australian Brush-Turkey, both of which belong to the megapode family of mound-builders, who scrape up leaf litter with their feet to create hummocks in which they lay their eggs. These mounds serve as incubation chambers, and the birds monitor them constantly, piling on or scraping off leaf litter to maintain an optimum temperature inside. Nearby, a pair of Bush Thick-knees stood rigidly to attention at the foot of a tree, perhaps hoping we wouldn't notice them on their sentry duty, while an Australian Koel revealed his presence in some dense foliage by calling his own name: '*koo-well*'.

Iain took us next to the popular Esplanade. Waders pottered about on the exposed muddy shore, totally unfazed by all the people so close by: Terek Sandpiper, with its jaunty upturned bill; Far Eastern Curlew, with its whopping great downturned bill; plus Red-necked Stint, Great Knot and Gray-tailed Tattler. We also added Little Black Cormorant, Australian Pelican, Black-necked Stork and Royal Spoonbill. This was just brilliant birding: thirty-two new species for the day. We wanted more.

But be careful what you wish for. Despite swearing that he would never set foot on a boat again as long as he lived, after his thirteen-hour marathon on the high seas off Cape Town, Alan was persuaded the next day to set sail once again, this time to the Great Barrier Reef and some of the cays, which were home to an exciting range of seabirds.

As usual, we boarded in the flat, calm shelter of the harbour while the sky remained cloudless and clear. Even then, Alan sat right beside the side rail in case of emergencies. 'Seastar bops along at 24 knots, getting to Michaelmas Cay in just over an hour' said the brochure. Well, maybe with a following wind, but the land was barely out of sight before the sky began to cloud over and the waves began to build up. Then one of the engines failed, so instead of bopping, we started a stately waltz in slow time, pitching forwards and backwards and swaying from side-to-side as we wallowed in the waves, barely making headway. By now, Alan had his eyes tight shut and was turning green.

'I get seasick myself,' said Iain, delighted by Alan's distress, 'unless someone else starts being seasick first. Then I feel fine!'

In fact, Iain felt so fine that he started up a sweepstake on how long it would be before Alan was sick over the side, donating a whole Mars Bar as the prize. Amazingly Alan held on until 9.05am, the exact time Len had predicted, when he turned and, with a groan, heaved the contents of his stomach over the side. Unfortunately the wind promptly blew everything back into the tender on the back of the boat, which we would be using to go ashore at Michaelmas Cay. Pity the poor crew-member who had to wash it down for us.

We dropped anchor, at last, about 500 metres from the shore of this little island, and piled into the now clean tender in batches of three at a time, to be ferried across to the cay. Alan was first to go ashore, where he collapsed onto the beach with a moan and covered his face with his hat.

The sand was pure white and wonderfully soft on the toes. This was a real desert island and a pretty special one, too, with its protected colony of Sooty Terns. Brown and Black Noddies also nested in close proximity to each other among the green bushes that covered the island's domed centre. Visitors here were kept to a strictly limited area of the beach to minimise disturbance. Not that the birds seemed too bothered by our presence. They covered every inch of ground, making an incredible din and commuting constantly back and forth between their nest sites and their fishing trips out at sea. I watched the frenzy for ages and took plenty of photos. Alan, meanwhile, took enough of a glance to register each species, then buried his face once more in his hands.

Soon it was time to rejoin the Seastar. There wasn't enough fuel in the tender's outboard motor to ferry us back three at a time, so the crew decided they'd just double us up and take us back in a single trip. This meant six of us plus two crew squashed into the tiny inflatable boat, which suddenly seemed very small and low in the water. Of course, the first wave crashed straight over the bow and covered our feet so we all shuffled towards the stern to keep the bow above water. Then the second wave came straight over the stern and swamped the engine. The sea was now sloshing about our knees. We made little headway through the water and the Seastar was still a long way off. The next wave crashed completely over us and it was obvious we were sinking. We were fully dressed in trousers and shirts, with expensive optics around our necks and heavy walking boots on our feet, and at least two of our group couldn't swim.

This was now getting serious. The crew, who were in a state of panic, radioed the Seastar for help. Surely we couldn't drown here, we thought. We're both pretty good swimmers, but I'd never tried to swim in walking boots before. But the Seastar had motored a little closer, and all her crew had assembled on the stern to haul us out of the tender and into the safety of the catamaran. Just as the bow of the tender dipped below the waves for good, Alan threw Ken bodily towards the boat where he was grabbed by the outstretched arms of the crew. I hurled myself at the catamaran next and landed in a crumpled heap on the deck. Then came Alan, and even in his sorry state he still turned to help Len and Linda onto the safety of the Seastar. Last came Iain, who was cackling with laughter, having hugely enjoyed the whole experience. There's nothing like a dice with death to put Iain in a good mood.

Alan staggered to the nearest bench, and collapsed in a heap, leaning back against a pile of life jackets. Where had they been a few minutes earlier? He closed his eyes and tried to sleep. Our ordeal had given us an appetite and, apart from Alan, we all tucked into the delicious cold buffet that had been laid out for us. Meanwhile the boat cruised over to Hastings Reef before dropping anchor in an area called the Fish Bowl.

This was my only chance to see the wonders of the Great Barrier Reef, but I didn't feel confident enough to snorkel by myself in these choppy waters. Help was at hand, however, in the form of a glass-bottomed boat. I had always thought these things looked pretty naff, but I was so wrong. Ken – who by now had recovered from being tossed aboard the Seastar like a beachball – joined me, and we both hopped on board.

It was enchanting exploring the fantastic landscape of the reef in the dry. An expert identified the different corals that we could see through the clear glass floor. They came in an amazing variety of shapes, colours and textures, with wonderfully descriptive names such as finger, boulder and brain coral, staghorn, spaghetti hair and soft elephant ears. Giant clams slowly opened and closed their corrugated 'hands', while sea cucumbers rolled sluggishly from side to side in the current. Among the many multi-coloured fishes nibbling at the coral were parrotfish, Six-barred Wrasse, Fusiliers and Sergeant-Major Fish – or was it Major-General Fish? Anyway, whatever their rank, they put on an entertaining show.

The motor back to the harbour was pretty uneventful: no one drowned and Alan wasn't even sick. This was probably just as well, given that we were no sooner back on dry land, than Iain had us in the minibus and driving along the winding road up the mountain into the tropical rainforest.

Our destination was Cassowary House, run by Sue and Phil Gregory, so no prizes for guessing our target bird here; apparently the creature even fed in Sue's garden. The next morning, as we set off to bird the rainforest, we arranged to take Sue's mobile phone with us. If the Cassowary turned up, she would call to let us know.

The plan worked like a dream. Of course, we were at the furthest point possible when Sue rang to tell us the bird was in her garden. Panic. Alan and I ran off at top speed but we had underestimated just how far we'd walked, and by the time we'd got back to Sue's property our legs were wobbly and our chests heaving. We sought to control our breathing so that our ragged gasps wouldn't scare the bird away. Sue pointed to the path that led under the balcony round to the back garden. We tiptoed along, as fast and as quietly as you can in walking boots.

Rounding the corner of the building, I found myself confronted by a huge shaggy mound. I was so surprised that I took a smart step back and crashed into Alan who was still travelling forwards at high speed, propelling me around the corner again and face-to-face with a creature that was considerably bigger than I was – a Southern Cassowary. This was no ordinary bird; this was a six-foot *Jurassic Park* monster. On the end of its sturdy legs were lethally-clawed feet that could reputedly disembowl you with a kick – and these birds have a reputation for being pretty bad-tempered. Protruding from the great mound of black feathers – its body – was a long neck, from which dangled two red fleshy wattles. Naked blue skin on the throat extended over the bird's face, on top of which was a naked, bony-looking grey helmet.

I have a very healthy respect for any bird that is bigger than me, so I was content to peer around the corner again at this monstrous beast while the rest of the group caught up. Once everyone had taken their first peek – and without fail this drew a sharp intake of breath from everyone – we all spread out in a semicircle to take photographs, keeping a respectful distance. What a bird!

The only way to follow an experience like that was with breakfast. Then we hit the road again. We were staying in the Daintree area for the next day or so. Once an important area for timber logging, this beautiful rainforest area is now a World Heritage listed area and, apparently, home to Australia's most life-threatening flora and fauna. If you want to be eaten by a crocodile, bitten by a snake or nipped by a killer spider, this is the place to be. No wonder Iain likes it so much.

Checking carefully under the bed and toilet seats, we moved into the Red Mill House for the night. This place is a birder's paradise. The owners, Andrew and Trish Forsyth, are keen birders themselves and knew just what a serious birding group needed: superb accommodation, delicious food served at odd times of the day or night, and excellent birding on the doorstep. In fact we could even bird and eat at the same time, enjoying scrumptious meals, up-to-date birding advice and glorious birds such as Green Orioles in the garden during the day, and bandicoots foraging in the spotlights by night.

Crack of dawn the next morning saw us taking a boat trip on the Daintree River with local riverman, Ian. The fact that he wore the largest glasses we'd ever seen didn't stop him having the sharpest eyes, and the lowly level of our flat-bottomed boat gave us an unusual perspective on the birds of this tree-lined tributary. Male and female Shining Flycatchers perched on an overhanging branch just above us, while tucked well into the shade of the trees on the bank was a Papuan Frogmouth, working very hard at making itself invisible with its cryptic plumage. At night, this stub of 'dead branch' would come to life, and swoop down on unsuspecting snails and small vertebrates as they foraged on the forest floor. Out on the broad Daintree River itself, we were very excited to see a Great-billed Heron perched on a stout overhanging branch. This bird lived up to its name, with a stonking great bill, and was an excellent addition to our list.

From Daintree we drove on to Mareeba and our home for the next couple of nights, the Jackaroo Motel. This part of Australia does very well for unspoiled forests, and Iain took us to another gem the next day, Mount Lewis, another World

Heritage site but one that is perhaps less visited. We had the misty forest all to ourselves as we drove along the track in amongst the dripping trees, but then it was only 4.30am. A great time for bird action, though – the early worm really does catch the bird – and we notched up Tooth-billed Catbird, Noisy Pitta and Fernwren.

Next we drove on to the Tinaroo Creek Road, but not without a brief pit stop in a small town to take advantage of the public toilets. Locking the door on the Ladies, I turned round to see the most bizarre sign on the wall: 'Photography is prohibited in these toilets'. What on earth did the locals get up to around here? Of course, I had to fetch the camera and record the sign for posterity.

By now our new team members were establishing their identities and revealing their idiosyncrasies. Ken, who'd been with us in the Outback, seemed to be coming out of his shell. He was an endearing, good-humoured and usually quiet gentleman who could always be relied upon to have the field guide handy. Somehow though, his possessions often seemed to get the better of him. His blue rain poncho, for example, ended up on him the wrong way round, with his arms backwards in the sleeves and the hood up over his face, leaving him staggering around with arms outstretched, as though in a game of blind man's bluff. Or his bum bag, which strapped itself around his waist upside down so that his water bottle and field guide threatened to throw themselves out at any moment.

Len and Linda, being at such opposite extremes of height, had to find their own separate places on the tour bus. Len, with his exceptionally long legs, needed to sit in the jump seat nearest to the sliding door on the minibus, but as he wasn't always the quickest out of the door, he frequently found the rest of us clambering over him in our desire to get onto the new birds as fast as possible. Linda, so much shorter, was usually in pole position nearest to Iain once we were on the ground, and Alan and I found that – providing she wasn't wearing her sunhat – we could stand back and still comfortably see over her head. Jackie made sure that Iain didn't fall asleep on the long drives, chatting amiably to him about birds, the universe and the meaning of life, while the rest of us dozed in the back. Politics also entered the conversation. We were sharing a minibus with a group of Americans who were heading for the most exciting presidential election in years. Luckily, for the sake of harmony on board, everyone was a Democrat – or at least that's what they were saying. Try as we might, though, Alan and I just couldn't get as excited as the others about the whole issue.

And then of course there was Iain Campbell himself. We'd already birded with him several times this year; in Ecuador, his adopted home country, where he was every bit as Latin-blooded as the locals; and in Ghana, where he'd once lived and birded, but was so laid-back on our tour there that he'd spent much of his time catching up on lost sleep. But out here in Australia he was a man on a mission. He wanted the highest bird score ever on this trip and was determined that Alan and I would smash the world record. Thus it seemed only right and proper that the record should be broken here and with him. This was never going to be an easy trip – Iain doesn't do easy – but if he drove us hard (and he did), then he drove himself even harder. We snoozed while he was still at the wheel, and in the evenings, long after even Alan and I had finished our computer homework for the day, Iain was still going strong. His red eyes in the morning gave away just how few hours' sleep he'd grabbed.

Iain was also going more native as the days passed. He was wearing the ubiquitous brown leather slouch hat, although his had been around the world so many times it probably had its own frequent flyer pass – and, judging by its smell, was definitely host to a whole universe of interesting microscopic life. His accent is a peculiar mixture of Aussie and American at the best of times, with the odd 'och' or 'aye' slipping out occasionally to betray his Scottish roots, but as the days went by, he and Rolf Harris seemed to have more and more in common – though, to be fair, I don't remember Iain ever waving his wobble board or asking 'Can you tell what it is yet?'

But back to birding. Australian Bustards were first on the menu the next morning, and we admired them strutting across some arable fields around Mount Carbine. The handsome male stalked around haughtily, standing about a metre tall from his three-toed feet to the top of his black-crowned head, his finely vermiculated white neck all puffed out to show just who was boss. Next up was a quick stop at a pool to admire some Double-barred Finches, dapper little birds, with black bands around their white faces that somehow gave them an owlish look. This was also a good place to catch up with some Galahs, cockatoos with a distinctive if rather effeminate colour scheme of bubblegum-pink and pale grey.

We birded our way back to Cairns, stopping off at likely sites along the way. These included Mount Hypipimee, a rainforest reserve dotted with road signs warning of Cassowaries crossing. A group of leather-clad bikers arrived and marched off down one of the trails. We overheard them discussing Cassowaries. 'They're just like little Roadrunners,' said one. Wow! The Roadrunners must be enormous where they come from.

We stopped at a little place near Yorkie's Knob where we wanted to bird a small track beside a railway line. We asked a nearby homeowner whether it was OK with him for us to walk there and whether he had noticed any finches around. Yes, it was fine to walk there, but no, he'd not seen any finches at all. So we wandered along the grassy track, seeing large numbers of Chestnut-breasted Munias, a stocky, brownish finch with a smart black face, and adding Crimson Finch to our list, an upright finch with a startlingly bright red face and breast. We wondered whether to tell the man about the birds, but decided not to disillusion him; he was probably happier believing he was living in a finch-free zone.

It was a brutal 3.30am start the next day to get to Cairns Airport for our flight down to Brisbane. Our new minibus looked remarkably like the previous one, so we immediately slipped back into our usual places: Len by the door, Linda in the front row, Alan and I asleep on each other in the next row, Ken amidst the luggage at the back, and Jackie keeping Iain awake at the front.

It wasn't long before we were adding more new birds at Nudgee Mangrove: Chestnut Teal and, appropriately, Mangrove Honeyeater. Then we headed south to the Koala Centre at Daisy Hill. I squawked in excitement when I spotted a largish grey-brown lump propped up against a side branch, but was disappointed to check with my binoculars and find it was a nesting Tawny Frogmouth complete with downy chick. The frogmouth was great, but I would have loved a Koala.

After a quick pie for lunch, we continued in the minibus to O'Reilly's Rainforest Retreat up in the Border Mountains. The twisting road wound its way up into the hills, with hairpin bends, blind corners, and plenty of traffic. At the top, an incredible spectacle met our eyes: first, hundreds of people – this seemed to be a popular spot for Sunday lunch with the family; and second, hundreds of gaudily coloured birds. There were red-and-blue Crimson Rosellas, and tomato-and-green King Parrots, and they were everywhere: on the ground, in the bushes, on fence posts and even perching on people's heads. These birds were so used to handouts that they would feed from your hand, sit on your hat or, as we were to find out later, even visit your bedroom in the hope of something to eat. That didn't stop them being stunningly beautiful, though, and it really was incredible to get such nose-to-beak views. Perhaps more authentically, a Regent Bowerbird popped up into view in a tree on the other side of the entrance road. And all this before we'd even checked in.

Dumping our luggage, we headed straight out into the field. We drove back down to a side track called Duck Creek Road looking for Bell Miner. We heard the bird first, as you might guess with a name like that. Its call – like a school bell ringing – led us up a forest-clad mountain until we laid our eyes on this green bird, with its bright orange legs and bill and yellow patch around the eye.

Target bird bagged, we returned to the hotel and this time followed the Border Trail, which led straight into the forest. It was late afternoon and the light was poor, but that didn't stop sharp-eyed Iain finding a pair of Logrunners, another of our target birds. Beautifully mottled, striped and barred in shades of russet, buff, black, grey and white, these birds lived up to their name, scurrying around on the dappled ground like a pair of feathered mice, over leaves, under branches and along logs – often coming very close, as we all froze on the spot.

The wildlife extravaganza at O'Reilly's didn't stop at birds. We also encountered Red-necked and Red-thighed Pademelons (no, not an exotic kind of fruit; these are small kangaroos), while a mother and baby Brush-tailed Possum fed under the spotlights just outside the restaurant.

It was no surprise to find other bird tours, including a group from the American company, Field Guides, also staying at this amazing place. The food was superb, the setting incredible and the wildlife right on your doorstep. Or sometimes even closer: we shared our balcony with more Crimson Rosellas, who liked to pick pieces of biscuit from Alan's fingers. From our raised vantage point, we watched the Field Guides group as they lined up in a row beside their leader and all scanned in the same direction looking hard for something. What they didn't realise was that while they were all looking one way, right behind them a Brush Turkey was tiptoeing past them down the road without anyone even realising it was there. You could almost hear it holding its breath as it crept on by, With my camera to hand, I couldn't resist firing off a shot of this comical scene – any more than I could resist showing it to their tour leader at dinner that night, who I'm glad to say took it in good humour. It just goes to show, though, that it pays to be with a tour company that gets you to face in the right direction.

We were out at dawn the next morning to walk the Border Trail again. We were quick to spot a Paradise Riflebird looking down at us from high up in the bushes, its gorgeous plumage a real contrast to its rough call. But bird of the day was definitely a mammal! Obviously harbouring no grudges about photographs, the Field Guides tour leader gave Iain a call to say they'd found a Koala down Duck Creek Road. Even though this wouldn't help our world record, we all piled into the minibus and bounced along to the site as fast as we could. Two trees back and three to the right, about ten feet off the ground, and there he was: our first Koala, propped up dopily in the fork of a eucalyptus, his back leaning against the trunk for support.

I must admit, this amazing mammal was as exciting as any new bird, although much easier to see, as he didn't move a lot. He looked around at us blearily as we scrambled a little closer. My relatives in Australia had given me a toy Koala when I was a small child and Fred, as he was known, was covered in a soft, pale grey fur, so that's what I assumed the real thing would look like. The real Fred was a quite different colour: almost chocolate brown on his back, with a cream throat and belly. But his ears were suitably round and tufted, and his peculiar egg-shaped black nose looked just right. Having doted on Koalas from a young age, I took photo after photo of Fred to make sure I had the perfect shot for the album. OK, so maybe 196 snaps of a creature that didn't exactly move a lot was slightly excessive, but it was so rare to get a photogenic subject that sat still in good light. So, if you need 196 slightly different shots of a very cute Koala turning his head slowly from one side to the other, crawling along a branch, eating some eucalyptus leaves and then falling asleep again, just give me a call.

A curious beast is your average Koala. It is a marsupial, that is, an animal with a pouch for carrying its young about, and it lives on eucalyptus leaves that most other species would find toxic, tucking into a tasty 500g of them a day. It takes around three hours to eat enough leaves to keep going, and has such a slow metabolism that it spends the rest of the day just sitting about, generally sleeping. This truly is a 'Bear of Very Little Brain', as A.A. Milne would have put it (and yes, I know Koalas aren't bears, but since their scientific name *Phascolarctos* comes from the Greek words *phaskolos* meaning 'pouch' and *arktos* meaning 'bear', I think I can get away with it). Apparently, the brains of modern Koalas have shrivelled to the size of a walnut, probably because their diet is so low in nutrition. Even more curious, the male has a forked penis, while the female has two lateral vaginas and two separate uteri. It is hard to imagine such a sleepy creature actually mating, but perhaps that's how it spends the remaining few hours of its day not already taken up with eating leaves or sleeping.

After another brief night in those oh-so-comfy rooms, we had to check out of O'Reilly's and drive back down to Brisbane airport, where we caught a plane to Sydney. Ignoring the opera house and the harbour bridge, we drove through the suburbs to our motel for the night, where we were each handed a room key and a bottle of milk for our breakfast. It was almost the end of October and we were on an incredible 3,618 species. That world record seemed almost touchable and we still had two months of the year to go. For the first time we dared to believe that we could really do it.

This confidence was underlined by newfound media interest. Thanks to our good friend, Sean Dooley, the Australian media was now enthusiastically following our progress. We'd first met Sean face-to-face at the British Birdwatching Fair in 2007 and had avidly read his book, *The Big Twitch*, in which he recounted the tale of his big year in Australia, when he'd blown his inheritance on setting a new Australian record of over 700 bird species; we had been thrilled to meet him in person as we bought a signed copy. Sean had kept in touch as we progressed around the world and used his excellent contacts to promote our cause. As a result, the local media got very excited about the fact that the world record was about to be broken on their turf. Alan recorded our first interview early in the morning with ABC Radio, as we huddled in the car outside a McDonalds while the rest of the group enjoyed coffee and muffins inside to warm up after our pre-dawn birding.

Our first birding stop on the edge of Sydney was Lady Carrington Drive in the Royal National Park. Here we saw a large bird lurking in the shadows under some shrubs. We were thrilled when it emerged from the undergrowth and strolled across the track right in front of us: a male Superb Lyrebird, complete with long tail trailing behind it like a chestnut-and-white wedding train. Who hasn't enjoyed that incredible clip on The BBC's *The Life of Birds,* of David Attenborough watching a Superb Lyrebird going through its courtship paces? The male attracts a mate by imitating other bird species, sometimes so realistically that the real thing may call by to see what's going on. But the Superb Lyrebird can also include in its repertoire any other noises it has heard, including car alarms, camera shutters and even the chainsaws that are destroying the forest around it. Sadly, our bird didn't feel like putting on a quick burst of chainsaw for our benefit, but it was fantastic to see nonetheless.

The Barren Grounds, our next stop, lived up to the name, as driving rain battered our faces and covered our bins. There was no point in trying to bird in this, so we drove down to a village and a warm café to thaw out. There I did another radio interview, this time with Sean Dooley himself and another female presenter. This was really fun, but I think the distinctive sound of an expresso machine in the background may have undermined my claims to be birding hard in the field at the time.

Then we all piled into the bus for a long drive to a town called Leeton, in the Riverina region of New South Wales. We dropped off our bags at the Town Centre Motel and headed out for Fivebough Swamp, designated a Ramsar site because it is home to the vulnerable Australasian Bittern. There we added some great birds to our list: Baillon's, Australian and Spotless Crakes, Australian Shoveler, Yellow-rumped Thornbill, and – proving the success of the Ramsar designation – an Australasian Bittern. Now we were just twelve birds short of the record.

Sleep is for wimps not world record-breakers, so Iain had us out on the road at 3.30am on 31 October to drive to Round Hill, an area of arid mallee scrub. Every species was now vital, so I recorded each bird in my notebook to make sure we didn't lose count during the day. Gilbert's Whistler was first up, with a great '*pooo-eee*' call which carried through the bushes. Next was Chestnut-rumped Thornbill, a small brown-and-cream bird with a chestnut-coloured rump. White-eared and Yellow-plumed Honeyeaters came soon after, then Southern Scrub-Robin, who gave us the run-around amongst the bushes, followed by Shy Heathwren (Hylacola), which proved not too shy to show itself.

Six birds down; six to go to equalise. The pressure was mounting. Bird number seven, Brown-headed Honeyeater, lived up to its name. Number eight, Black-eared Cuckoo, was calling from a spindly tree and attracting the attention of various honeyeaters, which mobbed it continuously, until it finally flew away in disgust. A Chestnut Quail-Thrush, with its striking black-and-white badger facial markings, strutted across an open patch of ground. Didn't it know it was supposed to be a skulking species? No matter, it was number nine for the day. Then Red-lored Whistler hopped onto the list as number ten, and we called a halt to have some breakfast in the field.

This was the cue for every fly within miles to make for us at top speed and explore every inch of our faces – in our eyes, ears and mouths, and up our noses. They landed on our cereal bowls, slid around the rims of our beakers and swooped onto our spoons.

Australia does flies very well. I don't. I hate them with a passion – particularly when I am trying to eat. A fly landing on my spoon just as I was putting it into my mouth was just too much, and I exploded, spitting out my mouthful of cereal and fly, and flinging down my bowl and spoon in disgust.

'They're disgusting! Filthy!' I shouted. 'They've just been walking on a pile of shit somewhere and now they're walking on my breakfast. Do you know what flies do? Do you? They spit on your food and then suck it up. It makes me sick. It's bad enough having to eat this crap food, without having flies all over it!'

The rest of the group was silent, not knowing what to make of my outburst. The normally calm and polite Ruth had turned into a furious hate-spitting harpy. Alan, knowing my short fuse, was totally unfazed. From behind me, I heard a loud snigger. I didn't need to turn round to see who it was.

'I'm so glad I amuse you, Iain Campbell,' I muttered furiously through gritted teeth.

'Oh, you really do!' he replied, cackling. This was too much even for me, and though I tried to keep a straight face a little longer for dramatic effect, I soon had to start giggling too, and soon the whole group joined in, laughing in relief.

Back to the serious business of birding, we tramped through the mallee looking for more birds. Three birders pulled up beside us in a car and reported that they'd had a couple of the birds we needed: White-fronted and Black Honeyeater. A striped bird swept into the tree and we peered through the branches at it. It was a juvenile White-fronted Honeyeater: bird number eleven for the day. That put us on 3,662 species – equal to the world record. It wasn't a particularly exciting bird, a brown and stripy juvenile, but it was an exciting moment. Now we just needed Black Honeyeater. This would make a cool record-breaker: according to the field guide, it had a black stripe like a tie down its white belly, and a long decurved bill. It had to be nearby. We checked the mallee scrub, trying to catch up with the individual that the other group had just seen. Suddenly a smallish black-and-white streak of a bird tore overhead and disappeared into the distance. Could that have been it? None of us had got a really good look, and despite searching hard, we couldn't relocate it. The bird had gone for good.

That was the cue for all new birds to disappear. As we drove and birded our way back towards Leeton through the afternoon, we saw plenty of great birds, but none of them new. Our list remained stuck firmly on 3,662 species. We were now joint record holders but we just couldn't edge past Jim Clements and into the lead. Alan and I were getting very tense.

We called in at Griffith Golf Course, a site that Iain visited regularly for a nesting Tawny Frogmouth. This wasn't a new bird for us – I'd misidentified one as a Koala at Daisy Hill a week or so earlier – but it was worth another look. Griffith was hosting a tournament that day, so there were golfers and golf carts all over the place. It was hardly a peaceful place to go birding, but that didn't bother the frogmouth, which was sleepily sitting on its nest on a branch overhanging the car park. We walked to the edge of the first tee, right in front of the busy golf club, and caught sight of six parrots feeding in the rough beside the fairway. We frantically focused our binoculars.

Cue a loud whoop of excitement: they were Bluebonnet Parrots, a new species. But not just a new species, they were bird number 3,663 on our list, which meant they were the world record-breaking species. It was 2.15pm on 31 October 2008 and we had broken Jim Clements' world record in just ten months. We had done it!

Ignoring the tournament going on around us, we moved in closer to watch our record breakers, who were now perched in a tree. Compared with the rainbow-coloured parrots we'd already seen, these weren't the most exciting birds to look at: mostly brown, with yellow and rust bellies and blue faces. But that didn't matter: right now, they were the most important birds in the world. Their instant fame didn't seem to bother them much, though. They went about their business regardless, cleaning their bills on the branches over our heads. We took photos, none of which came out too clearly, given the shaking hands, high emotions and poor light. But that didn't matter. To us they were very special.

I was bubbling over with excitement and wanted to jump up and down and give Alan a big kiss. But, miserable so-and-so, he was playing it cool, so I made do with squeals of delight and big hugs from Jackie and Linda instead. We needed a drink to celebrate, but we weren't allowed into the clubhouse, because of the tournament, so we drove back to the Town Centre Motel, picking up some champagne on the way. We all squashed into Iain's room, where we drank a toast to Alan and me, to our achievement together, and to the support that Iain and his colleagues at Tropical Birding – and all our birding friends around the world – had shown us so far, ever since we had mentioned our little idea back in 2006. And, of course, we drank a toast to the birds.

While the others grabbed a spot of downtime, Alan and I did another interview set up by Jenny, the proprietor of the Town Centre Motel, this time with journalists from *The Irrigator*, Leeton's leading local newspaper. They seemed delighted that we'd broken the record in their town, and asked us plenty of questions before taking our photo in the garden. We were the lead story on the front page of the next edition – though maybe sharing it with a story about a lost kitten did detract a little from our glory. World record holders or not, though, Iain lost no time in kicking us back onto the bus, and we returned to Fivebough Swamp, adding two more new birds before bedtime.

There was no chance of the next day being an anticlimax, as Iain had arranged for some very special birding for us with Phil Maher, the king of the Plains Wanderer. Phil had come across this odd bird in 1980, and made it his speciality, showing the bird to visitors from all over the world. We met up with him in the late afternoon at a pub in Deniliquin and headed straight out into the field.

Iain introduced us to Phil by saying we had broken the birding world record only the day before.

'Oh,' said Phil, before heading off into the woodland. He was a man of few words.

At first we played the game of 'kick the tree and rub it with a stick', until we found the right tree and a very cute Owlet Nightjar flew out of its nest in a hollow branch to see what was causing the noise. Its cryptic markings meant it blended in with the bark but its huge round eyes peered down at us from its high vantage point.

Then we drove out onto the open plains. First Phil and his mate John rounded up Australian Pratincole and Banded Lapwing amongst the short sparse grass, and then they tracked down Inland Dotterel: all good birds and hard to see. But the star of the show was going to be trickier. While we waited for darkness to fall, we tucked into our packed suppers and enjoyed a glorious sunset across the pancake flat landscape.

Eventually, Phil decided that it was dark enough to make a start. We piled into their two off-road vehicles and headed out across the plains, Phil and John sweeping their searchlights across the barren ground. Nothing. Then we tried driving round and round in circles to see if that would work. Still nothing. We were searching for a small brown bird in a large brown plain, a real needle in a haystack. Our spotlight picked out a dunnart, a tiny mouse-like marsupial, but still no sign of a Plains Wanderer.

By now we'd been driving in the darkness for two hours with a silent Phil Maher, so Alan decided to try a little conversation.

'Does it always take this long to find the Plains Wanderer?' he asked.

'Can do,' replied Phil, and that was that.

We continued our silent circling for another hour. Then Phil's walkie-talkie crackled: 'Gotta PW,' said John.

We bounced our way over to where John had his spotlight fixed on a patch of ground. There in the beam was a male Plains Wanderer. This bizarre wader is a real enigma. Some say it is related to seedsnipes, others maintain it is in a family all of its own. Whatever its taxonomy, it certainly appeared a curious bird as it froze motionless in the spotlight on its long, yellow legs, showing a rounded head, a short yellow bill, a big button eye and a slim body covered in mottled camouflage plumage. No wonder it had been hard to spot. This was a male; the more decorative female sports a black and white spotted scarf around her neck. But we didn't mind: Plains Wanderer was on the list and we were glad to head for home.

Our next birding destination was the Capertee Valley in the Blue Mountains. This beautiful area has allegedly the largest gorge in the southern hemisphere – or the whole world, depending upon which website you believe – with escarpments eroded into shapes reminiscent of South African kopjes. It is the 'centre of the universe' for Regent Honeyeaters, as one website put it. There are apparently only around 1,000 of these glorious birds, which cling on in the few areas of precious woodland – a habitat that has been cleared elsewhere in southeast Australia. At a trickling creek in Glen Alice, we spotted two birders we'd seen at O'Reilly's, and a female guide who approached us. We hopped out of the minibus and walked down to the creek. While Iain chatted to the guide, a fantastic bird suddenly flew into a tree right in front of us on the opposite bank. This was the elusive Regent Honeyeater. It was a male, with a black hood and bare pinkish patch around the eye. Its white breast feathers were black-edged, as though it was wearing a heavy diamond georgette, and its wings were a complex pattern of black and yellow, which made an exaggerated M shape as it flew. As we feasted on this gorgeous bird, another identical minibus turned up and a second birding group erupted. Clearly this was the group the guide had arranged to meet, so having filled our boots with satisfying honeyeater views we left them to it and drove back to Sydney airport.

After a short flight to Hobart, we collected another identical minibus and assumed our usual positions; this was becoming Groundhog Day. We liked what we saw of this city: it had a vaguely familiar feel, rather like a venerable Scottish university town, with its broad streets and reassuringly solid stone buildings. It had a Scottish climate too, pretty cold and blowy.

A local reserve was *the* place to see Forty-spotted Pardelote – and so it was that we found ourselves going round and round that roundabout as Iain tried to relocate the turning, throwing the map around in his fury.

With the birds duly recorded, we grabbed a McDonalds takeaway breakfast and drove at top speed to the ferry terminal to catch the boat over to Bruny Island. If Hobart was reminiscent of Edinburgh, then the scenery here was like British Colombia, with tree-covered hills sloping down to the clear water. We landed after a quick crossing and drove along the coastline. Stopping at an area of woodland, a cute Dusky Robin hopped up on a fence while Green Rosellas fidgeted in the trees, flapping about and hanging upside down as they ate the ripe fruit. Along a wooded track we added Pink and Flame Robins, the first with a rose-pink breast and the second bright red from belly to bill. This was a productive patch of woodland, giving us Crescent Honeyeater and Olive Whistler, among others, while Scrubtit and Tasmanian Thornbill were our rewards for ignoring the rain and following a footpath deeper into the forest.

Next we drove back down to the shoreline and restored ourselves with hot drinks at a café. While the rest of us walked a short way down the road to take advantage of the facilities, Alan set up the scope to scan the sea. I could hear his excited shouts while I was still inside the Ladies and was first on the scene, zipping up my trousers as I ran. He'd spotted a dark bird low on the water. Through the scope it was small but distinct: Little Penguin. As the others arrived, of course the bird disobligingly dived. They can swim quite a long way underwater, so it was a real challenge relocating it in the scope, but at last the whole group had a satisfying look at the bird bobbing about on the water's surface.

This great bird was our third penguin of the year. So, of course, what could we do but head back to the café for another hot chocolate to celebrate? This time, heading back to the Ladies before we set off, I finally succeeded in getting a photo of a Superb Fairywren as it perched on a low fence post. We could have carried on like this for some time – hot chocolate, bird, hot chocolate, bird – but Iain was having none of it.

Back on the Tasmanian mainland, we drove to the Ferntree Café, where Curry, the Grey Currawong, was a regular visitor and well known for his liking for salt-and-vinegar crisps. Sure enough, as we stood outside, he soon appeared, striding purposefully up to the largest crisp we threw on the ground for him, seizing it in his solid, oversized bill and flying off to savour his snack, before returning for the next.

Then we drove west towards Port Arthur to look for Cape Barren Goose. Some of these birds were in the area as part of a rehabilitation programme, but others were free flying – they weren't ringed, their wings weren't clipped – and were perfectly countable. But before we reached our destination, I caught sight of something that was even more exciting and had us leaping out of the minibus like the A-Team. It was shaped like a rugby ball, but with a pointy snout at one end, a stubby tail at the other and a thick carpet of spines in between. And it was trotting along the side of the road in full daylight.

'Echidna!' I screamed at full volume. Iain swerved onto the verge and we all piled out in hot pursuit of our spiny target. Realising we were after him, he rolled himself into a ball under some leaves to avoid detection. But we weren't giving up that easily, so we stood in a semi-circle and waited in silence. At last, tricked by our lack of noise, he cautiously unwound himself, his black nose whiffling in the air. His sense of smell can't have been very acute though, as he trotted right past Alan's left boot. What on earth was he doing out in broad daylight? Didn't he know he was supposed to be nocturnal?

Soon we reached our destination, the Tasmanian Devil Conservation Park, which is well known as a good place for Cape Barren Goose. We immediately saw some on the ground within the compound. These may or may not have been wild and free flying, it was hard to tell as they pecked at the ground, and we didn't feel comfortable ticking them. But a gaggle of five birds soon flew overhead and landed in some nearby fields. These were definitely countable, and they went straight on to the list.

Of course, you can't take a group of visitors to the Tasmanian Devil Conservation Park without letting them see Tasmanian Devils, so Iain disowned us as we paid our fees to take a peek inside. These are nocturnal animals in the wild, but they are also an endangered species so this was our best chance of seeing them. Tasmanian Devils are struggling to sustain a viable population, as large numbers have succumbed to a fatal cancer over the last decade, and while none of us particularly wanted to see captive animals, we were happy to support a centre that is helping to conserve the species and find a solution to their problem.

It has to be said, the devils were incredibly cute. Roughly poodle-sized, but not remotely fluffy, they are a dark chocolate brown all over, with a cream neck chain, and played together like overgrown puppies until it was feeding time. Then the cuteness vanished as though at the flick of a switch: suddenly it was every devil for himself, as the largest and most dominant one seized the piece of raw meat that was tossed into their enclosure and hurtled round the perimeter at top speed with the rest of the pack following him. Two, perhaps a little smarter than the rest, headed him off at the pass and snatched at the meat as he shot by. Now there were two pieces of meat in the game of tag, as the devils continued to charge round and round. Two seized opposite ends of a single piece in a furious tug-of-war, all snarls, flashing eyes and sharp teeth. Three others were caught in a three-way tie as each tried to bite off the best chunk without yielding a scrap. In no time at all they had demolished the lot, and calm resumed as they cleaned themselves up and relaxed, all peace and harmony once again.

And then it was all over. We'd come to the end of Tropical Birding's Eastern Australia Top to Bottom trip and we'd survived. No, we'd not only survived, we'd thoroughly enjoyed the most amazing tour and broken a world record to boot. I can honestly say I really loved this tour – and no, Iain hasn't bribed me. It was hard work but a real blast, and definitely one of the most fun parts of our year. I can't wait to go birding in Australia again.

But Australia hadn't quite finished with us. It was 4.30am as we left the hotel to go to Hobart Airport for our flight to Melbourne. On arrival, we just had time for a quick shower and freshen up before we met our date for the day: Steve Davidson, aka The Melbourne Birder. Steve is a bird guide and a good mate of Sean Dooley, who had put us in touch with him for a day's birding in the area. It started before we'd even left the hotel, with a Purple-crowned Lorikeet feeding in a tree right outside. As Steve drove us out of town to our first birding destination, we chatted away in the car. We clicked immediately and it felt as though we were birding with a good mate rather than a professional bird guide.

First stop was Werribee Sewage Works. This was a vast expanse of open settling pools and a real Mecca for waders, wildfowl and waterbirds. It was just heaving with birds and we could have stayed for ages, enjoying the massed armies of Red-necked Stints, Sharp-tailed and Curlew Sandpipers in the shallows, clouds of Red-headed Avocets overhead, Musk Ducks on the water and Brolgas flying in. We also added great new birds, including Stubble Quail and Lewin's Rail. But sadly we couldn't linger too long before it was time to move on to the next site and our most wanted bird of the day.

Steve drove us to a patch of wetland that was part of Seaford Swamp. We'd read about this area in Sean Dooley's book, *The Big Twitch*, as he wrote about the soggy place where he had cut his birding teeth as a young lad. Today, though, we wanted one particular bird: an Australian Painted Snipe, which had recently been seen here. Time ticked away, as we scanned and scanned the wetland, but still the scene remained snipe-less. Would we dip out on this lovely bird? Steve went to check out the hide that screened the lagoon from the car park. It wasn't open to the general public, but fortune was smiling on us. A local birder who volunteered at the reserve was just emerging from the hide. Steve managed to persuade him how important it was for us to see this bird. The volunteer kindly unlocked the hide to let us in. We tiptoed over to the windows and looked straight down. Crouching right below us in the shadow of the hide was the Australian Painted Snipe. Sensing our presence, it froze, so we had a perfect view of its striped crown and back. We didn't want to stress the bird unnecessarily so, after a good look, tiptoed away again, grinning from ear to ear. We thanked the volunteer for his kindness, and Steve drove us back to the airport hotel.

We'd had a fun day out with Steve and he'd helped us add some great birds. Now we had to knuckle down to some computer admin to make sure our Aussie bird list was up to date before we moved on to our next country. We wrote up our Melbourne birding and gave the Painted Snipe a good mention. So imagine our amazement when we received an email from the kindly volunteer, Andy Silcocks, and learned that we already knew him. He'd been in contact with Alan in the distant past when he had been the warden at Bardsey Bird Observatory, just off the North Wales Coast, and Alan had been running Birdline Wales. He knew Alan by voice, as they'd spoken many times on the phone, but they'd never met so it probably wasn't too surprising that he hadn't made the connection when we'd turned up at his hide. He was surprised to read about himself on our blog and was quick to get in touch, very pleased that he'd been able to help us score our last Australian bird of the trip.

We left Australia having reached a staggering year total of 3,718 species, and already had a good lead on the previous world record of 3,662. But still we were greedy for more birds. We had almost two whole months of the year to go, and some huge, bird-rich territories awaited us.

3,718 species

8–13 November, Malaysia (Alan)

Keith Barnes, from Tropical Birding, was waiting for us at Kuala Lumpur airport. He already had that mad look in his eyes that we knew so well. We gulped, and braced ourselves for the whirlwind.

But, first things first: Keith congratulated us on our world record, and once again we failed to get an ATM machine to work. Out into the chaos of the city traffic, Ruth bravely took on the map-reading duties while I sat safely in the back. Amazingly, we somehow found our way out of the metropolis, ticking off the mighty Petronas Towers, huge skyscrapers reaching for the clouds. We took a moment to remember the Twin Towers of New York and all who perished that horrendous day of 9/11.

Fraser's Hill, our first destination, immediately presented us with a problem. As its name suggests this is indeed a hill, a very steep one, and covered in lovely bird-filled forest. The road that winds up is very narrow, so traffic either goes up or down, but not both at the same time. The system was controlled from checkpoints, one at the bottom and one at the top. When we arrived the traffic had just switched to down and would stay that way for the next hour.

With an hour to kill there was only one thing to do: look for new birds. Apart from eastern Turkey this was *The Biggest Twitch*'s first venture into Asia, so – despite already being well past the world record – we were looking forward to an avalanche of new birds. We knew that with Keith's experience here we could boost our year list considerably during our brief visit.

We drove a few hundred metres from the bottom of the hill, jumped out and birded along the roadside. Here, lush gardens and forest edge produced plenty of birds: Ashy Bulbuls were busy stripping a fruiting tree, in which we also saw an Ochraceous Bulbul. Just around the corner we bumped into an Oriental Magpie-Robin that bounced along the forest edge. Next up was Fire-breasted Flowerpecker. Bluish-green above and pale buff below, with a scarlet breast patch, this tiny bird was a cracker.

With the traffic now switched to up only, we took the twisting road up Fraser's Hill to our hotel at the top, the Shahzan Inn. Here we dumped our bags and went straight out again; with so many amazing new birds available we did not want to waste a second. We drove the 'Telecoms Loop' road, which winds around the communication tower on the summit area. The birding was fast and crazy as we just kept hitting new and wonderful birds.

Many of these birds were lifers, as neither of us had birded in Malaysia before. A roadside Blyth's Hawk Eagle gave us great views as it heaved into the air and flapped slowly across the valley. Little Cuckoo-Dove flew in and landed low down, looking more cuckoo than dove, and we drooled over the exquisite colours of Blue-throated Bee-eater. Malaysia has barbets to spare and we particularly enjoyed Gold-whiskered Barbet gulping down fruit high above us. A flash of black and white and we had Little Pied Flycatcher, very like our familiar Pied Flycatcher back home in the woods of Wales. Keith called Black Laughingthrush and after a tense wait up it popped, its handsome black plumage set off by a sexy coral red bill and neat white mark just behind the eye.

If we thought the laughingthrush was good, the next bird was a mind-blower: Silver-eared Mesia just glowed with colour, painted in yellow, grey, red, black and, of course, silver. Then we came across a weird looking 'sunbird', with hardly any tail and the whopping bill of a curlew: a Long-billed Spiderhunter. Finally we just had time to find a Brown Shrike lurking in the damp vegetation when the heavens opened and torrential rain swept in. We dashed back to the hotel, where we feasted on wonderful Malaysian food while totting up our amazing day list. This far into the year, having already broken the world record, it was staggering to be adding forty-four new birds in just one day at just one site.

At 6am we were standing in the dark. We had no choice; the power supply had been knocked out during the storm. This gave us a few headaches: no computers could be charged and, worse still, Keith's iPod was dead; we needed this for bird calls. We also found that the mains cable for our laptop had split and would not have worked even if we had had power. Then we managed to lock ourselves out of our room, with no staff about. Only one thing for it: go birding.

First we drove to the bottom of the hill again. On the way down we saw a Malayan Whistling-Thrush feeding on the verge, though sadly he was not whistling. At the bottom we found a flock of six tiny Black-thighed Falconets; these sparrow-sized raptors were sitting in a dead tree, looking very dapper, with their black upperparts, white breast and orange vent.

It was still early; the bottom checkpoint looked unmanned as we headed back uphill. We stopped on the way to watch a stunning Red-bearded Bee-eater perched above the road. The trouble here is if you stop for one bird you quickly find more, and Ruth soon picked out a Green-billed Malkoha feeding in a tangle of vines.

We were having a wonderful time watching great birds. Then suddenly the peace was shattered by the blaring of a car horn. What was going on? The sound got closer as the vehicle responsible wound its way down the hairpins towards us. A police car swept into view with flashing lights and horn constantly pressed. It pulled up alongside us and thankfully the noise stopped too.

Then we found out what all the commotion was about: us! While we had been lost in our birding the road had switched to downhill mode and we, of course, were still heading up. That unmanned checkpoint had been manned after all; the guys at the bottom had radioed those at the top to tell them we were coming, but we had never appeared – and now a queue of traffic was waiting to come down. We apologised and the police were fine about it, though we got very hard looks from the people in the queue at the top. As we drove back we noticed huge signs proclaiming that no one should stop on the hill. Oops!

Back at the top we took to the jungle. This was with some trepidation, as we had heard horror stories about the leeches along these trails and did not relish the prospect of being eaten alive. But we had a weapon: very fetching leech socks. These giant, densely-woven socks, rather like over-sized Christmas stockings, are worn over your socks and trousers and come up to your thighs, their dense weave protecting you from the blood-suckers.

True, the leeches couldn't get through the socks. Instead, they just climbed past them and then got stuck in. Keith soon found a leech making its way up his trousers, and he flicked it at me, where it landed squarely in the eyecup of my bins. Yuk! These weird creatures make surprisingly fast progress as they loop along like caterpillars. But the birds here made it all worthwhile. A gorgeous Red-headed Trogon posed in the canopy as a pair of Pygmy Blue-Flycatchers flicked around him. Then a Blue Nuthatch nipped up the trunk above us.

Over another superb meal that night we went through the list of mouth-watering birds that we had seen and were very pleased to have chalked up another thirty-seven for *The Biggest Twitch*. Meanwhile Keith chuckled as he recalled our anxieties about leeches. 'You wait until we reach Taman Nagara,' he said, with relish, 'then you'll see leeches!'

The next morning we packed up and headed back down the hill. Yet again the roadside forest was alive with birds and we continually hit amazing feeding flocks. One of the many highlights was Wreathed Hornbills sitting in a dead tree. Through the scopes we marvelled at the huge yellow bills and bizarre yellow throat pouches of these monster birds. Meanwhile Edible-nest Swiftlets and Brown-backed Needletails competed for our attention overhead, and at eye-level a pair of Sultan Tits wowed us with their funky crests and smart livery of jet black and banana yellow. In a roadside ditch we found a Slaty-backed Forktail – far too good a bird to be in a ditch. Then Keith had us running down the road after the call of a Velvet-fronted Nuthatch: a pair of these lovely birds was climbing about on a dead tree, showing their bright blue upperparts, coral red bill and yellow eye-ring. As we watched these, a Black-naped Monarch flew in, this beautiful flycatcher decked out in blue and black. It was just one of those amazing birding episodes when you really did not know where to look next.

Time had flown by and we needed to hit the road for the long drive ahead. Of course we did not get far. At the second hairpin bend, I spotted two huge birds and shouted at Keith to stop. He slammed on the brakes, and we leapt out and dashed back to the bend. Now where were they? I had seen two huge lumps on a branch which I was pretty sure were birds. We peered through the trees and when we got the angle right, there they were: two enormous Barred Eagle Owls sitting motion-less, and staring at us from beneath their Groucho Marx eyebrows.

That afternoon, we passed through miles and miles of palm nut plantations; it was sad to think how much lowland forest has so recently been lost. This wildlife desert went on for as far as the eye could see. But eventually we reached the river opposite our next destination: Taman Negara resort. Here we left the hire car and took a boat across to reach our home for the next two nights, where we were greeted with a welcome drink and girls playing traditional flutes. The place was pretty upmarket, with lovely cottages in lush grounds and a very nice looking restaurant. We were sure we would like it here.

It was so hot and humid that we were sweating just standing still. With little light left we hurried down to an elevated hide overlooking a clearing, but too late to find any new species. Not too late, however, for a leech to find Ruth, somehow working its way up onto her neck. It looked like Keith was right about this place.

In the restaurant we tucked into mountains of wonderful food and again marvelled at the birds we had seen that day: 51 new species. As usual, we debated our 'bird of the day'. With so many new species, it was a long game and the debate was heated. Surely Rhinoceros Hornbill had to be the winner, a huge colourful bird with a ridiculous bill. But then, what about that Orange-breasted Trogon? Trogons are always classy birds and this one was a lifer. Black-and-yellow Broadbill would usually have won the game easily but today it had stiff competition. In the end no winner was declared. In fact, we were the winners, having experienced such an amazing day's birding.

At dawn the next day the jungle came to life with weird and wonderful calls floating on the humid air. We were dressed for combat, with our leech socks on and insect repellent generously applied. Our first new birds were in the lodge garden: Streaked Spiderhunter and Lesser Green Leafbird. Then we entered the jungle and even in the poor light we could see leeches: thousands of them. Every time we stopped to look or listen they came looping their way across the forest floor, hungry for blood. We continually flicked them off our boots and legs but it was a losing battle, sheer numbers were overwhelming us. A patch of blood spread across Ruth's lower neck; one had got through her defences. But, looking inside her shirt, we could find no leech; it had already feasted and fallen off without Ruth feeling a thing. These remarkable creatures inject an anaesthetic and anti-coagulant as they bite. But this first bleeding was a watershed: once we had survived without pain, the leeches no longer held such fear for us. By the end of day we all looked a real mess, with patches of blood all over our clothes, but we hardly cared.

Back to the birding, and we first heard then saw Black-and-Red Broadbill. Check out a picture of this beauty and you will see why we were in a state of panic when at first we could not lay eyes on it. A chunky bird, it has a solid blue bill and black head, with a slash of scarlet across the throat, scarlet underparts and black and white upperparts. Once we finally found it, we just stared in disbelief.

This was turning into yet another brilliant but exhausting day, with the heat and humidity taking their toll on us both. Red-naped and Scarlet-rumped Trogons, Checker-throated Woodpeckers, Blue-winged Pitta and eight species of babbler all found their way onto our list. But it was another broadbill that stole the show. Keith heard the call and, ignoring the leeches, we went off-trail with hearts pounding; we badly wanted this bird. The call got closer and suddenly there it was, sitting at eye-level before us: a luminous Green Broadbill. It looked unreal, the colours almost synthetic – like some child's toy discarded in the gloom of the jungle. The brilliant green plumage was set off by three narrow black wing bars, delicate black markings on the face and a large black eye. This dumpy, short-tailed little bird just sat there, turning its rounded head slowly from side to side, rather like a trogon.

We trudged back to the resort, reaching the restaurant after dark. We were famished. Foolishly we had forgotten just how driven Keith can be in the field and had not taken anything like enough food and water. In fact, we were so hungry and thirsty that we went straight to eat in our birding gear, not thinking about the effect on our fellow diners. The horror on their faces said it all. We had forgotten that our shirts were covered in blood from our numerous leech bites. For the poor tourists in the dining room, it must have looked like a scene from a war movie as we staggered in, muddy, sweaty and bleeding. Just to add to the horror, a leech dropped off Ruth's boot as we sat down and began looping its way across the restaurant floor. People at the next table screamed, but I just picked it up and showed it to them. They were amazed by how calmly we dealt with the blood-sucker, but a day on the trails here changes your outlook on these things: we had been just as jumpy a couple of days earlier.

Twenty-five new birds added and a fair bit of blood lost, but it had been another memorable day.

The next day we were up well before dawn and headed straight for a large breakfast; we had learned our lesson from yesterday's starvation. Ruth was yawning as we ate and already looked shattered. At sunrise we boarded a boat up river, where a Black-capped Kingfisher was a gorgeous bird with which to start the day.

Safe on dry land, after a decidedly dodgy landing on a rather rickety jetty, the birding was instantly amazing. Right above the jetty a Banded Broadbill sat calling. This was another wonderful creature, with a red body, dusky red head, black breast band, yellow and black wings, yellow rump and bright blue bill.

Once we set off we realised that the trails here were used much less than those around the lodge. The jungle pressed in on all sides, making visibility tricky. And guess what? More leeches than ever. Clearly we were in for a tough day; we were already soaked in sweat and wishing we had brought more water.

Keith, who had birded here before, was on high alert for pittas. We soon heard a Banded Pitta deep in the undergrowth but despite our best efforts crawling around on the leech-infested forest floor, it refused to show. Leeches were flicked off places leeches just should not have been, but already the blood was flowing freely. Next a Garnet Pitta called away, but again went unseen. However, we did lay eyes on a Black Hornbill and found two lovely White-crowned Forktails feeding around a small pool.

Suddenly Keith came to an abrupt stop and held his finger to his lips. We stood stock still and listened. What had he heard? Keith cursed loudly, something he does very well.

'I'm sure I just heard a Malaysian Rail-babbler,' he muttered.

Now it was our turn to curse spectacularly. This was a mind-blowing bird and we desperately wanted it. As the name suggests, it is a confusing creature: part rail and part babbler in appearance, it has a long tail, long slim neck and thin pointed bill, and its warm brown plumage is set off by a long black band from the base of the bill down the side of the neck. We had studied its image so often in the field guide and now there was one in this forest. Somewhere.

We crept forward, adrenalin pumping. Keith played the tape, and we listened to the long, thin, monotone whistle. The hair stood up on our necks. Then came the reply, a Malaysian Rail-babbler was calling just metres away. We crouched down and peered into the dense vegetation but it was impossible to see more than a few feet. The call came again, but it sounded further away. And when the next long low whistle was even more distant we knew we were not going to see this oh-so-special bird. We were gutted.

No one spoke for a while. The dip hurt badly. But soon another call had us looking hard again. This time it was a Blue-winged Pitta and it sounded close. We were determined to see this one and we stalked forward, scanning hard. The call came regularly and certainly sounded very close. Suddenly the bird was there. It jumped up on a fallen log and we had a clear view – for one second. A gang of noisy forestry workers came round the corner and the pitta was out of there in a flash of blue and red.

A quick leech check after our intense birding revealed three huge, blood-filled monsters on me. As I rolled down my waistband, following the trail of blood, I found that one had managed to get right down the front of my trousers. Luckily it hadn't got far, but it was still very unpleasant to peer down there and see blood flowing freely and a bloated leech guzzling away. Ruth joked, unsympathetically, that the leech's small size had made her think it was something else.

Back at the riverbank we slithered down to the tiny jetty and almost ended up in the river. Soon we were back at the lodge, exhausted, and drenched in sweat and blood in almost equal measure.

Despite the intense heat, and Ruth being shattered from her cystitis and lack of sleep, Keith was keen to try birding on the far side of the river opposite the lodge. We took the car and drove a little way to some trash habitat of small farms and scrub, where a few large trees remained to show that this area had once been a great forest. We struggled to find new birds out in the sun, it was just so hot. Ruth kept falling behind, exhausted and dehydrated. Keith and I at last found a feeding flock and we turned to look for Ruth, who was sheltering in a patch of shade some fifty metres back. I waved for her to join us, but she shook her head.

Keith went ballistic. He was ranting that he had not given up his precious time to help us find birds, just for Ruth to refuse to look when he found some. It was an unpleasant moment. I felt for Ruth, who was obviously suffering, but had to agree that Keith had a right to be mad. The guy was busting a gut to ensure we saw the maximum number of birds, and in true Tropical Birding style was not taking any prisoners. It was a tense few minutes as tempers flared, but thankfully the mood soon lightened and we put the incident behind us. Some more gentle birding followed, this time in mixed sunshine and shade, before we headed back, hot, thirsty and tired.

Early the next day, after a good breakfast, we left Taman Negara. It had been a short but very productive stay and yes, yet another place we insisted we would return to. We birded from the roadside as we headed for the airport, picking up Crested Goshawk, White-breasted Waterhen, Yellow-vented Flowerpecker, Asian Glossy Starling and White-rumped Munia. Our flat-out Malaysian birding had boosted our list to an incredible 3,904. We had seen two hundred species in just five days, nearly all of which were new for *The Biggest Twitch*.

It was a nice surprise when, checking in for our flight to Delhi, we were upgraded to business class. What a shame the flight was only five hours: it felt so good to stretch out in real comfort and actually get some sleep. The rest was probably just as well, though, as India and Peter Lobo were waiting for us.

3,904 species

14 November–17 December, India (Ruth)

At first, all we could see were the head-high grasses swaying gently. Then without warning, they parted like the Red Sea as a massive orange and black blur came charging through. Without even breaking its stride, the furious tiger leapt straight off the ground at the elephant, making for the humans sitting high on its back. So fast was the attack that this huge animal was instantly on top of the defenceless mahout, its mouth wide open in a snarl of fury before its teeth closed around his hand.

At this point the video screen went blank, and we all realised we'd been holding our breath for the last few minutes.

'And that's where we're going this morning,' said Peter with a chuckle.

Was that supposed to be reassuring? Peter, that's Peter Lobo, our friend and guide in India, had been showing us the YouTube footage of a tiger attack in Kaziranga National Park in northern India. And now we would be taking an elephant ride right through those very same grasslands. It certainly added a frisson of excitement to the prospect.

As the beasts materialised out of the gloom in the pre-dawn light, and the mist hung low over the grasslands, the atmosphere was magical. The first elephant lumbered over to the riding point, a sort of high-rise mounting block for jumbos. The mahout sat high on its neck with his legs dangling behind the elephant's ears; pressure behind the left ear meant turn left and behind the right ear meant turn right, while a metal hook pressed on the animal's forehead made it move forwards or backwards. More and more elephants appeared, until thirteen were lined up, steaming gently in the cool of the morning, waiting for their passengers.

We climbed the steps and were allocated our animal, a tall female loaded with a cosy seat for two. We sat astride her, facing forwards, with me in front, Alan behind and a cushion beneath us to provide padding over the backbone. We sat with our knees spread wide apart: not very elegant, but the ride was pretty comfortable – much like riding a horse, but with a slower stride and considerably higher off the ground.

Our elephant gave off a pleasant smell of mown grass, and the warmth that rose from her body kept us warm too. She seemed to be a racing model, as she quickly overtook the other animals to take the lead. As we brushed through the tall, wet grasses the elephants munched on the go, wrapping their trunks around the tussocks and ripping out a good bunch as they passed. There was much giggling and joking amongst the passengers, as their animals jostled for position and farted loudly. We seemed to be riding a senior elephant, or at least she had much longer legs than the others, as we were so much higher off the ground. The view was great, and we got down to the serious business of watching wildlife.

Soon we encountered our first Indian Rhinoceros, which was aware of the elephant but not the humans on top. He stood his ground and snorted. Little by little, our mahout edged us closer until we were only a few feet away from the armour-plated beast. Now the rhino became a little edgy; perhaps he had caught the scent of humans and decided enough was enough. He started to approach us menacingly, his head down low so that his horn was pointing directly at us. Our mahout put the elephant into reverse and we backed away slowly.

In all, we saw eleven rhinos, plus a wealth of other wildlife, including small Hog Deer hiding in the grass and a herd of larger Swamp Deer that seemed more relaxed. But of course, we were looking out for birds too, and our elephant flushed plenty as we progressed: Richard's Pipits were familiar but new for our list; Bengal Bushlarks were striking new birds; and best of all was the spectacular Bengal Florican, a large bustard-like bird that can be very hard to see – unless you're on top of an elephant.

We passed an open patch of tall grassland that looked vaguely familiar, but there were no big cats to be seen. Then, before we knew it, our time was up. We'd reached Riding Point Number Two and it was time to dismount. This was harder than it sounds, after sitting for an hour with legs outstretched at an unladylike angle, and certainly wasn't very elegant. I felt decidedly wobbly for a while afterwards, the ground seeming to buck and roll as though we'd been at sea.

It was now our 14th day with Peter Lobo in India, and elephant was just the latest in a long line of transportation methods we'd experienced. Peter was our guide and companion for the entire trip. We'd known him for several years, having kept in touch ever since we'd first met him at the BirdFair. So when we decided that India was an essential part of *The Biggest Twitch* he was naturally our first point of contact. Besides, Peter is the most well connected person we have ever met. As we travelled around his country, he had three mobile phones on the go, one for each ear and one for spare, and they all rang constantly. Wherever we went, people greeted Peter like an old friend. He was such fun and charming with it, with a ready smile and infectious laugh that made him very popular with his support team. We had hoped Peter would be able to help us arrange our trip to India, but we had never imagined he'd give up the time to be with us every single day. But that's Peter Lobo for you.

Just because Peter is such a nice guy, though, doesn't mean that he was going to let us take it easy. There were plenty of birds and Peter knew just where to find them. After collecting us at Delhi Airport on arrival on Day One in India, he had whisked us straight off to Corbett National Park where, despite our painfully early arrival and long drive, he had soon chivvied us out into the field.

We had then been joined by Hari Lama, a neat and tidy man, small enough to fold up into the back of our 4WD, and blessed with very sharp eyes and ears. The road beside the park was lined with hotels, guesthouses and elephant taxi ranks. But none of this was for us. Instead we headed out of town towards the river Kosi. This habitat, a mixture of woodland edge, private gardens and open scrubland along the riverbank, was teeming with birds, and in no time at all we had logged twenty-five new species. The river bed was broad here, even though the fast-flowing water itself was confined to a narrow channel, and the exposed gravel area, dotted with scrubby bushes, served as launderette, car wash and children's play area. We picked up White-capped and Plumbeous Redstarts on the rocks beside the water, Siberian Rubythroat in a bramble patch, and Rose-ringed Parakeets in the trees – the last of these looking decidedly more at home than they did in my friend Sara's garden back in Orpington in the UK. The list went on: Blue

Whistling-Thrush, Lesser Fish Eagle, Small Niltava, Golden-spectacled Warbler, Red-whiskered, Red-vented and Himalayan Bulbuls. This was exciting stuff. I was in love with India already.

The area was so good that we went back again the next day. I was a bit disappointed that we weren't going into the park itself as I had hoped to see a tiger, but Peter assured us that the birding was better outside. Leaving our guesthouse – called, ironically, Tiger Camp, but sadly with no tigers in residence – we drove a short distance up the road before birding a new stretch of river bank. The setting was uplifting: the sun rose to reveal layer upon layer of hill receding into the distance, while traditional Indian music began to play from a nearby house. The birds were pretty exciting too: yesterday's Siberian Rubythroat was upstaged by today's even more beautiful White-tailed Rubythroat, while a Slaty-blue Flycatcher was quickly abandoned in favour of a Black-lored Tit. I was especially excited to notice a pair of Ibisbills picking their way along the riverbank. Subtly camouflaged, greyish birds with a long decurved red bill, these were a great find – particularly as local experts had told us they were no longer in the area.

Heading to our next site, we found our way blocked by a makeshift market at a road junction. There was no point in getting fussed, life in India wouldn't be hurried, so we pulled over and watched the fun. Not that it was such fun for all the participants. Two black goats tethered by the roadside were suddenly reduced to one, as the first was grabbed, upended and had its throat slit – all in the time it took us to park the car. While the second animal looked on in mild confusion, the first was rotated over the fire to singe off its fur, opened up to remove its vital organs and then swiftly dismembered into a series of more manageable joints. It was the work of minutes to turn this fully functioning goat into a series of family-sized suppers.

Feeling slightly queasy, I looked across to the other side of the road. Here was a gaggle of chickens in wicker baskets, with just their heads popping up through holes in the top like milk bottles in a crate. I watched as a man spread his mat on the ground and carefully laid out his chopping block and knife. Oh, no. Not more carnage? But the chickens were spared for the moment as the man reached into his basket and drew out a large fish. Suddenly we didn't feel too hungry, and made do with a small tumbler of sweetly fragrant tea, known as *chai*.

Back at Tiger Camp, Hari Lama left us in order to guide a newly arrived, rather jet-lagged British couple and was replaced by our new local guide, Mr Singh, a very smartly dressed gentleman, with a military carriage and handlebar moustache that would have made Hercule Poirot proud. Unlike Hari, Mr Singh was not prepared to fold himself up in the boot. He commandeered the front seat and Peter joined us in the back as we headed out for more birding.

Birds were piling in so thick and fast that it seemed no time at all before we were celebrating bird number four thousand. This was an incredible landmark. When we'd set out in January, just breaking the record had seemed like enough of a challenge, and now here we were, way past the old record and still with six weeks to go.

Pulling off the road in search of a glimpsed Himalayan Flameback, we noticed a huge honeycomb suspended from a branch above us. This long oval clump was covered in a solid, crawling mass of bees. Movement caught our eye and we spotted a pair of gaudy Blue-bearded Bee-eaters swooping in to feed. One of these handsome birds, green all over apart from its blue throat patch, landed on a branch right next to the honeycomb. To eat, all it now had to do was turn its head sideways, snatch a bee and gulp it down; talk about fast food! Soon, however, the bees decided enough was enough, and started to swarm around the bird. This was our cue to make a run for it, just in case they thought we were party to the act. We may have been watching milestone bird number four thousand, but we didn't want to get attacked as accessories to murder.

Soon the road was gaining height rapidly as we headed towards the hill station of Nainital. Just before entering the town, we dived off left up a smaller road that wound uphill even more steeply. Rounding a bend, the most amazing vista opened up. No bird here, but we insisted on playing the tourist and pulling over to take a proper look from Snow View Ridge. The Himalayas were stretched out in front of us, a long range of pointed, snow-capped peaks looking like a row of uneven teeth glowing pink in the full rays of the sun. It was an awe-inspiring sight, and our cameras clicked furiously. Not surprisingly, a group of entrepreneurial locals was taking advantage of this natural opportunity, offering a look through their telescopes for a few rupees. Given that these brass contraptions looked like something straight out of Captain Pugwash, however, we politely declined their offer.

Peter rounded us up and we continued towards Jungle Lore camp in the little village of Pangot, our home for the next three nights. We dropped our luggage off in our cottage – very rustic, very cute and very cold – and grabbed a quick cup of tea, before heading out to see what was about. It didn't matter where you went here; everywhere was uphill. Even climbing the steps from our cottage to the dining room had us puffing and panting, so stopping off to admire the new Streaked Laughing-thrushes and Black-headed Jay in the garden was the perfect excuse to catch our breath.

We were after pheasants here – and knew we were in for a challenge. Our pre-dawn start saw us creeping through the forest in search of Koklass Pheasant but nothing was showing. Breaking out above the tree-line, we switched to checking the vertiginous cliffs for Cheer Pheasant. It was a spectacular spot, the narrow dirt track hugging the side of the cliff with a sheer wall towering above us on the one side and a very long drop on the other. But though we scanned and scanned, stripping off our layers as the sun came up, the Cheer Pheasants didn't materialise either. So we tried another spot of forest for a change of scene. Sharp-eyed Peter, now in the front again, with Mr Singh sharing the back seat with us, spotted movement between the trees ahead and there it was at last: Koklass Pheasant, standing up on a boulder and declaring his territory. Despite the gloom amongst the trees, his white collar and bottle green head and ear tufts glowed with colour.

The Sat Tal Forest area was next, its attractive combination of woodland and lakes also a popular local tourist attraction. Peter had promised us the full set of wren-babblers during our stay, and things got off to a great start here with Immaculate Wren-Babbler, looking as pristine as you might expect from its name. These dumpy, skulking birds, a speciality of northeast India, are notoriously hard to find, but Peter had a knack with them – as we were to find out.

It was thirsty work, so we were glad to stop for a double *chai* with milk. The first tasted so good we had a second. But maybe that second cup wasn't such a good idea, as by the time we returned to Jungle Lore, something was definitely not right with my insides. My belly was making ominous gurgling noises and I was feeling very achy and shivery. I didn't feel up to eating supper so went to bed early and shivered under the blankets until I made the first of many visits to the frosty bathroom during the night to be violently sick. I kept this up all night long at regular intervals, until I felt like I was turning myself inside out. Dawn came, and I still couldn't leave the bathroom long enough to get dressed, never mind go on another Cheer Pheasant hunt. Alan had had a pretty disturbed night too, thanks to my groans coming from the bathroom, so he and I left the others to track down those pheasants without us.

An awful lot of Imodium later, and I could at last leave the bathroom long enough to pile on warm clothes and stagger up to sit beside the blazing fire in the dining room. The first piece of news, that the Cheer Pheasant still hadn't materialised, made me feel slightly less bad. But learning that we had a long drive ahead of us to a railway station, where we would join an overnight train back to Delhi, would have had me crawling back under the blankets if I'd been allowed. Wimping out wasn't an option, though. *The Biggest Twitch* didn't have time to be ill, so I was dosed up with yet more Imodium and bundled into the car. I don't remember too much of the next few hours until we arrived at the station and I was prodded in the direction of the train.

The military Mr Singh left us here and we climbed on board. Peter had booked us three berths in a first class four-berth sleeping compartment. Just as we were bagging our bunks and wondering if we could commandeer the fourth one too, a noisy family party crashed onto the scene: mum, dad, baby and granny. We looked hopefully at granny as the best bet for a quiet companion, but sadly she was parked in another carriage and the family of three made themselves at home on the fourth bunk.

The baby promptly started crying and the mother crooned lullabies to soothe it. I climbed up into my bunk, rolled myself into the blanket and tried to pretend none of this was happening. Perhaps, if I shut my eyes tightly enough, it would all go away. No such luck. The baby cried and cried and cried, a piercing noise that in the close confines of the compartment went right through your head and out the other side. Then, a miracle happened: the baby fell asleep. Unfortunately, that was the cue for my stomach to start up again. I legged it down the corridor at top speed and, luckily, found the toilet unoccupied. It was nothing but a draughty hole in the floor of the carriage, through which you could see the tracks passing underneath, but I was in no position to complain.

I had no problem finding our compartment again – it was the one with the crying baby. Yes, I'd woken it up. This routine kept our whole carriage awake all night: baby crying, baby falling asleep, me running down the corridor, baby waking up and crying again – until at last we both caved in with exhaustion.

But it wasn't long before we were all awake again. This time it was dad. With all three of them squeezed into one berth, he was lying flat on his back and snoring his head off. I don't just mean a gentle rumble; I mean a full, belly-up, thunderous earthquake of a noise – the kind of snore an elephant with a blocked trunk would have been proud of – and it carried along the entire length of the carriage. I could even hear from the toilet, and I'm pretty sure the guys back at Jungle Lore could hear it too.

It was with some relief that we drew into Delhi Station at 5am. We got off the train and descended into chaos. There were people everywhere: passengers, families, porters, taxi drivers, tuk-tuk drivers, bus drivers, food sellers, cyclists, urchins, dogs and goats. I'm pretty sure I even saw a cow or two in the melee. Luckily, we were met by a very large man, who shouldered our luggage as though it were child-sized, and we followed in his wake through the crowds. Peter had thoughtfully arranged for us to have a few hours in a comfy hotel to rest and clean up, before we took a domestic flight to Bagdogra in the northeast. But despite this we were still pretty sleepy as we waited at the airport. In fact, we were so relaxed that it wasn't until we caught the words 'Peter Lobo' and 'Now!' over the tannoy that we realised our flight was about to leave without us.

We were met the other end by a smiling Sudesh, Peter's brother-in-law. Sudesh then drove us along another long and twisting road to Kalimpong. Here, Peter had a real treat in store for us. We were staying in his family home with Catherine, his wife, and Ron, his young son. Catherine was the kindest and most hospitable hostess you could possibly wish for. Ron, who was five, was thrilled to see his father again, and rushed around the house in great excitement, proudly getting out his own little binoculars and camera to show what he'd been up to. We had a day of birding the hills above Lava adding some fantastic birds, not least of which were Rufous-throated and Spotted Wren-Babblers. But all too soon it was time to move on.

Catherine really pulled out all the stops for us on our last night with a delicious supper: river fish, rice wrapped in leaves, chicken in a lightly curried sauce and 'tempura' aubergine, all beautifully cooked and presented. We were being so spoiled here that we were quite reluctant to leave the next day, even though we knew that Peter had more excitement lined up.

We flew to the Lokpriya Gopinath Bordoloi International Airport, or Guwahati Airport, as we found it easier to say, and from here drove just around the corner to the rubbish tip. As so often is the case in birding, the worse the habitat, the better the bird, and this was no exception, being a legendary site for the Greater Adjutant. This immense stork's numbers have long been in serious decline due to a loss of wetland and, sadly, its best habitat these days seems to be on this immense, reeking rubbish tip. Here, alongside people who were also scavenging for a living, the birds stalked through the detritus of rotting food and rubbish.

Nobody but its mother could consider a Greater Adjutant beautiful, and even she should really have her eyes tested. It is hideous: a bald pink skinhead of a hairdo, a dirty pink conical bill, and a bare pink neck with a hanging pouch that, I must admit, looked just like a giant scrotum. Beautiful or not, however, it was on the list. Now it was time to go: we had a five-hour drive ahead of us to Kaziranga National Park.

The park was back down at low altitude, and though it was pleasantly cool birding in the pre-dawn in T-shirts, we knew the heat was going to come later. We made quite a party: Peter and driver Hoon in front; Alan and me in the next row; Sudesh and another of Peter's protégé guides, Rafic, in the back. Soon we were driving though the entrance gates into what was to become one of my favourite areas in India. We spent several days birding here, and I loved every single minute of it.

The area of the park we explored first was a mixture of open water, marshland and woodland, and offered a wide variety of bird species. Given that rather ferocious animals wandered freely here, we had an armed guard to accompany us, although we weren't sure how much use his ancient gun would be in an emergency. The open water was heaving with birds, including some great new ones, such as Spot-billed Pelican, Bronze-winged Jacana and Lesser Adjutant. A Grey-headed Fish Eagle scooped up a fish from in front of us, taking it off to a nearby tree to rip it to shreds with its bill. Three Indian Smooth-coated Otters played together, while a fourth munched on a fish. We climbed a pavilion, which worked well as a look-out, and from our high vantage point counted up to thirty-seven Indian Rhinos dotted across the tall grasslands. More storks came in the form of Asian Openbilled Storks (or 'Asian-billed Openstorks', as Peter called them) and Woolly-necked Storks. This place was just brilliant.

We also visited the tea plantations, which looked just like the picture on the PG Tips box. In the shade of acacia trees, the dense bushes grew in rows, their height regulated by constant picking. The lower vegetation was dark green; the fresh new leaves and buds that made the best tea were brighter. Even the ladies looked the part, their bright red and orange saris a contrast to the greenery, and they looked so elegant as they daintily plucked the buds and threw them over their shoulder into the wicker basket on their back. We'd sampled plenty of the product on our way, both Darjeeling and Assam tea, so it was fascinating to see it being harvested.

As the light began to fade, we watched an Asian Barred Owlet hawking for moths over the tea bushes. It was dark as we drove back to the hotel, but still we found a Large-tailed Nightjar, which flew up from the warmth of the track in front of us.

And so, the next morning, after the first 14 days of our Indian leg had flown by, we found ourselves on a dawn elephant ride in Kaziranga National Park. I must admit, after Peter's build-up, that we were rather disappointed not to have any sort of encounter with a tiger – not even a hint of striped tail. But soon we were once more on the road to a new part of the country: Nagaland. This remote state in the northeastern corner of India is a hard place to visit: geographically, it is a long way from anywhere, lying on the border with Burma; and politically, it sees itself as independent. Even Indians need special permits to visit, and it was touch-and-go as to whether we'd be allowed in. But with Peter's excellent contacts, we sailed through the formalities and soon found ourselves chugging up the twisting main road. Then we headed into the even more remote hills up a narrow lane that quickly deteriorated into a bumpy dirt track. It felt as though we swayed and bounced our way along this for hours, and it was completely dark when we finally pulled up outside a small house in the village of Khonoma, where we were to stay for the next few days.

Khonoma offers accommodation to eco-tourists, bringing vital revenue to the locals. The welcome from our hostess and her tiny helper was very warm, though you couldn't say the same for the house itself, which was bitterly cold in the crisp mountain air. Facilities were basic: the kitchen had a rough stone floor; cooking was done on a simple range and in pots suspended over the fire; the beds were pretty hard; and the water in the tiny bathroom was icy. But if this was how the locals lived, then we were sure we could cope for a few days. Our hostess invited us to take the best seats beside the fire, while her young helper giggled shyly as she offered us tea. The people here looked almost oriental, with paler skin, high cheekbones and narrow eyes, and spoke in an unfamiliar-sounding local language. The local cuisine was particularly spicy, so while Peter tucked into a plate of dark-brown curry with relish, we were served rice and cabbage. Somehow, we were never able to convey the idea that we do actually like food with flavour, just not when it's burning hot with chillies. Still, at least rice and cabbage was likely to be safer on the stomach.

It gets light early this far east. Despite the great width of the country, India operates on only one time zone, so the sun was already beginning to outline the surrounding ridges at 4.30am as we sat in the kitchen sipping our tea. We spent the whole day happily birding the mountain tracks. Hills stretched uninterrupted as far as we could see, clad in a dense green cloak of pristine forest right to the skyline. After the hustle and bustle of the lowlands, the peace up here was incredible.

By the end of the day we had added some very special birds, too, including Mountain Bamboo-Partridge, Crested Finchbill, Red-faced Liocichla, and Grey-sided and Striped laughing-thrushes. Peter managed to whistle up two more of the promised Wren-Babblers: Long-tailed and the incredibly difficult Wedge-billed, the giant of the family. We also ticked off Yellow-rumped Honeyguide at a honey-comb that had been harvested by the local villagers; I sampled a piece dropped on the ground and the slightly-peaty golden liquid that ran out over my fingers was delicious. We even bumped into a Mithun, a huge domesticated form of the Gaur, also known as an Indian Bison, which had broad horns and white socks and was roaming freely around the hillsides.

The sun slipped behind the ridges early, so we headed back down to the village where we were joined for supper by the phenomenal American world lister, Peter Kaestner, whose life list stood at around a staggering 8,200 species. Not surprisingly, when you've seen so many birds, you have a few good tales to tell, and Peter kept us entertained all evening with stories of his best birds and birding destinations. He was an official at the American Embassy, which must be a pretty handy job to have if it posts you in good birding locations around the world.

Peter's tour in India was due to end shortly, and he had only 60 species still outstanding on the entire Indian list. He was here in Nagaland to tidy up a few stragglers, so naturally we were delighted to share our information with him. Unfortunately, work called Peter back to Mumbai early, but not before he had successfully ticked off his target birds, including Wedge-billed Wren-Babbler, and before he'd invited Alan and me to stay with him in Delhi later that month. How kind of him! Didn't he realise that, wherever possible, we took up all offers of hospitality, particularly if there was the likelihood of a good bird as well.

The road winding down out of Nagaland is full of twists and turns, and clearly speeding has led to some bad accidents. We spotted various road signs all encouraging drivers to take more care, such as 'Hurry spoils curry!', 'It's not a rally, enjoy the valley!' and 'Safety on the road, means safe tea at home!'

Our tea was at a comfortable hotel in the town of Tinsukia. But was it safe? First we heard of a bomb attack on the railway line just outside the town. Then, as we went downstairs to dinner, we passed a group of armed soldiers, plus a sniffer dog, rushing upstairs towards the bedrooms. Seconds later, the concierge hurriedly asked for our room key. After a while, the military boots clomped back down the stairs again and our key was politely returned. Presumably they'd had orders to check the rooms of all foreigners, but perhaps the sight of our laundry spread out to dry had convinced them that we weren't a terrorist threat.

If Nagaland was wild and remote, so too was our next destination: Mishmi Hills. Just getting there was an adventure. First we drove out across a broad area of marshland, dotted with scrubby bushes and scored with tyre marks. The tracks led right to the edge of the 'mighty Brahmaputra', as Peter called it, one of the greatest rivers in Asia. Here, it was a shallow, gentle waterway that sifted its way between wide sandbanks. Rotting hulks of ancient wooden barges were tied up beside it, and the mud made odd popping noises as it dried out in the sun. We had clearly reached a regular jumping-off point for people wanting to cross, and a gaggle of vehicles had already accumulated. To take advantage of this ready market, a series of shacks were offering *chai* and various spicy dishes.

By now we were travelling in a convoy of two vehicles, as Peter's team followed us to help with the camping that lay ahead. First there was Phurtey, who looked like a fourteen-year old, but was a hit with the ladies wherever we travelled and could rustle up a delicious meal out of thin air. Then there was his sidekick and our second cook, Manaj. Completing the team was Khanin Kalita, who towered over the other two. This trio always seemed to be having a whale of a time, as we travelled through the remotest parts of the country, and never failed to spoil us rotten.

As we waited for our ferry across the river, Peter and Sudesh headed off to inspect the cooking shacks while Alan and I scanned the river for birds. We were fascinated by the spectacle in front of us. Everything was being loaded onto a series of flat-topped wooden barges for the crossing: cases, boxes, bags, rolled up rugs, crates of chickens, loose goats, sacks of flour, bags of rice, traders, businessmen in suits, new brides and bicycles. It was all very entertaining.

When we turned back, a table and two chairs had been conjured up, complete with pink tablecloth, cups, bowls, plates, cutlery, condiments, sauces, spreads, jams and napkins. A thermos flask contained piping hot tea, and a metal container held a gently bubbling pot of porridge. Next to them a plate was piled high with neatly triangled sandwiches. Was this a mirage? Here we were, miles from anywhere, and Phurtey had conjured up a breakfast for us out of thin air.

Now it was our turn to provide the entertainment. While we tucked into delicious porridge topped with banana, a bus disgorged its load of passengers, who – ignoring the boats waiting to ferry them over the river – stood around us in a silent circle to watch the breakfast show. No doubt they were wondering just who these strange foreigners were and why were they eating so much.

We boarded the barges, as our drivers skilfully manoeuvred the trucks down two narrow planks onto the boat – taking care not to roll straight off the other side. As we set off, Peter, Alan and I sat out on deck to look for birds. A Sand Lark, a rather nondescript bird with a slightly finer bill than most larks, was pottering about on a sandbank, so we ticked him off. Suddenly our barge stopped abruptly, caught on a sand bar. This was obviously a regular occurrence, as a man in a red loincloth immediately jumped overboard carrying a tall pole attached to the barge by a long rope. He looked very small but was obviously full of wiry strength, as he planted the pole as firmly as he could into the riverbed and then hung onto it as a second crewman on the barge slowly wound in the rope to winch us off the sandbank. This was slow going, but inch by inch we made forward progress until the barge floated free.

Once we were unloaded on the far side of the Brahmaputra, we drove across the marshy river edges until we regained slightly firmer ground and a proper road. At the next town, we stopped while the crew bought some fresh produce. Again, Alan and I soaked up the scene: the colours of the saris; the rows of fruit and spices; the children shyly watching us; the pigs rooting around on the roadside. Of course, we were part of the spectacle too, and only when a middle-aged lady with no teeth dawdled past us for the fifth time did we realise that Alan had an admirer. Sadly for her, the attraction wasn't mutual, and once the boys were loaded up with food, Alan said goodbye to his lady friend and we were off, leaving Assam for the state of Arunachal Pradesh.

The Mishmi Hills area was another huge region of unspoiled mountains, and once again Peter was hoping to show us some very special birds. The road wound slowly upward into the forested hills, a sheer cliff on one side and a sheer drop on the other, while behind us were broad views back across the plain we'd just crossed. At last we reached our accommodation, a rather derelict rest house that had once been run by the government but now seemed to have been left to rot gently. We had expected to be camping, so were initially impressed with the sight of solid walls, wooden beds and a bathroom. However, there was no running water, electricity or heating, and very limited cooking facilities. The lads quickly lit a bamboo fire to take off the chill, wired up the van to provide lighting, put buckets of water in the bathroom and piled thick blankets on the bed. We would find it took more than a few blankets to dispel the chill of this neglected building, which almost seemed colder in than out, but by wearing hats, thermals and fleeces, piling up all the blankets and squeezing into one single bed to share body warmth and a hot water bottle, we somehow managed to survive the nights.

We headed up the mountain to the Mayodia Pass at 2,528m to see what birds were about. Tragopans and monals, exotic-looking members of the pheasant family, were key birds for this area, and there were various other specialist mountain species. But it was bitterly cold and deathly quiet: no sound of a single bird. Peter normally brought birders here in March, and this was November, so the birding was a bit of a gamble. Just to rub salt into the wound, our cheery crew arriving with breakfast gave the perfect description of a Sclater's Monal that had just run across the road in front of them. Still, the warming porridge cheered us up somewhat and we continued to bird our way back down to the resthouse, picking up a few new species, including Black-faced Warbler and Streak-throated Barwing.

Below the resthouse Peter whistled up a Mishmi Wren-Babbler, formerly known as Rufous-breasted Wren-Babbler. This is an incredibly hard bird to see, but with a bit of pishing we encouraged two birds to hop right out to the edge of a small bush at eye level. Maybe the birds weren't pouring in like the mixed flocks on the Manu Road, but we were certainly enjoying some very choice species.

There was another special bird lined up for us that night. Peter had noted from our visa applications that it was Alan's birthday and had asked me what was

Alan's favourite food. That's easy: duck. Unbeknown to us, a duck had been hidden amongst the shopping in the second truck, and Phurtey had worked his magic in the primitive kitchen, clutching a torch in his mouth to light his work in the dark, and served up a delicious whole roast duck, with mashed potatoes and vegetables. And, as if that wasn't enough, the team then marched into our candlelit dining room with a birthday cake, iced with 'Happy Birthday' lettering, while singing 'Happy Birthday to You'. How in the world had they created this spectacular food over an open fire in a derelict building? Afterwards we sat around the bamboo fire in the brazier, toasting each other's health with vodka and listening to Abba on Peter's iPod. It was surely a birthday that Alan will never forget.

The next day we birded down the track again, this time accompanied by the local headman and his cousin. At first things were very quiet, but as we lost altitude, so we started picking up new birds. Then we heard the call of a Blyth's Tragopan. This was a very special pheasant that we really wanted to see, not just hear. But try as we might, we couldn't catch even a glimpse. Soon another one called further up the track, so we jumped back in the vehicles. Reaching the spot, we all stood in a line staring intently at the slope as Peter played the call on tape. We could hear the bird's footsteps on the dead leaves as it crept down the hillside behind the bushes. At one point, I briefly caught sight of an outline as it passed behind a thin tree. Peter played the call again, this time from the other end of the line, and once more we heard footsteps as the bird cautiously approached the sound of the intruder. Again we had frustrating glimpses before it melted away into the undergrowth and we lost it altogether. But it was on *The Biggest Twitch* 'heard' list.

Two long driving days followed, as we left the peaceful Mishmi Hills and re-crossed the Brahmaputra. We were headed for the river in Kaziranga, where Peter had another means of transport up his sleeve: a spot of white-water rafting. Well, it wasn't quite white water, but we certainly covered a lot of rapids in our little rubber boats: Alan and me in one, Peter and Sudesh in the other.

Three of us had a very relaxing time, as we were paddled downstream, admiring River Terns, Great Thick-knees and Wreathed and Great Hornbills flying overhead. But one of us wasn't so sure. I thought it strange that Alan didn't seem excited by more Ibisbills, but unfortunately he'd discovered a whole new malady: river sickness. Thought this was not quite as bad as the full-blown pelagic version, he'd nonetheless found the bouncy ride over the rapids enough to upset his delicate balance and was starting to turn that familiar shade of green. He was very relieved to round a bend and see our car waiting for us. And even better, just a few hundred yards up the road was our accommodation for the next few nights: the very comfortable Eco-Lodge, sister lodge to the Jaipuri Ghar where we'd stayed at Kaziranga.

Our room was a very comfy tent, with a thatched roof and a brick-built bathroom, but there was no time to linger, as we had a birding game to play: hunt the Oriental Hobby at its regular roost in the tree in the middle of the grounds. Sounds easy, but it took us quite a while before Alan spotted it, quietly watching us from a high branch.

In the evening, some cultural entertainment arrived: a group of local singers and dancers. The men sang lustily and banged their drums to a powerful rhythm, while the women – beautiful wraithlike creatures in delicate red saris – whirled and danced around the fire on the lightest of toes. Unfortunately, audience participation was required, and while all the men hastily retreated out of reach, Pauline, another birder, and I weren't quick enough and found ourselves drawn into the swirling circle. Compared with the elegance of the dancers we felt very awkward, but then our fleeces and walking boots weren't exactly designed for the job.

The next day was spent birding the forest across the river in the company of an armed guard. Birds were everywhere, including the new-for-the-list Vernal Hanging-Parrot, a pocket-sized green parrot with a red bill and rump. On the path we saw the tracks of what our experts assured us were both leopard and tiger. Peter waited by a bench beside a ranger's hut with our kit while we thrashed through some rough habitat to check three pools for the very shy White-winged Wood-Duck, but without any luck. When we returned, we found him having a face-off with a large male Rhesus Macaque. The monkey was up on the roof of the hut and watched with great interest as we opened our bags and ate some snacks. I sat on the bench next to Peter's rucksack, eating a banana, and unwisely decided to throw the last bite towards the monkey. It leapt off the porch and snatched up the food. Then before I had a chance to react, it sprang straight at me, baring its sharp teeth and raking my arm with its nails.

The men chased the monkey off me and into the trees, but it wasn't afraid of humans at all and kept turning back and baring its teeth, until they'd chased it further and further into the forest. Meanwhile I cleaned up my arm, which had been badly scratched and was bleeding. Alan joked about amputation, but luckily a healthy application of antiseptic cream cleared up the wound and the only thing that was really hurt was my pride. That's the last time I share a banana with anyone.

Next we tried the trails further inland from the river. We heard what sounded like Wild Boar but saw no sign of the creature. Then, with a bit of bending and contorting, we added two more skulking Tesias, Gray-bellied and Slaty-bellied, which gave us the full set of these dumpy little birds. The path led us across a more open area, and although it was now late afternoon, the hot sun beat down on our heads. Mind you, being out in the open had its benefits, as we had wonderful unin-terrupted views of Great Hornbills flying overhead. These metre-long birds were truly impressive, with their huge yellow bill surmounted by a bony lump called a casque. We'd also heard that an Asian Painted Snipe had recently been seen lurking at a nearby pool, so insisted on thrashing through the long grass until we found the right pool and got a good view of the bird, thus completing our painted snipe set.

We'd been joined at Eco-Lodge by another birding couple, Philip from America and his partner Pauline, from Northern Ireland. Pauline and I had already shared the embarrassment of our Indian dancing experience, and we all got on very well together. We'd be birding with them for the next few days as we headed out with Peter's support crew again, this time to the remote mountains around Eaglenest Sanctuary. Truth be told, we were quite relieved to be joined by someone else, as we'd felt undeserving of all the attention that had lavished upon just the two of us.

So now we made a three-vehicle convoy as we wound our way along yet more serpentine roads to reach Dirang.

The view from our bedrooms in the Hotel Pemaling was spectacular: we could see straight down the length of the valley, which was enclosed by high mountain peaks on all sides. Marching in rows across the mountainside were armies of multi-coloured prayer flags on poles, all fluttering in the breeze. It was a stirring sight.

We could tell we were back up at high altitude again, as the sun disappeared early behind the lofty peaks and the temperature immediately plummeted. Back on went the two fleeces, hats and gloves. Was it only yesterday we had been burning up in the sun? It was bitterly cold at 3.30am the next morning as we headed out for the legendary Sella Pass. The weather looked grim and it was touch-and-go whether we'd actually be able to reach our destination. Ahead of us were many miles of bumpy and twisting road, and the low cloud and freezing drizzle made for a discouraging sight. In places, the road was covered with ice and the verges piled high with drifting snow. Elsewhere, it was just covered in a thick glutinous mud.

Despite the obvious hardship, small settlements were dotted along the road, and several times we passed people washing themselves and their clothes in the tumbling mountain streams, while a wisp of smoke rose from their simple wooden dwellings. Clearly the locals here were tough.

We pulled over frequently to allow army trucks to rumble past in the opposite direction. Peter explained that we were less than 150km from the Chinese border. Apparently the Chinese had invaded this part of India in 1962, and the Indian Army had established a huge presence in the area to discourage them from trying again. Of course, we'd like to think that they had birders in mind when they constructed this amazing vertiginous road up to the pass. How else were we expected to get great views of Himalayan specialities like Blood Pheasant? Ever since I'd seen Peter Lobo's presentation at the 2006 BirdFair, I'd lusted after these birds. And now here they were in the snow, just feet away from me, first on one side of the road then dashing madly across to the other. The males had funky grey cheeks and blood-red faces, and their white chests were splashed with red as though the colour had run. And, as if that wasn't enough, a gaggle of Snow Partridges wandered briefly onto the road as we scrambled back towards the vehicle.

It was a shock when we suddenly burst out of the cloud and found ourselves in a world of dazzling white and cobalt blue. By now we were well above the tree line, so the ground was cloaked in snow, while overhead the sky was completely empty of clouds and so bright that it made your eyes water. It was hard to believe that while the world below struggled in freezing grey mist and drizzle, up here, at 4,175m, we were enjoying bright sunshine and crisp mountain air.

We jumped out of the jeep to photograph the spectacular scenery, including the dragon gateway guarding the Sella Pass itself. We soon stopped though, as our limbs refused to work without oxygen. We'd driven up so steeply during the morning that we'd not had time to adjust to the altitude and suddenly we found ourselves struggling. How would we cope? Was Alan going to start seeing two of everything again?

A tiny wooden roadside shack turned out to be the world's smallest grocery store, but it had a wood-burning stove and offered noodle soup, so we piled in. Fortified on the inside, we decided to walk the track a little way but this time at a more sensible pace. Even so, we still had to keep stopping to gasp for breath every time the road made the slightest incline.

At first, we had the world up here all to ourselves. Around us was mile after mile of snow-clad, meringue-like mountain peaks. Somewhere out there in the distance lay China. To our left was the frozen Sella Lake with a pincushion of prayer flag poles around one side. Above us was an endless blue sky, and then a Snow Pigeon flew over and disappeared against the mountain-scape.

Of course, cold weather always makes you want to pee more, and in the middle of nowhere, without so much as a small bush to hide behind, Pauline and I were at a bit of a disadvantage. Hiding behind the vehicle while the menfolk carried on ahead was our only option. Just undoing all our layers took ages, and we found ourselves peeing at top speed just so we could pull our trousers back up as quickly as possible.

Not quite quickly enough though. Suddenly we were no longer as alone as we'd thought. With a rumble of engines, not one, not two, but forty identical army trucks thundered past us in convoy, roaring down the valley towards China. Probably never before in the history of the Indian Army have so many soldiers been mooned at in such a short time.

A Common Buzzard soared overhead, and then Peter caught sight of something more interesting that the raptor had flushed: a flock of Grandalas. This was a Himalayan resident that we could see only here. As fast as we could in the thin air, we chased after the flock. We could see them against the sky whenever they flew, but as soon as they landed they melted into the rocky background. How was this possible? They were supposed to be bright blue. We all focused binoculars rapidly, panting with the exertion. Yes, they were Grandalas all right, but sadly they were the rather streaky grey females. No wonder they'd been hard to spot. But if the girls were all here, where were the boys? Having seen the picture in the field guide, I wasn't going to be fobbed off with just a female so I suggested we walked a little further along the track. Good move: just around the next bend all the males were hanging out together, a gang of cool, royal-blue birds with black wings. That was more like it.

The next day we tried our luck down in the Sangti valley. This flat valley, with its snaking riverbed and patchwork of tiny paddy fields, was a known site for Black-necked Crane. Unfortunately a drifting mist filled the valley floor, and while it provided a very atmospheric setting, it didn't help the birding. During one brief break in the rolling mist, however, we managed to spot the outline of a large bird standing by itself in the middle of a field. And there it was: a beautiful Black-necked Crane in all its grey-bodied, black-necked glory.

Our next destination was the famed Eaglenest Wildlife Sanctuary. We'd heard so much about this place that we couldn't wait to see it for ourselves. Most birders visit the area in spring, so again we were taking a chance going in November, but Peter was pretty confident that we'd still be able to enjoy the key birds.

The November weather had caused a few problems. This area provides the first barrier to the monsoons heading towards Assam, and the resulting heavy rains had caused a number of major landslides along the track. With no military bases around here, keeping this road clear wasn't a priority, so we weren't sure how far we'd be able to get. However, we at least managed to bump and grind our way to Lama Camp, in the Bugun community area.

Once again we were birding in a remote mountainous area, with vertiginous drops on either side. However, this track had an unusual feature we'd not encountered elsewhere; Peter Kaestner had told us to look out for elephant footprints. We had already encountered mounds of dung and footprints along the road, but it seems these elephants were not averse to a little off-roading too. We'd follow their dustbin lid-sized footprints for a short distance along the road, and then marvel at how they suddenly plunged over the side of the mountain. How in the world did elephants manage to negotiate such steep slopes? We desperately wanted to see them in action, but though we once heard some crashing around in the bamboo we never actually caught sight of them.

Peter's support crew got to work, making the place as comfortable for us as possible. Here we were sleeping under canvas, but on wooden truckle beds, piled high with blankets, while a domed bamboo wicker roof provided protection for the tent. A row of bamboo cubicles enclosed our toilet and bathroom, while a separate wooden hut was our dining room, complete with log burner. We needed this going full-time, and we were very grateful for the scalding hot water bottles that Phurtey and his team provided. Lama Camp was certainly a very cold place to stay, but at least having to wear most of our clothes to keep warm at night saved us time getting dressed in the morning.

After a quick lunch on arrival, we started to bird our way back down the track on foot. We hadn't gone more than a few paces when Peter recognised the distinctive call of a Bugun Liocichla from behind us. This was a bird we just *had* to see. First discovered in 1995, it wasn't seen again for another ten years and was described as a new species only in 2006. It still does not feature in any field guide to the area and is thought to be endangered; only fourteen individuals have ever been counted and only three breeding pairs are known. With the species so scarce, scientists hadn't dared risk its future by killing one to make a full scientific description. Instead, they used a mist net to catch a pair, and any feathers that got stuck in the netting were kept for posterity.

There'd always been an outside chance of seeing this bird here, but we hadn't expected the opportunity to fall at our feet. Seven frantic birders – that's Alan, Philip, Pauline, Rafic, Sudesh, Peter and me – pounded back up the hill and pushed through the undergrowth until we were facing a small clump of bushes. Silently, Peter motioned us all to take up a place where we would get as good a view as possible. He paused for a moment to let us get our breath back – no point in scaring the bird with heavy breathing – and then spun the iPod.

With only thirteen others out there in the bush, I guess each Bugun Liocichla knows the voices of its mates pretty well. Or maybe when there's that few of you, you're really keen for new company. Whatever the reason, the bird shot straight out of the bush and perched up, looking around. Then there was a flurry in the the foliage and, amazingly, a second bird appeared. We were looking at around fourteen percent of the known world population of Bugun Liocichlas. It was an awe-inspiring moment.

Unaware of the emotional turmoil they were causing, the pair hopped around the bush, giving us incredibly good views. These stunning, multicoloured little birds were the size of a finch, with a spiky charcoal cap, a golden stripe through the eye, and russet, gold, black and red on wings and tail. The breast was a greenish-yellow and the rest of the body an ashy grey. We didn't want to disturb them unnecessarily so backed off quietly. Once we were a suitable distance away, however, we exploded with whoops and high-fives all round. Peter could retire now; he could never top that.

Of course Peter didn't stop there, but dedicated the next few days to finding us yet more fantastic birds. Our birding fell into a pattern again. Out at dawn, after a quick cuppa, and birding the trails until breakfast, when we either returned to camp or the magic table materialised in the middle of nowhere, laden down with steaming tea and bubbling porridge. Then on again along the track, with our vehicle following a short way behind, carrying the extra kit and ready to take us further up or down as needed, until the next meal in the field. At dusk we'd return to camp, where the lads would have a bamboo fire burning merrily and we'd sit and toast our toes while Phurtey conjured up yet another miracle meal.

But if Peter worked his team hard, he looked after them too, laughing and joking and constantly making sure all was well. He'd mingle with us for a while, then slip away to join them over a fiery curry while we tucked into something milder. In return, they repaid Peter's trust by pulling out all the stops for his clients. We might have been in the middle of nowhere, but we were certainly getting five-star treatment.

Whatever they were up to, the lads seemed to have great fun doing it, whether it was setting up camp, or shifting boulders to clear the track for our vehicles. It turned out that a digger had made it through the landslides, so we were able to continue to Sunderview Camp, deeper into the Eaglenest Wildlife Sanctuary. This was a more rustic affair, but still pretty organised, with camp beds under canvas, separate toilet tents, a bathing tent (for the brave), a dining tent and a warming bamboo fire. It didn't have the chill wind of Lama Camp, but nights were still pretty nippy. Even with the ready supply of hot water bottles, we were sleeping in thermal vests and long johns, two pairs of socks and a hat, and would wake in the morning so cold that we'd be glad to get out of bed to get the circulation going again.

On our last morning at Sunderview, I dashed over to the toilet tent first thing only to stop in my tracks as a Grey Nightjar swooped in display flight over the camp. I called out, and the heads of Alan, Philip and Pauline all popped out of their tents like rabbits from a burrow. Bodies and binoculars followed, and everybody got a good view of this new bird as it made a final flypast before disappearing into the forest.

At Eaglenest Pass, we stopped to look for Spotted Laughingthrush. Peter played the tape and we heard the birds call in reply, but from way up the hillside. Nothing for it but to plunge into the bamboo and follow the elephant trails. Our slog up the hill was rewarded with fine views of these birds, and then – just as we were about to leave – a flock of Brown Parrotbills appeared, passing close by as they flowed like a wave down the mountainside. Our birding came to an abrupt halt, however, when the crashing and cracking of bamboo announced that elephants were about. Much as we wanted to see the beasts, it was time to get out of there.

We took our time working back down the mountainside over the next couple of days, as we birded our way back down to Lama Camp and then continued to the valley bottom. Right until the end we were still enjoying great birds. At last, we had good views of the bizarre Slender-billed Scimitar-babbler, a brown bird with a scimitar stuck incongruously on the front of its face. The elusive Wedge-billed Wren-Babbler also put in another appearance, while new colour came in the form of Maroon Oriole and Scarlet Finch.

Back down in the hustle and bustle of the valley, we had to make a stop in the town to get some repairs done. We'd picked up a puncture so, while the lads took care of fixing it, the rest of us jumped out of the vehicles to stretch our legs. Above us loomed a high cliff of pale rock. A raptor wheeled overhead so, of course, we lifted our bins to watch it. Suddenly it folded its wings and swooped right in to the cliff face – only to swoop back out again and perch in a nearby tree. It repeated the process. What was it up to? Then we noticed another raptor – and another. We grabbed the scopes for a better look, and all became clear. They were Oriental Honey-buzzards, and they were all swooping in to raid a huge golden honeycomb against the cliff face. As each bird flew in, it broke off a piece of comb and took it to a nearby tree, where it plucked out the pupae from their cells. This was amazing behaviour and exciting stuff to watch, as again and again the three birds swooped down. There were a number of honeycombs clinging to the cliff face, and the birds always went for the unprotected golden-coloured ones, avoiding the browner ones, which were covered in a rippling mass of bees that would have attacked to protect the pupae.

Of course, a bunch of Europeans peering through telescopes in the middle of a border town also attracted some excitement, and we soon had a gathering of curious people around us. We showed them how to look through the scopes to enjoy these birds doing their stuff, and they exclaimed excitedly each time a bird performed its snatch and grab. It seemed they'd never noticed the drama that was happening right above their heads. One woman was so excited that she ran to the nearest hairdressers to get all her friends to come and look, and the women rushed out with their hair half-cut or held up in rollers to join in the excitement.

We were all quite disappointed when the repaired tyre was returned and we had to pack up and leave. But, of course, Peter had yet another gem up his sleeve for us. Back at low altitude again, we stayed in a residence just outside Orang National Park and at dawn we drove into the park in convoy. We were back in similar habitat to Kaziranga, open grasslands with head-high stems swaying in the gentle breeze, boggy areas with trickling streams and airy woodland. There were plenty of birds to look at as we bounced and swayed along the narrow track, but we were still missing two key species: Swamp Prinia and Marsh Babbler. Peter was confident that we'd be able to find both of them here.

We parked up at a likely spot above the swaying green sea of tall grasses, and Peter played the calls. Something called back from the grass on one side so he suggested we approached closer on foot. With the armed guard at the ready, we all scrambled down the embankment and the grasses closed around us. In just a single step, we had lost sight of the jeeps and could now see only the person immediately in front and behind. In crocodile fashion, we crept silently through the tall vegetation, the towering grasses making an impenetrable curtain either side us.

Peter was in front; we could hear him playing the tape for Swamp Prinia and a reply came from somewhere out in the grasses. At least the bird was a 'heard' for our records, but it would be nice to see it too. We forged further into the vegetation and came across a trampled area with huge dish-like footprints. Elephants had recently passed by. The thought made us huddle closer together, hoping for safety in numbers. Peter played the tape again. A reply came from very close by, but this time it wasn't a bird; it was a deep throaty grunt and snort. A rhino! Panic broke out. The guard cocked his gun to make a loud noise and, hopefully, scare the rhino away, but the rest of us didn't hang around to see it if worked; elbows flew as everyone jostled to be at the front of the high-speed retreat.

But our close encounter of the rhino kind hadn't put Peter off. He was determined we would tick Marsh Babbler too. This time we headed off into the sea of grass on the other side of the track and once again the grasses closed in around us. We reached a small clearing, just large enough for eight people to huddle together closely, and stood there in silence as Peter played the call of the Marsh Babbler on his iPod. A reply came from a short distance away so Peter played the call again. This time the reply was a little closer. Once again, and the bird replied from only a few feet away but we just couldn't make it out through the grasses. One final try with the iPod, but now the bird had obviously become bored and moved further away. We stood in silence in case it returned.

GRRRRRRAAAGH! A chilling sound ripped the air, making every hair on the back of my neck stand up. The deep, gravelly, unmistakable roar of a tiger. It came again. And again: a sound that you could feel reverberating through your body. It wasn't far away, in fact it sounded very close indeed, but all we could see was the impenetrable wall of grass. Just because we couldn't see the tiger, though, that didn't mean it couldn't see us. Maybe it was already eyeing us up and working out which one of us was lunch. I had a sudden flashback to the video Peter had shown us. I had desperately wanted to see a tiger, but maybe not as the last thing I *ever* saw. We didn't really want to end *The Biggest Twitch* in a horrible mess of blood and gore, so once again we high-tailed it back to the jeep. Marsh Babbler would have to stay as a 'heard only', but at least we'd all live to bird another day.

Orang National Park was our last destination with the rest of the group, and we toasted our success over supper. It had been great fun birding with Philip and Pauline, with whom we'd shared many laughs and hot water bottles over the past few days, but now we had to move on. We said our goodbyes and drove back with Peter to the airport. We all boarded the same plane, but Peter left us at Bagdogra to go home to Kalimpong, while Alan and I carried on alone to Delhi. It felt strange saying goodbye to Peter in such a rush. We didn't have time to thank him properly for looking after us so well and, of course, helping us add some staggering new birds to our list.

But India wasn't finished with us yet. Exchanging one Peter for another, we'd arranged to stay with Peter Kaestner in Delhi overnight before flying back to the UK, and he had been busy staking out one last key bird for us. We weren't sure what to expect when we arrived at Delhi Airport, but there was the man himself, standing out from the crowd in a smart suit, pink shirt and tie. Peter skilfully navigated the terrifying Delhi traffic back to his beautifully appointed pad, complete with a leafy garden and a spare apartment at the end of the lawn – just waiting to be occupied by a couple of dirty birders. We felt rather ashamed of our filthy gear as Peter invited us in for supper. We apologised to Peter's wife Kimberley for the intrusion, fed his boisterous black Labrador, Rocky, with peanuts, and hoped that we hadn't left too much mud on the carpets.

We were out at 5.40am the next morning for some rapid target birding with Peter before he had to head off to work. We walked to the Lodhi Gardens nearby, where the early hour and thick mist had not deterred the many walkers and joggers, nor the bizarre group of people practising laughter therapy under a tree. No birds here, so next we went to the Alkha Bird Park, an area of marshland beside the river. This protected area was, unfortunately, also a prime dumping ground for rubbish – even dead bodies, according to Peter – but we found birds aplenty, with Bar-headed Geese, Asian Openbills, Purple Swamphens, Spot-billed Ducks, Red-wattled Lapwings and a Brown-headed Gull – the last of these a new bird for our list. A red flash in a scrubby bush revealed itself as a Red Avadavat, another new one.

Peter had a particular bird in mind here, which he'd checked out regularly for us. Just as he was explaining exactly where he'd seen the bird on his last visit, there was a movement in a bush and hey presto: a male White-tailed Stonechat flew in and perched on top. We rushed back to the vehicle and Peter then drove us at top speed to the zoo, where we screeched to a halt in front of the locked gates. This was a known roosting site of Painted Storks, but there was no time to wait for the zoo to open: Peter had to get to work and we had a plane to catch. Thankfully, just as we were peering through the bars of the front gate, Peter spotted a single bird flying over. And, sure enough, a quick check through the bins revealed the black and white wings, orange bill and trailing red legs of a Painted Stork. This bird was heading out to find somewhere to feed, and as we watched, more and more began to follow it.

Four new birds for our list, but now we were out of time. We dashed back the house, where we thanked Peter and Kimberley profusely, before Peter headed out to work – probably late for his meeting – and we dashed to the airport. What a great guy!

We'd had an amazing time in India. The place had far exceeded our expectations. It had everything: colour, spectacle, scenery, wildlife and, of course, birds. Beautiful, intriguing and astonishing birds. We left with our year list on 4,226 species. And there was still one final stop before the end of the year: Ecuador. Again!

4,226 species

21–31 December, Southern Ecuador (Alan)

Back in January, when we had birded northern Ecuador, we had left the south untouched. There was a good reason for this: we had thought that, come December, we might still need a final species boost to break the world record. Since then, of course, we had not only broken the record but gone a good way past it; we could have rested on our laurels, finished the year early and gone home to north Wales. But this was the last month of what had been a life-changing experience and we just did not want it to end. We also wanted to post as big as possible a total in the hope that the record would stand for some time. So, here we were at Quito Airport with our great friend Nick Athanas from Tropical Birding, waiting for a flight south and anticipating a grandstand finish to *The Biggest Twitch*.

Arriving in Loja Airport, we were soon out and birding right by the perimeter fence. Nick was keen to find Drab Seedeater. A new bird, yes, but it hardly sounded very charismatic. It was also tough to find. We walked up and down, scanning the dry grass and scrub, and managed to add Peruvian Pygmy-Owl and Loja Hummingbird. This far south in Ecuador the birds had a Peruvian flavour, as the endemic-rich Tumbesian region of northern Peru spills over the border. It was one of the main reasons we were here.

Then Nick had the Drab Seedeater. We were quickly on to it and had to agree that this bird, one of the dullest of *The Biggest Twitch*, was very well named. But it counted the same as all the others. One more for the list.

It was a long drive to Copalinga Lodge, where the lush gardens were a relief after the dusty road. Catherine Vits welcomed us warmly and we gulped down a refreshing cold drink. The birding was under way immediately, with an Ecuadorian Tyrannulet whizzing about after tiny flies and a Lined Antshrike bouncing along a branch.

'Right, let's get going!' said Nick, who could see we were in danger of relaxing. 'We've lost time on the road; we need to get out and find birds.' Tropical Birding through and through!

A short drive took us to the entrance of the Podocarpus National Park and we walked the narrow forest trails in the late afternoon sun. New birds came easily: an Olive-chested Flycatcher sat above us, a Gray-chinned Hummingbird shot in and hovered up close, and White-necked Parakeets screeched loudly overhead. Meanwhile an Olive Finch crept through the undergrowth and a Black-streaked Puffbird, lured by the tape, just sat there peering down at us.

Back at the lodge we enjoyed a wonderful meal and fell gratefully into our beds, exhausted but well pleased with our first day in the south. Seventeen new birds had taken us to 4,244 species for the year. Even in bed the total continued to inch up, as we awoke to hear a Band-bellied Owl calling above our cabin.

A pre-dawn breakfast and then we returned to the park. Feeding flocks bustled through the trees and we struggled to keep pace. Lafresnaye's Piculet, a miniature woodpecker, hung from a vine; a Western Striped Manakin displayed vigorously; and an Ecuadorian Pied-tail, a small hummingbird, fed right over the path. Next came a Chestnut-crowned Gnatcatcher, quickly followed by Foothill Elaenia and Foothill Antwren. All these birds were new – which was exactly why we had come south.

As we neared the truck, Nick was a little way ahead of us on the narrow trail. Ruth noticed a small warbler feeding deep in a tangle of vines below the path. It looked different. I pished, both to encourage the bird to show and also to get Nick's attention without frightening it. This worked perfectly. Nick came striding back just as the bird popped up. It was a Connecticut Warbler, not only new for *The Biggest Twitch* but also only the third record for Ecuador and, even better, a life bird for Nick. After all the wonderful birds Nick had helped us to see in 2008, it was great to find a good one for him. Incredibly, Nick is originally from Connecticut, so this seemed only right.

Back at the lodge we watched a gorgeous male Spangled Coquette humming-bird feeding on the flowering shrubs right by the veranda. Now we could feel the clock running down on our wonderful year of birding and wanted time to stand still so we could keep this amazing experience going for ever. We savoured each bird, new or not, trying not to think that in a few days 2008 would end – and with it *The Biggest Twitch*.

It was on Christmas Eve that we thanked Catherine and said our farewells to the wonderful Copalinga Lodge. We birded slowly back down the old Samora road, finding some great feeding flocks. A highlight among these was cracking views of the tiny Black-and-white Tody-Tyrant. Nick was thrilled that we had got this rarity – and, at the same time, he enjoyed his best ever views.

Next we made our way up the twisting mountain drive to the other side of the Podocarpus National Park. Entering by the Cajanuma gate, we slowly climbed the dirt track to the dead end near the summit. Soon we heard the loud song we were hoping for and, after some careful stalking, had great views of Plain-tailed Wren. It was nothing spectacular to look at but it was on the list and we were heading down.

Our next bird could not have been more different. Nick instructed us to scan the treetops below the road for a blob of colour.

'That's it!' he said, excitedly, as a call drifted across the forest. 'It must be sitting up somewhere!'

We scanned harder. At last I had a red-and-yellow blob in my bins – but what was it? Through the scope, it became a stunning Red-headed Tanager, glowing in the sun. This was a mega bird and we drooled over its amazing colours. The head was a luminous scarlet and the body a deep yellow, like a plastic banana. It stood out like a beacon, and we wondered how it did not fall prey to a passing raptor.

Leaving the park, we headed for our hotel at Madre Tierra at Vilcabamba, in the 'Valley of Longevity'. This name was promising; perhaps we could extend our year here and not finish next week?

In Ecuador Christmas is celebrated on 24 December, so we had been looking forward to some partying that evening. But, although we had a turkey dinner, complete with cranberry sauce, the party amounted to no more than a couple of limp fireworks. Christmas morning began at 4.15am. There was no sign of Santa, no presents at the foot of the bed and breakfast was a cup of lemon tea.

Oh well, we thought, forget the festivities. Instead, we drove back into the park and headed high up into the Paramo. Jumping out, we were shocked by the bitter cold. We wandered around, a tad grimly, and luckily were quickly able to find our target species: Mouse-coloured Thistletail and Neblina Metaltail, the latter a small hummingbird that whizzed around like an angry bee. Job done, we jumped back into the vehicle and headed down, just as the sun was beginning to warm the slopes.

This mountain road was handy, allowing us to look down on birds that would usually have given us neck-ache from peering up into the canopy. Red-faced Parrots circled over the forest, quickly followed by Masked Mountain-Tanager and Golden-crowned Tanager, both showing very well.

With all our target species safely on the list, we took the long drive to Tapichalaca, where we were to stay at Casa Simpson. This comfortable new lodge was missing just one thing. Food. It was Christmas Day, and there was nothing for lunch. We did manage to get a cup of tea and broke out some snack bars, but thought longingly of family and friends back home tucking into their Christmas feast.

Lunch over (it didn't take long), we headed out to look for more birds. But upon reaching the truck we saw we had a problem: a very flat tyre. Nick and I quickly worked to put on the spare, but sadly this was also very low on air – not yet completely flat but well on the way. Great. Driving these tough mountain roads with a dodgy tyre and no spare was out of the question.

We made our way slowly down the hill to the nearest town in the hope of finding a garage. Not surprisingly, given that it was Christmas Day, the first place we saw was all locked up. As it was only a small town we did not hold out much hope of another. We met two cops, however, who told us about a second garage. We followed their directions and, lo and behold, there was a mechanic working on a tyre.

Nick jumped out and greeted the man in his usual fluent Spanish, but soon returned to the truck, looking shaken.

'The guy is an ignorant pig!' he explained. 'I asked about him fixing the tyre and got a load of abuse. Maybe he's drunk, or perhaps he doesn't like gringos. Either way, we'll get no help from him.'

Happy Christmas to you too, pal, I thought.

The recently fitted spare now looked even softer and we now noticed that one of the 'good' tyres had an egg-sized bulge in the side-wall. It did not look as though we would be driving anywhere very far.

Undaunted, Nick suggested we look for Marañon Thrush, which he thought would be a garden bird around here. After a brief downpour we drove slowly out of town scanning. Soon Nick slammed on the brakes. He'd seen a thrush but it had disappeared behind a hedge. We bailed out and searched the area, finding not only our thrush, sitting high in a treetop, but also three fine Black-faced Tanagers.

Back at the lodge the staff were sure that one of them would be able to get the tyre fixed in town the next day. All we could do was hope. Luckily, supplies had now arrived so we ate well that night. Meanwhile, we were entertained over dinner by an Israeli birder, Noam Shing, who was also staying there. He had a colourful past and had been involved in South American birding for many years. Much of his time had been spent in Peru, where he had been instrumental in producing the field guide and helping many conservation projects. He had even birded with Jim Clements, whose world record we had just smashed.

Early next morning we were out birding the trails around the lodge – on foot, of course – and looking for a very special bird. This reserve had been established to protect the recently discovered Jocotoco Antpitta, and today was our chance to see one. Given that the reserve staff had been feeding the antpittas along one of the trails we fancied our chances of success.

We rounded a bend on the forest track and a clearing opened up, complete with a shelter and benches. Our Israeli friend, Noam, had beaten us to it and was sitting quietly on a bench, grinning broadly. And soon we saw why. A Jocotoco Antpitta bounced out onto the path just a few metres ahead of us. It stood upright on its long legs, revealing its black head, white cheeks, chestnut back and pale grey breast, and looked very comical as it stood there giving its hooting call.

Then it was gone, back into the forest. We moved slowly forward to join Noam and sat in silence. Seconds later out hopped another one – and then a third came bouncing along. This was mind-blowing: these birds had only recently been discovered and were very rare.

A member of staff from the lodge appeared but the antpittas stood their ground: he was carrying a bowl of worms and they were ready for breakfast. As the worms were scattered on the path, more antpittas came out of the forest to gobble them up and soon we had a whole family at our feet. We were mesmerised. We set up a photo opportunity by placing our mascot Toco the Toucan on the path and waiting for an antpitta to hop alongside him. It was very funny watching these amazing birds peering up at Toco, totally unafraid: Toco meets Jocotoco.

Back at the lodge we learned that the tyres had been fixed. The mechanic had, apparently, sobered up and was in the mood to work. This was good news, as we had another huge drive ahead, travelling even further south towards the hot, dusty border town of Macara, just a few miles from Peru.

We were a little worried about our stay in Macara, as we knew it was our friend Iain Campbell's favourite town in Ecuador. Iain likes to party hard and live close to the edge, so we knew this might be a rather wild place. And indeed it looked like a cowboy town from the Wild West, with plenty of dodgy characters hanging around the dusty streets and rundown shops and bars. But our hotel in the centre, though a little shabby, was fine; the rooms even had air-con. Tired and dirty after our long, dusty drive in the baking heat; we showered, ate and crashed out. No partying for us.

Up before dawn to take advantage of the cooler air, we drove out of town to the nearby reserve managed by the Ecuadorian conservation group, Fundacion Jocotoco. This area of dry sand forest was a new habitat for us and as the light came so did new birds. First a pair of Red-masked Parakeets flew in calling loudly, giving us one of our main target species within seconds of leaving the car. We then set off up the trail into the forest, soon finding Gray-and-gold Warbler, Pale-browed Tinamou and Black-capped Sparrow.

Then loud calls from further up the hill had us off in search of Rufous-headed Chachalacas. These long-tailed, pheasant-sized birds were making a right racket but were hard to see – until we went off-trail, whereupon one burst from a tree above us and half flew, half fell down the slope to another tree top. A whole flock of chachalacas followed, raining down on the forest as though a chicken coop had just exploded.

Back on the trail, Nick picked out a Henna-hooded Foliage-Gleaner and we dashed to his side but it had ducked out of sight. A tense wait followed, then up it jumped to give us a good, if brief look. Loud drumming above us led to a pair of Scarlet-backed Woodpeckers really hammering a dead branch in the sunshine. Tumbes Swifts cruised overhead, Watkin's Antpitta called from the undergrowth and, as we headed back to the car, a White-tailed Jay swept up into an open tree above the track. For a while we stood and watched this lovely bird – a real stunner, with its blue, back and white plumage. Then, with the temperature now approaching 40°C, we retreated to town, with its promise of cold drinks and air-con.

Mid-afternoon, we set off again and did some exploring. Nick wanted to scout out new habitat that might be useful for future Tropical Birding tours, and so we headed for an area of semi-desert scrub. Birds were in short supply in the intense heat, and while Ruth and I watched a pair of Tropical Gnatcatchers, Nick wandered on in search of more exciting fare.

Sticking with the gnatcatchers, we noticed a movement in the scrub beyond. Pishing, we moved round to see it in better light. Out jumped a cracking little bird. It was a small flycatcher, but not one of the usual drab brown tyrannulets that usually gave us such headaches over identification. This one had a bright yellow breast and forehead, and a dark mask through the eye, plus white wing bars and outer tail feathers. We grabbed the field guide and hurriedly thumbed the pages to flycatchers, but couldn't find anything like it. What was going on here? Meanwhile Nick had returned to see what we were up to.

'Shit! exploded Nick, as the bird popped up in front of us. Then 'Jesus!' as he started blasting off photos like some demented paparazzo who had just stumbled on an A-list celeb in a compromising position. We were guessing this must be something good.

'So what is it?' we asked, once Nick had calmed down a little. 'We can't find it in the field guide.'

Nick's answer left us stunned. 'You won't find it in the Ecuadorian guide,' he said, 'because it is a new species for Ecuador!' This is a Tumbes Tyrant. It's meant to be a Peruvian endemic.'

Wow! Ecuador already has over 1,600 species on its list and the field guide weighs a ton. It doesn't really need any more. Nicking one of Peru's birds will not be popular, we realised. Countries are very protective of their endemics and losing one is painful. But for us it was a wonderful moment. You don't often add a new bird to a country list. What a coup for *The Biggest Twitch*! And luckily Nick had some brilliant, frame-filling photos to back up the record. As we wandered back, elated, we also added Tumbes Sparrow, Tumbes Hummingbird and Superciliated Wren to the list, taking our total to 4,315. But, of course, it was the tyrant that had completely stolen the show.

That night Macara came to life, with thumping disco music that shook the hotel until the small hours. The town was partying hard and sleep was impossible, as the pounding bass was overlaid with fireworks, screams, laughter and drunken shouting. We could see why Iain loved it here.

On 28 December we were out before dawn and into the warmth of a Macara night. A long drive took us to the peace and quiet of another Fundacion Jocotoco Nature Reserve, at Bosque de Hanne. On the way up the mountain we picked up some good birds in the mist, including Hepatic Tanager, Rufous-necked Foliage-Gleaner and Line-cheeked Spinetail. We were still missing one major target bird, Black-cowled Saltator, and had just decided that we should give up when it flew across the trail and landed in full view. Now we could move on happy.

We climbed higher and higher, soon breaking out of the mist into a clear high-land morning. Here we birded the cloudforest ridge and got rather lost in the maze of trails. At last we found a sign declaring the 'Black-crested Tit-Tyrant Trail' and, even better, we soon found the bird itself. What a cracker! About the size of our European Great Tit, it was decked out in black and white stripes, with a white face and jaunty black crest. We also picked up Gray-headed Antbird, Jelski's Chat-tyrant and the weird Pirua Hemispingus, all new.

At some hummingbird feeders we sat down to see what might show up. A lovely Rainbow Starfrontlet soon zapped in. Orange and green with a whopper of a bill, this was one of our favourites. Then two new hummers arrived: Purple-throated Sunangel and Mountain Velvetbreast. The last was a bird we had missed in the north back in January, so it was great finally to nail it. We headed back to town well-pleased.

We moved on from Macara before dawn, heading for a dry forest at El Empalme, where we arrived at first light. We had come to this site for White-headed Brush-Finch and there it was, just like that. Our target bird, however, was immediately overshadowed by the appearance of a stunning Elegant Crescent-chest. Although not a new bird, these were our best views yet and we could now see just what a beauty it was, totally up-staging the brush-finch, with its bold black, white and chestnut markings.

The rest of the day was spent birding protected patches of forest at the Buenaventura Jocotoco Reserve. Raptors were a feature of the afternoon, with both Gray-backed and Barred Hawks eventually found in the damp forest. We also really enjoyed the Bay Wren, although, not a new bird, which belted out its loud song in the open, showing off its richly barred, reddish plumage. Our last new bird of the day was Uniform Antshrike, bringing us to 4,331 species. Then we checked in at our accommodation in the hill town of Zamora, where we found the Hotel Roland very comfortable, if a long hike from the car to our room down hundreds of steps.

The penultimate day of *The Biggest Twitch* started well before dawn, as we slipped out of the hotel and headed back to the Buenaventura Reserve. Fittingly, it was one of those mornings when the birds really behaved for us. Each time we targeted a new species, out it popped. Considering this was 30 December and we had birded hard non-stop for twelve months, it was brilliant to be picking up an amazing nine new species.

First came Rufous-breasted Wood-Quail, quickly followed by Whiskered Wren. Then a noisy gang of Blue-fronted Parrotlets landed in the canopy, exciting Nick, who had not seen them at this site before. An Ochre-breasted Antpitta began to call somewhere up ahead and, despite Nick's warnings that we were unlikely to see this elusive bird, we found it sitting in full view at eye level. An Ecuadorian Tapaculo was next to call, but this bird was so deep in the forest that we had to be content with a 'heard only'. Then a feeding flock gave us Spotted Barbtail and Russet Antshrike, both new, before – making our way down to the lodge – we jammed in on a Striped Woodhaunter, an elusive, russet-tailed relative of the foliage-gleaners.

At the lodge we enjoyed a well-earned cup of tea and settled down to watch the busy hummingbird feeders. Literally dozens of hummers were crowding around the sugar-water dispensers, fourteen different species commuting in from the forest for a free feed. White-whiskered Hermit was impressive, with its long drooping bill and white tail streamers, but Velvet-purple Coronet was definitely the smartest. Green Honeyeaters were also common here and were joined by jaunty Bananaquits. There were no new species, but it was great entertainment – and soon the action heated up still further, as a flock of Pale-mandibled Araçaris whirred out of the forest like guided missiles, their huge bills protruding menacingly as they swooped in for bananas laid out on a sturdy bird table.

Nick was ready to move on. Reluctantly we tore ourselves away from the bird-table show and followed him heading uphill into another area of forest to search for one special bird. We scanned and listened. Then came our last new bird of the day; the one we had waited for: a flock of El Oro Parakeets came screeching in, circled and thankfully landed. The scope gave us a great view of these green birds, with their reddish tails and red frontal band above the bill. It was with mixed emotions that we trudged back down the hill. We were elated at picking up nine new species today, but sad that we had just one day left of *The Biggest Twitch*.

The last day of 2008 began, like so many others, with us up and out well before dawn. At 4.30am we left our hotel and stepped out into the low cloud and steady rain. It somehow fitted our mood: we had not wanted this day to come and certainly did not want it to end.

Nick had lined up a very special bird for our last day and we were really looking forward to seeing it. But would the weather allow? The drive back to the reserve was very slow, along a twisting road and through dense fog. At last we parked by a trailhead and hiked downhill into the dense forest. The rain and the steep slope meant we were more sliding than walking, and we were caked in mud by the time we reached more level ground. The rain got heavier and the trail muddier. Had we really said we did not want this to end?

But Nick knew the exact spot where we needed to wait, and we stood in the pouring rain listening for the weird mooing of a Long-wattled Umbrellabird. All we could hear was the rain falling heavily on the leaves. We waited and waited, getting steadily wetter. A movement low down revealed a Brownish Flycatcher feeding in the damp under-storey and we struggled to get clear views through soaking wet bins. It was no looker, but still a new bird for 2008 – and still counted the same as an umbrellabird.

Eventually even Nick had to admit that the umbrellabirds were just not going to show in this downpour. And so it was in a sombre mood, and somewhat bedraggled, that we finally struggled through the mud back up to the vehicle and headed for the airport.

So that was it. We were finished in Southern Ecuador and had raised our list to an amazing 4,341 species, totally smashing the previous world record of 3,662. We felt numb. It had not sunk in. Neither did it yet feel over, as we were still in Ecuador, thousands of miles from home, and about to board yet another flight. We had been through this routine time and time again over the year, and each time it had been the beginning of a new fantastic adventure. Now we faced the last few hours of 2008 and then the weird prospect of heading home – whatever that might be.

A short flight had us back in Quito, where we met up with Iain Campbell, his wife Cristina and their children Gabriel and Amy. That night, New Year's Eve, we partied with them and Nick at their beautiful house on a hill above the city. We popped bottles of champagne to toast our success and all the people who had helped make the *The Biggest Twitch* possible. It still didn't really feel over and in fact it wasn't. Iain regularly sees Band-winged Nightjars from his roof top terrace, and as we watched the skies over Quito light up with fireworks, we scanned in vain for one last new bird. Then the bells rang out. It was midnight and *The Biggest Twitch* was over.

4,341 species

Epilogue: Life after *The Biggest Twitch* (Ruth)

We awoke to see sunlight filtering through the curtains. Alan sat bolt upright in panic. Had we overslept? Shouldn't we be out birding? Then he remembered, and slid back under the duvet. As of midnight last night, *The Biggest Twitch* was officially over. At first it felt great to roll over and go back to sleep again, but the novelty soon wore off. It was a real anticlimax – like being eight years old and waking up on Boxing Day, with Christmas Day over and no more presents under the tree.

We paced around Iain's spacious apartment in Quito like a pair of caged tigers, and when he suggested spending a couple of days back in the cloudforest at Tandayapa Bird Lodge with him and Nick, we jumped at the chance. It was great to be out birding again, surrounded by buzzing hummingbirds and multicoloured tanagers – and now, at last, with the time to photograph and enjoy them.

But we could only put off the inevitable for so long. All too soon it was time to pack up all our gear, say goodbye to Iain and his wife Cristina, and fly back to the UK. It felt very odd to arrive at our flat in Llandudno and know that this time we were home for good. At first it was great to catch up with our friends and family, but soon the reality of normal life kicked in.

We had deliberately made no plans for our return, as we hadn't wanted to divert any of our energy from the challenge of our travels. We were sure that something would turn up if we looked in all the right places, and luckily we were soon proved right. Neil Rylance from blah d blah design, the friend who had created our website, contacted me as soon as we returned and offered me a job as their marketing consultant. How lucky was that? And Alan was soon offered a contract job with the RSPB, researching the best places to find and film birds for a TV programme. This part-time work at least helped us keep the wolf from the door, as we juggled all the other activities on our long to-do list.

We were quickly in demand as guest speakers, invited to talk about *The Biggest Twitch* to a wide variety of groups both at home and overseas. Our audiences ranged from local Women's Institutes in the UK to the American Birding Association's conference at Corpus Christi, Texas, where we shared a stage with birding legend, Kenn Kaufman, one of our heroes. The Club 300 of top-notch Swedish birders invited us to talk to them at Öland on the Baltic coast at just the right time to enjoy spring migration, and even invited us back for more in the autumn. The Finnish twitching group, Bongarililitto, invited us over to Helsinki, and the Dutch Birding Association asked us to speak at their AGM in Amsterdam.

Alan, meanwhile, was signed up for a flurry of guiding around North Wales, taking small groups and individuals around the best birding spots in the area to see our local specialities. Now the tables were turned, as he worked hard to make sure other people saw as many new birds as possible during their time in North Wales.

And then we started writing the book. We had always intended to commit *The Biggest Twitch* to paper. So many people around the world had asked us about it that we knew there would be a ready market for our story. But rushing around the world looking at birds every day was easy compared with sitting down at the computer every day trying to write about them. Alan and I had spent 366 days in each other's pockets, and in doing so had compressed about ten years of married life into just one, but amazingly we were still best friends. That is, until we started writing. We both knew exactly how to write each chapter, and we both knew that the other was wrong. This led to so many arguments that the only thing we could agree on was that we should write separate chapters in separate rooms. Did it work? Well, having got this far, you're best placed to judge, but at least Alan and I are still on speaking terms.

We hope you've enjoyed sharing the highs and lows of our incredible journey with us. Would we do it again? Absolutely! Tomorrow, if possible. But this time we might need some sponsorship, as we've no money left in the bank. We've been lucky enough to see a staggering number of birds, 4,341 species, but that's not even half the world's total. Why stop there? There are over 5,000 more weird, wonderful, beautiful, skulking and showy new bird species still to see.

So if you try to call us and there's no reply, don't worry: we might just have gone birding.

Glossary

ABA	American Birding Association.
decurved	(of a bird's bill) curved downwards.
digiscope	photograph at high magnification by attaching a camera to a telescope.
dip	fail to see a bird that you are searching for.
jam in on	find by chance.
jizz	essential suite of characters unique to each species of bird.
mega, mega bird	rare or thrilling sighting.
paramo	high-altitude habitat of the Andes, at 3000–5000m elevation, comprising steep grasslands with bogs, lakes and small forest patches..
pishing	making a repeated soft, sibilant noise, '*pish, pish, pish*, in order to encourage small birds into view.
primaries	long flight feathers that make up the 'hand' of a bird's wing.
primary projection	the length that the tip of a bird's primary wing-feathers project when folded.
Ramsar site	a wetland site protected under the International Convention on Wetlands, signed in Ramsar, Iran in 1971.
RSPB	The Royal Society for the Protection of Birds (UK-based bird conservation charity).
string	claim to see a bird that you haven't; misidentify one species as another.
secondaries	flight feathers that make up the 'arm' of a bird's wing.
supercilium	pale stripe above a bird's eye, also known as its eyebrow.
trash birds	birds too numerous or common to be of interest to a birder.
trash habitat	a habitat spoiled by development, though potentially still of interest to birders.
tertials	wing feathers between the secondaries and the body.
vent	area of bird between its belly and undertail.